# Prairie Kitchen Sampler

## By E. Mae Fritz

# Preface

# Prairie Kitchen Sampler

A sixty-six-year personal history of midwestern farm kitchens from the recipes and stories of Alice Mickish Hendrickson as told to her daughter, Ethel Mae Hendrickson Fritz.

# Acknowledgements

*Artist* — Linda Fritz Corkery

*Editorial Consultant* — Krista Fritz Rogers

*Special Thanks to* — Wilma Huffstutter Hendrickson, Kathleen Hendrickson Colburn and Connie Swift Hendrickson

*And to Alice Hendrickson* — A heartfelt thanks for all the good times cooking and remembering

Printed in the United States of America

Illustrations by Linda Fritz Corkery

---

Publisher's Cataloging in Publication Data

Fritz, E. Mae
Prairie Kitchen Sampler

1, Cookery, American
Recipe index 435 pages
TX715 F91 641.5 89-107450
ISBN 0-9620404-0-1 Hardcover

First printing, December 1988
Second printing, June 1989
Third printing, November 1989

iv

# Contents

*Artwork*

# Map of Buffalo County, Nebraska

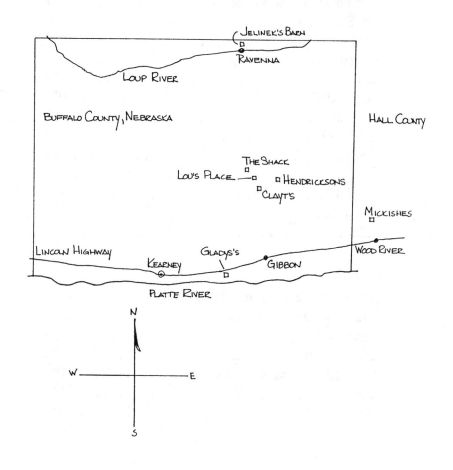

# Prologue

More than a cookbook, Prairie Kitchen Sampler is a storybook, too.

It contains more than three hundred of Alice Mickish Hendrickson's recipes "layered," "frosted," "marinated" and "garnished" with stories about a black monster cookstove, a pretty new cookstove, freezing ice cream in a snow bank, Lilac Day on the original Hendrickson homestead, electricity coming to the farm house and many other reminiscences. Recipes and stories are "folded" and "kneaded" together in a brief personalized history of midwestern farm kitchens since 1922 as Alice cooked, first with corncobs, then kilowatts and now with microwaves.

I grew up on Alice's cooking and though fate moved me away the farm, I still get homesick for my mother's kitchen—the yeasty smell of bread rising and baking, the crunchy sound of crisp cabbage being raked across the sauerkraut cutter, the feel of farm-thick-cream ice cream melting on my tongue, the sight of tree-ripened, fresh, juicy red cherries oozing between blankets of tender flaky pie crust and the taste of a warm, apricot-filled—my favorite—*kolache* from the oven of the cob-fired cookstove.

It's been said that each time an old recipe becomes extinct, we sacrifice part of our heritage. In preserving the past, we need not always aim for a recipe to be prepared exactly the way grandmother made it; we may, instead, make it with whatever adaptations are necessary in order for it to be prepared in today's kitchens so it may be served and enjoyed today and in all of the tomorrows to come.

Family backgrounds of the Fialas, Millers, Mickishs, Cheevers, Lathrops and Hendricksons reflect Czechoslovakian, German and Irish heritages which have become thoroughly blended in Alice's kitchen. Her "signature" recipes, those she is best-known for, are breads, pies and cakes, many of which are made from of her oldest recipes. She shares her tips for preparing those and other recipes in a Special Reminders and Tips section.

Alice admits to not caring if she has "to render lard...turn corn into hominy... milk a cow... pluck a chicken... ever again." And while she is glad she "knew how to do all those things when it mattered," she's just as happy to be cooking now in an age when foods defrost, simmer, broil or bake in minutes, even seconds by the push of a button, the flip of a switch or the turn of a dial. Her idea of "fast food" is baking with Master Mix or pulling a frozen packet of home-processed food from the freezer and zapping it in the microwave.

In Prairie Kitchen Sampler, Alice passes on recipes and stories that for her continue to make cooking for family and friends a genuine pleasure, an adventure and a labor of love.

E. Mae Fritz

# WITH THIS CAKE...

I remember the exact date. On Monday, August 7, 1922, using pen and ink and my best penmanship, I painstakingly wrote "Brown Stone Front Cake. Boil together slowly 2 squares of chocolate, the yolks of 2 eggs and 1/2 cup sweet milk..." on the lined pages of a string-stitched, five-by-eight-inch Universal notebook. That was the very first entry in my collection of recipes that would cover more than sixty years of cooking.

I remember the date because it was the day after my eighteenth birthday, and on that day, August the sixth, I had a date to go to an afternoon neighborhood baseball game with Walter Hendrickson, a young, redheaded farmer. After Sunday dinner, my sister Opal and I made quick work of clearing the table and doing dishes and I changed into a new dress I'd made—a soft Copenhagen blue voile with floating, elbow-length sleeves. I perched on the arm of a chair near a window in the front parlor where I had a clear view of the street to watch for Walter's car—a brand new, shiny black, four-door, Model T Ford with red tires.

I was lucky to see Walter more than once a week that summer. My parents had sold their farm near Ravenna, Nebraska that spring and while they waited to take possession of a farm they'd bought near Wood River, we lived in Kearney. It was more than a twenty-mile, two-hour round trip in a Model T from Walter's farm nine miles north of Gibbon, too far for him to drive on weeknights after he'd worked all day in the field. He made the trip every Saturday night and sometimes, for a special occasion like my birthday, he made it again on Sunday.

That particular Sunday, I hoped he'd arrive early so there would be time to show him snapshots taken at my May graduation from Ravenna High School. He did. We sat at one end of the dining table and I lined the pictures up in front of him. We laughed and talked, remembering family and friends who'd been present for the ceremonies, and as I chattered on about the pictures, Walter turned sideways to face me and fished a little gray velvet box out of his shirt pocket.

"I have something for you," he said, handing me the box. I opened it and there, sticking out of the velvet ridges, was a ring, a diamond solitaire in a pierced white gold mounting! Was I surprised! I was so surprised, I couldn't say a word! I wasn't surprised that Walter was giving me a birthday gift, secretly, I expected one; after all, we'd known each other nearly two years. We met the fall of 1920 at a Saturday night barn dance at Joseph and Tressie Jelinek's farm just north of Ravenna. I was there with my family and Walter came with a couple of his baseball-playing friends. From that night on, Walter had been my favorite dancing partner and boy friend. Marriage had never been mentioned, so I had no reason to expect an engagement ring. The only ring I was expecting was the ring of the school bell. By September, I expected to be a teacher in a one-room country school. It was common practice in the 1920s for rural school districts to hire high school graduates to teach grades one through eight, and with that in mind, I'd taken "normal training," courses educating and preparing teachers for the classroom, and did student teaching to earn a two-year teaching certificate. It was generally "understood" school boards didn't hire married women but there were no such "understandings" about hiring engaged women.

While I was very happy wearing Walter's ring on the third finger of my left hand and I understood that at twenty-three, he was ready to get married, maybe more ready than I was, I did feel shy when our friends at the ball game noticed the ring.

"When are you getting married?" We heard that question over and over.

"Oh, I'll be teaching this fall," I said and turned away any further questions by joking, "I can't get married, I don't have a hope chest."

It was true. Most of my girl friends had embroidered dish towels, crocheted edgings on pillow cases and sheets, and collected dishes, silver, pots and pans to stash away in their "I-hope-I'm-going-to-get-married chests." Not me. I worked as a waitress at Kearney's Midway Hotel that summer, earning money to buy teaching supplies and a teacher's wardrobe.

Still, every sparkle from that ring flashed "hope chest…hope chest…" Part of me longed to start collecting things and part of me wanted to stick to my first plan, getting ready for the classroom. Before I fell asleep that birthday night, I'd thought of a collection a newly engaged girl like me could start, one that wouldn't cost money, one that would be free—recipes.

The next day, on my morning break between the breakfast and lunch crowds, I walked two blocks from the hotel to Woolworth's and spent a nickel for Notebook Number 239 with red sketches of an eagle soaring over two globes, a ship and a train on its mottled beige cover. Those sketches suggested the little book was for travel records, but in the sixty years I've had it, that little notebook hasn't been out of Buffalo County.

I didn't tell Walter about the book right away. For more than a year, he'd listened to me talk about prospective schools, teacher's contracts and salaries and, though he didn't mention it when he gave me the ring, he'd been working out another plan for me. Slipping a ring on my finger was just the first step in his plan. With that done, he took the second step and signed a contract to rent a larger farm and the next Saturday night, he came to Kearney, ready to take the third step.

He waited until we were in the car headed for the weekly dance at Yanda's Pavilion south of Ravenna before he brought the subject up. Once he started talking, he never stopped. He kept his eyes on the road and his hands on the steering wheel, except when he clutched and shifted the Model T, coaxing it first up one hill and then letting it coast down to the bottom of the next hill. There must have been at least seventeen hills on the graveled roads between Kearney and Ravenna. Some were "quick dips" between low hills, dips that swirled and dropped your stomach, those the Model T skimmed over easily, but in order to "top" the steeper, longer hills, the car had to be "clutched down." Walter was clutching and talking, talking and clutching. He talked about the contract with the new landlord, the better, not-so-hilly farm land, the big, two-story house on the farm, the need to buy more livestock, and he covered each point so thoroughly and so deliberately and emphatically, I suspected he was at last delivering a speech he'd practiced for days. He talked non-stop for miles before he paused for a second and then, in a burst, out came the words about how he needed me with him on the bigger farm.

"If you sign a contract to teach school September through May," he said, "that wouldn't work. Moving day, March first, comes right in the middle of the spring school term and if you teach school, we won't be able to get married and make the move together."

"Get married!"

That was the first time I'd heard Walter say anything about getting married. Those words sounded very much like a marriage proposal to me and that sounded like pretty serious talk coming from a man who'd kept me laughing with his wit and two-stepping, fox-trotting and waltzing for nearly two years.

All the while, Walter talked, I didn't let myself look at him. Just like him, I, too, stared straight ahead at the road. But when he got to the part about "get married," I *had* to look. I had to see his face to be sure he wasn't joking. He wasn't.

"When do I go on the payroll?" That was all I said, but I knew right away I'd said the right thing. Walter eased the Model T to the side of the road on the crest of the last hill, the one overlooking the pastures and cornfields of the Loup River Valley. The car chugged and gulped to a stop. Walter looked at me with a great big grin on his face.

"You pick the date," he said.

I took my time picking the date for our wedding, or so Walter thought, but as I explained to him, I'd been getting ready to be Miss Mickish handing out reading, writing and arithmetic assignments for so long, I had to have some time to get ready to be MRS. Hendrickson dishing out three meals day. What I didn't tell him was, I needed a few more waitressing paychecks and tips to stock a hope chest I wanted to outfit as a surprise. "Have you set the date?" He asked me that question every time I saw him.

"What's the matter," I'd say, "you tired of your own cooking? Or maybe you're just tired from driving back and forth to your folks' for your meals."

Walter had started farming on his own that spring and, like a lot of young men, he'd thought "batching," living alone, having his own place, was going be a cinch. He'd eat what he wanted, when he wanted. He hadn't considered that, if he was going to eat, first he'd have to cook. After a couple of days of eating his specialties—scrambled eggs, fried potatoes, bread and butter— three times a day, he cranked up the Model T and, as his mother told it, "just kinda showed up around suppertime" at his parents' house three-and-a-half miles away.

As far as Walter was concerned, it was a trip well worth taking. He got a good meal, there were no dishes to wash afterwards and when he was ready to leave and go back to the "Shack," as he called his place, his mother gave him "a little something"— cookies, a jar of canned peaches, sliced roast beef in gravy, a loaf of baked-that-day bread—enough to see him through until the next time he "showed up" for some of her cooking.

I may have teased Walter about going home to eat but I

certainly didn't blame him. I'd been invited to dinner and supper at Hendricksons' many times and I knew what a good cook Carrie, his mother, was. She managed her kitchen very well, I saw that, and I also saw how important it was to her to have her whole family sit down together at mealtime. It was the family custom, when a child was big enough to sit in a grown-up chair, that child was expected to be at the table, hands and face washed, hair combed and ready to eat by the time Carrie had "taken up the food." It was a custom Walter and I would carry on in our own family.

That fall, while I assembled my hope chest and copied recipes, Walter struggled to harvest his first corn crop in what turned out to be an unusually wet season. Even under ideal warm and sunny conditions, before mechanical pickers and harvesters were invented cornhusking was hard work. Every single ear of corn had to be manually yanked from the stalk and stripped of its shucks by ripping it through a set of curved metal husking hooks strapped to the palm of the picker's hand before it was then tossed against the bangboard and fell into the wagon. Wet corn, picked and cribbed too soon, spoiled and rotted and couldn't be sold, so Walter held off picking until the corn was mature and dry enough to be safely cribbed. Still the rains kept coming. Fields became soggy and muddy; wheels of loaded wagons mired down in the muck so deep it took two teams of horses to pull the wagon through the rows.

Picking dragged on and on as the days grew shorter and shorter. The dawn's early light came a little later each morning and darkness, a little earlier each evening. Walter carried a kerosene lantern with him to see to do morning and evening chores. After evening rounds—feeding the livestock, unharnessing and brushing down the horses, milking the cow—and before he fired up the cookstove to fix himself a quick supper, he scooped the picked corn from the wagon into the crib. "It'd sure be nice," a weary Walter remarked on a Saturday night date late in October, "if I had a cook who'd have a hot meal ready for me when I came in from the field."

That did it. I didn't wait for him to ask me one more time if I'd set the date.

"How about November 22?" I asked and Walter nodded his head in agreement and the date was set.

It wasn't a spur of the moment pick. I'd had my eye on that date—November 22, 1922—for our wedding day. I liked how the numbers 11-22-22, indicating month, day and year, looked and sounded together. To me, they seemed right and special.

With the date set, Walter bought the wedding band that matched my diamond ring. I wondered but I didn't ask how, in the middle of his first year of farming and before he'd marketed his crops, he was able to buy my rings. Later, when I heard him say how glad he was that his father had taught him how to shock grain, I decided Walter probably had hired out to other farmers as a "shocker" that summer. "Shockers" followed horse-drawn binders through grain fields, stacking cut and tied bundles of wheat, oats or barley in upright positions with grain heads up, eight to ten bundles to a shock. Properly shocked bundles rested against each other at just the right angles to protect kernels of grain so they were not shelled out and lost on the ground before the threshing crew got to the field. A skilled "shocker" could earn several dollars a day during grain harvest.

On Wednesday, November 22, after morning chores, Walter put on his dark gray, three-piece suit, a white shirt and a new maroon tie, a dark grey brushed felt hat and tucked the wedding band in a vest pocket. He drove, first, to a nearby farm to pick up our attendants, his sister, Ruth, and her husband, Lyle Sherard; they'd agreed to "stand up" with us when we got married. The three of them called for me at my parents' home at eleven o'clock.

I wore a simple, collarless navy blue wool dress with long, tapered sleeves. The bodice of the dress buttoned from the left shoulder to a dropped waistline. Five narrow pleats, or "plaits," as the sales clerk called them, formed in the skirt in line with the bodice closure. The store-bought dress cost just over ten dollars; I bought it at Ruter's, one of Kearney's nicest stores. In my new dress, a new black hat trimmed with a narrow satin ribbon and flat

bow and new black kid leather pumps, I slipped into my black
plush coat, ready for the ten-block drive to the Buffalo County
courthouse on south Central Avenue where for two dollars, the
County Clerk issued us a marriage license. We recited our vows
in chambers before Judge J. M. Easterling. After the ceremony,
we descended the courthouse steps into bright sunshine and a light
breeze. Walter checked his gold pocket watch and announced,
"It's time to eat."

Getting married hadn't spoiled his appetite.

"It's such a nice day," he said, "let's take a drive and find some
place to eat." We weren't expected back at my folks' until
evening, so the afternoon was ours. Walter followed Central
Avenue south past the courthouse, out of town, over the Platte
River bridge and took graveled roads east and south through the
low sand hills to Minden were we had lunch at the hotel.

Back in Kearney, we took the Sherards on a sightseeing tour
over the town's newly paved streets, the sure sign of an up-and-
coming 1920s town whose population topped seven thousand. By
sundown, we sat down to the wedding dinner Mother had prepared—roast pork with dressing and gravy, canned green beans,
carrots, potatoes, pickles, rolls, strawberry jam and for dessert, not
a wedding cake, but warm, fresh apple pie.

With dessert came my parents' wedding gift to us—silver
flatware, service for six. The card told us "to pick out dining room
furniture to be delivered to your new home."

The note reminded Walter that he had a check from his parents
in his billfold for us. It also came with instructions "to buy
furniture."

And that seemed to be the perfect time to surprise Walter with
my hope chest. One by one I showed him twenty-one bleached
flour sacks I'd turned into dish towels by first hemming them and
then embroidering and cross-stitching fruit, vegetable and flower
designs in one corner of each towel. With money earned as a
waitress, I'd bought a set of fine china dishes, table linens, sheets
and pillow cases, bath towels and small kitchen utensils—rotary
egg beater, potato masher, a set of Old Hickory knives—items I
wasn't likely to find in a bachelor's kitchen. And I mustn't forget
all of the potholders and aprons Mother made for me—every bride

had to have plenty of those.

The real treasure in the chest was a blue and white quilt Mother had hand-pieced and quilted in the Star Pattern. I recognized many of the cotton prints in the quilt. There were blue triangles and squares from scraps of fabric Mother had used to make dresses for me, dresses I'd worn to my first piano recital, my fifth grade Christmas program, the last-day-of-school picnic when I finished eighth grade—it was a quilt of memories. Only Mother could have made it for me.

All the pleasure I'd had putting the hope chest together doubled when my new husband saw it.

"You did all of this?"

"How did you ever buy all of this?"

"I can't believe you did this, that you bought all of this!"

"You did this for us...for our home..."

He was more than surprised, he was impressed. The more he exclaimed, the more I blushed. I was truly the blushing bride. The next day, we made the rounds, calling on Walter's parents and aunts and uncles in both of our families. By Friday, after missing two days of cornpicking—his brothers, Roy and Elmer, had "chored" for him while he'd taken time off to get married— Walter was ready to load up the car and take me, my clothes and the hope chest and head for the Shack.

We piled clothes in the back seat and strapped the chest on to the running board but not until Walter had covered every inch of the chest with old blankets. The "chest" was in reality a big box, two feet deep, two feet wide and four feet long. Mother and I had padded it inside and out with a pink cotton print.

"It's too pretty to let it get mud-spattered," Walter said, and he was right. The rains that had made a muddy mess of the cornfields had left the roads riddled with big, sloshy, water-filled chuck holes.

Loading the car took all morning, Walter saw to that.

"I want to leave your house with a full stomach," he told my mother as he winked at me, "I don't know how long it'll be before my next good meal."

After noon, right after we'd eaten, Walter eased the loaded Model T out onto the street and we were off for the Shack.

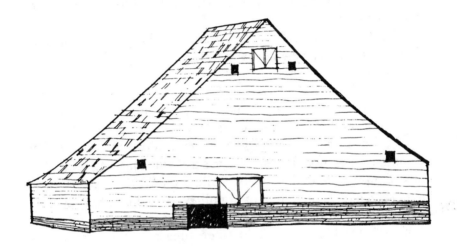

## Jelinek's Barn

*The barn where Alice Mickish and Walter Hendrickson met at
a dance in 1920.*

# GETTING TO KNOW MY STOVE

"Better get a fire going in the old stove," Walter said after the car was unloaded and my things were in the Shack. I knew he meant the old cast iron cookstove; it was the only stove in the place. It did the cooking and it also heated the Shack, and if ever there was a stove big enough to do two jobs, it was that stove; being iron, it was particularly efficient in dispersing and retaining heat. To me, it was the Black Monster. "I guess you'll want to watch so you can learn to run it," Walter said. I smiled to myself. He was saying what Mother had been telling me...

"You have to learn to *run* your stove before you can learn to cook with it."

I stood next to Walter, ready to face the Monster, ready to begin getting acquainted with my first stove.

Other than being the biggest stove I'd ever seen—the grace-less black hulk had no legs, its base sat flat on the floor, making it seem even longer and wider than six-by-three-feet—it looked and worked like other cookstoves of its kind. Everything about it was big, from its eight-lid cooking surface (most cookstoves I'd seen had only six), to its cavernous oven, its two big warming ovens perched two feet above the cooktop at the back of the stove, and its six-gallon reservoir, a galvanized tin-lined tank attached to the right-hand end of the stove. The reservoir held an ever-ready supply of hot water for cooking or washing dishes, clothes and people. On the coldest winter nights indoor temperatures often dropped below freezing and when that happened, it wasn't unusual to get up in the morning and find a skim of ice on the "hot" water in the reservoir.

The four tools needed to operate and clean the stove hung on the stove's backside. There was a lid lifter. It looked like a sawed-off screwdriver with its fat handle and short, notched, blunt, stubby blade. The blunt end of the blade was made to fit into slots on the lids so the lids could be lifted or removed. There was a poker, a long rod used to stir and spread burning corncobs in the firebox and there was a soot scraper, a one-by-six-inch rectangular blade attached to the end of a long wire handle. It was used to pull ashes out of the ash basket and soot out of the air spaces under the cooktop and around the oven. And there was a short-handled, grate bolt crank. It fit over a bolt on the front of the stove and, by jerking the bolt back and forth, the grates were tipped over, spilling cold ashes out of the firebox and into the ash pan directly below.

The first step in building a fire in either a heater or a cookstove is "Shake down the grates." Walter did that. With the grates cleared, he went to the second step, "Lay up the cobs." Walter grabbed a handful of cobs, seven or eight in all, from a nearby basket and poked them through the small door of the firebox located under the two front lids at the left-hand end of the stove. He left the cobs where they fell in a loose, criss-crossed pile. The third step, "Open the draft and damper," was next. The draft, a metal plate on the end of the stove, just in front of and below the firebox, slid back and forth exposing holes. When it was open, air was fed into the fire by being drawn through the holes underneath the cobs. The damper, a metal disk in the stovepipe just above the cooktop, allowed smoke from the firebox to go up the chimney. Walter double checked the draft and damper to be sure they were wide open before he struck a match, a two-inch, Blue Diamond wooden stick match, igniting the few scattered shucks still attached to the cobs; when shucks were sparse, crumpled newspapers were used to get a fire going.

Walter didn't have much to say as he fired up the stove, he didn't give me a list of instructions. It may have been the first time I'd seen a fire built in the Monster, but it wasn't my first lesson in starting a fire in a stove. Walter knew that. He simply did each step in the order it had to be done and I watched.

After the cobs were engulfed in a high dancing, yellow-red flame, he added more cobs until the firebox was almost full and there was a good bed of fire. Next came the tricky part—adjusting the draft and damper. If the draft were left wide open, there'd have been a roaring hot fire but all the heat would have gone up the chimney. Shut the draft down too much, lack of air would have squelched the blaze and the stove would've belched smoke out into the room. It was a delicate balance, one that varied from stove to stove and one that also varied from day to day, sometimes hour to hour, depending on the weather. There were no markings on the draft or damper. Once Walter had them balanced, I took note of the position of the draft's plate over the holes and the angle of the damper handle. Those two things would serve as guides and help me control and manage the stove.

And so ended Walter's demonstration. There was more, much more, for me to learn but I would have to learn it by actually using the stove. With patience and practice, I set out to take charge of the Monster.

The stove had first claim on any heat it generated. Closing the damper and draft slowed the rate at which the cobs burned, kept heat inside the stove until the stove itself, the stovepipe, chimney and flue were all sufficiently heated before heat was then radiated to the cooktop, oven, reservoir or out into the room. From Mother I'd learned the cooktop got hot enough to cook on much sooner than the oven got hot enough to bake in and that the reservoir and warming ovens were the last to get any of the stove's heat.

On clear, sunny and breezy, high-pressure days, a corncob-fired cookstove could be cooperative and quick to heat. On damp and stormy or windless days when the air was heavy, a stove might be temperamental, contrary and cranky. On those days, the draft needed to be almost fully open to keep a fire going. How much heat a stove generated depended on the arrangement of the stove and stovepipe in relation to the chimney, outside air currents, the height of the chimney, the cleanliness of the chimney and the stove's interior and that included a clean ash box.

"First, you carry in the cobs, then you carry out the ashes." That was one of Mother's old laments. Carrying out ashes wasn't one of her favorite chores or mine either, but she'd taught me that the ashes weren't to be wasted. They were scattered over vegetable and flower beds to be spaded in along with a generous covering of barnyard litter where they furnished valuable mineral supplements as well as loosened the soil.

Scraping soot accumulations out of air chambers surrounding the oven was another messy chore and, thankfully, it only had to be done twice a year. Stovepipes and the chimney were cleaned once a year. Cleaning the chimney was easy. Walter climbed onto the roof, dangled a log chain down the chimney and wiggled it from side to side, jarring soot loose. Stovepipes were taken down and carried outdoors where the sections were separated at the joints and gently rapped, knocking soot out.

Taking care of the stove's exterior, especially the Monster's, was a daily nuisance. It took a lot of scrubbing just to get the black, cast iron surfaces clean and even when it was clean, that old stove never looked even halfway decent unless it was rubbed all over with a coat of "blackener," an exhausting job that called for a lot of "elbow grease."

The National Fire Protection Association may have had a set of specifications on the correct procedures for setting up stoves, but if they did, we didn't have a copy. From common sense and the experience of others, we knew a stove should be placed eighteen inches from any wall, that stovepipes should be made of blackened tin or blued (tempered) steel and that they should be assembled in spans which took the shortest, most direct line to the chimney.

The Association and stove manufacturers assumed the "fuel" burned in stoves was either going to be wood or coal but out on the prairie, that wasn't always the case. I've heard and read the stories about how early settlers burned bundles of dry grass or dried cow dung, sometimes called "prairie coal," in the stoves or fireplaces of their dugouts and sod houses but, by the time my mother was a child, the sod busters had come to the prairie in such numbers and turned so many acres into cornfields that corncobs had become the primary fuel for cookstoves.

As renters, we didn't have the right to cut down trees for firewood. Few trees grew naturally on Nebraska farms and many of those that were planted were fruit trees. The only time a fruit tree was ever used as firewood was if a tree died or was blown down in a storm, then we were free, actually, as a good renter, we were *expected*, to clear away the fallen tree. Then it was permissible to saw up the tree and chop it into logs to fit our stove's firebox.

Mostly we burned cobs, the bare, rough and dented, rusty-red core, all that was left after kernels of corn were shelled from an ear. Cobs varied in size but were usually as big around as a broomstick handle and ranged in length from six to twelve and sometimes as much as fourteen inches long, depending on the variety of corn or the amount of rain or temperatures during the growing season. It'd be hard to find cobs like that today. After an ear of corn passes through one of today's mechanical picker-shellers, the cob falls onto the ground in little bits and pieces. Cobs used to be used on the farm as a mulch or fertilizer, so it's appropriate that they now are left in the field where they are eventually plowed back into the ground. Today, a few cobs might become corncob pipes but the majority of them go into cork substitutes, cleaning and polishing compounds. They are also combined with other waste plant products, such as hulls from cottonseed, oats and rice, to be made into furfural, a liquid chemical used to make plastic and nylon products.

I was well acquainted with cobs. I could say I had a close working relationship with them, not the cobs of industry but the cobs of the kitchen. As a child growing up on a farm, I probably hand-gathered hundreds, maybe thousands of bushels of cobs. Getting married didn't change that, at least not right away, not until we had children and they were old enough and big enough to load cobs into one-bushel, wooden slat baskets—the kind peaches were shipped in—and then carry the baskets from the cob house or cob pile to the house.

Each spring when corn was planted, we hoped for a good harvest in the fall. A good crop meant there would be plenty of grain to feed our livestock and even more to shell and sell. It also meant, though this was seldom mentioned by anyone other than the cob carrier in the family, there would be fresh piles of clean new corncobs.

At harvest time, shucked corn was stored either inside in permanent cribs or outside in temporary open cribs made by stacking slat cribbing two and three rounds high in circles fifty to sixty feet in circumference. Corn was usually shelled during the winter when, hopefully, the market price was the highest. The first corn sheller I remember seeing was powered by a four-horse team driven in a circle by a driver standing on a center platform. As the horses went 'round and 'round, they pulled the sheller gears that rubbed ears of corn until the kernels fell off the cobs. By the time Walter farmed, gasoline engines had replaced horses as power for the corn sheller but the shellers still worked the same. Shelled corn poured out of a spout into a waiting wagon on one side of the sheller and cobs spewed from a trough on the other side. Cobs were either caught in a wagon to be unloaded later into a cob house or they fell from the trough and formed a pointy stack on the ground beside the sheller.

To a city cousin, carrying cobs might not seem like a very important job. Country kids knew better. Cob carriers were responsible for refilling "empties" every day—and there was more to it than just tossing cobs helter-skelter into a basket. Neatness counted. As the oldest child in the family, Mother taught me, and I in turn taught my sister and brothers, the correct way to load a basket of cobs. When cobs were gathered from a cob pile out in the open, it was very important to pull cobs only from one side of the pile and it was just as important that the cobs from that side of the pile not slide down but that the side stay as straight up and down as possible, so that when it rained or snowed, dry cobs could still be found by burrowing into the pile from that straight side. Getting a fire going with wet cobs was next to impossible; at best, it was a slow and a smoky ordeal.

Regardless of whether cobs came from an open pile or a cob house, cob carriers had to be on constant alert for "stowaways." Cobs offered warm, dry and cozy housing for nests of field mice and every now and then one of them would hitch a free basket ride into the house. The trouble didn't start until the stowaway crawled out of the basket to explore the house, presumably looking for a new nest. After the first round of screams and yells subsided, the cat was brought into the house, mouse traps were set and this cook didn't rest easy until the hunt ended with a gray, furry and a very dead little body.

There was an art to loading a cob basket. After every three or four handfuls of cobs, the basket needed a good, side-to-side shake to settle the load and make room for more cobs. A basket might appear full but it could be made to hold still more cobs by standing a row of cobs upright around the rim of the basket like a fence. Filling in that ring of cobs with more cobs increased the basket's capacity by thirty percent.

When corn prices stayed low, as low as fourteen cents a bushel in 1932, shelling was postponed in hopes the price would go up. During the postponement, sometimes our supply of "clean cobs" ran out and we had to resort to "pig pen cobs." Pigs weren't fed shelled corn, they were fed whole ear corn and, in the process of eating the corn off the cobs, pigs rooted the cobs off the feeding platform, scattering them all over the pen. Picking up those cobs was smelly, dusty, unpleasant and a very slow-going job. As much as I disliked gathering pig pen cobs, I disliked having them in my kitchen even more. They had their own "di-STINK-tive" odor, one that became even more offensive when the cobs were burned. Thankfully, the Shack's previous renter had left behind a generous supply of cobs, so, as a bride, I didn't have to deal with pig pen cobs.

In the winter we kept the fire burning from the time we got up until we went to bed. I went through six or seven big baskets of cobs every day and sometimes more on those nights when we "banked the fire." To "bank a fire," we first built up a big bed of red hot, glowing cobs. Then we put on a log, the largest one the firebox would hold. We opened the draft to let in extra air to ignite the log. When it was burning well, the draft was almost closed. It was left open just a crack. In the morning, just by adding cobs to the coals, I could have a full-fledged fire going so quickly, that in no time at all, I was flipping pancakes and frying sausage and eggs.

In the summer, I got by on two baskets of cobs a day, except, of course, on wash days and then the stove was hot most of the day, first to heat the boiler to boil sheets, towels and white shirts and then to heat the "sad irons" used to iron the sun and wind-dried clothes.

It's my guess those old irons got their name because of how one felt after spending hours standing over the ironing board bearing down on them. The irons came in sets. There were two oval iron bases and one clip-on wooden handle in each set. As you ironed with one base, the other base heated on the stove. When a base cooled off and no longer did a good job of pressing out wrinkles and creases, that base was set on the stove to reheat, the handle was removed and clipped onto the base that was hot.

Winter or summer, there was always plenty of wind to dry the wash. On sub-zero days, I braced myself against strong north winds and felt my fingers turn into icicles in order to hang out my wash so it could freeze-dry on the clothesline. Freezing seemed to make whites whiter and colors brighter; then, too, the clothes that had frozen stiff as boards outside dried much faster when they were brought into the house and hung on lines stretched back and forth across the kitchen in front of the stove. Freezing acted as a fabric softener and made clothes easier to iron.

When I could, I avoided firing up the stove on hot, stuffy, breezeless summer days, but its fever could never be completely escaped. I had to "stand the heat in the kitchen" at least once a day—at noon—and even then, I was stingy with the cobs. I tried not to add one more cob than was absolutely necessary to cook the meal. Summer suppers were usually cold leftovers from a hot and hearty noonday dinner.

A cob-fired stove took careful and constant watching and the Black Monster called for extra patience and attention. Because it was so big, it took longer to get hot, and once it was hot, it stayed hotter longer. Even when the stove was hot, the fire couldn't be neglected. It had to be watched and tended to keep it burning at the right level for whatever kind of cooking or baking was being done. I couldn't turn a knob, flip a switch or punch a button to make the stove do what I wanted it to do. It was a case of me learning to recognize when the stove was ready to do what I wanted it to do. Every stove had its own rhythm and the cook adjusted to that rhythm. Timing varied from dish to dish. Many old recipes contain the phrase, "Remove pan from *fire*," and that's an accurate description of how cooking was done on a cob-fired cookstove where there was, for a fact, a fire.

To say "build a fire" suggests a roaring inferno, but that's not what's called for in cooking and baking with a cob-fired stove. What's needed is a steady, well-controlled fire, one that is past the blazing-flame stage.

Even with an established, steady bed of fire, a cook had to keep in mind the level of heat was not the same over the entire cooktop surface. The cooktop was surprisingly versatile and flexible. It was possible to find all intensities of heat from searing hot to barely simmering even on the cooking surface of a relatively small stove. Pans were shifted around on the cooktop to raise or lower the heat. And, just as there wasn't one correct setting for either the damper or the draft, there were no hard and fast rules about where the hottest or the least hot spots on the cooktop were. After I'd boiled potatoes dry a few times, I knew exactly where my stove's hot spots were and I never forgot them.

The two lids directly over the firebox were the hottest ones and that was true for most cooktops. That's where coffee was started, where the teakettle sat and where pans and skillets were set when food needed to come to a quick boil or where meats were fried or braised. To grill a steak or sear a roast in a hurry, a front lid could be removed so the bottom of the skillet or roaster was in direct contact with the fire.

Moderate heat was found near the center of the cooktop. That was where a pan of potatoes, for example, might be set after the potatoes had come to a full boil and needed just enough heat to keep them cooking in a steady but a gentle boil until they were tender.

The far right-hand end of the cooktop, the portion next to the reservoir and farthest from the firebox, provided heat similar to today's crock-pot. There, on the back of the stove, soups and stews simmered and barely bubbled away for hours, mingling flavors and tenderizing stews and roasts. When the lowest heat on the cooktop was still too hot, a pan was set on a trivet raising the bottom of the pot an inch or two above the hot surface. Coffee pots usually needed trivets. Once coffee perked, placing the pot on a trivet at the back of the stove kept the coffee piping hot without simmering it.

Walter had very little cookware in his cupboard, but what he had, a couple of skillets and a couple of pots, was made of heavy cast iron, the perfect cookware to use on cob-fired stoves. They had iron handles—the intense heat of the old cookstoves would have scorched and burned wooden handles—and while they weren't fancy, those cast iron utensils did a super job of cooking. They heated evenly and they retained heat very well. If they were well-seasoned, they were also easy to clean.

A new cast iron skillet, pot or griddle was seasoned by coating its cooking surface with two or three tablespoons of lard and setting it on a hot stove or putting it in a moderate, 350 to 400 degrees Fahrenheit, oven for ten minutes or until the lard got hot and smoked. Then the utensil was allowed to cool on the back of the stove or in the oven until it could be touched without a potholder. When the cookware turned a dull black, that meant the pores were sealed and it was "seasoned." To preserve the seasoning, after each use, the pot was allowed to cool completely before it was wiped with a dry cloth or paper—seasoned iron cookware was never washed with soap and water—and then rubbed with a thin coat of lard.

Throughout each cooking and baking procedure, I checked constantly to see when and if and how many cobs should be added to the fire to maintain, lower or raise the level of heat.

Learning to use the oven proved to be a bigger challenge than stove-top cooking. Except for quick baking—things that baked in twenty minutes or less—oven baking and roasting called for an even, steady fire. Roasting meats and poultry was easier than baking bread, biscuits, cakes, pies or cookies because meats were less likely to be adversely affected by slight oven temperature irregularities. Managing oven temperatures took experience and there were as many ways to do that as there were cooks to tell about it.

Some cooks claimed they could touch the outside of the oven door and tell if the oven temperature was "low," "moderate," "hot" or "scorching hot." Others placed a small piece of white writing paper in the oven for *five minutes* and then estimated the oven's temperature according to the paper's discoloration. If the heat turned the white paper a rich chocolate brown, the oven was considered "quick and hot," just right for biscuits, muffins or pie crust; if it was a dark yellow, the oven was "moderate," right for cakes and breads; and, if it was a light yellow, it was "slow," right for sponge cakes. And others used flour to find the approximate oven temperature. A tablespoon of flour was sprinkled on a piece of plain brown paper and placed in the oven for *five minutes*. From the degree of browning shown by the flour, the oven temperature was judged to be within these ranges: If the flour was light brown, it was a "slow" oven; medium golden brown, "moderate"; dark brown, "hot"; and, very dark brown, "very hot."

Forget browning a piece of paper or flour or feeling the oven door. I didn't use any of those tests. I merely waved my hand inside the oven. That was Tillie's test, it was Carrie's test and it became my oven test, too. Here's how it worked: If I could stand to have my hand inside the oven and wave it around for fifteen seconds, it was a "very hot" oven; twenty seconds, "hot"; thirty seconds, "moderate"; and, sixty seconds, "slow or low." It wasn't long before I could just open the oven door and with one quick hand wave inside, I knew how hot the oven was without even timing myself.

Putting those oven temperatures in Fahrenheit degrees, the ranges would be something like this: Slow oven—250 to 350 degrees; moderate oven—350 to 425 degrees; hot oven—425 to 450 degrees; and, very hot oven—450 to 500 degrees and over.

Except for "a very hot oven," most oven temperatures were best achieved with a full bed of glowing coals rather than with leaping flames. A steady fire produced oven temperatures that were no longer on the increase, temperatures that could be held level so there was less chance of food over-browning or burning.

It was difficult to guess the length of time it took from the time a fire was built in a stove until that stove's oven reached, say, 350 degrees Fahrenheit, hot enough to bake a cake. The time varied from stove to stove; it even varied from one time to the next in the same stove. A cake made from the same recipe, baked in the same pan, in the same oven might take twenty to forty minutes to bake, depending on the weather and on the cook's ability to judge how many cobs to add and when to add them in order to bring the oven up to temperature and then hold it there until the cake tested done. Reaching and holding a perfectly constant 350 degree oven on any cob-fired stove was next to impossible. It didn't matter if the stove had an oven thermometer, the kind where the indicator was mounted on the outside of the oven door; those thermometers were far from accurate. As the old joke had it, a thermometer like that didn't tell how hot the oven was, it only told how hot the oven *door* was.

Along with judging oven temperatures, it was equally important to locate an oven's "hot spots," those small areas which were always hotter than the rest of the oven. Every cob-fired cookstove oven had them and they weren't in the same location in all ovens, though usually they were found in the upper half of the oven near the side wall next to the firebox. I took Carrie's advice on how to find the "hot spots" in my stove's oven. I made a big batch of baking powder biscuits, enough to fill a large cookie sheet and by studying the tops of the baked biscuits, I was able to pinpoint the oven's "hot spots." Typically, a baked biscuit has a light, golden brown top. That's how most of the biscuits in my test looked; a few got too brown; they were close to being burned. From the location of the over-browned biscuits on the cookie sheet, I could determine their exact location in the oven. I made a mental note of those spots and from then on, whenever I baked a pie, cake, cookies or muffins, I rotated pans and cookie sheets, moved them around in the oven once or twice during their baking time so the baked goods browned and baked evenly and, at the same time, avoided being in any of the "hot spots" too long. Sometimes, if after rotating the pans, the bread, rolls or pie crusts still browned too quickly, I placed pieces of plain brown paper lightly over the pans. The food continued to bake under the paper yet the paper protected it from over-browning and burning.

There are some foods that benefit from high oven heat at the beginning of their baking time. High heat during the first few minutes in the oven is crucial to breads baked in loaves or rounds on a cookie sheet rather than in a pan. It sets the crust and helps the bread hold its shape throughout the baking time. To "turn up the oven heat," so to speak, five minutes before the bread was ready for the oven, I added a handful of cobs to the fire. And when the bread went into the oven, I made sure it was placed in or near one of the oven's "hot spots," on a rack in the top position. Some ovens had three rack positions; the Monster's oven had only two. Lowering the rack or placing food on the lowest rack in the oven lowered the oven temperature ten to twenty degrees.

Two-crust fruit pies were started in a "hot" oven, near the back, on the upper left-hand side of the oven. After ten minutes in that position the lower crust was "set" and the upper crust was barely brown. Then the rack was lowered to the middle position and the pie was moved to the center of the rack where it finished baking as long as it continued to bake and brown uniformly; otherwise, it was rotated, moved side to side, front to back in the oven as necessary to make sure it baked evenly.

When the oven overheated, the oven door could be left ajar for a few minutes to let some of the heat escape but that method of "turning down the heat" became very tricky if there was a cake, pie or cookies already in the oven. It was much better to avoid letting the oven get too hot in the first place.

After a few tries, I knew how many cobs to add to maintain a "low," "moderate" or "hot" temperature range and that was the closest any cook could hope to come when regulating the oven of a cob-burning cookstove. Cooking and baking times and temperatures given for recipes were never taken as absolutes; they were "suggestions." There were too many irregularities and uncertainties from one cook to another, from one stove to another, from one day to another, not to mention the lack of standardized pan sizes, to ever be able to state precisely the time or temperature for any recipe. From a practical standpoint, I found it very helpful once I was able to recognize how a particular food looked, smelled or felt as it cooked or baked and when it was done. Of course, I could always stick a toothpick in a cake and if the toothpick came clean, free of crumbs, I knew the cake was done, but there were times when a cake baked so quickly that by the time I tested it, it was already overdone and it was dry. I learned to "catch" the cake just as it began to pull away from the sides of pan, when the top of the cake looked firm and, if it were a plain or a white cake, its top was barely golden brown; with a chocolate cake, the top turns a darker shade of brown. When cakes reached that stage, then I reached for a toothpick and if the cake tested done, I could expect that it would still be moist and light. As a beginning cook, I tested meats for doneness by poking them with a sharp, two-tine cooking fork to see if they were tender, but each time they were tested they lost some of their juices. Later, by observation, I was able to tell when meat was done by the color of the pan juices—if they ran clear and were no longer pink, the roast was done—and by touching them— if there was some "give" when a roast was pressed lightly, it was done. I checked the color of pan juices, too, when I roasted fowl, and also I gently twisted leg joints; if they moved easily, the chicken, turkey, goose or duck was done.

Learning to cook on a cob-fired cookstove took time and it took practice. But when you cook three meals a day, day in and day out, you get plenty of opportunities to practice and perfect your kitchen skills. Breaks in the daily routine were few. A cook "made do" with what she had on hand. There were no drive-through windows at the Colonel's, McDonald's or Wendy's in the 1920s. An occasional sack of six-for-a-quarter hamburgers from the corner diner was a BIG treat back then, so was a Sunday dinner with the Mickish or Hendrickson family.

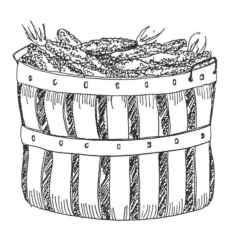

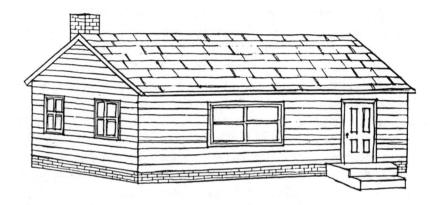

# The Shack

# THE SHACK

The Shack was our first home. We lived there together only three months. Walter moved into the one-room house after he rented the 160-acre Kriha farm March 1, 1922, and "batched," a 1920s word describing a young man who lived alone, for nearly eight months before we were married in November of that year.

The farm was located halfway between Gibbon and Ravenna, four miles northwest of Walter's parents, and, like all the farms we rented or owned the next sixty years, it was in Buffalo County, Nebraska. The buildings of the farmstead were laid out between a pasture and plowed fields about an eighth of a mile from a graded dirt road.

"Does it have running water?" was one of my first questions about the house.

"Sure it's got running water," Walter answered. "When the water pail is empty, you *run* out to the windmill, fill the pail and *run* back to the house."

And every pail of water carried into the house had to be carried out as dish water, bath water, wash water or it went out in the slop pail. That pail did the job of a garbage disposal. It collected potato and apple peelings, pea hulls and other kitchen scraps—anything the dog or cat wouldn't eat.

There was no need to ask if the house had a bathroom; without running water, somewhere, out behind the Shack, there'd be a two-hole privy.

The windmill stood as a sentinel in the center of the farmyard about a hundred yards from the house. Water from its pump ran to tanks in the corrals through underground pipes, except, of course, when temperatures fell below zero in the winter freezing the iron pump solid. Then we ran to the windmill with a teakettle full of boiling water which was poured slowly over the pump to thaw it out and get the water flowing again.

The November day we moved me and my things into the Shack wasn't the first time I'd seen the place. I'd seen it earlier in September. I was spending the weekend at Hendricksons' when, right at the dinner table in front of his whole family, Walter asked if I'd like to see his "batching quarters," meaning the Shack. Before I could answer, it was arranged that his older sister, Jessie, would go to the Shack with us, because, as Walter's mother pointed out, "It wouldn't look right to take your girl to your place *alone.*"

As we approached from the east, I had to look twice to see the squatty, little white house surrounded on three sides by apricot and apple trees. Next to a full-sized barn, corncrib and other sheds, the house looked even smaller than twelve-by-twenty-four feet.

A giggling Jessie led the way through the Shack's only door.

"I'll go first and make sure Buzzer made the bed," she said.

Jessie had been two years old when Walter was born and "Buzzer" was the closest she could come to saying "brother." The nickname stuck but it was always understood that it was for family use only. No one else dared to call Walter "Buzzer," not unless that someone was looking for a fight.

Inside, the Shack was wall-to-wall furniture. The door, near the north end of the east wall, opened between the bedroom and kitchen ends of the room, beside a high, broad, double-door oak wardrobe in the northeast corner, near a small dining table and four chairs under a big east window. On the other side of the table, in the southeast corner, was an oak kitchen cabinet. Its four-foot zinc work surface topped two pull-out bins which held flour and sugar; on its upper shelves, Walter stored cereals. The south end of the room was *all* stove—a huge, dull black cookstove. In the southwest corner, crowded behind a tall, wide and handsome oak cupboard with etched glass upper doors, was a small, three-drawer walnut chest. It held a pail of water and wash basin and served as a wash stand. A rocking chair stood beside the bed. Linoleum covered the kitchen area of the floor and a trail of rag rugs went from the door to the bed and to the wardrobe.

Another bachelor farmer had lived in the Shack ahead of Walter, so before her son moved in, Carrie scrubbed the place down thoroughly, fumigated it and brushed a beige-colored, watery Kalsomine wash over the walls and hung marquisette sash curtains over cloth roller shades on the big window on the east wall and two narrow windows on the south.

A "tour" of the place took less than five minutes.

As each Hendrickson son or daughter married Will and Carrie gave them a team of horses, a sow and a cow. Two families who were long-time friends and neighbors of the Hendricksons went together on their wedding gift for us—a dozen laying hens. None of the "gifts" came boxed or adorned with fancy paper and ribbons. They came wrapped with lots of practical and genuine good wishes and affection and we were mighty happy to get them. Having our own livestock and our own milk and eggs—that was all a farm couple just getting started could wish for.

What little machinery Walter had—a plow, harrow, corn planter, "go-devil" (a tillage tool), and cultivator—he bought secondhand at farm sales. What he couldn't afford to buy the first year he farmed—a grain drill, mower, rake, hay buck and other hay-making tools—he borrowed from his father.

# 1922 - 1934

Babies and moving dominate memories of our first twelve years of marriage. We lived on four different farms and our children, a boy, William Wayne, and a girl, Ethel Mae were born during those years. Between 1923 and 1930, we moved from the Shack to Lou's, to Clayt's and to Gladys's. I'd just get us settled into one house and I'd be packing us up to move into another. I knew how to drive a car and that was a big help when we moved.

The summer I turned sixteen, my father taught me to drive the family car—a dark green, four-door, Buick touring car with isinglass side windows. The car was an "easy starter"; it only took a couple of quick spins of the crank to get the motor running and from then on it was a matter of coordinating the stick shift with the clutch pedal to get the car in motion. To my father, it was a necessity that, as the oldest child, I knew how to drive; I considered it a privilege. I drove Mother to town for groceries on Saturdays so Dad could stay in the field and I drove her and my two brothers and sister to afternoon *kolache* and coffee visits with her widowered father or to see her sisters, Anna and Julia.

One day, not long after we were married, when we were getting ready to go for a drive, my new husband motioned for me to get into the driver's seat of his Model T Ford.

"It's your car, too," he said, "you may as well start driving it."

Driving the Ford was a little different than driving the Buick. For one thing, the Ford didn't start as easily. As one of our neighbors put it, "Spinning hard the crank was the only way to get 'her' going." And shifting gears on the Ford was also different. It had five gears—first, low, high, second and reverse—the position of the clutch pedal determined which gear the car's transmission was in. Once I got the hang of finding each gear, besides trips to town for groceries and other shopping, Walter soon had me running errands for him. I picked up medicine from the drugstore to treat livestock, took plow shares and cultivator shovels to the blacksmith to be sharpened and, when there was a machinery breakdown, I was the one who ran to the implement dealer's shop for repairs. On moving days, I made several trips with the car packed with dishes, pots and pans and other housewares—towels, bedding, clothes, mirrors, framed pictures—any items not well-suited to an open-air wagon ride.

Each move took us to a larger farm, one with more tillable acres where the "lay of the land" and the soil was better. The last move, the move to Gladys's, was to an irrigated farm. We were willing to move whenever and wherever the farming prospects appeared more promising. And while the houses on the four farms varied in size and appearance, their facilities were standard for farmhouses of the time—cob-burning cookstoves in the kitchen, wood and coal-burning basin heaters in the dining room and "front room" (living room or parlor), kerosene and gasoline lamps and lanterns and outdoor privies. Until we installed utilities in the house on Gladys's farm, none of the houses had hot and cold running water, central heating, electrical service or basements though each farm did have a cave or cellar, none of which were directly under the house. They were thirty to fifty feet from the kitchen door. Some were dug into the side of a hill and some were covered with a low, earthen dome. Either way, a cave might have gone completely unnoticed except for a wooden door laid at about a thirty degree angle over the cave's stairwell and a small chimney-like air vent which protruded out of the ground above the cave.

My kitchen routine ran smoothly and almost constantly, day in and day out. I baked pies, cakes or cookies nearly every day; bread, every other day; rolls, two or three times a week; and churned butter once or twice a week.

Churning was, admittedly, a monotonous job but it had one redeeming value—you could sit down and do it. I'd fill the one-gallon glass jar of my Daisy churn with thick sour cream—butter can be made from either sweet or sour cream but I preferred the flavor of butter made from sour cream—then I'd sit down with the churn on my lap and begin turning the crank, rapidly at first, to get the cream thoroughly agitated and frothy. Thirty or forty minutes later, as the cream thickened and turned to butter and the crank became harder to turn, the cranking pace slackened. When butter held together in large clumps in the churn, the buttermilk was drained off and the soft butter was turned into a bowl where excess water and buttermilk were "worked out" and salt was "worked in." "Working" the butter, a continuous stirring, pressing and kneading of the butter, was done with a flat, six-inch wide wooden paddle. When no more moisture could be "worked out" of the butter, the butter was pressed into a one-pound block-shaped, wooden butter mold. A gallon of rich, heavy cream made about a pound and half of butter. If, when I churned, I knew we would be having company, I packed some of the fresh-churned butter into a round, wooden butter mold with a fancy flowery design on the top. The mold was one of my mother's; she'd slipped it into my hope chest along with a butter paddle my father had whittled for me.

How much and how often I baked or churned depended on how many people I guessed might pull their chairs up to my table for breakfast, dinner or supper on any given day. Walter's folks and several of his brothers and sisters lived nearby and we ate meals together quite often. Sometimes they were invited but more likely than not, our "guests" came unexpectedly but they were always welcome.

With a well-stocked cave and pantry, putting an extra plate or two or three or more on the table was never a problem. Each winter I processed home-butchered pork and beef and each summer I canned hundreds of quart and pint jars of fruits and vegetables. Shelves lined with sparkling glass Mason and Kerr jars filled with green beans, corn, tomatoes, pickles, sauerkraut, peaches, cherries, applesauce, pickles, jams and jellies made a colorful fall mosaic in the cellar's filtered light. There were potatoes in the bins, apples in baskets and carrots and parsnips buried in tubs of sand. With one trip to the cellar even in the middle of winter, I could put a meal together to feed a six-man corn shelling crew with half a day's notice.

Shelling crews were about half the size of grain threshing crews and there was one other difference—threshers got two meals a day and shellers got only one.

In 1929, at the time we lived on Clayt's in the smallest of all the houses we ever lived in, we entertained the Hendrickson family—fifteen adults and five children—on Christmas Eve. It was a full house but it wasn't too crowded to squeeze in Santa Claus and his bag of goodies for our gift exchange.

The New York stock market had crashed that October and while the jolt could be felt out here on the prairie, it probably didn't hit farmers quite as hard as it did city folks. Farmers had been walking around with empty wallets in their overall pockets for so long, they didn't notice any big financial slumps, at least not right away. We felt lucky to be able to draw names so every one in the family, kids and grown-ups alike, got at least one gift for Christmas. There was a one-dollar limit on the price of each gift but in 1929, a dollar bought something—a purse, a tie, a pair of gloves, a small doll, a baseball glove...

The next year, 1930, we moved to Gladys's. The new decade got underway with the country in fiscal shock. Two years later, it was bogged down in the Great Depression. Under President Franklin Delano Roosevelt many "lettered" programs spewed out of Washington—PWA, WPA, NRA, TVA, NIRA and the AAA. That last one, the Agricultural Adjustment Act, was aimed at helping the farmer. Recovery was slow to come. At the same time the economic outlook was under clouds of financial gloom and doom, the Great Plains states were under dark and dirty clouds of the Dust Bowl. Topsoil from the Dakotas, Nebraska, Kansas, Oklahoma and Texas filled the skies, drifted across fields and roads burying fences; it sifted through closed windows and under closed doors. Not even the drought-proof, irrigated valley escaped the dusty and gritty onslaught.

It was a lucky thing for me that we had purchased the new and used household furnishings we did while we lived on Lou's farm. In the "dirty thirties," we could barely eke out five dollars from the cream-and-egg money to buy a much-needed used icebox. We had our hands full trying to pay for the one brand new tractor we'd bought in 1930. It was a gray International Harvester Farmall Regular. It looked like an over-sized tricycle with its two small, close-set, iron rimmed wheels on the front end and two, big open-lugged iron wheels on the rear. It cost somewhere around six hundred dollars and it took us more than two years to pay for it. We couldn't afford to buy any of the machinery manufactured especially for use with the Farmall—planters, cultivators, grain binders and plows. Walter adapted horse-drawn machinery to pull behind the new tractor, and since that was long before tractors and machinery were equipped with hydraulic lifts, someone—sometimes that someone was me—had to ride on the planter or the cultivator to manually drop and lift shovels in and out of the ground at the start and the end of the rows.

Hard times didn't stop recipe collecting. Recipes seldom appeared in the small, local newspapers or farm magazines that came in the mail, and if there were food columns and recipes in the popular women's magazines of the time, like other farm women I knew, I couldn't afford subscriptions to those magazines. Instead, we shared family recipes among ourselves. I got them from my mother and mother-in-law, sister and sisters-in-law and neighbors and friends. Some of those old, home-tested recipes written on scraps of note paper, backs of used envelopes or brown wrapping paper are still in my collection.

# RECIPE GUIDE

Recipes from decades past have been updated for use with today's standard measuring utensils, bowls, pots, baking pans, casseroles and food mixers, blenders and other electrical appliances including ranges, ovens and cooktops with uniform temperature ranges and controls.

"Flour" means "all-purpose flour" and "sugar," "granulated sugar."

For "light cream," use Half and Half, for "thick cream," whipping cream and for "sour cream," commercially soured cream. Commercially soured milk is not available; buttermilk may be substituted for sour milk or add vinegar to sweet milk, one teaspoon of vinegar to one cup of milk, and set aside a few minutes for the milk to "sour."

Use only butter, when a recipe specifies "butter." Do not substitute margarine. In recipes where margarine can be substituted for butter with little or no appreciable effect on the taste, texture or appearance of the final product, "butter or margarine" will be indicated.

# BREADS

One of my earliest childhood memories is of my mother baking bread. She always started bread in the evening, after the supper dishes were done. It was made in what she called a "bread raiser," a heavy tin bowl which sat on an attached footed base. The raiser was deep and round, twenty inches in diameter, and ten or twelve inches deep with tapered sides. She used the sponge method and she did not have a recipe. With her hands, she scooped six or seven cups of flour into the raiser. In a small bowl, she worked four cakes of compressed yeast into a cup of warm water to which she had added half a teaspoon of sugar. The sugar wasn't spooned in with a measuring spoon but with a spoon ordinarily used to stir sugar into a cup of coffee or tea. When the yeast was dissolved and activated, she added another cup and a half of warm water. If we'd had boiled potatoes for supper, she saved the potato water and used it as part of the liquid for the bread mixture and she might also have held back one of the cooked potatoes to mash and stir in with the potato water.

Mother NEVER put milk or eggs in yeast bread dough.

When the yeast and liquids were thoroughly blended, she made a hole in the center of the flour and added the liquid all at one time; it made a fairly thin mixture. At that point, using a big wooden spoon, she gave the mixture a very hard beating. When the surface was all bubbly, she added two teaspoons of salt and, if the mixture appeared a little too thin, she added another cup of flour, just enough to make a light sponge mixture.

Then the raiser bowl was wrapped, first, in a clean, dry tea towel and then in several thicknesses of heavy flannel and was placed on the lid of the stove's reservoir where there was just enough warmth to keep the yeast "working" all through the night.

The next morning, after breakfast, and again using the wooden spoon, she stirred in more flour, just enough to make a stiff yet light dough but a dough that was not sticky. While the dough was still in the raiser, she kneaded it until it was smooth and satiny and divided it into quarters which were then shaped into loaves and placed side by side in a greased four-by-ten-by-twenty-four-inch black tin baking pan. The loaves were covered with a tea towel and set either inside of or on top of the stove's warming oven. After the loaves doubled in bulk, they were ready for the oven. Bread baked first for fifteen minutes in a "hot oven," about 400 degrees Farenheit. Once bread was in the oven, the fire was allowed to die down to a bed of embers and was maintained at that level by adding only one cob every fifteen to twenty minutes. Taking care to slow-bake the bread another forty-five to sixty minutes prevented the loaves from getting too brown and their crusts too thick. Mother tested the bread for doneness by thumping the upper crust with her thumb. If it sounded hollow, it was done. To Mother, the perfect loaf of bread was white, light and feathery, with the top crust free of cracks and creases and when the bread was sliced, the holes in the bread's interior were very tiny and uniform in size.

By mixing up the bread the night before, Mother did save some time the next morning; still, the final mixing, kneading, shaping, rising and baking took up an entire morning. In winter months, when the day started a little later, the baked bread would be coming out of the oven about the time I got home from school after having walked a mile across the fields. I remember that wonderful yeasty aroma that hit my nose and made my mouth water when I walked in the door. Is there *anything* that smells as good as homemade bread baking?

Bread was on the table for EVERY meal so it was essential that I acquire the "knack" of making bread and that I be able to do it simply, quickly and well.

Though Mother tried her best to teach me, I never quite got

the hang of making bread in the raiser and I thought starting the dough the night before with the "sponge method" was a nuisance. So Mother skipped that and concentrated on teaching me the "straight method" of bread baking. If I wasn't going to make bread in a raiser, then she insisted, I had to make it in a large, heavy crockery bowl. She claimed the earthenware retained heat generated by the "working" yeast and also protected the rising dough from cool drafts better than a bowl made of a thin, lightweight material, such as tin, aluminum or enamelware. As I practiced making bread under her direction, together we were able to come up with a recipe with more accurate measurements and more specific directions for me to follow so I was able to turn out the same quality of bread every time I baked.

## WHITE BREAD I

The home baker's goal in 1922 was to turn out a bread that was as white, fine grained and as airy in texture as the bread that came from the bakery. This basic method of bread making came very close. I hadn't been married very long before I began doubling this recipe to make four loaves at one time. All four loaves were baked in the bottom of a big, heavy aluminum roaster, one large enough to roast a turkey in—

1 cake of compressed yeast
1/4 teaspoon sugar
1/2 cup warm water
1-3/4 cups warm water or lukewarm potato water
3 tablespoons sugar
1 tablespoon salt
2 tablespoons lard, melted
7 to 7-1/2 cups flour

In a small bowl, soften yeast in 1/2 cup warm water to which 1/4 teaspoon of sugar has been added. Work water into yeast with the back of a spoon. Set aside 5 minutes. In a large bowl, combine 1-3/4 cups of remaining liquid, 3 tablespoons sugar, salt, lard and half the flour. Beat hard with a spoon until mixture is smooth and bubbles burst on the surface. Add only as much of remaining flour as is needed to form a soft dough. Turn dough out onto a well-floured board or pastry cloth. Cover with inverted bowl and let rest 5 minutes. Knead until smooth and elastic, about 10 minutes. Place dough in a well-greased bowl; turn to grease surface. Cover; let rise until double in bulk. Punch dough down in the bowl. Cover; let rise again until double in bulk. Grease two 9 x 5 x 3-inch loaf pans. Turn dough out onto lightly floured board or pastry cloth. Divide in half. Shape into loaves and place in prepared pans. Cover lightly; let rise until almost double in bulk. Preheat oven to 350 degrees F. Bake bread one hour or until tops of loaves are golden brown and bread tests done. Turn bread out of pans onto cooling racks; brush tops with melted butter. Makes 2 loaves.

This is still my favorite basic bread recipe though through the years there have been some changes in the list of ingredients. I now use dry yeast and add one-fourth teaspoon of sugar and a dash of ginger to the water in which the yeast is dissolved. The larger portion of the water has been replaced by milk which makes a whiter bread and one with a softer crust. And, to improve the bread's flavor, butter or margarine has replaced lard as the shortening.

## WHITE BREAD II
Made with today's enriched flour, this white bread is nutritious as well as delicious—

2 packages of dry yeast
1/2 cup warm water
1/4 teaspoon sugar
Dash of ginger
1-3/4 cups milk, scalded
3 tablespoons sugar
1 tablespoon salt
2 tablespoons melted butter or margarine
7 to 7-1/2 cups flour
1 tablespoon melted butter or margarine

In a small bowl, soften yeast in warm water to which 1/4 teaspoon sugar and a dash of ginger have been added. Set aside 5 minutes. Let scalded milk cool to lukewarm. In a large bowl, combine lukewarm milk with sugar, salt and 2 tablespoons butter. Add yeast mixture together with 2 cups of flour. Beat hard with a spoon or with an electric mixer at low speed until mixture is smooth and bubbly. Add only as much of remaining flour as is needed to form a soft dough. Turn dough out onto a lightly floured board or pastry cloth. Cover with inverted bowl; let rest 5 minutes. Knead until smooth and elastic, about 5 minutes. Place in greased bowl; turn to grease surface. Cover; let rise until double in bulk. Punch dough down in the bowl. Cover; and again, let rise until double in bulk. Grease two 9 x 5 x 3-inch loaf pans. Turn dough out onto lightly floured board or pastry cloth. Divide in half. Use hands to flatten each portion into an oval, tuck ends under and place in prepared pans. Cover; let rise until *almost* double in bulk. Preheat oven to 350 degrees. Bake loaves 1 hour or until bread tests done. Turn out of pan onto cooling racks; brush tops with 1 tablespoon melted butter. Makes 2 loaves.

Seventy-five years ago, the closer a family was to the old sod, the more that family seemed to cling to the foods of their old country. This was evident in my mother's and father's families, especially when it came to breads. My mother, Tillie Miller Mickish, was born in Iowa and lived most of her life in Buffalo County, Nebraska. Both of her parents, Paul and Mary Fiala Miller, were born in Bohemia, now a part of Czechoslovakia. Paul's mother died when he was fourteen and in 1857, his father moved his family, one son and six daughters, to the United States. They settled first on a farm near Salone, Iowa. Paul enlisted in the Union Army in 1863 and fought in several Civil War battles before his 1865 discharge. He and Mary married in 1867 and had six children, four of whom lived to make the move to a Nebraska homestead in 1879 where they lived in a sod house near other families in the growing Czech colony in Sherman County.

Mary Fiala Miller died when Tillie, her youngest daughter, was twelve years old. At twelve, Tillie was already an accomplished baker. She made rye bread, *Kolaches*, *Rohlicky* and *Houska* just the way her *Mamincina*, mother, had taught her so that she might please her *Tatinek*, father, and her younger brother, William. I never knew *Babicky*, grandmother, Miller, but I knew *Deoecek*, grandfather, Miller very well and I remember how he enjoyed coming to our house to eat when my mother, his daughter, baked these old Bohemian favorites. For him, the old breads were tender reminders of a homeland he'd left behind. These updated versions of the Old World recipes are the result of adaptations made by five generations of cooks but they still can fill a kitchen with sweet, yeasty, memory-making fragrances.

## *BABICKY'S* RYE BREAD
Rye bread with caraway seeds, the way Czechs liked it best—

2 packages dry yeast
1-1/2 cups warm water
1/4 teaspoon sugar
Dash of ginger
1/4 cup molasses
1/3 cup sugar
1 tablespoon salt
2 tablespoons softened margarine
1 teaspoon caraway seeds
2-1/2 to 3 cups flour
2-1/2 cups rye flour

In a large bowl, dissolve yeast in warm water to which 1/4 teaspoon sugar and ginger have been added. Set aside 5 minutes. Stir in molasses, sugar, salt, margarine, caraway seeds and 2-1/2 cups of flour. *Use all-purpose, white flour only at this point.* Beat well with a spoon or with an electric mixer until mixture is smooth and bubbles burst on the surface. Use a spoon to blend in rye flour. Turn dough out onto lightly floured board or pastry cloth. Cover with inverted bowl; let rest 5 minutes. Knead 5 minutes; take care not to knead in any more flour than is absolutely necessary; rye flour is stickier than wheat flour and by combining the two flours, the resulting bread has the look and taste of rye but with a lighter texture. Place dough in a well-greased bowl; turn to grease surface. Cover; let rise until doubled in bulk. Punch dough down while it is still in the bowl. Cover; let rise again until doubled in bulk. Grease a cookie sheet generously. Turn dough out onto lightly floured board or pastry cloth. Divide in half. Shape dough into two round loaves and place on prepared sheet. Cover lightly with a damp cloth to prevent a hard crust from forming on the dough as it rises. Let rise until *not quite* doubled in bulk. Preheat oven to 375 degrees F. Bake bread 35 minutes or until it tests done. Remove from baking sheet and place on cooling racks. Makes 2 loaves.

My father loved music and he was anxious that I learn to play an instrument. I started with an accordion when I was seven years old but I wasn't big enough, my arms weren't strong enough, to pump out the notes so I switched to the piano. My music teacher lived in Hazard, twelve miles west of Ravenna. She rode a train to Ravenna every Saturday morning and gave lessons in the home of friends who owned a grocery store and bakery. A half-hour lesson cost fifty cents and when my lesson went well, I was rewarded with a nickel to spend at the bakery. When plums were in season, I bought a warm slice of Fresh Plum Coffee Cake.

### FRESH PLUM COFFEE CAKE
Use Italian or any red plums—

3 packages dry yeast
1/2 cup warm water
1/4 teaspoon sugar
Dash of ginger
1 teaspoon salt
1/2 cup sugar
1/2 cup lukewarm milk
1/3 cup melted butter or margarine
4 eggs
1/2 teaspoon freshly grated orange peel
1 teaspoon vanilla
4-1/2 to 5 cups sifted flour
1 teaspoon light cream, Half and Half
3 pounds fresh plums, quartered

Streusel Topping:
1/4 cup butter or margarine
1/3 cup sugar
1/2 teaspoon cinnamon
1/2 teaspoon vanilla
3/4 cup flour
3/4 cup chopped walnuts

In a large bowl, sprinkle yeast over warm water to which 1/4 teaspoon sugar and ginger have been added. Set aside 5 minutes. Add salt, 1/2 cup sugar, milk and butter. Mix thoroughly. Beat in 3 eggs, orange peel and vanilla. Use a wooden spoon to stir in 3 cups of flour; blend well, then beat hard 3 minutes. Add only as much of remaining flour as is needed to make a soft dough. Turn dough out onto a lightly floured pastry board or cloth. Cover with inverted bowl; let dough rest 10 minutes. Knead 10 minutes or until smooth and elastic. Place dough in a well-greased bowl; turn to grease surface. Cover; let rise until double in bulk, about 40 minutes. While dough rises, make topping. In a small bowl, cream margarine. Add sugar, cinnamon and vanilla. Cream until light and fluffy. Add flour; blend thoroughly. Stir in walnuts and blend well. Punch dough down then turn out onto lightly floured pastry board or cloth and knead 2 minutes. Preheat oven to 350 degrees F. Grease a 9 x 13 x 2-inch baking pan. Press dough into bottom and sides of pan. Beat remaining egg with cream and brush on dough. Top with plums and sprinkle with Streusel Topping. Bake 45 minutes or until crust and topping are both golden brown. Cool coffee cake in pan 10 minutes before slicing. Serves 12.

## KOLACHES

When I found this recipe, it was made with two cakes of compressed yeast and lard. It has gone through many changes to become the all-time favorite dough for making old-fashioned Czech *"kolachy"* —

2 cups milk, scalded
1/4 cup margarine
1/4 cup shortening
1/2 cup sugar
2 teaspoons salt
2 packages dry yeast
1/2 cup warm water
1/4 teaspoon sugar
Dash of ginger
2 eggs, well beaten
6 to 7 cups flour
1/2 cup melted margarine

To scalded milk add margarine, shortening, sugar and salt. Cool to lukewarm. In a small bowl, dissolve yeast in warm water to which 1/4 teaspoon of sugar and ginger have been added. Set aside 5 minutes. In a large bowl, combine milk and yeast mixtures. Add eggs. Add 2 cups of flour. Beat hard with a spoon or with an electric mixer at medium speed 2 to 3 minutes to form a very soft, bubbly dough. Gradually add 4 cups of flour, 1 cup at a time; beat well after each addition. Add only as much of the remaining cup of flour as is needed to form a soft dough. Turn dough out onto lightly floured board or pastry cloth. Cover with inverted bowl; let rest 5 minutes. Knead 5 minutes. Place dough in greased bowl; turn to grease surface. Cover; let rise until double in bulk. Turn dough out onto lightly floured board or pastry cloth. Cover with inverted bowl; let rest 10 minutes. Grease four cookie sheets. Use a sharp knife to cut off pieces of dough the size of a large walnut and gently, without any pressure on the dough, roll it between well-floured palms of the hands until it is smooth and round. *Cut and roll rounds one at a time.* Place rounds 2 inches apart on prepared cookie sheets. Brush tops lightly with melted margarine. Cover with waxed paper; let rise until double in size and dough is so light that a dent remains after the dough is touched lightly with a finger. With the first two fingers of each hand, make an indentation in the center of each round; stretch dough slightly to form a hollow to hold apricot, prune or poppy seed filling. For variation, top some of the apricot and prune fillings with a Cottage Cheese Topping. Cover filled and topped rolls lightly with waxed paper; let rise until dough is almost double in bulk and light to the touch. Preheat oven to 400 degrees F. Bake 10 to 12 minutes or until rolls are a very delicate golden brown and test done. Remove rolls from cookie sheets but do not put on cooling racks; cool on several thicknesses of newspaper covered with waxed paper. Makes 90 to 100 *kolaches.*

Apricot Filling:
1 1-pound box of dried apricots
Water to cover
1/4 to 1/3 cup sugar

In a small saucepan, combine apricots and water. Cook over medium heat until fruit is soft and most of the water has been absorbed. Add sugar. Cook until mixture thickens. Mash to a fine puree. Set aside to cool.

Prune Filling:
1 1-pound box of dried prunes
Water to cover
1/4 to 1/3 cup sugar

In a small saucepan, combine prunes and water. Cook over medium heat until fruit is soft and most of the water has been absorbed. When prunes are cool enough to handle, pit, add sugar and return to medium heat. Cook until mixture thickens. Mash to a fine puree. Set aside to cool.

Poppy Seed Filling:
1/2 pound poppy seeds, ground
1 cup water
1/2 cup milk
1/2 cup sugar
1 tablespoon butter or margarine
1 teaspoon vanilla
Dash of salt

In a small saucepan, combine poppy seeds and water. Cook over low heat until most of water is absorbed, about an hour. Add milk and sugar. Return to low heat and cook 10 minutes. Watch sauce carefully so it does not scorch. Stir in butter, vanilla and salt. Set aside to cool.
Canned commercial fillings may be used in place of homemade fillings.

Cottage Cheese Topping:
1 cup cottage cheese, small curd style, do not use creamed style
3 tablespoons sugar
Dash of cinnamon

Press as much moisture as possible out of cottage cheese. In a small bowl, combine cottage cheese, sugar and cinnamon. Blend well.

## HOUSKA

Though it's often called a Czech Christmas *cake*, this loaf is really a rich yeast dough. My grandmother insisted *Houska* had to be made with a wooden spoon and that the almonds and raisins had to be worked into the risen dough with the hands, and that's exactly how my mother and I always made it. The original old recipe has been updated many times, but even in this, its latest version, I still use ONLY BUTTER, *never* margarine, and I use only *freshly* grated lemon rind—

4 cups unsifted flour
1 teaspoon salt
1/2 cup sugar
1/2 cup butter, *no margarine*, please
1 package dry yeast
1/4 cup warm water
1/4 teaspoon sugar
Dash of ginger
1 egg, slightly beaten
1 cup milk, scalded
1 tablespoon freshly grated lemon peel
1 teaspoon vanilla
1/4 cup slivered, blanched almonds
1/4 cup seedless raisins

Butter Icing:
2 tablespoons butter
1 cup sifted powdered sugar
1/4 teaspoon vanilla
1 to 2 tablespoons milk
1/4 cup chopped almonds

In a large bowl, combine flour, salt and 1/2 cup sugar. Add butter and with a pastry blender or two table knives, cut butter into dry ingredients until mixture resembles coarse cornmeal. In a small bowl, dissolve yeast in warm water to which 1/4 teaspoon sugar and ginger have been added. Set aside five minutes. Combine egg, milk, lemon peel and vanilla and add to yeast mixture. Blend thoroughly before adding to flour mixture. Beat hard with a wooden spoon until all ingredients are thoroughly combined and the soft dough forms a ball in the bowl. Turn dough out onto lightly floured board or pastry cloth. Cover with inverted bowl; let rest 5 minutes. Knead until smooth, about 10 minutes. Place dough in a well-greased bowl; turn to grease surface. Cover; let rise until double in bulk, about 1-1/2 to 2 hours. Grease a cookie sheet. While dough is still in the bowl, punch down and sprinkle with almonds and raisins. Lightly flour hands and using only the fingers, gently blend and work nuts and raisins evenly into the dough. Turn dough out onto lightly floured board or pastry cloth. Divide into nine equal portions. Using the hands and *a very light touch*, roll each portion into a 20-inch strip; try to make all nine strips identical in diameter and length. Twist, braid and layer the nine strips of dough to make *one* big loaf in this manner: Use *four* strips to make bottom layer; twist two strips together twice, pull and stretch dough ever so slightly to taper the ends and then gently pinch ends of strips together; and, place the two resulting strips less than an inch apart, side by side on the cookie sheet. Use *three* strips to make the middle braided layer; start braid by placing three strips side by side on top of bottom layer; work from the center of the strips; gently pull and stretch to taper ends of the strips; lap strands one over another; and, braid to each end of the strips. Use *two* strips for the top layer; twist two remaining strips together; pull dough slightly as it is twisted to taper the ends to seal smoothly. As loaf is assembled, shape, stretch and fit each layer gently into place to form a long pyramid. Pinch edges as necessary to hold each layer firmly in place. Cover loaf lightly with a damp cloth; let rise until *it is not quite doubled in bulk*. Preheat oven to 350 degrees F. Bake 35 minutes or until bread is golden brown on all sides and tests done. While loaf bakes, make Butter Icing. In a small bowl, cream butter with 1/2 cup powdered sugar. Add vanilla and milk; blend thoroughly. Gradually beat in remaining powdered sugar until icing reaches desired spreading consistency. Remove loaf from cookie sheet. Place on a cooling rack. Drizzle hot loaf with Butter Icing. Sprinkle with chopped almonds. Makes one large loaf. If *Houska* is to be reheated and served later, do not add icing or almonds until after the loaf has been reheated. Makes 1 loaf. Serves 20.

"Where there are Czechs, there's music and where there's music, there's dancing..." That's how it was in our neighborhood. Dances usually took place during spring, summer and fall months for two reasons: One, after a winter of feeding livestock, there was less hay and straw left in the loft and that meant more room for dancers and, two, it was too cold to dance in unheated barns in the wintertime. The wooden floors of the lofts were polished slick by the straw and hay. They glistened and shone and called out for dancing feet to whirl through waltzes and fast-stepping polkas and slide gracefully into the slower tempo of schottisches as played by a four-piece Czech band. Sometimes a four-piece band consisted of *four* accordions.

Dances were family affairs, no baby sitters were needed. Sleeping babies and very young children napped under coats and jackets on benches or in the hay while their mamas and papas danced the afternoon away.

For a Sunday dance, everyone dressed in their "Sunday best," women and girls in their dressiest homemade dresses and men and boys in white shirts and neckties under dark suits or jackets and trousers. Young people learned to dance at the barn dances. Fathers and uncles taught the little girls in the family and mothers and aunts coaxed shy little boys out onto the floor. Everyone danced, young and old alike. My parents were very good dancers. They won a waltz contest once and ever after, their friends called them "The Waltz Champions." Their prize was a five-dollar bill.

The host family furnished the barn and music and those who came to dance brought the food—deep, round dishpans piled high with roast beef sandwiches, fried chicken, dill pickles and sweet rolls—*kolaches* and *rohlicky*. There were no plates, not even paper napkins—everyone took the food up and ate it right out of their hands. Everyone furnished their own coffee cup or beer mug. The home brew flowed in a steady trickle from the spigot of its wooden keg.

Saturday night dances were just as much fun though not quite as festive. They were more spur-of-the-moment affairs, and while everyone wore clean, freshly ironed clothes, no one "spiffed up" quite as much as they did for Sunday dances. Boys and girls wore school clothes; women, everyday house dresses; and, men, work shirts and overalls. No refreshments were served and the music was seldom more than one man squeezing out the old favorite songs—"Baby Face," "Alice Blue

Gown," "Let Me Call You Sweetheart," "My Blue Heaven"—
on his accordion. It was at one of these Saturday night dances
that Walter and I met. I was there with my family and he was
there with two of his baseball-playing friends. The first time he
asked me to dance it was to the tune "Chicago, Chicago, That
Toddling Town."

After we started going out together, we continued to go to
the neighborhood dances but we also went to dances at
Yanda's and upstairs at the Ravenna Opera House where they
charged an admission fee. When we said "good-bye" at the end
of one date, we usually set the day and time for our next date
and, when we didn't, Walter called me. Both of our families
had telephones, but it was a long distance call. The call had to
go through two exchange operators, called "Central," one for
Hendricksons' phone line and one for our line.

In all the time we dated, I called Walter only once. I'd
heard there was going to be a big dance at Hazard and I
doubted that Walter would have heard about it, so I called to
tell him when and where it was going to be and to ask him to
go with me. He answered me with a high, squeaky, girlish
voice and said what I always said when he called me for a date.

"I'll have to ask my mama."

He was a kidder. It was one of the things I liked best about
him. He took everything about farming very seriously. He was
particular about every job he did from setting straight fence
lines, plowing straight furrows, planting straight rows, mowing
fence rows and grader ditches to keeping the farmyard neatly
trimmed, but when the sun went down and the cows were
milked and chores were done, he was ready to have a good
time. We didn't spend all of our dates dancing. We played
cards with our families, went to ball games and went to "picture shows" or "flickers." We saw romantic movies—Con-
stance Talmadge in "Polly of the Follies," Herbert Rawlson in
"Cheated Hearts," and Jean Paurel in "The Great Lover," or
dramas like William Farnum in "Perjury." But best of all, we

loved to laugh at a Harold Lloyd, Charlie Chaplin or Laurel and Hardy show.

Food was a part of every date. It might be a hamburger and coffee at a diner after a show, a meal with my family or his before a game, and after a Sunday dance, we finished off the leftover slices of Mother's *Rohlicky*.

## *ROHLICKY*
Sweet Bohemian nut-filled rolls—

1 package dry yeast
1/4 cup warm milk
1/4 teaspoon sugar
Dash of ginger
2-1/2 to 3 cups flour
3 tablespoons sugar
2 teaspoons salt
1 cup butter or margarine
1 teaspoon freshly grated lemon peel
1/2 cup sour cream
1 whole egg plus 1 egg yolk, well beaten

Filling I:
2 egg whites
2 tablespoons sugar
Dash of salt
1 cup finely chopped walnuts

Filling II:
2/3 cup strawberry or apricot jam
1/4 cup finely chopped walnuts

Frosting:
2 cups sifted powdered sugar
1/2 teaspoon lemon extract
3 to 4 tablespoons milk

Grease two cookie sheets. In a small bowl, dissolve yeast in warm milk to which 1/4 teaspoon sugar and ginger have been added. Set aside 5 minutes. In a large bowl, combine 2 cups flour, sugar, salt, butter, lemon peel, sour cream and eggs; blend thoroughly. Add yeast and milk mixture; beat well. Add only as much of remaining flour as is needed to form a soft dough. Turn dough out onto lightly floured board or pastry cloth. Cover with inverted bowl; let rest 5 minutes. Divide in half. Roll each portion into a rectangle 1/4-inch thick. To make Filling I: In medium bowl, beat egg whites until stiff peaks form. In a small bowl combine sugar, salt and nuts. Fold into egg whites. To make Filling II: In a small bowl, combine jam with nuts; blend thoroughly. Spread each rectangle with half of one of the fillings. Start with a long side and roll up as for a jelly roll. Seal edges well. Place loaves on prepared cookie sheets; make sure sealed edges are underneath. Cover; let rise until almost double in bulk. Preheat oven to 350 degrees F. Bake 30 to 40 minutes or until loaves are golden brown and test done. Prepare frosting while loaves bake. In a small bowl, combine powdered sugar, lemon extract and enough milk to make a thin frosting. Beat until smooth. Remove baked loaves from cookie sheets, place on cooling racks and drizzle lightly with frosting. At serving time, use a serrated bread knife to cut loaves into half-inch slices. Makes 2 loaves.

## HOLIDAY *STOLLEN*

Fruits and nuts should be at room temperature before they are added to the dough—

2 packages dry yeast
1/2 cup warm water
1/4 teaspoon sugar
Dash of ginger
1 cup shortening
1 cup milk, scalded
1 cup sugar
2 teaspoons salt
1 cup flour
1/2 teaspoon nutmeg
1/2 teaspoon allspice
3 eggs, well beaten
1 teaspoon vanilla
6 to 7 cups flour
1 cup diced dried apricots
1 cup golden raisins
1/2 cup chopped blanched almonds
2 tablespoons melted butter or margarine
2 tablespoons sugar
1/2 teaspoon cinnamon

Orange Sugar Frosting:
1 cup sifted powdered sugar
2 tablespoons fresh orange juice
2 teaspoons freshly grated orange peel

In a small bowl, dissolve yeast in warm water to which 1/4 teaspoon of sugar and dash of ginger have been added. Set aside 5 minutes. In a large bowl, combine shortening and scalded milk; stir until shortening melts. Add sugar and salt; stir to dissolve. Cool to lukewarm. Stir in yeast mixture. Add 1 cup flour, nutmeg and allspice; beat hard. Add eggs and vanilla; stir to combine thoroughly. Add only as much of remaining flour as is needed to make a very soft yet easy to handle dough. Turn dough out onto well-floured board or pastry cloth. Cover with inverted bowl; let rest 5 minutes. Knead 10 minutes or until dough is smooth and elastic. Place dough in a lightly greased bowl; turn to grease surface. Cover bowl with a damp cloth; let rise until double in bulk. Turn dough out onto lightly floured board or pastry cloth. Gradually knead in apricots, raisins and almonds. Divide dough into three portions. Cover lightly with damp cloth; let rest 10 minutes. Pat or roll out each portion of dough to make an 8 x 12-inch oval. Brush ovals with melted margarine. In a small bowl, combine 2 tablespoons sugar and cinnamon. Sprinkle one-third of mixture on each oval. Fold ovals in half, pinching to seal edges. Grease two or three cookie sheets generously; two *stollens* can be baked on one cookie sheet if the sheet measures at least 13 x 18 inches, otherwise bake on separate cookie sheets. Place filled and sealed *stollens* on prepared cookie sheets and shape into crescents. Cover; let rise until *almost* double in bulk. Preheat oven to 350 degrees F. Bake 20 to 25 minutes or until loaves are golden brown and test done. While *stollens* bake, prepare frosting. In a small bowl, combine powdered sugar, orange juice and peel. Beat until smooth. Remove baked *stollens* from cookie sheets, place on cooling racks and drizzle with frosting. Makes 3 *stollens*. Serves 24.

In the three months before we moved, Walter finished picking corn and I started cooking. I soon discovered it wasn't as easy as my mother had made it look in the two-month, crammed cooking course she gave me before I was married. In daily kitchen drills, she attempted to teach me all she could as fast as she could. She was forty-four years old at the time and she'd cooked every day of her life since she was twelve when she became the family cook upon her mother's death.

Her kitchen moves were instinctive; there was no wasted motion, no last-minute panic. She switched from gently folding cake batter to patting out biscuits to vigorously whipping mashed potatoes to whisking lump-free gravy and got a meal on the table with little apparent effort.

"How long will it take, how many meals will I have to cook," I'd wondered, "before I feel as comfortable and confident in my kitchen as Mother does in hers?"

At first, I spent most of every day in the kitchen. If I wasn't preparing food, I was washing dishes. Our everyday dishes were Walter's batching dishes—a set of heavy, white English ironstone in the Bronze Tea Leaf pattern. The china dishes I bought for my hope chest were saved for company.

My kitchen equipment was limited. Even after I'd stowed my hope chest utensils on the shelves and in the drawers beside Walter's rag-tag assortment of kitchen gear, the cupboard was still quite bare. I'd use a bowl or a pan and then I'd wash it and use it over. I might do that several times in the course of fixing one meal. Nothing was washed more often than one medium-sized, aluminum mixing bowl. It was my "do everything bowl." I couldn't have cooked without it. It was one of only two mixing bowls I had; the other one, a big, broad, deep crockery bowl was for mixing bread dough. For everything else—stirring up cakes, cookies, biscuits, pancakes, waffles or pie dough, beating eggs, rinsing leaf lettuce, snapping green beans, shelling peas—I used the aluminum bowl and I'm still using it. After sixty years of service, it should be declared an heirloom.

Another indispensable item in my kitchen then and now is a another aluminum metal pan. It's shallow and straight-sided, four inches deep, twelve inches in diameter and because it has a flat bottom, it doubles as an extra pan in the oven or on top of the stove. It was the pan I took to the orchard to pick a few apples, apricots or cherries, to the garden to gather fresh vegetables or to the cave to carry up stored fresh apples, potatoes, carrots, onions and parsnips.

Skillets and pans, heavy black cast iron ones, I had two of each, a small one and a medium-sized one; only the pans had lids.

All of my hand tools fit in one narrow drawer. There were two forks, a heavy-tined one with a long handle and a short one with narrow, stubby tines; two spatulas, a long-handled, thin one and short-handled, square one; three knives, one for paring, one for slicing meat and one for slicing bread; three measuring cups, a one-cup, half-cup and quarter-cup; and, three measuring spoons, a tablespoon, teaspoon and half teaspoon.

Even as a beginning cook, I didn't need a lot of recipes and most of those I did collect were for baked goods. It was enough if a cook "had in mind" general directions for preparing beef, pork and chicken—season lightly with salt and pepper and roast in the oven for three or four or more hours according to weight—and knew how to pan-fry steaks, chops and chicken. It was also very important to know how to make gravy from either roasting pan drippings or from skillet scrapings. Vegetables were usually boiled in lightly salted water on top of the stove; a few, like parsnips, were lightly browned in butter in a skillet; and, occasionally, squash and potatoes were baked. It was simple, good tasting, hearty "stick to the ribs" cooking.

Cooks like Tillie and Carrie, my mother and mother-in-law, rarely used a recipe and when they did, it was one they had used so often and for so long, they had it memorized. Some of my mother's recipes—biscuits, bread, pie dough—had never been written down until I wrote them in my recipe book. In many cases, it was the first time Mother had ever bothered to actually *measure* the ingredients using standard measuring cups and spoons. When she said, "Add a spoonful," she might have meant a stirring spoon, serving spoon, soup spoon or teaspoon. "A cupful," meant a coffee cup. A tablespoon, teaspoon or half teaspoon of any dry ingredient was determined by the size of a small mound of, say, baking powder, baking soda or salt in the palm of her hand. Her "pinches" were sized "small," "medium" and "big." As we worked together on the recipes, she measured and I recorded. Sometimes it took several tries for her to come up with what she judged to be the correct amount, one I could record. When I had the ingredients for a recipe listed, then we tackled the procedure—"stirring," "whipping," "folding," "cutting in," "mixing," "beating," "kneading," etc. Very few old recipes came with written instructions but, by being right there at Mother's elbow, seeing her combine the ingredients, watching the action as a mixture was "beaten," "stirred," "folded," "kneaded," etc., I had a very clear picture in my mind of how to prepare each recipe; I didn't need to jot down a bunch of instructions in my notebook.

# QUICK BREADS

As Mother saw it, a girl didn't dare get married without knowing how to make a batch of respectable baking powder biscuits.

"You *have* to be able to make a *decent* biscuit," she said. "They're quick. When you run out of bread, there's no time to whip up a batch. Bread takes four or five hours from start to finish. And you certainly can't drop everything and run to town just for a loaf of bread. Biscuits can be stirred up, patted out, cut and be in and out of the oven in twenty minutes. And, when you've got bread, you can make a meal around it." She convinced me—my first cooking lesson was biscuits.

### BAKING POWDER BISCUITS FOR TWO
Tillie's stand-by and my first biscuit recipe—

"1 heaping cup flour. 1 large or 2 level teaspons baking powder. Lard the size of an egg. Pinch of salt. Enough milk to mix and hold ingredients together."

It may not look like much of a recipe but it was all the information I needed to make six or seven two-inch biscuits. On my first try, I put the ingredients together and handled the dough in the same way I'd seen Mother do it and I turned out what she rated as "a pretty good biscuit."

"Now watch...see how I do this...see what happens..." I heard those words over and over and soon I, too, was able to let my eyes tell me "how much...," "how long to cut, stir, beat, mix, fold, knead...," or "when to add..."

Mother had lots to say about making biscuits: "Measure flour, salt and baking powder into the bowl and stir them together before adding the lard...it's easier to cut in lard if you use a straight-sided bowl large enough to allow ingredients to be easily combined... use two table knives like scissors to cut in lard...continue cutting in lard until mixture looks like coarse cornmeal...make a well in the center of the mixture...add milk, about two-thirds of a cup, all at once...stir milk in with a fork, working quickly...stop after three or four stirs and add another tablespoon or two of milk only if needed...continue stirring...stop when all ingredients are moistened."

She counted the strokes out loud each time the fork circled the bowl.

"...and ten! *Never stir biscuit dough more then ten times!*" It was no idle statement. It was a command.

When dough pulled away from the sides of the bowl and followed the fork around the bowl to form a very loose ball, she pronounced it "ready for kneading" and turned it out onto a lightly floured bread board.

"The lightest hand makes the flakiest biscuits," she lowered her voice and all but whispered the words. "Handle the dough gently. Use only the fingertips." After seven or eight light, quick kneads, giving the dough a one-quarter turn after each one, and the dough was no longer "knobby or sticky," she patted it out gently with her fingers until it was half an inch thick and cut the biscuits.

Mother gave me a biscuit cutter just like hers—a tin can. Can openers available at that time cut lids off below the seal ridge, leaving the can with a knife-sharp edge. Not just any tin can could become a biscuit cutter; it had to be one that measured two and a quarter inches in diameter and four inches tall. Air holes were punched in the bottom end of the can so the cut biscuit fell out of the can easily without the dough sticking to the can. The can's cutting edge was dipped in flour before each biscuit was cut.

Cut biscuits were placed half an inch apart on an ungreased baking sheet. Placing the unbaked biscuits close together allowed them to rise to their fullest height and produced a biscuit with soft, tender sides.

Biscuits baked ten minutes in a "very hot oven," the equivalent of 450 degrees, until their tops were a rich golden brown and they tested done when stuck with a toothpick.

My mother-in-law made baking powder biscuits in what she called her "biscuit bowl," a broad, shallow, round wooden bowl with tapered sides. With her hands, she scooped in the amount of flour she guessed she needed to make the number of biscuits she wanted based on the number and the size of the mouths she would be feeding. She made a well in the flour, added lard, salt and baking powder and cut the lard into the dry ingredients with a short-handled, cooking fork. When the mixture looked "coarse and mealy" and resembled cornmeal, the fork was put aside. The rest of the process, adding milk, "enough to make the dough stick together," mixing the milk into the flour mixture and then patting out the dough was all done with the fingers and hands and it was all done right in the bowl. The biscuits were even cut right in the bowl. Carrie's biscuit cutter was also made from a tin can.

## BAKING POWDER BISCUITS
Makes an even dozen—

2 cups flour
1/2 teaspoon salt
3 teaspoons baking powder
1/2 cup shortening
2/3 cup milk

Preheat oven to 450 degrees F. Have an *ungreased* cookie sheet at hand. In a medium bowl, sift flour, salt and baking powder together. Add shortening. Use a pastry blender or two forks to cut in shortening until mixture looks like coarse cornmeal. Make a well in the center of the mixture and add milk all at one time. Use a fork to stir quickly no more than *10 times* or until dough cleans sides of bowl. Turn dough out onto lightly floured board or pastry cloth. Knead gently and quickly no more than *10 times*. Pat out the dough with hands or roll with a cloth-covered rolling pin until dough is 1/2-inch thick. Cut with 2-inch biscuit cutter dipped in a little flour. Place cut biscuits 1/2-inch apart on cookie sheet. Bake 12 to 15 minutes or until biscuits test done. Makes 2 dozen.

Among the first quick bread recipes I collected were Carrie's Irish Oatmeal Bread and Corn Bread, two quick breads that were favorites of her families, the Lathrops, Cheevers and O'Haras. The families immigrated from Ireland in the early 1800s and settled first in New York, and though genealogy searches have not yet placed the families precisely in any one southern state, it has been speculated that they spent time in Virginia or Georgia and maybe Tennessee before stopping in Illinois. It was from Illinois that Carrie's parents, William and Lydia Cheever Lathrop, traveled by covered wagon, crossed the Mississippi River and settled for a time in Iowa before moving on to Kansas and later to Nebraska. They arrived in Buffalo County when Carrie was six years old.

Oats, the small rolled grains they cooked and ate as a breakfast cereal on the trail, found their way into cookie dough, cake batter and quick breads when they had established homes and had kitchens with stoves and ovens to bake in. In addition to nutritional value, oats contributed flavor and texture to baked goods. Quick breads, breads made without yeast, need to have at least one egg in their list of ingredients, otherwise, they would be heavy, dense, compact loaves. Adding one or two eggs makes a finer textured bread, one that is airy and light. Neither oatmeal nor cornmeal contain sufficient gluten to be used alone in a bread; they must be used in combination with all-purpose wheat flour. They do have great absorbency and therefore produce relatively thin batters, ones that need a bit more salt and other flavorings than are usually called for in recipes using only all-purpose flour.

### CARRIE'S IRISH OATMEAL BREAD

This recipe has been changed many times in the last six decades. In its latest revision, it's made with quick-cook oatmeal—

3 cups flour
1-1/4 cups quick-cook oatmeal
1-1/2 tablespoons baking powder
1 tablespoon salt
1 egg
1-1/2 cups milk
1/4 cup honey
1 tablespoon margarine

Preheat oven to 350 degrees F. Grease generously a 9 x 5 x 3-inch loaf pan. In a large bowl, combine flour, oatmeal, baking powder and salt; stir lightly to blend. In a medium bowl and with a rotary beater, beat egg and milk together. Beat in honey. Pour into flour mixture all at once. Stir with a wooden spoon just until dry ingredients are moistened; mixture will appear lumpy. Spread batter into prepared pan. Bake 1 hour and 15 minutes or until loaf tests done and the top is brown and crusty. Turn loaf out of pan onto cooling rack and brush top with margarine. Makes 1 loaf.

Carrie's families may have been Southerners for only a brief time but it was long enough for them to have acquired a cornbread craving they never outgrew.

## CARRIE'S CORN BREAD

A hot bread for a cool, rainy day supper or a chilly day dinner of ham hocks stewed overnight with white Northern beans. Walter liked corn bread so much that he ate it with his meal like bread. Then he put a square of it in a cereal bowl, sprinkled it with sugar, poured over cream, ate it with a spoon and called it "dessert"—

1 cup yellow corn meal
1 cup flour
4 teaspoons baking powder
1/4 cup sugar
1/2 teaspoon salt
1 egg
1 cup milk
1/4 cup margarine, softened but *not melted*

Preheat oven to 425 degrees F. Use margarine or butter to coat an 8-inch square baking pan generously. In a large bowl, combine corn meal, flour, baking powder, salt and sugar; stir lightly until well blended. In a small bowl, beat egg and milk together and blend in softened margarine. Pour into prepared pan. Bake 20 minutes or until top is slightly brown and bread tests done. Serves 4.

Fritters made Sunday and birthday breakfasts special at Hendricksons'. Stirring up the batter was the easy part; frying the puffy, egg-shaped cousins to the doughnut in deep, hot fat took some practice. Before I tried them in my own kitchen, I took a lesson from Carrie.

In a deep, heavy cast iron saucepan, she melted lard.

"Don't skimp on the lard. Make sure it's at least two-and-a-half to three inches deep," she said, "so the fritters can move freely and turn over on their own as they brown and cook. The pan should be half full of melted lard to allow room for the hot lard to 'bubble up' when the batter is dropped in." She judged the fat to be hot enough to begin cooking fritters when it turned a one-inch cube of bread golden brown in one minute. To do that, the fat had to be about 375 degrees.

"And NEVER LET FAT GET SO HOT IT SMOKES!"
Carrie gave every word a mid-air down beat with the pointer
finger of her right hand and went on to explain, "If batter is
dropped into overheated fat, the fritters will be burnt to a crisp
on the outside and still be raw batter on the inside. And don't
start before the fat is hot or you'll get grease-soaked fritters."

After each round of fritters was fried, she skimmed out the
crumbs and gave the fat a couple of minutes to regain the
proper frying temperature. Left in the fat, the crumbs burned,
discolored the fat and affected the flavor of successive rounds
of fritters.

Each fritter will take on its own unique shape as it fries and
every effort should be made to drop fritters that contain equal
amounts of batter. Carrie's tip for dropping uniform portions of
fritter batter from a spoon was "...to dip and drop batter from a
*clean spoon*." She dipped the spoon, first, into the hot fat, and
then into the batter, and sure enough, the batter slipped cleanly
from the fat-coated spoon and for each fritter thereafter. Fritters
were given the toothpick test for doneness. If the toothpick
came out free of crumbs, the fritter was done. Fried fritters
were kept hot on a brown paper-lined pan in a low oven.

Eventually lard was replaced by solid commercial shortenings, like Crisco, and still later, Crisco was replaced by liquid
shortenings, like Wesson or Mazola oil. More absorbent paper
towels replaced brown paper under the fried, ready-to-eat fritters being held in a warm oven.

## CARRIE'S FRITTERS

Don't crowd fritters in the pan. Give them room and they'll twist and turn and brown evenly on all sides unassisted—

1 egg, well beaten
1/4 cup sugar
2 tablespoons melted butter or margarine
2 cups flour
3 tablespoons baking powder
1/4 teaspoon salt
2/3 cup milk

In a wide heavy saucepan, deep heavy skillet or a deep electric skillet, heat 2-1/2 to 3 inches of fat to 375 degrees F. In a medium bowl, beat egg. Add sugar; mix well. Stir in butter and milk. Sift flour, baking powder and salt together and add all at one time to egg mixture. Stir just until flour is moistened; batter may appear slightly lumpy. If it should appear too thin to drop easily from a spoon, add more flour, a tablespoon at a time, until batter reaches proper consistency. Drop batter, a slightly rounded tablespoonful per fritter, into hot fat. REMINDER: First dip *clean* dropping spoon into hot fat before dipping it into the batter. Watch fritters carefully. Give those that don't turn on their own a gentle nudge with a cooking fork so they turn before they get too brown and overcooked on the underside. Fry until fritters are golden brown and test done. Serve hot with warm maple syrup. Makes 10 to 12 3-inch fritters.

During my first several years of cooking, a farmer could still take bags of his home-grown wheat to the mill to be ground into flour. Walter hauled our wheat to the Gibbon Roller Mill, a four-story reinforced concrete structure built beside the Union Pacific Railroad track on the west edge of town. It had all the latest in electric-powered grinding machinery, making it one of Nebraska's most modern mills.

The ground flour was for family use only; we were not allowed to sell it.

As the miller milled the wheat, he would, upon request, add dry leavening agents to one or two bags turning the flour into "pancake flour." Pancake flour, in its day and in its way, was the forerunner of all the many boxed baking mixes that now take up more and more grocery store shelf space with every passing year. Along with the ground flour and pancake flour, farmers had the option of also taking home the "shorts and bran," the "leavings," after the wheat was milled. "Leavings," mixed with whole grains—corn, wheat, barley and oats—were fed to livestock, which led some nutritionists to claim the pigs, cows and horses were better fed than their masters because they got more of the wheat's most valuable nutrients.

So far as I know, there wasn't a recipe for making pancakes from pancake flour. If there was, I never saw a copy of it. I didn't need a recipe to stir up a batch of pancakes, all I needed to know was how many people I'd be feeding. When I knew that, then I guessed at the size of their appetites, and if I was making pancakes for cornhuskers, I'd better make plenty, enough to hold them through a cold winter morning of hard work in the field. No matter how much they ate for breakfast, those huskers would be back at the dinner table at noon, hungry again.

On the farm, the noon meal was "dinner," it wasn't lunch. "Lunch" was the mid-afternoon snack in a twelve or fourteen-hour day, a common occurrence during planting and harvesting seasons. "Lunch" might be a sandwich, a cold chicken leg or wing leftover from dinner, an apple with a wedge of cheese or a handful of cookies, enough to tide the men over until supper, the evening meal. A farmer's breakfast was a big meal, as big as dinner or supper. Along with four to six six-inch pancakes slathered with butter and drizzled with syrup, a man might eat several strips of home-cured bacon or a slice of ham or pork sausage patties, hash browned potatoes, and fried eggs, and he drank milk along with cup after cup of hot coffee.

Once I'd decided how many pancakes I was going to make, then I knew how many eggs I needed to crack into my all-purpose, aluminum "do everything" bowl. By using the same bowl every time I made pancakes, I could judge levels of the mixture at various stages. The bowl was sort of like one giant, un-

marked measuring cup. After I'd cracked the eggs into the
bowl and saw the level they reached in the bowl, I knew about
how much milk to add, and when I saw the level of the egg-
milk mixture in the bowl, I knew about how much pancake
flour to add to make the right amount of batter for the number
of pancakes I planned to bake. I never actually measured the
ingredients. If I had, the proportions would probably have read
like this:

## GIBBON MILL PANCAKES
Makes eighteen to twenty light, fluffy pancakes six inches
across and about three-eighths-inch thick—

4 eggs
2 cups milk
4 cups pancake flour

In a medium bowl, combine eggs, milk and pancake flour. Beat hard
with a spoon until batter is smooth. Allow 1/4 cup batter per pancake; my
big mixing spoon level full equaled 1/4 cup. For thinner pancakes, increase
the amount of milk and for thicker pancakes, decrease the amount of milk.
Bake on a hot griddle. To test the griddle to see if it is hot enough to begin
baking pancakes, sprinkle it with water. If the water "dances" across the
griddle and vaporizes in an instant, the griddle is hot. Brush hot griddle
lightly and quickly with shortening and spoon on batter. When pancake tops
are bubbly and edges are lightly browned, carefully lift an edge of the first
pancake poured. If the underside is golden brown, flip the pancake. *Turn
pancakes only once during baking time.* Continue to check and flip until all
pancakes test done. Another way to test pancakes for doneness is to nick the
center of each cake with a sharp edge of the pancake turner. The "nick"
allows a peek inside; if no "wet or moist" batter can be seen, the pancake is
done. Serve hot. Makes 24 5-inch pancakes.

Before I stirred up the pancake batter, I prepared syrup to
go with the pancakes. We bought thick—too thick to pour—
dark, maple-flavored corn syrup by the gallon. It came in a
small, lidded-pail with a wire bale handle. The thick, viscous
syrup was diluted to make a lighter syrup, one that poured easily.

## PANCAKE SYRUP

2 cups undiluted syrup
1/2 cup water
2 cups brown sugar

In a heavy medium saucepan, combine syrup, water and brown sugar. Stir to blend and dissolve brown sugar. *Do not boil.* Allow mixture to heat at the back of the stove until thoroughly combined and hot. Makes about 3 cups.

I took over the stove my first morning at the Shack, built the fire and set out to make breakfast while my new husband went out to the barn to do morning chores. After the coffee pot was on the stove and perking, I got out my recipe book. I'd taken a quick look through the cupboard the night before to see what I had to work with and I'd seen a round, black, cast iron waffle iron. Pancakes were a fairly typical farmer's breakfast and so was French toast, but waffles? Sounded pretty fancy for a bachelor farmer. I asked Walter about the waffle iron, how he happened to have it and if he'd used it.

He said, "No," he'd never used it and that "It came in a box of kitchen stuff from Dinglers." Dinglers lived on a neighboring farm.

I wanted our first breakfast together in our own home to be one to remember, so, if Walter hadn't been making waffles, I decided waffles were the very thing I would fix—never mind the fact I'd never made waffles. I'd watched Walter's mother make them and I had her recipe—"WAFFLES 1 cup milk 2 eggs pinch of salt 1/4 cup melted butter 2 scant teaspoons baking powder flour to make soft batter, about 1-1/2 cups. Beat flour and milk, add butter and beat. Add well-beaten yolks and beat, then add b. powder and salt and beat very hard for a few minutes, add beaten whites."

The directions were sketchy, but I knew from watching Carrie the eggs were separated before they were beaten and that the whites were beaten until they "held stiff peaks," and then, after all the other ingredients were thoroughly combined, the beaten whites were folded in *very carefully*.

Before I prepared the batter, I poured syrup into a small saucepan and set it on the back of the stove near the hot, perked pot of coffee. Then I removed the left front stove lid and set the waffle iron directly over the fire to preheat. Once the iron was hot, the stove lid was replaced. The closed iron had to be swiveled and turned, so its two sides alternated in being next to the fire, allowing the waffle to bake and brown evenly on both sides. During the ten minutes the iron preheated, I swiveled it a few times to make sure both sides of the iron were good and hot, then I tested it to see if it was hot enough to begin baking the waffles. I used the same test I'd learned to test a hot pancake griddle—I flicked a few drops of water on it with my fingers. When the drops danced, scattered, turned into steam and disappeared in an instant, I knew the iron was hot. The stove lid was replaced and the top and bottom sides of the grid were swished with a little lard and the batter was spooned on. If the cast iron baker got too hot or wasn't quite hot enough, either way, the baked waffle stuck to the grid. Only the middle two-thirds of the grid was covered with batter; when the lids were closed, they pressed the batter out to the sides of the iron, filling in the circle. After one side of the waffle baked one minute next to the fire, I swiveled the iron to let the other side bake one minute next to fire. From that point on, the iron was swiveled every thirty seconds until steam no longer puffed out between the lids, the sign the waffle was done. Total baking time was generally three or four minutes. *THE WAFFLE IRON WAS NEVER OPENED UNTIL THE WAFFLE STOPPED STEAMING.*

Ridges in the grid marked the waffle into quarters or four servings. Once baking was underway, waffle eaters couldn't keep up with the waffle baker—a fresh, hot waffle was ready every three or four minutes. To some cooks, the first waffle in a batch is always a "throw-away"; they expect it will be either under-baked or burned to a crisp, but I have seldom tossed out the first waffle. When a baked waffle was removed from the iron, the empty iron was swiveled to put the hottest side in position to receive the batter for the next waffle.

I waited until Walter was back from his chores before I started baking the first waffle. He had washed up and was seated at the table, waiting for the waffle to come out of the iron when there was a rap at the door. Walter jumped up from the table, anxious to see who our first caller was. It was Martin Prohaska, a bachelor farmer who lived about three hills away.

"I've come to meet the new missus," he said to Walter.

"Good," Walter said. "Have you had breakfast yet?"

"No," Martin laughed, "I wouldn't be here if I'd already eaten."

Walter laughed, too, and said, "Come on in and pull up a chair."

That was the first of what must have been thousands of spur-of-the-moment invitations my husband issued in our fifty-two years together.

Later, that first waffle recipe was revised so it now reads:

## WAFFLES

1 cup sifted flour
1/2 teaspoon salt
2 teaspoons baking powder
2 eggs, separated
1 cup milk
2 tablespoons melted butter or margarine

Preheat waffle iron. Into a large bowl, sift together flour, salt and baking powder. In a small bowl, beat egg yolks and milk together. Add to dry ingredients all at one time; beat well. Stir in butter or margarine; blend thoroughly. In a small, steep-sided bowl and with a rotary beater or an electric mixer, beat egg whites until stiff peaks form. Fold gently into prepared batter. Bake in hot waffle iron 3 to 5 minutes or until steam no longer puffs out from sides of iron and waffle is golden brown and tests done. Serve with butter and warm syrup. Makes 4 8-inch waffles.

As a school girl, Memorial Day, also called "Decoration Day," marked the beginning of summer. It was the first holiday after school was out. It struck a somber note with a morning parade of war veterans, marching bands and groups of little girls all dressed in white marching down Ravenna's main street. Grandfather Miller, a Civil War veteran, and I represented our family in the parade. Like the other girls, I carried a basket of iris blooms which, at the end of the march, were ceremoniously tossed, one by one, into Beaver Creek at the edge of town.

The solemnness of the day lightened when the family gathered back home at noon for a pork roast dinner complete with Mother's dumplings.

## TILLIE'S FEATHERLIGHT DUMPLINGS

There are two secrets to light dumplings: Keep them steaming on top of *simmering* stock and never crowd them in the pan. Serve with roast pork and sauerkraut, stewed chicken or beef—

2 cups flour
2 teaspoons baking powder
1 teaspoon salt
1/2 cup milk
1 egg, well beaten

In a medium bowl, sift flour, baking powder and salt together. Add milk to beaten egg. Add all at one time to flour mixture; blend to form a soft dough. Drop dumpling dough into deep, hot bubbling stew or broth with a silver serving spoon. *To prevent dough from sticking to spoon, first dip clean spoon into hot broth.* Cook dumplings uncovered 8 minutes, then cover and cook an additional 10 to 12 minutes or until dumplings test done. Test dumplings with a toothpick; if the toothpick comes out clean, dumplings are done. Or, break open one dumpling and take a look; make sure there's no moist or wet batter inside. Remove dumplings from cooking liquid and quickly prick each with a sharp fork to let steam escape so dumplings will be feathery and light and not soggy inside. Makes 10 to 12 dumplings.

## TILLIE'S LIVER DUMPLINGS
A firmer textured dumpling—

2 or 3 chicken livers, finely chopped
2 to 3 tablespoons shortening
2 tablespoons flour
1 cup chicken broth
2 cups flour
2 teaspoons baking powder
1/2 teaspoon salt
1/4 teaspoon pepper
1 egg, well beaten
1 small onion, grated

In a skillet, combine chopped livers and shortening; cook until liver is browned and tender. Remove liver from skillet and set aside. Add 2 tablespoons flour to fat remaining in skillet and cook over low heat until flour is a dark brown but not burned. Gradually stir in chicken broth; cook until sauce is quite thick. Return livers to sauce; stir to blend well. Set aside to cool. In a medium bowl, sift flour, baking powder, salt and pepper together. Add egg, onion and liver-sauce mixture; stir quickly to mix well. Drop dough into deep, hot bubbling stew or broth with a silver serving spoon. *To prevent dough from sticking to spoon, first dip clean spoon into hot broth.* Cover pan. Cook dumplings 10 minutes or until they test done. Makes 12 dumplings.

# CAKES

It wasn't long, even as a beginning cook, until I no longer relied on recipes. Meals were planned around roasts—beef, pork or poultry—or chops, steaks and stews supplemented with fresh or canned vegetables depending on what was growing in the garden or was stored in the cave. Once I had developed "an eye" for judging proportions and for recognizing when pie crusts and fillings, biscuits and breads "looked right," I only needed recipes for cakes, cookies, candy and desserts.

That should explain why half of the first forty recipes I collected were for cakes and twelve were for candy, cookies and desserts.

Cakes were the yardstick by which a woman's cooking skills were measured. To have any chance of turning out a top-notch cake every time you baked the same cake, you at least had to start with a "bare bones" written recipe. If you were lucky and had a choice of pans—either eight or nine-inch round or square pans, a nine by thirteen-inch loaf pan or a nine by five by three-inch loaf pan, and even though those pans didn't necessarily conform to today's "standard" pan sizes— they greatly improved your chances of becoming a great cake baker.

Besides recipes and pans, there were many other variables that had to be taken into account every time I stirred up a cake. I had the very freshest eggs to bake with, eggs gathered from nests in a chicken coop a few hundred feet from my kitchen but those eggs were not uniform in size. In the fall when the pullets, young hens, were just beginning to lay eggs, their eggs were very small, about half the size of eggs laid by mature hens. Those variations in the eggs made it difficult to be very exact in predicting just how much liquid the eggs contributed to the cake batter. The fat content in milk from our own cows varied, too, according to the breed of the cow and according to what the cows ate, and that varied each season of the year. All of these factors played a part in determining the richness of the cream or home-churned butter that went into cakes. Because salt was added to home-churned butter, most old cake recipes did not call for any additional salt. The word "flour" in a cake recipe always meant "all-purpose flour," and in some of those old recipes, it is still best to use all-purpose flour. In those recipes where switching to "cake flour" resulted in a better cake, the updated version of the recipe will specify "cake flour." That same guide applies in recipes where lard has been replaced by butter or margarine: when a substitution improved or gave equal results, that substitution appears in the updated, printed recipe.

Most of the time when I wanted to bake a cake, the stove was already fired up, but when I had to fire up a cold stove and a cold oven, I found that by the time I shook down the grates, laid up a full bed of cobs, got a good blaze going, washed my hands, measured out the ingredients, greased the pans, stirred up the batter and poured it into the pans—about ten minutes in all—I could give the oven my "hand wave" test, and nine times out of ten, the oven was hot enough to bake the cake.

"Don't slam the door!"

When my family heard that yell, they *knew* there was a cake in the oven. The richer the cake—the higher the proportion of cream and butter to other ingredients in a recipe—the more tender the cake's texture will be and the more sensitive it will be to jarring. The slightest jolt or tremor of the old cookstoves could cause a half or fully risen cake to "fall." The cake actually collapsed, leaving a gaping hole in the center. Houses and stoves are supposed to be more stable today and therefore cakes should be less susceptible to vibrations caused by slamming doors and household bumps and thumps. Still, I am very careful how I treat certain cakes while they are in the oven and I never open the oven door during a cake's first fifteen minutes in the oven. The rush of room temperature air into the oven during the early stages of the baking time can lengthen the baking time and diminish the texture of a particularly light and delicate cake.

Midway through my first year as a bride, a Watkins Man showed up at my door and was I happy to see him. My mother-in-law had promised to send him to my house the next time he called on her. The reputation of his products preceded him. All the good cooks I knew, especially those who were renown for their cake-baking skills, claimed they "had to have his vanilla."

He traveled a regular route going door to door selling a full line of Watkins products. For nearly twenty years, I bought vanilla and other extracts almost exclusively from a Watkins Man. I could expect to see him three times a year. He came carrying an oversized, brown leather satchel—the kind doctors carried only much larger. Near the top of the box-like satchel, the two sides slanted together in a peak and closed under the handle. When the case was snapped open, it displayed for easy selection rows and rows of upright bottles of vanilla and other extracts standing in close formation with rows of spice cans and jars of liniments, ointments and other non-prescription medications.

Of all the door-to-door salesmen who made their rounds through the countryside during those years, the Watkins Man probably got the most sincere welcome because he sold quality products. His prices weren't necessarily less; an eight-ounce bottle of vanilla cost about the same at the grocery store, but Watkins' vanilla and their other flavorings were fresher and had more strength. The amount of vanilla a recipe called for could be cut almost in half if Watkins vanilla was used, making Watkins vanilla go farther and last longer, and that made it cheaper in the long run.

## CARRIE'S BROWN STONE FRONT CAKE

A chocolate delight and the lead-off recipe in my first hand written recipe notebook—first, as it actually appears in the notebook—

"Boil together slowly 2 squares chocolate, the yolks of 2 eggs and 1/2 cup sweet milk. Mix butter the size of an egg, 1 cup sugar, 1/2 cup sweet milk, 1 teaspoon soda dissolved in boiling water flavor with vanilla. Stir in first part boiling hot and add 1-1/2 cups flour." That was it, that was the complete recipe as I copied it from Carrie's card. This is the updated version—

2 ounces unsweetened chocolate
2 egg yolks
1/2 cup milk
1/3 cup butter or margarine
1 cup sugar
1/4 teaspoon salt
1/2 cup milk
1 teaspoon baking soda
3 tablespoons boiling water
1 teaspoon vanilla
1-1/2 cups flour

Preheat oven to 350 degrees F. Grease and lightly flour two round, 8-inch cake pans. In a small saucepan over low heat, melt chocolate; watch carefully so it doesn't scorch. In a small bowl, beat egg yolks with 1/2 cup milk. Add to melted chocolate. Cook over low heat until mixture is thick and bubbly. Set aside. In a large bowl, cream butter and sugar until light and fluffy. Add salt and remaining 1/2 cup milk. In a cup, dissolve baking soda in boiling water. Add vanilla to baking soda-water mixture and stir half of mixture into creamed butter and sugar; blend thoroughly. Add half of flour; beat well. Add remaining baking soda-water mixture; blend thoroughly. Add remaining flour; beat well. Pour batter into prepared pans. Bake 25 to 30 minutes or until cake tests done. Cool cake in pans 10 minutes before turning out onto cooling racks. When cool, frost with a chocolate icing. Serves 16.

## BROWN SUGAR SPICE CAKE

I was sixteen the first time I baked a cake and it was this old family favorite. The revised recipe can be made with an electric mixer—

2 cups brown sugar
1/2 cup butter or margarine
3 eggs
1 teaspoon vanilla
1 cup sour milk
1-1/2 cups flour
1/2 teaspoon salt
1/2 teaspoon cinnamon
1/2 teaspoon nutmeg
1 teaspoon baking soda

Preheat oven to 350 degrees F. Grease and lightly flour two round 9-inch cake pans. In a large bowl, cream brown sugar and butter until light and fluffy. Add eggs; beat well. Blend in vanilla. Sift flour, salt, cinnamon, nutmeg and baking soda together. Add alternately with sour milk; start and end with dry ingredients. Beat well after each addition. Pour batter into prepared pans. Bake 25 minutes or until cake tests done. Cool cake in pans 10 minutes before turning out onto cooling rack. When cake is cool, frost with Caramel Icing. Serves 16.

On our first trip to town after we were married, we stocked up on candy bars—Baby Ruths, Snickers, Milky Ways—we wanted to be ready to "pass out the treats" in case we were "shivareed." A "shivaree" was an Old World custom. It usually took place within a week or two after a wedding when family and friends gathered at the home of the newlyweds after dark and hopefully after the couple had gone to bed. The shivaree gang circled the house in a noisy mock serenade, honking car horns, ringing cow bells, tossing empty tin cans on the roof, whistling, singing, banging wooden spoons on pots and pans, crashing pan lids together as though they were cymbals—anything to make a lot of noise to rout the sleepy bride and groom out of bed. The couple was expected to provide "treats" and then announce the date and place of their wedding dance.

One night, after we'd been married about ten days, Walter's folks asked us to their house for supper and late in the evening, just as we were leaving to go home to our shack, a shivaree erupted. The Hendricksons had been in on the plan all along, they'd inveigled us over to their house because they didn't think there would be room in the Shack for everyone who wanted to be on hand to shivaree Walter when he got married. He'd been the instigator of lots of tricks pulled on cousins and friends when they were shivareed, and now those same cousins and friends had their chance to get back at Walter. Fortunately for us, the December night they picked to shivaree us was so cold, no one pulled any pranks on us. Carrie and Willie let the ruckus go on until the noisemakers began to wear down and lose their volume, then they called the crowd inside, there were about thirty in all, and passed out treats.

Their serenade was over, they had their treats and then the gang wanted to know "When's the wedding dance?"

Walter and I were ready for that question.

"It'll be Saturday night, December 16 at Sharon Hall," we told them.

No bride ever forgets her wedding festivities and for me and for Walter, too, our wedding dance was "THE" event to remember. Sharon Township Hall was a long, narrow, white frame building set in a grassy swale between two low hills a couple of miles west of the Shack. Township halls were often mistaken for one-room schoolhouses. Inside, there were two small cloak rooms on either side of the double front doors and one big main room whose long walls were lined with a single row of straight-backed chairs. Every twelve-square-mile township had a hall. It was where we cast our ballots on election day but mostly it was the scene for Saturday neighborhood dances and, of course, wedding dances—although occasionally a traveling preacher might hold Sunday services there.

A 1922 wedding dance was somewhat like a wedding re-

ception today, except there were no written invitations. After a
dance was announced, news of it spread by word-of-mouth.
For Walter and me, it was an evening of music, food, fun and
dancing shared with more than eighty relatives and friends.
What a wonderful way to celebrate our marriage.

The very popular Skala Band provided the music. It was a
four-piece group, a father and his three sons; they played an
accordion, a clarinet, a saxophone and the drums. Their first
tune of the evening, "Moonlight and Roses," was danced only
by Walter and me and, oh, how we danced with pride and
pleasure, me in my navy blue wool wedding dress and him in
his best gray suit.

The groom's family furnished the food for wedding cele-
brations and Carrie and her daughters had piled baking sheets
high with sandwiches made of home-canned, cold-packed beef
ground and seasoned with Carrie's mayonnaise and her home-
grown, canned sweet pickles spread on thick slices of homemade bread. For two days before the dance, they baked dozens
of pies— pumpkin, apple, raisin and cherry pies—and cakes—
Chocolate Loaf Cake, Carrie's Easy Devil's Food Cake, and
Ruth's Sour Cream Spice Cake, just to name three of the assorted cakes that filled two long serving tables. And there was
plenty of hot coffee for adults and bottles of orange, grape and
cherry soda pop for children.

## CHOCOLATE LOAF CAKE
A "good traveler"—

1 cup sugar
1/2 cup butter
4 eggs, separated
1/2 cup milk
2 cups flour
1/4 teaspoon salt
2 teaspoons baking powder
1/2 cup shaved unsweetened chocolate
5 teaspoons boiling water

Preheat oven to 350 degrees F. Grease a 9 x 5 x 3-inch loaf pan generously and line with waxed paper; grease the waxed paper also. In a large bowl, cream sugar and butter until light and fluffy. In a small bowl, beat egg yolks with a rotary beater. Add to creamed mixture; blend well. Stir in Milk. Sift flour, salt and baking powder together 3 times. In a small bowl, dissolve shaved chocolate in boiling water. Add to creamed mixture alternately with flour mixture; start and end with dry ingredients. Beat well after each addition. In a large bowl and using a rotary beater, beat egg whites until soft peaks form. Gently fold into chocolate batter; blend thoroughly. Ease batter into prepared pan. Bake at 350 degrees 40 to 45 minutes or until cake tests done. Cool cake in pan 10 minutes before turning out onto cooling rack. When cool, drizzle top and sides lightly with favorite chocolate icing. Serves 16.

## CARRIE'S EASY DEVIL'S FOOD CAKE
Chocolate Devil's Food Cakes were very popular in the 1920s, so of course, there had to be at least one for our wedding dance refreshments. This recipe was easy to convert to the quick-mix electric mixer method—

1 cup heavy whipping cream
1 teaspoon cider vinegar
1 cup sugar
1-1/4 cups cake flour
3 tablespoons cocoa
1 teaspoon baking soda
Pinch of salt
2 eggs, well beaten
1 teaspoon vanilla

Preheat oven to 350 degrees F. Grease and lightly flour two round 9-inch cake pans. In a large bowl, combine whipping cream and vinegar. Set aside. Combine sugar, cake flour, cocoa, baking soda and salt and sift together 3 times. In a small bowl, combine eggs and vanilla. Stir into cream; blend thoroughly. Add dry ingredients to egg-cream mixture. Beat at medium speed 3 minutes. Pour into prepared pans. Bake 25 minutes or until cake tests done. Cool cake in pans 10 minutes before turning out onto cooling racks. When cake is cool, frost with Fudge Frosting. Serves 16.

## RUTH'S SOUR CREAM SPICE CAKE

Ruth, Walter's sister, baked this cake, her specialty, for the cake table at our wedding dance—

1 cup sugar
2 eggs
2 cups flour
1/4 teaspoon allspice
1/4 teaspoon ground cloves
1/2 teaspoon cinnamon
1/2 teaspoon nutmeg
1/2 teaspoon salt
1 teaspoon baking soda
1 cup sour cream

Preheat oven to 350 degrees F. Grease and lightly flour two round 9-inch cake pans. In a large bowl, beat sugar and eggs together. Sift flour, allspice, cloves, cinnamon, nutmeg and salt together 3 times. In a small bowl, dissolve baking soda in sour cream. Add to sugar-egg mixture alternately with flour-spice mixture; start and end with dry ingredients. Beat well after each addition. Pour into prepared pans. Bake 25 to 30 minutes or until cake tests done. Cool cake in pans 10 minutes before turning out onto cooling racks. When cool, frost with Caramel Icing. Serves 16.

## APPLESAUCE CAKE

Fragrances of winters past fill the kitchen when this cake is in the oven. Top it with yesterday's Hot Vanilla Sauce or today's Hot Caramel Sauce—

1 cup raisins
1-1/2 cups thick, tart applesauce
1 cup sugar
1/2 teaspoon cinnamon
1/2 teaspoon nutmeg
1/2 cup butter or margarine, melted
2-1/2 cups flour
2 teaspoons baking soda
1/2 teaspoon salt

Preheat oven to 350 degrees F. Grease a 9 x 12-inch baking pan. In a small bowl, "plump" raisins by covering with boiling water for 5 minutes. Drain thoroughly on paper towels. In a large bowl, combine applesauce, sugar, cinnamon, nutmeg and butter. Cream together thoroughly. Sift flour, baking soda and salt together; reserve 2 to 3 tablespoons and sprinkle over raisins. Stir dry ingredients into applesauce mixture; beat well. Stir in flour-coated raisins. Pour into prepared pan. Bake 30 minutes or until cake tests done. Cut into serving portions and serve right from the pan. Serve cake warm or cold. Top with Hot Vanilla Sauce or Hot Caramel Sauce. Serves 16.

Hot Vanilla Sauce:
2 tablespoons butter or margarine
2 tablespoons flour
1 cup boiling water
2 tablespoons sugar
1 teaspoon vanilla

In a small saucepan, melt butter, add flour. Cook over medium heat until mixture bubbles; stir constantly. Add boiling water and sugar. Cook over medium heat until smooth and satiny; stir constantly. Remove from heat and stir in vanilla. Place sauce over hot water to keep it warm.

Hot Caramel Sauce:
1/2 cup light corn syrup
1-1/2 cups brown sugar, firmly packed
1/4 cup butter or margarine
Dash of salt
1/2 cup whipping cream
1 teaspoon vanilla

In a small saucepan, combine syrup, brown sugar and butter. Bring to a full boil over low heat; stir constantly. Remove from heat. Stir in whipping cream, salt and vanilla. Place sauce over hot water to keep warm.

Farm wives seldom went to town during the winter months. Whatever groceries they needed were bought at the store and brought home by their husbands when they hauled wagon loads of grain to town to sell. Walter's father was fond of bananas and whenever they were available, he brought home a whole stalk of the tropical, mostly-green fruit which was hung from a floor joist in the dirt-floored cellar under the kitchen. The bananas curved upward making the stalk appear to be hanging upside down, but that's exactly how bananas grow naturally in the tropics and that's how the grocer recommended they be hung while they finished ripening. At first the fruit ripened slowly, banana by banana by banana, but about halfway through the stalk, ripe bananas began to out-number banana eaters. Carrie used the ripest ones to make Banana Oatmeal Cookies and Banana Nut Cake, two old family favorites that are still very popular.

## CARRIE'S BANANA NUT CAKE

This old recipe has been revised and can now be made with an electric mixer in the "quick-mix" method. When Carrie made the cake, the walnuts were considered optional. Nuts were expensive to buy, so unless she was able to gather walnuts in a nearby grove, they were omitted—

2/3 cup butter or margarine
2-1/2 cups cake flour
1-2/3 cups sugar
1-1/4 teaspoons baking powder
1 teaspoon baking soda
1 teaspoon salt
2/3 cup buttermilk
1-1/4 cups mashed bananas, 4 medium bananas
3 eggs
2/3 cup chopped walnuts

Preheat oven to 350 degrees F. Grease and lightly flour two round 9-inch cake pans; line pans with greased and lightly floured waxed paper. In a large bowl, cream butter at high speed until light and fluffy. Measure cake flour, sugar, baking powder, baking soda and salt into sifter and sift over margarine. Add half of buttermilk and all of the bananas. Beat 2 minutes at medium speed. Add eggs and remaining buttermilk. Beat 2 minutes at medium speed. Use a spoon to fold in nuts. Pour batter into prepared pans. Bake 30 minutes or until cake tests done. Cool cake in pans 10 minutes before turning out onto cooling racks. When cool, frost with 7-Minute Icing or with Butter Frosting to which 1/8 teaspoon of nutmeg has been added. Serves 16.

## CARRIE'S BURNT SUGAR CAKE

This is the cake Carrie took to Hendrickson reunions. All the Burnt Sugar Cake lovers in the family counted on this cake being there. By the time Carrie was no longer able to bake it, her daughter Elsie had made the cake one of her specialties, so she took over for her mother and she now carries the wonderful old, caramel-frosted cake to the annual family gathering in her cake basket. Labeled "temperamental," "difficult to bake" and a "high risk cake" by many, the original old recipe for Carrie's

Burnt Sugar Cake was definitely not for beginning cake bakers. Over the years, by making some additions and revisions, I've been able to minimize some of the risks—

1/2 cup sugar
1/2 cup boiling water
1-1/4 cups sugar
1/2 cup margarine
2 eggs, well beaten
1 teaspoon vanilla
1 cup sifted cake flour
1 1-1/2-ounce packet of Dream Whip
1 cup water
1 cup sifted cake flour
2 teaspoons baking powder
1/4 teaspoon salt

Preheat oven to 350 degrees F. Grease two round 9-inch cake pans. In a small heavy saucepan or skillet over low heat, melt and "burn" 1/2 cup sugar until it is a rich, dark brown color. Stir constantly. Add boiling water and cook until a medium syrup forms. Reserve 3 to 4 tablespoons of syrup. Set aside to cool. *Do not rinse or wash pan or skillet used to "burn" the sugar; set it aside and use the syrup residue in the pan to make the frosting.* In a large bowl, cream 1-1/4 cups sugar and margarine until light and fluffy. Add eggs and vanilla; beat well. Add 1 cup cake flour; beat well. Add Dream Whip directly from packet; blend thoroughly. Sift remaining 1 cup flour together with baking powder and salt. Add alternately with water; start and end with dry ingredients. Beat well after each addition. Stir in reserved burnt sugar syrup; blend thoroughly. Pour into prepared cake pans. Bake 25 to 30 minutes or until cake tests done. Cool cake in pans 10 minutes before turning out onto cooling racks. When cake is cool, fill and frost with Burnt Sugar Frosting.

Burnt Sugar Frosting:
1 cup sugar
1 cup light cream, Half and Half

Combine sugar and light cream and put into the same saucepan or skillet in which sugar was "burned" to make syrup for cake. Bring to an easy boil over medium heat. Boil until mixture reaches "soft ball stage." Cool until the bottom of the pan or skillet is warm to the touch, then beat hard until frosting reaches desired spreading consistency. Frosting "sets up" fast. Work quickly to fill and frost top and sides of cake lightly. Serves 16.

## DEVIL'S FOOD CAKE
A big, delicate textured, hard-to-resist cake—

1 cup sugar
3/4 cup cocoa
1 egg, well beaten
1 cup milk
1 cup sugar
3/4 cup margarine
2 eggs, well beaten
2 cups cake flour
1/8 teaspoon salt
1 teaspoon baking soda
1 teaspoon vanilla
1/2 cup milk
2 cups large marshmallows

Preheat oven to 375 degrees F. Grease two round 10-inch cake pans; line pans with greased and lightly floured waxed paper. In the top of a double boiler, combine 1 cup sugar and cocoa. Add 1 beaten egg. Stir in milk. Cook mixture over boiling water until smooth and thick. Set aside to cool completely. In a large bowl, cream 1 cup sugar and margarine together until light and fluffy. Add 2 beaten eggs. Sift flour, salt and baking soda together twice. Combine vanilla and milk. Add to creamed mixture alternately with flour mixture; start and end with dry ingredients. Beat well after each addition. Add cooled cocoa mixture; beat thoroughly. Pour into prepared pans. Bake 25 minutes or until cake tests done. Cool cake in pans 5 minutes before turning out onto cooling racks. While cake cools in the pans, use kitchen shears dipped in warm water to cut marshmallows in half horizontally. When cake layers are on cooling racks, *IMMEDIATELY* cover top of each layer with marshmallow halves. The warm cake will melt marshmallows slightly. When cake has cooled completely, frost with Fudge Frosting, taking care not to dislodge partially melted marshmallows. Serves 20.

In the late 1920s, as the country edged deeper and deeper towards a depression, farm families looked for ways to supplement their farm income. From July until late October, Walter worked on road gangs. For one dollar a day, he hired out as a driver and also furnished four of his own horses to pull contractor-owned slips, graders and blades being used to build the first graded, graveled road from Gibbon to Ravenna. Later, he worked on a stretch of road from U. S. Highway 30 to the little town of Poole, southwest of Ravenna. Still later, in the early 1930s, he and his horses prepared culvert "beds" when U. S. Highway 30, also known as "The Lincoln Highway," was re-graded and paved.

When he was on that job, Walter was able to live at home but on his first two road jobs, he was away from home from Monday morning until Friday night. The road gangs lived in tents pitched beside the working sites. The contractor provided a cook's shack and a cook.

I did my part to earn extra spending money, too, by "keeping the schoolteacher." For five dollars a week, she had her own private bedroom (at some small sacrifice on our part, considering that at the time we had two children and were living in a four-room, two-bedroom house) and was furnished all of her meals, including five box lunches each week. As a rule, school-teachers went home to their families over the weekend, but since "our" teacher was Laura Croston, a longtime personal friend of ours (she had graduated from high school with me), she quite often skipped the trip home and tended to her personal laundry and other weekend tasks at our house. Any loss of privacy we felt by keeping the teacher was more than offset by the fun we had having her there. After she'd graded papers and prepared the next day's lessons, she was always ready for a game of cards after supper and maybe another piece of cake.

## CARRIE'S ONE-EGG DEVIL'S FOOD CAKE

During the years that I kept the teacher, I baked a cake every single day of the school year. This is the updated version of Miss Croston's favorite—

1/3 cup butter, melted
2 tablespoons cocoa
1 teaspoon baking soda
1 egg
1 cup sugar
1 cup milk
1 teaspoon vanilla
1-1/2 cups flour
1/4 teaspoon salt
1 teaspoon baking powder

Preheat oven to 350 degrees F. Grease and lightly flour two round 8-inch cake pans. In a small bowl, combine melted butter, cocoa and baking soda. In a large bowl, beat egg, then beat in sugar; beat hard to dissolve sugar thoroughly. Combine milk and vanilla. Sift flour, salt and baking powder together 3 times. Add to egg-sugar mixture alternately with milk-vanilla mixture; start and end with dry ingredients. Beat well after each addition. Pour into prepared pans. Bake 25 to 30 minutes or until cake tests done. Cool cake in pans 10 minutes before turning out onto cooling racks. When cake is cool, frost with Caramel Frosting. Serves 16.

## BROWN SUGAR DEVIL'S FOOD CAKE

A tall, dark, moist cake—

1 cup brown sugar
1 cup milk
3 1-ounce squares unsweetened chocolate, shaved
1/2 cup milk
1/2 teaspoon cider vinegar
3 cups cake flour
1/2 teaspoon baking soda
1/2 teaspoon salt
1 cup brown sugar
1/2 cup butter
3 egg yolks
1 teaspoon vanilla

Preheat oven to 350 degrees F. Grease three round 8-inch cake pans; line pans with greased and lightly floured waxed paper. In a small saucepan, combine 1 cup brown sugar, 1 cup milk and shaved chocolate. Cook over medium heat until chocolate melts. Set aside to cool. In a small bowl, combine milk and vinegar. Set aside 5 minutes. Sift flour, baking soda and salt together. In a large bowl, combine 1 cup brown sugar and butter and cream until light and fluffy. Add egg yolks; beat well. Blend in vanilla. Add flour mixture alternately with sour milk; start and end with dry ingredients. Beat well after each addition. Pour into prepared pans. Bake 25 minutes or until cake tests done. Cool cake in pans 10 minutes before turning out onto cooling racks. When cake is cool, frost with Caramel or Fudge Frosting. Serves 20.

## CARRIE'S DEVIL'S FOOD FRUIT CAKE

A large, round, three-layer cake, one which was always part of a Hendrickson Christmas. This fruit cake is not supposed to be "aged." Carrie served it fresh from the tall, crystal cake plate she reserved for her tallest and most elegant cakes, cakes that had earned her the reputation of being a superb cake baker—

Half of 1-ounce square of unsweetened chocolate, melted
1 cup sugar
1 egg, lightly beaten
1/2 cup milk
3/4 cup butter, do *not* substitute margarine
1 cup sugar
3 eggs, separated, reserve egg whites for frosting
2-1/2 cups flour
2 teaspoons baking powder
1/2 teaspoon salt
1 cup milk
1 cup raisins
1 cup seeded and chopped dates
1 cup chopped walnuts

Preheat oven to 350 degrees F. Grease and flour three round 9-inch cake pans. In a small saucepan, combine melted chocolate, 1 cup sugar, lightly beaten egg and 1/2 cup milk. Bring to a boil over medium heat; cook until thick. Set aside to cool. In a large bowl, cream butter with 1 cup of sugar. In a small bowl, beat egg yolks. Add to creamed mixture; beat until light and fluffy. Sift flour, baking powder and salt together 3 times. Add to creamed mixture alternately with 1 cup of milk; start and end with dry ingredients. Beat well after each addition. Stir in cooled chocolate mixture; blend thoroughly. Stir in raisins, dates and walnuts; blend thoroughly. Pour into prepared pans. Bake 35 minutes or until cake tests done. Cool cake in pans 10 minutes before turning out on to cooling racks. When cake is cool, frost with Boiled White Icing. Serves 20.

## CARRIE'S WHITE FRUIT CAKE

A delicate loaf fruit cake and one that is not supposed to be "aged" but should be eaten fresh—

1 cup white (golden) raisins
1 cup butter, for a whiter cake, use shortening
1-1/2 cups sugar
4 eggs
2 cups flour
1 teaspoon salt
1 teaspoon baking powder
1/4 cup pineapple juice
1-1/4 cups pineapple chunks or tidbits, drained and halved
1 cup sliced almonds

Preheat oven to 275 degrees F. Grease a 9 x 5 x 3-inch loaf pan. In a small bowl, "plump" raisins by covering with boiling water 5 minutes. Drain thoroughly on paper towels. In a large bowl, cream butter and sugar until light and fluffy. Add eggs, one at a time. Beat well after each addition. In a small bowl, coat raisins and pineapple with 1/2 cup flour. Combine remaining flour, salt and baking powder and sift together 3 times. Add alternately with pineapple juice; start and end with dry ingredients. Beat well after each addition. Stir in almonds, raisins and pineapple. Stir gently until well-blended. Pour into prepared pan. Bake 1-1/2 hours or until cake tests done. Cool cake in pan 10 minutes before turning out onto cooling rack. Drizzle cooled cake with a thick powdered sugar icing. Serves 16.

## CARRIE'S GLASS CAKE

This cake got its name from the fact that a glass tumbler was used as the measuring utensil. The original recipe as I wrote it in my notebook read: "Use a glass that will hold 1-1/2 cups of liquid. Place 1 egg and butter the size of an egg into glass then fill glass up with milk. Sift together 1 cup sugar, 2 teaspoons baking powder, 2 cups flour. Add the contents of the glass to this and beat well. Place in 2 9" layer pans that have been greased and floured. Bake in moderate oven until done, about 25 minutes." Here's the recipe as a quick-mix cake made with an electric mixer—

1 egg
1/3 cup butter or margarine, softened to room temperature but *not* melted
About 1 cup milk
1 cup sugar
2 cups flour
2 teaspoons baking powder
1/4 teaspoon salt
1 teaspoon vanilla

Preheat oven to 350 degrees F. Grease and flour two round 9-inch cake pans. In a two-cup glass measuring cup, combine egg and butter. Add enough milk to raise the level of the mixture in the cup to the line marked "1-1/2 cups." Pour into a large bowl. With an electric mixer, beat at medium speed 2 minutes. Sift sugar, flour, baking powder and salt together 3 times. Add to egg-butter-milk mixture. Beat at medium speed 2 minutes. Blend in vanilla. Pour into prepared pans. Bake 25 minutes or until cake tests done. Cool cake in pans 10 minutes before turning out onto cooling racks. Frost cooled cake with Butter Cream Frosting. Serves 16.

## TILLIE'S HARDTIMES CAKE

Stir this cake up just like Tillie did—with a spoon and in the same saucepan in which the raisins are cooked. This recipe saw the Miller-Mickish families through a couple of wars and two depressions—

1 cup water
1 cup sugar
1 cup dark, seedless raisins
1/2 cup butter or margarine
2 cups flour
1 teaspoon baking soda
1/4 teaspoon salt
1 egg, well beaten
Dash of cinnamon
1/2 cup chopped walnuts

Preheat oven to 350 degrees F. Grease a 9 x 13-inch baking pan generously. In a medium saucepan, combine water, sugar and raisins. Bring to a boil over medium heat; boil 2 minutes. Remove from heat. Add butter; stir until butter melts. Sift flour, baking soda and salt together 3 times. Add to raisin mixture. Use a spoon to blend thoroughly. Add egg and cinnamon; beat well. Stir in walnuts. Pour into prepared pan. Bake 15 minutes or until cake tests done. While cake bakes, prepare glaze.

Glaze:
Juice of one lemon
1/2 teaspoon freshly grated lemon peel
1/2 to 2/3 cup sifted powdered sugar

In a small bowl and with a spoon, combine lemon juice, lemon peel and powdered sugar. Beat hard to completely dissolve sugar. Pour glaze over hot cake as soon as it comes out of the oven and while it is still in the pan. Cool cake in pan. Serves 16.

## TILLIE'S PLAIN CAKE

Every cook had one cake she could whip up on short notice and this was my mother's stand-by—

1 cup sugar
1/3 cup butter
1 egg
1-1/2 cups flour
1-1/2 teaspoons baking powder
Pinch of salt
1 cup milk
2 teaspoons vanilla

Preheat oven to 350 degrees F. Grease and lightly flour a 7 x 11-inch baking pan. In a medium bowl, cream sugar and butter until light and fluffy. Add egg; beat well. Sift flour, baking powder and salt together 3 times. Add to creamed mixture alternately with milk; start and end with dry ingredients. Beat well after each addition. Blend in vanilla. Pour into prepared pan. Bake 25 minutes or until cake tests done. Cool cake completely in pan or cool in pan 10 minutes and then turn out onto cooling rack. Frost with any flavor frosting or serve with Lemon Sauce. Serves 12.

Though she was younger than me, my sister Opal began baking sooner than I did. She liked to vary recipes and never hesitated to change a tried and true recipe. On one occasion she had the batter for this loaf cake stirred together, ready to pour into the baking pan when she decided to turn it into a chocolate cake by adding a one-half cup of shaved sweet chocolate. When the cake came out of the oven, instead of a chocolate cake, she had a white cake with lots of little chocolate flecks in it. Grandfather Miller was having supper with us that evening and when he saw the specks of melted chocolate shavings in the cake, he teased Opal by asking, "Did the flies get in your cake?"

## OPAL'S WHITE LOAF CAKE
Without chocolate shavings—

1 cup shortening
1 cup plus 2 tablespoons sugar
1 teaspoon vanilla
2 cups flour
2 teaspoons baking powder
1/4 teaspoon salt
1 cup milk
4 egg whites

Preheat oven to 350 degrees F. Grease and lightly flour 9 x 12-inch baking pan. In a large bowl, cream shortening and sugar until light and fluffy. Add vanilla. Sift flour, baking powder and salt together 3 times. Add to creamed mixture alternately with milk; start and end with dry ingredients. Beat well after each addition. In a medium bowl and with a rotary beater, beat egg whites until soft peaks form. Gently fold into prepared batter; blend thoroughly. Pour into prepared pan. Bake 35 to 40 minutes or until cake tests done. Cool cake completely in pan or cool in pan 10 minutes and then turn out onto cooling rack. Frost with a favorite icing or serve with Lemon Sauce. Serves 12.

Lemon Sauce:
1 cup sugar
3 tablespoons butter
1 tablespoon flour
1 cup water
Juice of 1 lemon

In a small saucepan, combine sugar, butter, flour and water. Bring to a boil over medium heat; cook until mixture forms a thick syrup. Remove from heat. Add lemon juice and stir to blend thoroughly. Serve hot or cold.

## TILLIE'S WHITE CAKE WITH WALNUT FROSTING

Only five words accompanied the list of ingredients in the original recipe: "Save out...cream...beat...and fold." This was another one of Mother's recipes that you had to *see* being made before you could believe it was correct. Now I let the mixer do some of the beating—

1/2 cup flour
3 teaspoons baking powder
2 cups sugar
1/2 cup butter
1 teaspoon vanilla
1 cup warm water
2-1/2 cups flour
5 egg whites

Preheat oven to 350 degrees F. Grease and lightly flour two round 9-inch cake pans. Sift 1/2 cup flour and baking powder together. In a large bowl, cream sugar and butter together at high speed until light and fluffy. Add vanilla. Add warm water. Stir in 2-1/2 cups flour. Beat hard 5 minutes. In a medium bowl and using an electric mixer or a rotary beater, beat egg whites until stiff peaks form. Use a rubber spatula to fold beaten egg whites along with flour-baking powder mixture into creamed mixture; blend thoroughly. Pour into prepared pans. Bake 25 minutes or until cake tests done. Cool cake in pan 10 minutes before turning out onto cooling racks. When cake is cool, frost with Walnut Frosting.

Walnut Frosting:
1/3 cup butter
4 cups sifted powdered sugar
1 egg yolk
1-1/2 teaspoons vanilla
2 tablespoons light cream, Half and Half
1/2 cup finely chopped walnuts

In a medium bowl, cream butter at high speed. Gradually add half of powdered sugar at low speed; blend thoroughly. Beat in egg yolk and vanilla. Add light cream alternately with remaining powdered sugar; add only as much sugar as is needed to reach spreading consistency. Beat hard after each addition. Sprinkle walnuts over the top of the frosted cake. Serves 20.

## TILLIE'S WHITE HOUSE CAKE

Whether or not this cake actually was baked in the White House kitchens during Woodrow Wilson's residency there, I can't say, but that was what Mother and her friends believed as they passed the recipe around neighbor to neighbor. A very delicate and light cake—it was my mother's choice for her birthday cake—

1-1/2 cups sugar
3/4 cup butter
1 teaspoon vanilla
2-1/2 cups flour
1-1/2 teaspoons baking powder
1/2 teaspoon salt
1 scant cup milk (1 cup less 1 tablespoon)
5 egg whites
1/4 teaspoon cream of tartar

Preheat oven to 350 degrees F. Grease and lightly flour two round 9-inch cake pans. In a large bowl, cream sugar and butter until light and fluffy. Add vanilla. Sift flour, baking powder and salt together 3 times. Add to creamed mixture alternately with milk; start and end with dry ingredients. Beat well after each addition. In a medium bowl and with a rotary beater, beat egg whites until foamy. Add cream of tartar. Continue to beat until stiff *but not dry* peaks form. Gently fold beaten whites into batter. Pour into prepared pans. Bake 25 minutes or until cake tests done. Cool cake in pans 10 minutes before turning out onto cooling racks. When cool, frost with Butter Cream Frosting. Serves 20.

Before there was an icebox or gas or electric refrigerator in a farm kitchen, there were mainly two places where milk and cream would stay fresh and sweet even for a few days—in a deep, cellar or cave during summer months or, during winter months, in a closed-door pantry, preferably one with at least one outside wall. "Sour cream" could still be sold or "traded" at grocery stores for a price determined by the amount of butter fat in the cream. A ten-gallon can of cream brought six to eight dollars a can. That "cream money" together with the "egg money," a thirty-dozen crate of eggs at twenty cents a dozen sold for six dollars, provided the extra cash for kitchen staples, incidental clothing and shoes, gas for the car and occasionally paid for machinery repairs. Some of the sour cream found its way into baked treats, such as rich, light and moist cakes.

Before we had our own cream separator, cream was skimmed off the top of whole milk; cream, being lighter than milk, rose to the top of whole milk when it was allowed to stand a few hours. Skimming wasn't a very efficient technique; you could only capture sixty to seventy percent of the cream in the milk. Forty years had gone by since Sweden's Carl Gustaf de Laval had patented a home-sized, mechanical separator but not every farm home in America could afford such a machine. A separator had a large, open steel tub on top. Whole milk was poured into the tub and coursed down through a series of fast spinning disks where centrifugal forces separated cream from milk and sent the two liquids out of the machine through separate spouts and into separate containers. Cream from the separator was very thick, as thick as today's commercially available whipping cream. When I make cakes from old recipes calling for "sour cream," I turn commercial whipping cream into sour cream by stirring a teaspoon of cider vinegar into the heavy whipping cream and allow it to stand five minutes before adding it to the cake batter. Adding vinegar to today's pasteurized milk will cause it to "turn sour" though I prefer to use commercial buttermilk as a substitute for sour milk in the old recipes.

## SOUR CREAM CHOCOLATE CAKE
A fabulous dessert when cloaked in Fudge Frosting—

1-1/2 cups thick whipping cream
1 teaspoon cider vinegar
1-1/2 cups sugar
1-3/4 cups flour
2 heaping tablespoons cocoa
Pinch of salt
2 eggs, well-beaten
2 teaspoons baking soda
4 tablespoons hot water
1 teaspoon vanilla.

Preheat oven to 350 degrees Farenheit. Grease and lightly flour two round 9-inch cake pans. In a small bowl, combine whipping cream and vinegar. Set aside 5 minutes. Sift sugar, flour, cocoa and salt together 3 times. In a large bowl, combine eggs and sour cream. Beat 2 minutes with electric mixer at medium speed or until batter is smooth. Add dry ingredients. Beat 2 minutes at medium speed. Dissolve baking soda in hot water and add. Stir just until well blended. Blend in vanilla. Pour into prepared pans. Bake 25 to 30 minutes or until cake tests done. Cool cake in pan 10 minutes before turning out onto cooling racks. When cool, frost with Fudge Frosting. Serves 20.

## CARRIE'S TROPICORONA CAKE
A towering two-toned creation which Carrie baked for her husband, Willie, on his birthday—

1/2 cup butter or margarine
1-1/4 cups sugar
2 eggs, well beaten
1-1/4 cups sifted flour
4 teaspoons baking powder
1/4 teaspoon salt
1 teaspoon cinnamon
1 teaspoon nutmeg
1 cup milk
1-1/4 cups sifted flour
1 tablespoon cocoa
1 tablespoon water

Preheat oven to 350 degrees F. Grease and lightly flour three round 8-inch cake pans. In a large bowl, cream butter and sugar until light and fluffy. Add eggs; beat well. Sift 1-1/4 cups flour, baking powder, salt, cinnamon and nutmeg together 3 times. Add to creamed mixture along with milk; beat well. Add remaining 1-1/4 cups flour; beat well. Reserve one-third of batter. Divide remaining batter between two prepared cake pans. Dissolve cocoa in water. Stir into reserved batter; blend thoroughly. Pour into remaining prepared pan. Bake 20 to 25 minutes or until cake tests done. Cool cake in pans 10 minutes before turning out onto cooling racks. When cool, assemble cake layers with a spice layer on the bottom; spread with half of Mocha Filling; top with the cocoa layer; spread with remaining filling; and, top with remaining spice layer. Frost top and sides of cake with favorite chocolate frosting.

Mocha Filling:
1 tablespoon cocoa
2 tablespoons butter
1 teaspoon vanilla
3 tablespoons strong coffee
2 cups powdered sugar, sifted

In a small bowl, cream butter and cocoa until light. Add vanilla. Add powdered sugar alternately with a few drops of coffee until filling is thick yet spreads easily. Serves 20.

## CARRIE'S PEANUT LOGS

Bars cut from a simple sponge cake, dipped in icing and rolled in chopped, roasted and salted peanuts make these finger-licking good "logs"—

3 eggs
1-1/2 cups sugar
2 cups flour
2 teaspoons baking powder
1/2 teaspoon salt
1 cup water
1 teaspoon vanilla
3 cups finely chopped roasted, hulled and salted peanuts

Preheat oven to 350 degrees F. Grease and lightly flour a 9 x 13-inch baking pan. In a large bowl, combine eggs and 1/2 cup sugar. Beat until light and fluffy. Gradually beat in remaining sugar; continue to beat a total of 5 minutes. Sift flour, baking powder and salt together 3 times. Combine water and vanilla. Add to egg-sugar mixture alternately with *half* of flour mixture; start and end with dry ingredients. Beat well after each addition. Add remaining flour mixture; beat until thoroughly blended. Pour into prepared pan. Bake 25 minutes or until cake tests done. Cool cake in pan until it is *completely cool.* Cut into 16 bars; each bar should measure about 1-1/2 x 4-1/2 inches. Remove bars from pan. Work quickly to coat bars on *all sides* with icing, then roll in chopped peanuts and place on waxed paper. Makes 16.

Icing:
1/4 cup butter
4 cups sifted powdered sugar
1/2 cup milk

In a small bowl, cream butter and 2 cups powdered sugar. Add remaining powdered sugar alternately with milk. Beat hard after each addition. *Icing will be thin, similar to a glaze.*

## CARRIE'S UPSIDE DOWN CAKE
Must be made in a cast iron or oven-proof skillet—

1 cup brown sugar
1 tablespoon butter
Home-canned peach halves or pineapple rings, enough to cover
    bottom of 10-inch oven-proof skillet
1 tablespoon fruit juice
1 cup sugar
2 tablespoons butter
1 egg, lightly beaten
1 cup flour
1 teaspoon baking powder
1/4 teaspoon salt
1/2 cup milk

Preheat oven to 350 degrees F. *Butter* generously a 10-inch oven-proof skillet. Sprinkle brown sugar evenly over bottom of skillet. Dot with 1 tablespoon of butter. Top with peach halves, cut side down, or pineapple rings. Drizzle with fruit juice. In a medium bowl, cream sugar and 2 table-spoons butter until thoroughly blended. Add egg; beat well. Sift flour, baking powder and salt together 3 times. Add flour mixture to creamed mixture alternately with milk; start and end with dry ingredients. Beat well after each addition. Pour over fruit in skillet. Bake 25 minutes or until cake tests done. Let cake stand in skillet 10 minutes before turning out onto a serving plate. Serve warm or cold with sweetened whipped cream. Serves 8.

I knew school was about to begin for me the summer of my fifth birthday when Mother laid claim on an empty, rectangular, red tin box that had held Union Leader tobacco for Grandfather Miller's pipe. She gave it a daily scrubbing and set it out in the sun with its hinged lid ajar so it could "air out." Without Mother telling me, I knew that tin tobacco box was going to be my school lunch box. Ordinarily the empty tins went to the shop where they held nuts, bolts, washers, screws and other small, easy-to-lose shop items. The night before my first day of school she used a nail to scratch the letters "A-L-I-C-E M-I-C-K-I-S-H" on the bottom of the tin.

My first day of school, my father drove me there in the horse-drawn family spring wagon, but from that day on, rain or shine or snow, I walked the one mile across the fields, following the fence rows to Karel School, District 42, a one-room school northeast of Ravenna. I can't remember whether my sandwich for the first day of school was cold roast beef, pork or chicken, but I do remember there was an apple and also a wonderful little cupcake in my lunch box.

## TILLIE'S SCHOOL DAYS CUPCAKES

These school lunch box treats were moist, tender and light though they were not quite as delicate as a fine-textured layer cake. The little cakes were baked directly in a muffin "tin"— cake, pie and muffin pans were all referred to as "tins"—and were seldom frosted but were eaten plain. Through all the years I carried my lunch to school, whenever one of these little cupcakes showed up in my box, I knew it was a special treat baked by Mother especially for me and later for my sister and my brothers when they were in school—

1 cup sugar
1-1/2 cups flour
1/2 teaspoon salt
1-1/2 teaspoons baking powder
2 egg whites, unbeaten
1 rounded tablespoon butter, softened to room temperature but *not* melted
1/2 cup milk
1/2 teaspoon vanilla

Preheat oven to 350 degrees F. Grease and lightly flour one 12-muffin pan. Sift sugar, flour, salt and baking powder together twice, the last time into a medium bowl. Make a hole in the center of the dry ingredients. Add egg whites, butter, milk and vanilla all at one time. Beat hard with a spoon 2 to 3 minutes; batter should be light, fluffy and thoroughly blended. Spoon into prepared pan. Bake 15 minutes or until cakes test done. Cool cakes in pan 5 minutes before removing to cooling rack. Makes 12 cupcakes.

# FROSTINGS

## CARAMEL ICING

1/4 cup margarine
3/4 cup brown sugar
3 tablespoons milk
2 cups sifted powdered sugar

In a medium saucepan over low heat, melt margarine. Stir in brown sugar. Cook over low heat 2 minutes. Add milk. Bring to a rolling boil then remove from heat. Cool to lukewarm. DO NOT STIR DURING COOLING TIME. Add powdered sugar. Beat hard until frosting is smooth and of a spreading consistency; will lightly frost a two-layer, 8 or 9-inch cake or a 9 x 13-inch cake.

## CARRIE'S BUTTER ICING

A quick glaze suitable for bars, cookies or single layer or loaf cakes—

1-1/2 cups sifted powdered sugar
1 tablespoon butter
1 tablespoon white corn syrup
1 teaspoon vanilla
1-2 tablespoons milk

In a small bowl, cream 1/2 cup powdered sugar with butter. Add syrup and vanilla. Gradually add remaining powdered sugar alternately with milk until icing reaches desired spreading consistency.

## BROWN SUGAR FROSTING

1 cup brown sugar
1 cup sugar
1 cup light cream, Half and Half
2 tablespoons flour
1 teaspoon vanilla

In a small saucepan, combine brown sugar, sugar, cream and flour. Mix well. Bring to a boil over medium heat. Boil until mixture reaches "soft ball stage." Cool slightly. Add vanilla. Beat hard until frosting reaches desired spreading consistency; will lightly frost a two-layer 8 or 9-inch cake or a 9 x 13-inch loaf cake.

## EASY FUDGE FROSTING

6 tablespoons sugar
2 tablespoons butter or margarine
6 tablespoons milk
2 tablespoons cocoa
1 teaspoon vanilla
3 cups sifted powdered sugar

In a small saucepan, combine sugar, margarine, milk and cocoa. Bring to a full boil over medium heat; boil 2 to 3 minutes. Remove from heat. Add vanilla. Gradually beat in powdered sugar until frosting reaches desired spreading consistency; will frost a two-layer, 8 or 9-inch cake or a 9 x 13-inch loaf cake.

## TILLIE'S BUTTER CREAM FROSTING

1/3 cup butter or margarine
4 cups sifted powdered sugar
1 egg yolk
1 teaspoon vanilla
1/8 teaspoon lemon extract
2 tablespoons light cream, Half and Half

In a small bowl, cream butter with 2 cups powdered sugar. Beat in egg yolk, vanilla and lemon extract. Gradually beat in remaining powdered sugar alternately with cream until frosting reaches desired spreading consistency; will frost a two-layer, 8 or 9-inch cake or a 9 x 13-inch loaf cake.

## FUDGE FROSTING

2 1-ounce squares unsweetened chocolate
3 cups sugar
3 tablespoons white corn syrup
1/4 teaspoon salt
1 cup milk
1/4 cup butter or margarine
1 teaspoon vanilla

In a two-quart saucepan, combine chocolate, sugar, syrup, salt and milk. Cook over low heat; stir just until sugar is dissolved and chocolate melts. DO NOT STIR DURING REMAINING COOKING TIME. Cook until mixture reaches "soft ball stage." Remove from heat. Add butter but DO NOT STIR. Cool until a hand can be held comfortably on bottom of pan, then add vanilla. Beat hard until frosting reaches spreading consistency; will frost a two-layer, 8 or 9-inch cake or a 9 x 13-inch loaf cake.

## BOILED WHITE ICING

2 cups sugar
1 cup water
2 egg whites
1/8 teaspoon salt
1/8 teaspoon cream of tartar
1 teaspoon vanilla

In a small saucepan, combine sugar and water; stir until sugar dissolves. Bring to a boil over medium heat. Cover and cook 3 minutes, until steam washes down any sugar crystals which may have formed on sides of pan. Uncover and continue cooking until syrup spins a very thin thread, so thin it almost seems to disappear. In a small bowl, combine egg whites and salt. With a rotary beater, beat until frothy. Gradually add syrup in a thin stream. Add cream of tartar. Continue to beat until stiff peaks form and frosting reaches spreading consistency. Beat in vanilla. Fill and frost cake immediately, before icing sets up; will frost a two-layer, 8 or 9-inch cake or a 9 x 13-inch loaf cake.

## NUT ICING

Fold 1/2 cup chopped walnuts into Boiled White Icing just before filling and frosting cake or sprinkle chopped nuts over top of a cake freshly iced with Boiled White Icing.

# CANDY

Of all the candy recipes I've tried and collected, none have surpassed Carrie's Fudge and Aunt Minnie's Divinity from my first recipe notebook. Since 1922, I've made hundreds of batches of both candies for Christmas, birthdays, anniversaries and other special occasions.

Along with her fudge recipe, Carrie passed along these candy-making tips: Cook sugar and liquids in a *heavy* saucepan. Stir just until sugar is dissolved, then continue boiling WITHOUT STIRRING OR MOVING OR SHAKING THE PAN.

Aunt Minnie and Carrie didn't use a candy thermometer and neither do I. Like them, I drop a few drips of the boiling syrup into a cup of cold water making sure to USE A FRESH CUP OF COLD WATER FOR EACH TEST to determine if the syrup has reached the necessary sugar concentration called for in the recipe, such as a "soft ball," "firm ball," "hard ball," "soft crack" or "hard crack" stage.

## AUNT MINNIE'S DIVINITY

A soft, white cloud-like candy that sets up quickly once it's poured into a pan—

2-1/2 cups sugar
1/2 cup white corn syrup
1/2 cup water
1/8 teaspoon salt
2 egg whites, beaten stiff
1 teaspoon vanilla
1/2 cup finely chopped walnuts

Butter a square 9-inch pan. In a small heavy saucepan, combine sugar, syrup, water and salt. Cook over medium heat until syrup spins a fine thread as it runs back into the pan from the spoon. Remove pan from heat. Pour half of syrup over beaten egg whites in a small steady stream; beat constantly with a rotary beater or a whisk. Return pan to heat. Cook remaining syrup until it reaches "hard crack" stage. Again pour syrup into egg whites in a steady stream; beat constantly with a rotary beater. Use a spoon to fold in vanilla and walnuts. Continue to beat with spoon until mixture holds its shape and loses its gloss. Pour into prepared pan. Before candy cools completely and sets, cut into 1-inch squares.

## CARRIE'S FUDGE

This recipe makes a small amount of candy, but take it from one who has tried, THIS RECIPE CANNOT BE SUCCESSFULLY DOUBLED—

2 cups sugar
1 scant cup milk
1 heaping tablespoon cocoa
1 tablespoon butter
1 teaspoon vanilla
1/2 cup chopped walnuts (optional)

Butter a 3 x 6-inch pan. In a small heavy saucepan, combine sugar, milk and cocoa. Bring to a boil over medium heat. Boil until mixture reaches "soft ball stage." Remove from heat. Add butter and vanilla. Beat hard with a spoon until mixture thickens, 3 to 5 minutes. Fold in nuts. Pour into prepared pan. Candy sets up quickly. Cut into squares before it cools completely.

# COOKIES

## GRANDMOTHER LYDIA LATHROP'S OATMEAL COOKIES

The window in the pantry off of Carrie's kitchen opened onto a side porch. After a night out dancing, Walter made a practice of slipping through that little window and raiding the cookie jar before he headed on upstairs to bed. He counted it a lucky raid when these cookies made from his maternal grandmother's recipe were in the cookie jar—

1 cup raisins
1 cup sugar
1 cup butter
2 eggs
1 teaspoon vanilla
1 teaspoon baking soda
5 tablespoons raisin water
2 cups flour
1/2 teaspoon cinnamon
1/2 teaspoon nutmeg
1/2 teaspoon allspice
1/2 teaspoon salt
2 cups quick-cook oatmeal
1/2 cup chopped walnuts

Preheat oven to 375 degrees F. Grease cookie sheets. In a small saucepan, cover raisins with water. Bring to a boil over medium heat; boil gently 5 minutes. Drain; reserve hot liquid. In a large bowl, cream sugar and butter until light and fluffy. Add eggs; beat well. Add vanilla. Dissolve baking soda in 5 tablespoons of reserved hot raisin liquid. Add to creamed mixture; blend thoroughly. Sift flour, cinnamon, nutmeg, allspice and salt together. Add to creamed mixture; mix thoroughly. Add oatmeal and walnuts; blend thoroughly. Drop by teaspoonfuls onto prepared cookie sheets. Bake 10 minutes or until cookies are lightly browned and test done. Makes 3 dozen.

## CARRIE'S FILLED DOUBLE-DECK COOKIES

Changing the original recipe from all-purpose to cake flour resulted in a softer, more cake-like cookie—

3/4 cup butter or margarine
1 cup sugar
2 eggs, well beaten
3-1/2 cups cake flour
3 teaspoons baking powder
1/2 teaspoon salt
1/3 cup milk
1-1/2 teaspoons vanilla

Preheat oven to 400 degrees F. Grease cookie sheets. In a large bowl, cream butter and sugar until light and fluffy. Add eggs. Sift cake flour, baking powder and salt together 3 times. Combine milk and vanilla. Add alternately with flour mixture; start and end with dry ingredients. Mix well after each addition. Divide dough in half. On a lightly floured board or pastry cloth, roll out each portion of dough until 1/8-inch thick. Cut with a 2-1/2-inch round cookie cutter. Place rounds on prepared cookie sheets. Top each round with a teaspoon of filling. Roll and cut remaining dough. Use a thimble to cut out the center of each round; place "ring" of dough over filling on bottom rounds. Seal edges of cookie layers together by pressing lightly with fork tines. Bake 10 minutes or until cookies are lightly browned and test done. Makes 5 dozen.

Filling:
1-1/2 cups sugar
1 cup hot water
2 tablespoons butter or margarine
1 tablespoon flour
1/4 teaspoon salt
1/2 cup raisins

In a small saucepan, combine sugar, water, butter, flour, salt and raisins. Cook over low heat until mixture thickens to the consistency of thick jam. Cool thoroughly.

## CARRIE'S BANANA OATMEAL COOKIES

When bananas ripened on the stalk in the cellar faster than they could be eaten, Carrie selected the ripest ones, those with lots of big, brown freckles on their skins, and baked them up into these cookies. Five generations later, they are still one of the most requested cookies in our family—

1-1/2 cups sifted flour
1/2 teaspoon baking soda
1 teaspoon salt
1/4 teaspoon nutmeg
3/4 teaspoon cinnamon
3/4 cup butter or margarine
1 cup sugar
1 egg
1 cup mashed ripe banana, 3 medium bananas
1-3/4 cups quick-cook oatmeal
1/2 cup chopped walnuts

Preheat oven to 400 degrees F. Grease cookie sheets. Sift flour, baking soda, salt, nutmeg and cinnamon together 3 times. In a large bowl, cream butter and sugar until light and fluffy. Add eggs; beat well. Add mashed banana alternately with flour mixture; start and end with dry ingredients. Beat well after each addition. Stir in oatmeal and walnuts. Blend well. Drop by teaspoonfuls onto prepared cookie sheets. Bake 10 minutes or until cookies are lightly browned and test done. Makes 3 dozen.

## CARRIE'S DATE PINWHEEL COOKIES

Long before we had refrigerators, these cookies were made only at Christmas or during winter months when the dough could be chilled in a covered box on the porch—

1 cup butter or margarine
1 cup sugar
1 cup brown sugar
3 eggs, well beaten
4 cups flour
1 teaspoon baking soda
1 teaspoon cinnamon
1/4 teaspoon salt

In a large bowl, cream butter, sugar and brown sugar until light and fluffy. Add eggs; beat well. Sift flour, baking soda, cinnamon and salt together 3 times. Add to creamed mixture; mix thoroughly. Divide dough into four portions and wrap each portion in waxed paper. Chill dough at least an hour before rolling. While dough chills, prepare filling.

Filling:
1 pound seeded, chopped dates
1/2 cup sugar
1/2 cup water
1 cup chopped walnuts

In a medium saucepan, combine dates, sugar and water. Cook over medium heat until mixture is well-blended and thick. Remove from heat. Stir in walnuts. Cool thoroughly. On a lightly floured pastry cloth or board, roll each chilled portion of dough into an 8 x 10-inch rectangle; dough will be about half an inch thick. Spread with cooled filling. Start with a long side of the rectangle and roll up as for a jelly roll. Wrap each roll in waxed paper and refrigerate until firm, at least an hour or overnight. At baking time, preheat oven to 375 degrees F. Grease cookie sheets. Cut rolled, filled rolls into 1/4-inch slices. Place on prepared cookie sheets. Bake 10 minutes or until cookies are lightly browned and test done. Makes 6 dozen.

Laborers, including farmers, whose jobs require them to be outdoors, working in summer's heat and humidity, needed plenty of drinking water to ward off dehydration and heat exhaustion. Burlap-covered, crockery jugs swung from levers on cultivators, go-devils, grain binders or whatever piece of machinery a farmer might be riding. Soaking the burlap thoroughly with water kept the water inside the jug surprisingly cool for several hours. It was the closest thing we had to a thermos bottle or jug and the next best thing to having a drink and lunch delivered to the field.

Before we had children, I took Walter his mid-afternoon lunch. After we had children but before they were old enough to find their way to the field by themselves, taking lunch to Daddy was a high point in our day. The children rode in their little red wagon and I pulled it through the newly worked ground along the end of the field. Immediately before we set out on our trek, I filled a quart fruit jar with cold, fresh water straight from the pump, wrapped the jar in several thicknesses of newspapers for insulation and slipped it inside a brown paper bag. Lunch, sandwiches or cookies, was in another bag. Sometimes the cookies were Carrie's Molasses Cookies, Walter's favorite.

## CARRIE'S SOFT MOLASSES COOKIES
A good-keeping cookie—

1 cup milk
1 teaspoon cider vinegar
1/2 cup butter
1/2 cup plus 2 tablespoons shortening
1 cup sugar
2 eggs
2 cups molasses
4-3/4 cups flour
3 teaspoons baking soda
1 teaspoon cinnamon
1 teaspoon ginger
1 teaspoon ground cloves

Preheat oven to 375 degrees F. Grease cookie sheets. In a small bowl, combine milk and vinegar. Set aside. In a large bowl, cream butter, shortening and sugar. Add eggs; beat well. Stir in molasses. Sift flour, baking soda, cinnamon, ginger and cloves together twice. Add alternately with milk; start and end with dry ingredients. Blend thoroughly after each addition. Working with one-third of dough at a time, turn dough out onto lightly floured board or pastry cloth and roll until 1/4-inch thick. Cut with a 2-1/2-inch round cookie cutter. Place cookies on prepared sheets. Bake 12 to 15 minutes or until cookies are *very lightly* browned and test done. Cool baked cookies on racks. When completely cool, store in air-tight container. Makes 5 dozen.

## TILLIE'S PRESSED CURRANT COOKIES
The best-remembered cookie from my childhood—

2 cups sifted flour
3/4 teaspoon baking powder
1/2 teaspoon salt
1/2 cup butter or margarine
1/2 cup sugar
1 egg
1 teaspoon vanilla
1/2 teaspoon almond extract
1/2 cup dried currants

Preheat oven to 400 degrees F. Grease cookie sheets. Sift flour, baking powder and salt together twice. In a large bowl, cream butter and sugar until light and fluffy. Add egg; beat well. Stir in vanilla and almond extract. Add flour mixture; mix thoroughly. Add currants; blend thoroughly. Chill dough an hour. Shape dough into walnut-size balls; place on prepared cookie sheets and press down with a table fork. Bake 8 to 10 minutes or until cookies are lightly browned and test done. Remove cookies to cooling racks. Cool completely before frosting. Makes 3 dozen.

Frosting:
1 cup powdered sugar, sifted
1/4 teaspoon vanilla
2 to 3 drops almond extract
Few tablespoons of milk

In a small bowl, combine sugar, vanilla and almond extract. Add milk a tablespoon at a time; beat well after each addition and continue to beat until frosting is smooth and of spreading consistency.

# DESSERTS

My first Thanksgiving Day in the Hendrickson family came a week and a day after Walter and I were married. I didn't want to go empty-handed to my new in-laws' house but as my new mother-in-law saw it, I was still "company," and as such, I wasn't expected to contribute food.

All seven Hendrickson children were there—four sons, Walter, Albert, Roy and Elmer, and three daughters, Jessie, Ruth and Elsie—plus Ruth's husband, Lyle, and Walter's wife, me. Ruth and Walter were the only children married at the time and there were no grandchildren yet. The gathering also included several aunts and uncles and cousins—anyone who didn't have a place to go knew they were always welcome at Willie and Carrie's house for the holidays. The square oak dining table was stretched to seat sixteen, six on each side and two on each end, and we ate in shifts—the first seating was men and boys and the second, women and girls. The meal was planned around a big, eighteen-pound rump roast and two fat baked hens. There were bowls of mashed potatoes, canned beans and corn, baked squash, bread dressing, gravy, plates of thick-sliced, fresh homemade bread and home-churned butter. Assorted jams and jellies and relishes, pickled beet rounds, sweet pickles and spiced whole apples and peaches were mounted as jewels in crystal compotes and relish trays.

Desserts waited on the side porch where it was cool until platters and bowls had circled the table two or three times for each shift of diners to take second and sometimes third helpings. The treats of the day, tall, thick slices of rich, moist assorted cakes and fat slices of fall fruit pies were passed as diners protested, claiming they were "stuffed" and "couldn't eat another bite" and then proceeded to devour every crumb of their chosen desserts before requesting "just a sliver" of some other dessert that had caught their eyes or another diner recommended they "had to try."

There was never a crumb of Carrie's Date Pudding left. Squares of that dessert were gone after the first round.

## CARRIE'S DATE PUDDING

Dates were not homegrown and that qualified them as a treat, a luxury reserved for Thanksgiving and Christmas—

6 eggs, separated
1 cup sugar
1/2 cup plus 1 tablespoon fine, dry bread crumbs
2 teaspoons baking powder
1/2 pound dates, pitted and chopped
1 cup chopped walnuts
1 cup whipping cream
2 tablespoons powdered sugar
1 teaspoon vanilla

Preheat oven to 350 degrees F. Butter generously a 7 x 10-inch baking pan. In a small bowl, beat eggs yolks until light. Gradually beat in sugar. In a large bowl, combine bread crumbs and baking powder. Add egg yolk-sugar mixture; blend well. Add dates and walnuts; stir gently until thoroughly blended. In a small bowl and with a rotary beater, beat egg whites until soft peaks form. Gently fold into crumb-date-nut mixture; blend well. Spread mixture into prepared pan. Bake 20 to 25 minutes or until pudding is firm to the touch and knife inserted halfway between the sides of the pan comes out clean. Cool in the pan. At serving time, cut into squares and top with lightly sweetened whipped cream flavored with a few drops of vanilla. Serves 8.

## BREAD PUDDING

Wash day was a good day to make Bread Pudding. The cookstove was already fired up and set to go full blast all day, no need to let a hot and ready oven stand empty. The pudding can be made with store-bought bread but it's better if it's made with firm-textured, homemade bread that's *two to three days old*—

2 cups dark, seedless raisins
Boiling water
12 slices white bread, do not use fresh bread—
6 eggs
1-1/2 cups sugar
1/2 teaspoon salt
3 cups milk
1 teaspoon vanilla

Preheat oven to 350 degrees F. Butter a 9 x 12-inch baking pan generously. In a small bowl, "plump" raisins by covering with boiling water 10 minutes. Drain thoroughly on paper towels. Trim crusts from bread slices. Arrange half of slices in pan. Sprinkle raisins over bread and top with remaining bread slices. Make sure no raisins are exposed or they will burn during baking. In a large bowl and with a rotary beater, beat eggs until light. Beat in sugar and salt. Stir in milk and vanilla. Pour mixture over bread. Bread should be completely covered; add more milk if necessary. Bake 45 minutes or until top of pudding is lightly browned, the pudding is firm to the touch and a knife inserted halfway between the sides of the pan comes out clean. Serve warm or cold and pass a pitcher of light cream. Serves 12.

## CARRIE'S PINEAPPLE TORTE

A Sunday "company's coming" dessert—

3 eggs, separated
1 cup sugar
1 cup fine, *fresh* bread crumbs, crumble fresh bread gently between the fingertips
1/2 cup chopped walnuts
1 cup crushed, drained pineapple

Topping:
1 cup whipping cream
2 to 3 tablespoons sugar
1/2 teaspoon vanilla

Preheat oven to 350 degrees F. Butter a 7 x 11-inch baking pan generously. In a large bowl, beat egg yolks until light and fluffy. Gradually beat
in sugar. Add bread crumbs, walnuts and pineapple; blend thoroughly. In a
small bowl, beat egg whites until stiff peaks form. Gently fold into crumb-
nut-pineapple mixture; blend thoroughly. Spread into prepared pan. Bake 25
minutes or until torte is lightly browned and firm to the touch. Cool. At
serving time, cut into squares and spoon on whipped cream topping. To
make topping: In a small chilled bowl and with chilled beaters, whip cream
until it begins to thicken. Gradually beat in sugar; beat until cream is stiff.
Blend in vanilla. Serves 8.

## *OMA'S* POPPY SEED PANCAKES

Grandmother Louisa Mickish used a lot of poppy seeds in her baking. They were a staple in her kitchen. She bought them in the bulk and always kept a bag on the shelf right beside bags of flour and sugar. When her husband, William, got homesick for Germany, she made him this special dessert with the break-fasty-sounding name. This is her recipe as it was told to me: "Put poppy seeds through coffee grinder or put seeds in cloth bag and pound bag with a mallet to open seeds. Place seeds in a pan and add water to cover. Cook about an hour. Most of the water will be absorbed. Add some milk and sugar and a little butter and a pinch of salt. Bake a batch of pancakes. Keep baked cakes in warming oven. Cut pancakes into narrow strips. Put strips in a serving dish and pour poppy seed sauce over."

Now here's my version—

1/2 pound poppy seeds, ground
1 cup water
1/2 cup milk
3/4 cup sugar
1 or 2 tablespoons butter or margarine
1 teaspoon vanilla
Dash of salt
12 5-inch pancakes

In a small saucepan, combine poppy seeds and water. Cook over low heat until most of water is absorbed, about an hour. Add milk and sugar. Return to low heat and cook another 10 minutes; watch sauce carefully so it does not scorch. Add butter, vanilla and salt. Keep sauce warm while pancakes are baked. Place baked pancakes in a very low oven until all are baked. Cut cakes into 2-inch strips, place in serving dish and pour over poppy seed sauce. Serves 6 to 8.

Before Walter's folks gave us a two-quart, hand-cranked ice cream freezer with its own wooden tub, we made ice cream in a one-gallon, tin syrup pail with a bail handle and a tight-fitting lid. An egg-sugar-milk-cream mixture was poured to within two inches of the top of the pail, its lid was sealed in place and it was set down inside a six-quart galvanized tin pail and alternate layers of crushed ice—sometimes we used snow instead of ice—and salt were packed around it. We took turns gripping the handle of the syrup pail to rotate the pail back and forth in 180-degree turns in the ice-salt mixture. Every five minutes, we removed the lid of the syrup pail v-e-r-y carefully so no ice or salt got into the ice cream and scraped the frozen mixture away from the sides of the pail with a table knife. Near the end of the freezing—it took thirty to forty minutes to freeze ice cream in that little contrivance—the ice cream was stirred vigorously to break-up the frozen crystallized mass in an effort to make the finished ice cream as smooth and creamy as possible.

Farm families made and ate more ice cream in the winter than they did in the summer. Except for sugar, ice cream "makings," the eggs, milk and cream, were always on hand the year around, but in the wintertime we didn't have to buy ice because there was plenty of ice available "free of charge" in the livestock water tanks. Card games, welcome diversions anytime, were particularly popular pastimes during long winter evenings. There were no prizes, no money stakes. We might play to see who had to fetch an extra basket of cobs or do supper dishes and we often played to see who had to make ice cream for a midnight dessert. It was not unusual to see "losers" chipping ice from a tank and milking a cow by lantern light to pay-off the "winners" of that night's game.

One enterprising "loser" milked a cow, got ice from the horse tank and mixed up a freezer of ice cream—yes, the man mixed it up himself, his wife wasn't one of the "losers," so she couldn't help him out. He poured the ice cream mixture into the can, iced and salted it down in the freezer tub and then, just when we thought everything was set for him to start cranking, without a word, he abruptly carried the freezer outdoors. Next thing we knew, he'd driven his Model T Ford right up next to the kitchen door. He jacked up one of the car's rear wheels, stuck the ice cream freezer's crank handle between two spokes of the wheel, cranked up the car engine and got in the car, ready to put the gears into "forward." Up until that point, all of us watching from the kitchen windows were thinking it was all a joke, a prank, a stunt. When we realized the guy was serious, the other fellows rushed outdoors and tried to get him to call it off.

"Cut it out!"

They had to shout to be heard above the clatter of the car.

"You'll wreck the freezer...the crank'll rip the spokes out of the wheel...stand back, that freezer'll flip, hit your leg and break it..." None of shouts phased the "inventor" of the first "powered" ice cream freezer. Well, it was the first power ice cream freezer we'd ever seen. After he'd set the car wheel in motion, he calmly went back inside the warm kitchen, pulled a chair up to the window and sat down to keep an eye on the operation. The car motor purred, the wheel spun, turning the freezer at a good clip and in no time at all, he'd cranked out the ice cream and was serving it to a bunch of flabbergasted "winners."

Birthdays were always celebrated with ice cream and for summertime birthdays, we bought a fifty-pound chunk of ice at the ice plant and carried it home in a gunny sack in the trunk of the car or wedged between the car's back bumper and a rear fender. Then we'd drive as fast as we could—thirty-five miles an hour—to try to get the ice home before too many pounds melted away.

As the number of guests for our ice cream parties grew, so did the size of our ice cream freezer. We went from a two-quart to a one-gallon to a one-and-a-half-gallon freezer—all hand-cranked. But the last thirty years I've been making ice cream, I haven't turned a crank. I have an electric ice cream freezer, a small motor powers its dasher. For a large group of eight or more, I use the electric freezer and for a small group of two, three or four, I can make ice cream in a one-quart electric freezer that plugs into a wall outlet and sits inside my home food freezer.

Regardless of the recipe being followed or the size and type of freezer being used there are some basic directions for making ice cream:

Use the freshest eggs, milk and cream available.

Rinse and chill freezer can, lid and dasher.

Don't fill freezer can too full. Allow for expansion as ice cream mixture freezes. For best results, the can should be between three-quarters full or to within two inches of the top; it should never be filled clear to the top.

When the can is in place in the freezer tub and the dasher and can lid are secure, add cracked ice until freezer tub is one-quarter full, adding alternate layers of ice cream or rock salt and ice, six parts of ice to one part salt.

*Pack ice and salt up to, NOT OVER, the freezer can lid.*

Add more ice and salt as needed throughout freezing time. When it becomes too difficult to turn the crank, or, as in the case of an electric freezer, the motor stops, the ice cream should be frozen solid enough to serve or to pack. Packing allows ice cream to "ripen," improving its texture and mellowing the flavor.

To pack frozen ice cream, drain off accumulated salt water and remove ice to a level well below the lid of the can. Remove crank or motor head.

Thoroughly wipe the lid and top of can to remove all traces of salt and ice.

Carefully ease dasher out of the can, scraping ice cream from dasher back into can. Stir ice cream down in the can to remove large air pockets.

It was an unwritten rule at our house: "The one who cranked the ice cream got to lick the dasher." Now that an electric motor turns the gears for our homemade ice cream, licking the dasher goes to the one who gets there first after the motor stops signaling the ice cream is frozen.

Place a cork in the hole in the can's lid, replace lid and re-pack tub with alternate layers of ice and salt, six parts of ice to one part salt. Wrap freezer tub with heavy cloths—for years we had the perfect ice cream freezer cover, one of Walter's old discarded sheepskin coats. Several layers of newspapers covered with a large sheet of plastic serves the same purpose. "Ripening" ice cream should stand at least two hours before it is served and it can be held for as long as four hours.

## TILLIE'S ICE CREAM
A quick-mix, there's no cooking—

6 eggs
2 cups sugar
1-1/2 pints whipping cream
1 tablespoon vanilla
2 drops lemon extract
About 2 quarts of milk

In a very large bowl, beat eggs until light and fluffy. Add sugar and beat thoroughly until sugar dissolves. Add cream, vanilla and lemon extract; blend thoroughly. Pour into freezer can. Add enough milk to fill can to within 2 inches of the top. Makes 1 gallon.

## FRESH PEACH ICE CREAM
As smooth and refreshing as the Peach Ice Cream Aunt Marie Mickish Kaspar cranked out on hot and humid August days—

1 cup sugar
1 tablespoon unflavored gelatin
2 quarts light cream, Half and Half
2 eggs, slightly beaten
2 teaspoons vanilla
1/2 teaspoon almond extract
Dash of salt
12 to 14 fresh peaches, enough to make 3 cups of mashed pulp
1-1/2 cups sugar

In a medium saucepan, combine 1 cup sugar and gelatin. Stir in 2 cups light cream. Cook over low heat. Stir constantly until gelatin dissolves. In a medium bowl, beat eggs. Slowly blend small amount of hot mixture into beaten eggs. Return mixture to saucepan. Cook over low heat; stir constantly until mixture thickens, about a minute. Cool. Add remaining cream, vanilla, almond extract and salt. Peel, seed and mash enough peaches to make 3 cups of pulp. IMMEDIATELY add 1-1/2 cups sugar to prevent peaches from darkening. Add peaches to cooled cream mixture. Pour into freezer can. With this recipe, the freezer will be only about two-thirds full. Makes 1 gallon.

Under the Homestead Act passed by the United States Congress May 1862, John Hendrickson, Walter's grandfather, filed a claim to 160 acres in the Sodtown community of Gardner Township in Buffalo County, Nebraska. Being a person "over twenty-one years of age, who was the head of a family and either a citizen or an alien intending to become a citizen," he agreed to live on the land and to make "certain improvements." Since Nebraska had a noticeable lack of trees, improving land in this state carried an implied directive to plant trees and since John's wife, Mary Ann Dobson Hendrickson, was a flower-lover and was particularly fond of the fragrant, purple spiked flower head of the lilac bush, John hauled baskets of spindly, pencil-sized lilac shoots across the Missouri River from Iowa and on into Central Nebraska where he set them in dense rows around the homestead's farmyard.

Seedlings from the original lilac bushes have been transplanted throughout the Midwest at new home sites established by John and Mary's children, their children's children and *their* children's children for six generations. Each spring the shrubs bloom in the yards of Hendricksons everywhere, filling the air with a flourish of happy reminders and drawing the family back, if only in their minds and hearts, to their Nebraska roots.

For several years after I was in the family, John and Mary's descendants gathered at the homestead for what came to be called "Lilac Day." It was a Sunday late in April or early May.

The exact Sunday varied from year to year, depending upon when the lilacs bloomed.

Their first years on the homestead, the family lived in a dugout, a cave recessed in a hillside with the exposed side crudely framed in with wooden timbers. Later, they built a small, two-room house and still later, a large, two-story house was erected. The original two-room house was left standing and it became reunion headquarters for the family, which by the late 1920s numbered more than fifty. The couple's three sons, David, Abner and William, and their daughter Katie had married and had grown children of their own and there were half a dozen great-grandchildren by then.

The reunion came early enough in the season so flies and insects were not a problem for the potluck picnickers. Food was spread out inside the little house on an old oak table; that table and a few chairs were all that remained of furnishings from the old house. The chairs were reserved for older women in the party. Men and children sat outside on the grass or they sat around the outer edge of the open front porch, feet dangling over the side of the porch.

There came a time when the homestead was no longer farmed by a Hendrickson and that caused a lapse in the annual reunions. They were resumed in about 1940 and since then, the families have met in parks or halls at Gibbon, Grand Island, Mason City and Cairo, Nebraska. Such reunions, valued for giving meaning to life and giving it continuity, were once an established part of American life. Over the last forty years, with more and more Americans moving to where the jobs are, families have had a hard time keeping the tradition going. They try to bridge the gap to their past and their present by staging a reunion, if not every year, maybe every other year or every five years. It's one way to say "We matter to one another...we miss you...let's keep in touch."

Lilac Day was all of that and more for the picnicking Hendricksons. It was also an exhibition of good foods. The hungry crowd circled the old table, loaded their plates from platters of roast beef, baked ham, deviled eggs, pans of scalloped potatoes, baked beans, bowls of potato salad and home-canned vegetables and later came back to the table to choose a dessert from an assortment of cakes, pies, sometimes a freezer or two of homemade ice cream and Aunt Katie's Strawberry Shortcake.

## AUNT KATIE'S STRAWBERRY SHORTCAKE

Aunt Katie lived in the fast-growing, railroad city of Grand Island where grocery stores offered the first fresh strawberries of the season. It became a Lilac Day tradition for her to bring large bowls of hulled, washed and sugared berries and trays of her home-baked, sweet-biscuit-type shortcakes. At serving time, berries were ladled over the shortcakes and pitchers of light cream were passed to top the classic American dessert—

2 cups flour
2 tablespoons sugar
3 teaspoons baking powder
1/2 teaspoon salt
6 tablespoons butter or margarine
3/4 cup milk

Preheat oven to 400 degrees F. Have an *ungreased* cookie sheet at hand. Into a medium bowl, sift flour, sugar, baking powder and salt together. Add butter. Cut in with two forks or a pastry blender until mixture resembles coarse crumbs. Add milk. Stir with a fork just to moisten and until dough begins to come together in a loose ball. Turn dough out onto lightly floured board or pastry cloth. Knead dough very gently 4 or 5 times. Use fingers to gently pat dough out until it is 1-inch thick. Cut shortcakes with a 2-1/2-inch round cutter and place 1/2-inch apart on cookie sheet. Bake 15 minutes or until shortcakes are lightly browned on top and test done. Makes 6 to 8 shortcakes.

## JAMS AND JELLIES

Fruit ripened at the peak of the summer canning season when there was no time to make jelly and jam. That didn't mean the fruit was lost or wasted or that jelly and jam weren't made that year. It just meant the final steps in the process were postponed a few months. Fresh ripe fruit was sorted, washed, cooked in water to cover until the skins burst. Then the hot fruit pulp and juice went into hot, sterilized half-gallon jars and was canned. The jars were opened later at a more convenient time and the fruit juice and pulp were finished as jelly or jam.

The hunt for jelly and jam makings wasn't limited to our own garden and yard or to those of our neighbors. I followed creek beds and fence rows, searching for wild plums, grapes and chokecherries that were free for the gathering.

Turning fruit into jelly or jam requires two slightly different methods but once hot, freshly cooked and sugared juice has "jelled" and hot, freshly cooked and sugar fruit pulp has "jammed," and the finished products are ready for the final processing step of being sealed into jars, they are treated just the same.

Matched jelly jars are nice, they make an attractive picture on the pantry shelf but when it comes to sealing and protecting the jelly and jam, they aren't necessary. Small odds-and-ends glass jars, peanut butter jars, mismatched drinking glasses— they all work just fine. And it doesn't matter if the jars or glasses have lids or not, because after the hot jelly or jam has been poured into hot sterilized glass containers, the containers are immediately sealed with paraffin and that's all the protection jelly and jam need.

Paraffin is purchased at the grocery store in large blocks and must be melted over simmering water so it can be poured. I shave the paraffin into a clean, one-quart can and then set the can in a saucepan in three inches of water. By pinching the top rim of the can with a pair of pliers, a spout can be formed making it easier to pour the hot paraffin in a slow, narrow stream.

Fill jars to within one-quarter inch of the top. Wipe jars with a damp cloth to remove particles of jelly or jam, paying particular attention to the rims where the slightest speck of fruit or a drop of jelly can interfere with getting a tight, secure seal. Pour a thin layer—about one-eighth of an inch thick—of melted paraffin over the jelly or jam. When that layer sets, pour on another layer of paraffin, filling the jar to the rim. Cleanliness and proper sealing—putting HOT jelly or jam into a HOT jar and pouring HOT paraffin over it—protect the sweet spreads from molding or fermenting during storage.

## FRESH STRAWBERRY JAM
Everybody's favorite—

3 pints fresh strawberries
1/3 cup sugar
3 tablespoons lemon juice
2-1/2 cups sugar

Wash and hull berries carefully so they remain whole. Place berries in a large bowl. Sprinkle with 1/3 cup sugar and lemon juice. Let stand overnight. The next morning add 2-1/2 cups sugar and transfer mixture to a large heavy saucepan. Bring to a gentle boil over medium heat. Continue to boil over low heat *7 minutes*—COUNT TIME FROM THE MOMENT THE MIXTURE STARTS BOILING. Pour hot jam into hot sterilized jars and seal immediately with melted paraffin. Makes 1-1/2 to 2 pints.

## WILD PLUM BUTTER

Pawing through plum thickets, suffering scratched and nicked hands, arms and legs to pick one of nature's wild jewels of summer will seem well worth the effort later when this wonderful stuff is spread on thick slices of homemade bread or hot biscuits—

3 quarts of wild plums
1/2 cup water
9 cups sugar

Wash and sort plums; select only the ripest, unblemished ones for stewing. In a large heavy saucepan, combine plums and water. Bring to a slow simmer over low heat. Simmer until plums burst. Rub plum pulp through a fine sieve. Three quarts of fruit should yield about 9 cups of thick plum puree. Add sugar. Return to saucepan and simmer over low heat until thick. Pour hot jam into hot sterilized jars and seal immediately with melted paraffin. Makes about 4 pints.

## WILD PLUM JELLY

To make jelly instead of butter or jam, use only strained plum juice and process only four cups of juice at a time. Measure carefully. Use three-fourths to one cup of sugar for every cup of juice. In a heavy medium saucepan combine juice and sugar and bring to a slow simmer over low heat until mixture thickens and reaches "jell stage." It takes experience before a jellymaker learns to judge how much sugar to add, how long to cook the jelly and how to recognize when the mixture has reached "jell stage." It takes constant sampling and testing. One test calls for dipping a table fork into the simmering jelly. If the jelly forms a film or thin sheet between the tines of the fork, it's cooked long enough. My mother had her own way of testing jelly—she dripped a few drops of the simmering mixture onto a clean, cool jar lid. If it set up as soon as it hit the lid, the jelly was done, ready to be poured into hot sterilized jars and sealed immediately with melted paraffin.

## CORN COB JELLY
A sweet surprise from the cob basket—

1 dozen 10-inch red corn cobs
8 to 9 cups water
1 box Sure-Jell
3 cups sugar

In a large heavy saucepan, combine cobs and water—yes, that sounds like a LOT of water, but the cobs will absorb most of it. Bring to a simmer over medium heat. Lower heat; simmer 30 minutes. Strain. There should be about 3 cups of juice. In a medium saucepan combine juice, Sure-Jell and sugar. Bring to a boil over medium heat. Boil *2 minutes*. Pour hot jelly into hot sterilized jars and seal immediately with melted paraffin. Makes 1-1/2 to 2 pints.

## CARRIE'S RED TOMATO PRESERVES
After we'd eaten our fill of sliced fresh tomatoes and I'd canned a stock for winter eating, then I made preserves—

5 pounds firm, ripe red tomatoes
5 pounds sugar

Wash and skin tomatoes. To skin tomatoes easily, place them in a large kettle or bowl and cover with boiling water 1 MINUTE. Plunge into cold water. Quarter skinned tomatoes; remove heavy cores. In a large heavy saucepan, combine tomatoes and sugar. Bring to a slow simmer over medium heat. Lower heat; simmer until preserves are very thick. Stir frequently throughout simmering to prevent scorching. Pour hot preserves into hot sterilized jars and seal immediately with melted paraffin. Makes 6 to 8 pints; amount depends on degree of thickness preferred and how long mixture is cooked.

## TILLIE'S YELLOW TOMATO PRESERVES

Of all the canning and preserving chores assigned to us, my sister and I liked to help Mother make Yellow Tomato Preserves the best because it was so easy—the little yellow, pear-shaped tomatoes did not have to be skinned or quartered—

4 pounds small yellow tomatoes
3-1/2 pounds sugar
1 tablespoon mace

Wash and prick each tomato several times with a sharp fork. Place in a large heavy saucepan. Add sugar. Tie mace in a small muslin bag so it can be removed at the end of cooking. Bring mixture to a slow simmer over low heat; simmer until mixture reaches desired thickness. Stir frequently throughout simmering to prevent scorching. Pour hot preserves into hot sterilized jars and seal immediately with melted paraffin. Makes 4 to 6 pints; amount depends on degree of thickness preferred and how long mixture is cooked.

Damson Plum Jelly was Carrie's most prized jelly. It was made with fruit from a small, thin-limbed, fifteen-foot tree in the side yard next to her vegetable garden. Damson jelly was a taste treasure dating back to Carrie's mother, Lydia, and her childhood in New York State where the little plum trees grew naturally. Grandmother Lydia's last years were spent with Carrie and her family and it was during that time that Carrie ordered a Damson seedling from a local nurseryman. What she got was a very unpromising looking, skinny, leafless twig whose bare roots were swathed in damp straw wrapped in burlap. Yet with heavy protective straw mulching every winter and a generous feeding of manure each spring, the little tree withstood the cold Nebraska winters and thrived. In its fourth spring, it bloomed—tiny, dainty white blossoms—and late that summer, blue-black, mat-finished, plums not much larger than grapes hung in grape-like clusters on its scrawny upright limbs.

The plums weren't good to eat; even the birds and insects left them alone, and, as far as Carrie was concerned, that was good news. At least, as she remarked, she didn't have to worry about her children eating the plums right off of the tree before she even had a chance to get them picked and made into clear, sparkling, garnet-colored jelly.

On cold but sunny winter days when snow clogged the roads, making it impossible to get around in cars, Walter and I did our evening chores early and hitched Dan and Queen, the team of grays, to our one-seat bobsled and took a five-mile sleigh ride to Carrie and Willie's in the last rays of the sun as it sparkled and glistened on the snowy hills. We bundled ourselves and our two children under cowhide robes pulled up close to our chins. Tippy, our black part-spaniel, piled in on top of the robes and stood watch, front paws on the dashboard. Wherever Dan and Queen went, Tippy was sure to go, barking all the way. He especially liked a sleigh ride. One time, he spied a jackrabbit and instinctively made a big dive out of the sleigh and ended up headfirst in a snowbank. Digging him out and wrestling him back into the sled delayed us; we were afraid we were going to be late for supper. We wanted to get there in time to "get our names in the pot," so to speak, before Carrie fixed supper, a supper of home-cured ham served with fresh fried potatoes, hot baking powder biscuits and Carrie's Damson Plum Jelly. As she herself put it, when she put out her Damson Plum Jelly, she felt she was putting out her very best.

## CARRIE'S DAMSON PLUM JELLY

This shimmering gem of a jelly served in a tall, crystal compote made an ordinary country supper something special—

5 to 6 pounds Damson plums
5-6 cups water
2 cups of sugar for every 2-1/2 cups of strained plum juice

In a large heavy saucepan, combine plums and water. Bring to a boil over medium heat; lower heat and simmer until plums are soft and pulpy, about 30 minutes. Strain through several thicknesses of dampened cheese-

cloth placed inside a strainer or colander. Measure juice into a heavy saucepan and return to medium heat. Bring to a gentle boil. Cook 2 minutes before gradually adding the appropriate amount of sugar. Stir until sugar dissolves and mixture returns to a gentle boil; cook until mixture reaches "jell
stage," about 15 minutes. Pour hot mixture into hot sterilized jars and seal
immediately with paraffin. Makes 3 pints.

## BEEF, PORK and POULTRY

Butchering day was a sight, and quite truthfully, as a child,
it was a day I dreaded for two reasons. One, because I found it
hard to reconcile the fact that a hog or a calf I regularly fed and
cared for, might have named, might even have petted and
talked to while I did chores that morning, was by that afternoon, "dressed out," wrapped in a clean white sheet and hanging out to cool in the alley way of the corncrib or in the garage.
Secondly, butchering day put a few of my least favorite foods
on the table—liver and onions and fried heart, to name two.

Butchering was man's work. My father did the slaughtering, split the carcass and cut it into serving portions. Except for
making Blood Sausage, Mother didn't get involved until it was
time to process or preserve the meat.

To make Blood Sausage, she had to be right there on the
spot the very moment the hog's throat was slashed in order to
catch the blood as it spurted from the hog. She sprinkled salt
over the bottom of the pan before she began collecting the
blood and added salt intermittently, beating the salt and blood
together constantly throughout the collecting time so the blood
wouldn't clot. The salted blood was set aside and later made
into sausage.

Intestines from the slaughtered animal provided casings for
the uncooked sausage. They were emptied, washed and scraped
inside and out and soaked in a lye water solution after which
they were washed again and again before being set aside and
held in salt water.

Link sausages were only made in the winter when storage wasn't a problem. Cooked sausages were coiled inside a deep crockery jar and the jar was set in a snowdrift next to the north side of the house. A wooden plank weighted down by a rock kept dogs or other snoopy animals from getting into the frozen sausages.

## BLOOD SAUSAGE

Contrary to what might be expected, this sausage is not red. Blood becomes a dark brown during cooking—

1 cup pork meat from neck, leg or shank bones
1 cup uncooked barley
2 tablespoons lard
1 onion, chopped fine
2 cups fresh pork blood
1/4 teaspoon pepper
1/4 teaspoon allspice
1/8 teaspoon ground ginger
1/8 teaspoon ground cloves
Clean, salted casings

In a medium saucepan, cook pork meat and bones in lightly salted water until meat falls away from bones. Drain; reserve liquid. Use the finest blade of a meat grinder to grind the cooked and cooled pork meat. In a small saucepan, cook barley in reserved liquid. In a small heavy skillet, melt lard and saute onion until light golden brown. In a large bowl, combine blood, ground pork meat, barley, onion, pepper, allspice, ginger and cloves; mix thoroughly. Use a sausage stuffer to pack mixture into prepared casings. Tie each end of the casing closed and ease sausage into a large kettle of deep, salted boiling water. Simmer 1 hour.

## LIVER SAUSAGE
Made by the same process as Blood Sausage—

1-1/2 to 2 pounds fresh pork liver
1 cup fresh pork meat
1 cup uncooked barley
2 tablespoons lard
1 onion, chopped fine
1/4 teaspoon pepper
1/4 teaspoon allspice
1/8 teaspoon ground ginger
1/8 teaspoon ground cloves
Clean, salted casings

In a small saucepan over low heat in lightly salted water to cover, gently simmer liver until tender. In a separate medium saucepan in lightly salted water to cover, simmer pork meat until tender. Reserve liquid. Use the finest blade in a meat grinder to grind enough cooked liver to make 2 cups and enough cooked pork to make 1 cup. In a small saucepan over medium heat, cook barley in reserved liquid. In a small heavy skillet, melt lard and saute onion until just golden brown. In a large bowl, combine liver, pork, barley, onion, pepper, allspice, ginger and cloves. Mix thoroughly. Use a sausage stuffer to pack mixture into prepared casings. Tie ends of casing closed and ease sausage into a large kettle of deep, salted boiling water. Simmer 1 hour.

## PORK SAUSAGE
The only way to have sausage seasoned just the way you like it is to make it yourself—

4 pounds coarsely ground fresh pork
1 pound coarsely ground fresh pork fat
5 teaspoons salt
2 teaspoons pepper
3 to 4 teaspoons ground sage
Clean, salted casings

Spread ground pork and fat on a cookie sheet. Sprinkle with salt, pepper and sage. Use hands to mix thoroughly, then put mixture through the meat grinder again. Use a sausage stuffer to pack mixture into prepared casing. Tie casing off in desired lengths and ease sausage into deep, boiling salt water. Simmer 10 minutes. Remove cooked sausage from hot water and plunge into cold water for a few minutes. Drain and cool completely. Sausage will keep 2 weeks in a cool place. At serving time, heat sausage in a skillet or in the oven.

## CARRIE'S PORK SAUSAGE

Cooked, ready to reheat sausage processed in round, metal, lidded one-pound coffee cans—

5 pounds medium ground pork, 4 parts lean to 1 part fat
5 teaspoons salt
1 tablespoon ground sage
2 teaspoons pepper

Preheat oven to 325 degrees F. Spread ground meat on a cookie sheet. In a small bowl, combine salt, sage and pepper. Sprinkle evenly over meat. Use hands to knead seasonings into meat; mix thoroughly. Pack bulk sausage into coffee cans to within an inch of the top of the can. Bake *uncovered* 1 hour or until meat pulls away from sides of can and top is lightly browned. Cool completely. Pour melted lard over cooked sausage to a depth of 1 inch; put lids on cans. Store up to six months in a dark, cool cellar. At serving time, remove lids and place uncovered can in a 350 degrees F. oven 20 to 30 minutes. *Do not overheat.* Heat until fat melts so it can be poured off and sausage slips easily out of the can yet is still cool and firm enough to slice easily. Cut into 1/2-inch slices and brown in a heavy skillet; no additional shortening is necessary. The same ingredients can also be formed into 2-inch balls rather than being packed in coffee cans. Brown balls in a heavy skillet, then pack into wide-mouthed quart canning jars with two-piece metal lids. Set lids and rings in place with rings screwed tight, then turn rings back half a turn and process an hour in a hot water bath with water over tops of jars or process in a pressure cooker according to directions.

## OLD-FASHIONED SCRAPPLE

Hash browned potatoes *must* accompany this cereal-sausage dish—

2 pounds seasoned pork sausage
4 cups *cooked* cornmeal, oatmeal, Farina or Cream of Wheat

In a heavy *cold* skillet, crumble sausage. Fry over medium heat until sausage is lightly browned, not hard and dry. Pour off drippings. In a large bowl, combine cooked cereal and fried sausage. Stir with a fork to blend thoroughly. Rinse a 9 x 5 x 3-inch loaf pan in cold water. Pack cereal-sausage mixture into pan and chill overnight. To serve, unmold loaf and cut into 1/2-inch slices. Dip slices lightly in flour or cornmeal and fry slowly in a skillet lightly greased with bacon drippings or shortening until scrapple is golden brown. Serve with warm maple syrup and hash browned potatoes. Serves 8.

Butchering was done mostly between November and March when the cooler weather made it easier to keep meat fresh longer. Chops, steaks and roasts were used fresh as long as possible before the meat was processed and preserved by frying it down and storing it in its own fat renderings, by canning, by putting it in a brine or by smoke-curing it. There was a lot of grinding involved in processing meats, especially in making sausage. There was no way my little, Universal Number 2, hand-powered food chopper with the one-cup hopper could handle the really big meat grinding jobs. Until I had a larger capacity grinder, one with a three-cup hopper, I borrowed one from Tillie or Carrie. The big grinder took more strength than I could muster. It took *man*power. Walter had to crank it, and even for him, it was hard cranking. To get the best leverage, he secured the grinder in place on the seat of a kitchen chair, braced himself with one foot on a rung of the chair, one hand on the back of the chair and with the other hand, he turned the grinder's handle. Later, much later, not long before we stopped processing our own meats, we had a large capacity, electric grinder.

After dressed pork cooled twenty-four hours, it could be processed. Beef, however, needed to hang in a cool place to "age" a week or two or more after it was butchered in order for it to develop its full flavor before it was eaten or processed.

## PORK IN LARD

Oven-roast pork loins, shoulders and hams.
Pack and stack them on top of each other in 2 and 3-gallon crock jars.
Cover with melted lard.

The lard provides an airtight seal that protects the meat, so it can be
stored three months or more in a deep cellar or cave preferably one that is
away from the house; an unheated cellar or basement under a house is generally not cool enough to store meats preserved in this manner. When a
roast is removed from the jar, it is very important to re-spread the lard carefully over the remaining meat in the jar to maintain a good seal. To serve,
reheat roast in a 325 to 350 degrees F. oven an hour or more, depending on
the size of the roast.

## BRINED PORK AND BEEF

Pork shoulders, hams and sides of bacon which are to be
smoke-cured must first be soaked at least a week in a brine, a
salt-water solution. Meat which is to be brined should be kept
cool but *must not be allowed to freeze*; freezing hinders curing
and results in uneven penetration of the brine.

Pack meat into crockery jars.
To make a brine for 25 pounds of pork or beef, dissolve 2-1/2 pounds
of salt and 1/2 ounce of saltpeter, available at a drugstore, in 4 quarts of
boiling water. When salt solution cools, pour over meat. Fit a stoneware or
pottery plate down inside the jar directly on top of the meat and place a
weight, a 1-quart fruit jar filled with water works fine, on the plate to hold
the meat submerged in the brine. Store brined meat in a cave away from the
house, not in a cellar or basement under the house. Meats will keep several
months in a brine. To serve brined pork, soak in cold water to remove some
of the saltiness then roast or braise the whole roast or cut it into slices and
pan fry. Brined beef should also be soaked to remove some of the saltiness.
It may then be prepared as a corned beef by simmering it in deep water with
1/2 cup of mixed pickling spices tied in a muslin bag. Allow 30 minutes per
pound.

## SMOKED PORK

Some farms had a small building used exclusively as a smokehouse. None of the farms where my family or Walter and I lived had one. We rigged up our own make-shift smokehouses. Sometimes our smokehouse was a large wooden, salt barrel and sometimes it was two, fifty-gallon steel barrels stacked together to make an air-tight seal. A hole drilled in the top of the top barrel served as an air vent allowing excessive smoke to escape. Two other holes were drilled directly opposite each other in the sides near the top of the barrel. A pipe was passed through the holes and hams and bacon slabs were suspended from the pipe by a couple of heavy wires. It was important that the pieces of meat did not touch each other during processing and that smoke circulated freely on all sides of each piece of meat. A fire pit was dug a short distance from the smoking barrel and a shallow trench covered with a length of sheet metal directed smoke from the pit into the barrel. The burning wood chips were supposed to smolder and burn without creating a blaze. Occasionally they were sprinkled with a handful of water, causing the fire to give off even more smoke. Home-smoking was and is a "guess and by gosh" operation. The color of the meat determines the length of time the meat is smoked—it may take several days—during which time every effort needs to be made to keep the fire embers smoking and glowing day and night.

Once meat was sufficiently smoked, the chunks were wrapped in clean cotton flour sacks and were buried in the oats bin. The oats kept the meats cool in the summer and yet protected them from freezing in the winter.

At serving time, smoked meats were used just as they are used today. They were baked, sliced and fried, or diced and added to egg dishes and casseroles. The skin of smoked pork was cut away and saved to be used to season soups, stews and vegetables.

## COLD-PACKED BEEF

Not many cooks keep jars of cold-packed beef on pantry or cellar shelves any more but they could. With home-cooked, home-canned beef on hand, beef that is not loaded with excessive salts and preservatives, a cook has the makings for any kind of a meal from sandwiches to a hearty dinner or supper. Canned beef has the texture and flavor of oven-baked stew—

In a heavy skillet over high heat and in melted lard, brown serving portions of steak on both sides. Pack steak pieces into hot sterilized jars. Deglaze skillet with water and pour the hot liquid over the meat; the liquid adds flavor and provides a stewing liquid during the water bath. Before jars are sealed, sprinkle 1 teaspoon of salt on top of meat. Set rings and lids in place. Screw lids on tight, then turn back half a turn. The half turn back allows air to escape during the water bath. Place filled jars in canner and cover with water to a depth of an inch over tops of jars. Bring to a boil over high heat. Lower heat and maintain a strong simmer for 45 minutes. Remove jars from hot water and seal lids.

At serving time, set a jar in deep warm water to loosen meat chunks in the jar so they are less apt to crumble and fall apart when they are removed to a skillet and heated in their own juices.

Beef may also be ground, seasoned with salt and pepper, shaped into meat balls or patties and then placed in shallow baking pans and browned in a hot oven, 375 to 400 degrees F., 15 to 20 minutes. Turn patties halfway through browning time; to turn meatballs, simply shake the pan. Pack browned meat in wide-mouthed canning jars. Deglaze baking pan and pour juice over meat in jars. Sprinkle with salt. Set lids. Screw lids on tight, then turn back half a turn. Place filled jars in canner and cover with water to a depth of an inch over tops of jars. Bring to a boil over high heat. Lower heat and maintain a strong simmer for 45 minutes. Remove jars from hot water and seal lids.

At serving time, set jar in deep warm water to loosen meatballs or patties so they slide out easily and unbroken. Add to prepared tomato sauce to make spaghetti and meat balls or to cooked noodles in beef broth to make beef and noodles.

Before I owned a regular canner, a large enameled pot with an inside rack to holds jars up and away from the bottom of the canner and which is also used to lift jars out of the canner, I used my copper wash boiler as a canner. Jars sat on a piece of wood cut to fit the bottom of the boiler so they didn't have direct contact with the metal boiler which had direct contact with the top of the red-hot cookstove. The boiler was filled with water to a depth of at least an inch over the tops of the jars. The water was brought to a full boil and then held at a strong simmer for an hour at which time jars were removed from the boiler and lids were sealed tight.

## LARD

To render lard from pork fat trimmings, cut fat into 1-1/2-inch cubes. In a large heavy saucepan, cook fat over very low heat several hours. It is crucial that the mixture never reaches the boiling point of water and that it is stirred frequently with a wooden spoon to prevent scorching or burning. Once lard is scorched, it is ruined and cannot be used in baking and cooking because it will give food an "off" flavor. During cooking, remove light brown cracklings as they form and float on the surface. Cracklings were either saved to be used in making soap or they were fed to the chickens. Remove from heat and let cool until it can be handled safely but before it sets. Stir frequently as it cools to prevent it from separating. Strain into a crockery jar through clean muslin cloth or several layers of cheesecloth. Cover jar with a clean dish towel and store in a cool place.

## ROAST BEEF

Use rib, loin or sirloin tip roasts with good fat covers—

Preheat oven to 425 degrees F. Wipe roast with a damp cloth. Place on a rack in an uncovered roaster. Put in hot oven for 15 to 20 minutes to sear. When meat is well seared, sprinkle with salt and pepper and return to oven. Lower oven temperature to 325 or 350 degrees F. Continue to roast covered or uncovered until meat is done to taste, "rare," "medium" or "well done"— all meat used to be cooked until it was "well done,"which required roasting it 25 to 30 minutes per pound. Covering the roaster eliminates basting, however spoon-basting a roast with its own pan juices every 20 minutes throughout the roasting period improves flavor and juiciness.

## BEEF POT ROAST

For less tender cuts of beef—chuck, shoulder, brisket, top and bottom round and rump roasts—

Preheat oven to 400 or 425 degrees F. Wipe meat with a damp cloth. In a small bowl, combine a teaspoon of salt, 1/4 teaspoon pepper and 3 or 4 tablespoon of flour. Rub into entire surface of roast. Place in roaster. Sear roast 15 to 20 minutes. Add 1 cup of water to bottom of roaster. Cover and return to oven. Lower oven temperature to 325 or 350 degrees F.; allow 40 to 45 minutes per pound. Bake until beef is tender and well done. After a pot roast has been rubbed with seasoned flour, it may be seared in a heavy skillet over high heat in a small amount of shortening before it is placed in the roaster. Deglaze skillet with 1 cup of water and pour over roast. Cover and place in preheated 325 to 350 degree F. oven; allow 40 to 45 minutes per pound baking time.

## BEEFSTEAK

One-inch thick rib, loin and sirloin steaks—

Wipe with a damp cloth. Trim off extra fat; reserve larger pieces. Heat heavy skillet over high heat until skillet is very hot. Rub hot skillet with reserved beef fat and add steak. Over high heat quickly brown steak on both sides. Lower heat and continue to cook until steak is done to taste, 10 to 15 minutes.

## SWISS STEAK

Bake in the oven or simmer on top of the stove—

Use a round steak cut one and a half inches thick and bake in the oven or simmer on top of the stove.

If steak is to go into the oven, preheat oven to 325 or 350 degrees F. Wipe steak with a damp cloth and cut into serving pieces. In a small bowl, combine 1/4 cup flour, 1 teaspoon salt and 1/4 teaspoon pepper. Rub into steak pieces. With the edge of a saucer pound flour mixture into steak. In a small amount of lard in a hot, heavy, oven-proof skillet or Dutch oven with a tight-fitting lid, quickly brown steak on both sides. Add 1 to 1-1/2 cups water. Cover. Simmer over low heat or bake 1-1/2 to 2 hours or until steaks are tender and well done.

## PORK ROAST
Ham, loin or shoulder cuts—

Preheat oven to 450 degrees F. Wipe meat with a damp cloth. Sprinkle with salt, dredge with flour and roast uncovered 10 minutes. Lower oven temperature to 325 or 350 degrees F. Continue to roast until meat juices run clear; allow 30 to 35 minutes per pound. *Pork must be thoroughly cooked until it is well done.*

## PORK CHOPS
Cut 1/2 to 3/4-inch thick—

Wipe chops with a damp cloth. Trim off extra fat; reserve. Heat heavy skillet over high heat until skillet is very hot. Rub hot skillet with reserved fat and quickly brown chops on both sides. Lower heat and continue to cook covered or uncovered until chops are tender and well done.

## SCRAMBLED EGGS WITH BRAINS
*Oma* and *Opa* Mickish always came for supper the day after butchering day. They knew there'd be a supper of hash browned potatoes, raw onion rings in vinegar, hot corn bread and butter and Scrambled Eggs with Brains. Brains are very fragile and cannot be frozen; they must be used fresh within two days—

1 fresh pork brain
Cold water
1 teaspoon salt
1 tablespoon vinegar
6 eggs, beaten well
1 teaspoon salt
Dash of pepper
1 teaspoon Worcestershire sauce
3 tablespoons butter or margarine
1 teaspoon minced onion

Wash brain, remove membranes and veins. Soak in a bowl of cold water to cover to which salt and vinegar have been added. This solution draws out blood and leaves the brains a creamy white color. In a medium saucepan, simmer brain in water to cover for 15 to 20 minutes. Remove brain from hot water and plunge into cold water. Cool completely, drain and cut into cubes. Combine beaten eggs, salt, pepper, Worcestershire sauce. Note: Worcestershire was not in the original recipe. In a medium skillet over medium heat, melt butter. Add eggs mixture. Cook until eggs are partially set. Stir in brain cubes and onion; cook until eggs are done. Serves 4.

Christmas Day with the Hendricksons was very much like Thanksgiving—there was a house full of people and a table full of food. There were a few changes in the menu. Roast Christmas Goose was added and so were Carrie's White Fruit Cake and Devil's Food Fruit Cake.

Turkey was not a regular feature of holiday meals on the farm. Except for sugar, spices and occasional fresh fruits, farm families still grew everything they ate and in the 1920s, few farmers raised turkeys. In the first place, turkeys weren't very compatible with other fowl commonly raised on the farm— chickens, ducks and geese—and in the second place, they were susceptible to many diseases, not to mention their reputation of being "unpredictable...difficult to raise...too stupid to come in out of the rain."

## ROAST CHRISTMAS GOOSE
Pre-baked in water to get rid of excess fat—

1 10-12 pound goose
Cold water
Salt and pepper
1 onion
1 carrot

Preheat oven to 350 degrees F. Put goose in a roaster. Add cold water to fill the roaster to within an inch of the rim. Cover and bake 2 hours. Drain goose thoroughly. Season generously with salt and pepper inside and out. Peel and slice onion; peel and split carrot; place in body cavity. Return goose to roaster. Cover. Lower oven temperature to 325 degrees F. Bake 2 to 2-1/2 hours or until juices run clear and leg and wing joints move freely. Serves 8.

## CREAMED HERRING AND POTATOES

When I saw "one gallon of herring in salt brine" written on Mother's grocery list, I knew it was almost spring and soon we'd be enjoying this old German supper. The herrings were about seven inches long and came with their heads, tails and fins on. They were packed in wooden kegs and were available in the markets only during Lent. Creamed herring *had* to be served at suppertime because it took most of the day to soak the excessive salt brine out of the fish. Potatoes accompanying the cold fish *had* to be, as *Oma* Mickish put it, boiled in their "jackets"—

8 whole herrings
1 large onion, peeled, sliced and separated into rings
2 cups sour cream
1 cup light cream, Half and Half
2/3 to 3/4 cup cider vinegar
Pepper
8 medium potatoes, boiled in their skins

Early in the day, put herrings to soak in deep, cold water. Change the water 5 or 6 times during the day. Allow a total soaking time of 10 hours. At the last change of water, about 2 hours before serving time, remove fins, heads and tails and cut each fish in half crosswise. In a large serving bowl, layer fish halves and onion rings. In a medium bowl, combine sour cream, light cream and vinegar; blend thoroughly. Pour over fish and onion mixture. Sprinkle lightly with pepper. Let stand at room temperature until ready to serve. An hour before serving time, cook potatoes until tender; drain and serve immediately. At the table, pass potatoes first; each person may peel or not peel the potato before mashing it. Then pass herrings and onions in cream sauce. Serves 4.

## JELLIED PORK LOAF

"B. R.," *Before Refrigerators*, this old Mickish recipe could be made only during the cool months. "A. R.," *After Refrigerators*, it became the main course for a cool supper on a warm summer evening—

Fresh pork hocks, neck or leg bones
Water
1 bay leaf
Vinegar
Salt and pepper

In large saucepan, combine pork bones and water to cover. Bring to a boil over medium heat. Reduce heat so liquid barely simmers; simmer until meat falls off the bones and is tender. Reserve cooking liquid. Remove bones and meat and cut meat into very fine pieces. Return meat to reserved liquid. Add bay leaf, vinegar, salt and pepper. Heat over low heat until mixture is hot *but not boiling*. Pour into a *glass baking dish*; *do not use a metal container*. Chill several hours or overnight. At serving time, cut into 1-inch slices. Serves 6.

## EASY SCALLOPED OYSTERS

A traditional side dish for holiday dinners—

2 8-ounce cans of whole oysters
1-1/2 cups coarse saltine cracker crumbs
1/4 teaspoon salt
1/4 teaspoon pepper
1/2 cup whipping cream
1/2 cup butter or margarine, melted

Preheat oven to 400 degrees F. Lightly butter one-quart casserole. Drain oysters. Reserve liquid. Sprinkle one-third of cracker crumbs over bottom of prepared casserole. Arrange half the oysters in a single layer over crumbs. Sprinkle with half the salt and pepper. Cover with another one-third of crumbs. Sprinkle with remaining salt and pepper. Combine whipping cream with reserved oyster liquid and pour over all. Top with remaining crumbs. Drizzle with melted butter. Bake uncovered 30 minutes or until sauce is bubbly and crumbs are browned. Casserole can be assembled, covered and refrigerated up to 2 hours before baking. Serves 6.

The first time I cooked for a threshing crew was in August 1923, the first summer I was married. Besides the owner-operator of the tractor-thresher rig and his assistant, there were ten to twelve other men in a crew—shock loaders, bundle pitchers, grain haulers and scoopers. Some of the men were neighbors who exchanged work with each other and some were extra hands hired just for threshing—either way, they all had to be fed two meals a day, dinner and supper, on each of the two days it took them to thresh our grain.

As soon as a crew finished on one farm, they moved immediately to the next one. The huge, black, box-shaped machine was pulled into our place the middle of the afternoon by a hissing and belching steam engine. After the thresher was stationed near the barn, the engine was unhooked and repositioned facing the thresher to be belted up to power the thresher and set its internal gears and shaker beds into motion. Soon team after team of horses pulled hayrack loads of bundles along both sides of the thresher and men began pitching bundles into the thresher's hopper. The bundles were carried down inside the thresher where its shake, rattle and roll vibrations separated grain from straw. Straw spewed out the far end of the thresher from a long, telescoping tube and grain streamed out of a side spout into a waiting wagon.

When I was a youngster, the day threshers came to our place was one of the high points of summer. As a bride about to feed for threshers for the first time, I felt excited but it was a different kind of excitement than I had known as a child. I'm not sure what I felt, maybe it was apprehension, but whatever it was, one thing for sure—I was about to be tested as a cook.

Because I had a good-sized flock of young chickens and because chicken could be fried and ready to serve in an hour, I planned supper that first day around fried chicken, six or seven of them. The rest of the meal included plenty of potatoes and gravy, corn on the cob, green beans, cabbage slaw, home-baked bread and freshly churned butter with cake and fresh, sliced peaches for dessert, along with pitchers of lemonade and a twenty-cup pot of coffee. I borrowed the big coffee pot and two extra skillets from my mother-in-law. She also contributed several jars of canned beef to be served with noodles for the noon meal on the second day of threshing. She offered to come and help in the kitchen but I already had offers of help from my fifteen-year old sister, Opal, and from my sixteen-year old sister-in-law, Elsie. Now, that I think back to that day, I realize I had a kitchen crew made up of *three teen-agers*! I'd just had my nineteenth birthday a few days earlier.

Our working day started at dawn. While my helpers baked cakes, I started a batch of bread dough. When their cakes came out of the oven, my bread went in. We gathered corn, beans and cabbage from the garden, and they churned butter while I caught and dressed the chickens.

Chickens, from the baby chicks to the laying flock, were my responsibility. I fed and watered them, gathered the eggs and, when it came time to catch and kill and "dress" a fat hen to roast or stew or a young fryer for the skillet, I did that, too. Killing and dressing chickens had been one of my jobs before I was married while I still lived at home; I'd been doing it for several years. As the oldest child in the family, I was "privileged" to be the first to get to do or *have* to do many things— killing and dressing chickens was another one of those "oldest-child privileges."

There's more than one way to kill a chicken. My method was the same as my mother's: hold the fowl tightly by the legs; lay the head on the chopping block; and, with one clean swipe of a sharp hatchet—actually, we used a sharp long-bladed corn knife—chop off the head. It was quick and the bird bled profusely, a very important and desirable factor in any slaughtering process. A few minutes later, after the bleeding subsided, the chicken was held by the legs and dipped in and out of a pail of hot *but not boiling* water. The quick hot dip made it easier to "pick" the chicken, pull off the feathers. Only chickens were scalded before they were "picked," never turkeys, ducks or geese.

The next step was "singeing"; that was done in the kitchen at the stove. A front lid of the cookstove was removed so the chicken could be held close to the open flames in the firebox or sometimes a newspaper ignited by the stove's fire was laid on the cooktop and the chicken was passed through the open flames of the burning paper—either way, singeing a chicken was a very unsafe practice, not one that I can in good conscience recommend, still it got the job done. It singed off any long, stray, hair-like feathers that might have been left after a chicken had been "picked." A singed chicken was thoroughly rinsed and allowed to rest ten to fifteen minutes in cold water before it was "drawn."

If a chicken was to be left whole for roasting, "drawing" consisted of first making two incisions: one under the neck to remove the crop and one under the rump to remove the innards and the gizzard, being extra careful not to break the gall and to extract the liver in one piece. The "drawn" chicken was rinsed many times through several changes of water. Fryers, young chickens about ten weeks old and weighing a pound-and-a-half to two pounds, those that were going to be cut going into individual pieces—drumsticks, thighs, breasts, wings, backs and ribs—were split open with one long, neck-to-rump incision.

I don't remember how long it took me to dress all those chickens that day—probably a couple of hours—but it was a job that had to be done that day, it couldn't be done ahead of time. Before refrigerators, it was a hard fast rule on the farm: *Chicken had to be eaten the same day it was killed.*

While I got the chicken skillet-ready, Opal and Elsie stretched the table to its full length, covered it with a white damask cloth and set it with just about every single plate and all the silverware I owned. They set up an outdoor washstand under a big elm tree. Besides a wash basin, they put out several pails of water to warm in the afternoon sun and piled stacks of clean towels nearby. They even hung a mirror from the branch of the tree in case any of the crew members wanted to comb their hair or see how well they'd washed their faces.

At sundown, when we saw the men water and feed their horses and head for the yard, the girls and I flew into action. In a rush, I "took up the chicken," removed it from the skillets to a cookie sheet, and set the cookie sheet at the back of the stove where the chicken would stay hot while I made gravy. My helpers sliced bread and filled serving bowls with vegetables from steaming pans on the stove. As they shuffled and shoved hot pans around on the cooktop, the tray of fried chicken was pushed farther and farther back on the stove, where suddenly, in one quick back flip, it fell off the end of the reservoir, landing upside down on the floor.

"Mercy!" I said.

I looked at the girls. After giggling and girl-talking their way through the long, busy day, there they stood, stunned and speechless, their faces caught mid-gasp, looking accusingly at each other, wondering which one had given the tray one shove too many. I looked at the crispy, golden brown chicken pieces scattered over the linoleum.

"Get the platters," I said, speaking as calmly as I could. "The men *have* to eat and they *have to have meat*."

Piece by piece, the chicken was picked up and looked over carefully before it went on a platter.

Fortunately the men entered the dining room through a door off the back porch without having to pass through the kitchen so they were unaware of the mishap.

After the threshers had eaten, the girls and I ate our suppers at the kitchen table and yes, we all ate chicken, maybe a little warily at first bite, but as both girls said over and over, "There wasn't one thing wrong with the chicken."

By eleven o'clock that evening, after they'd washed and dried the last of the dishes, Opal and Elsie were back to laughing. They joked about the "chicken catastrophe" and confessed "the big spill" to Walter.

"Don't worry about it," he told them, "Alice's kitchen floor is so clean, nobody should be afraid to eat off of it."

## "REAL" FRIED CHICKEN

There's only one right way to fry chicken and that's in a skillet, one with a tight-fitting lid. Coat chicken pieces with flour seasoned only with salt and pepper and fry in one-quarter inch of hot shortening. Forget soaking chicken pieces first in milk, buttermilk, lemon juice or vinegar and forget dipping chicken in beaten egg and then coating it with bread, cracker or cereal crumbs—many delicious chicken dishes are made with lots of other seasonings and coatings, but they should not be mistaken for "REAL" FRIED CHICKEN—

1 1-1/2 to 2-pound chicken, cut into serving pieces
1-1/2 cups flour
2 tablespoons salt
1/2 teaspoon pepper
Butter or margarine
Shortening

In a shallow bowl, combine flour, salt and pepper. In a large heavy skillet, combine equal portions of butter and shortening. When butter and shortening are melted, fat should be 1/4-inch deep. Heat until a drop of water sizzles when it is flipped into the hot fat. Dredge chicken pieces with seasoned flour and place in skillet; take care not to crowd the pieces. Brown until chicken is the color of honey oak on one side; then turn and brown the other side. Brown meaty pieces first. Allow 20 to 30 minutes to brown chicken on both sides. Cover. Cook on low 30 minutes or until chicken is tender. For crispy chicken, remove cover and increase heat last 10 minutes of cooking time; turn chicken as necessary to prevent over-browning. Serves 3 or 4.

# PICKLES

Home-canned pickles add color, spice and variety to any meal but they were especially welcome at winter tables when garden-fresh radishes, green onions, cucumbers and tomatoes weren't available.

To be a successful pickle maker, you must use fresh, the very freshest, cucumbers. Stick by the old rule of "twenty-four hours from the vine to the brine." And there's one other old pickle-making rule that must be respected: Do not use metal utensils, except, of course, for the cooking steps.

From Tillie, Carrie and my own pickle-making experience I've found it is best to work with small batches of pickles; small quantities of cucumbers cook faster and more evenly and they retain a clearer color. Take time to prepare brine accurately. Watch the clock when cooking pickles and time the cooking periods carefully. Overcooking softens pickles and so does a weak brine. Undercooking, short-cutting brining time, using too much salt or too much sugar—any one of these can cause pickles to shrivel and be tough instead of crisp and crunchy. Hollow pickles may be due to growing conditions or they can result from not using fresh cucumbers. Use a medium to coarse pure salt. Do not use table salt; it contains chemical additives intended to prevent lumping.

## SWEET PICKLED BEETS
Begin with whole, fresh beets—

Wash beets thoroughly and carefully. *To prevent "bleeding" during cooking, do not cut off root tails and leave two to three inches of the tops on.* Place in a large saucepan in water to cover and boil until almost tender. Plunge into cold water. Cool completely. Remove skins. Small beets, those less than an inch in diameter, may be left whole; quarter or slice larger beets into rounds 1/4-inch thick.

Syrup for 4 pints of cooked beets:
4 cups sugar
2 cups vinegar
2 teaspoons salt
1 tablespoon whole cloves
1 teaspoon whole peppercorns
2 sticks of whole cinnamon

In a saucepan, combine sugar, vinegar and salt. Tie cloves, peppercorns and cinnamon in a muslin bag and add to sugar-vinegar mixture. Add cooked beets and bring to a full boil over medium heat. Boil 5 minutes. Use a slotted spoon to pack hot beets into hot sterilized jars. Pour hot syrup over. Seal jars and process in hot water bath 30 minutes.

## DILL PICKLES
Never use over-sized, over-ripe cucumbers to make "dills." Use only fresh, firm, solid cucumbers—

Dill pickle-sized cucumbers, 4 inches long, 1-1/2-inch in diameter
2 quarts water
1/2 cup pickling salt
2 cups dark cider vinegar
Carrots, peeled and halved lengthwise
Small onions, peeled and halved
Fresh dill heads

Wash cucumbers. In a medium saucepan, combine water, salt and vinegar. Bring to a simmer over medium heat. Lower heat and keep mixture hot but not boiling throughout packing time. Begin by placing a dill head in the bottom of each *cool* sterilized two-quart jar. Stand cucumbers, *blossom ends down*, in vertical layers in the jars. Wedge carrot and onion halves into spaces between cucumbers. When a jar is full, top with another dill head. Fill jars with vinegar solution; make sure all cucumbers are completely covered. Seal jars tight. Some of the pickling solution may ooze out of the jar during storage but that is not a concern; it will not in any way threaten the quality of the pickles. Allow pickles to stand 6 to 8 weeks before serving.

## TILLIE'S SWEET GREEN TOMATO PICKLES

Mother used so much vinegar at pickling time that she bought it in one-gallon crock jars—

1 peck, 2 to 3 gallons, of firm, fresh green tomatoes
1 cup pickling salt
2 quarts water
1 quart cider vinegar
4 quarts cider vinegar
2 pounds brown sugar
3 tablespoons dry mustard
2 tablespoons ground ginger
2 tablespoons cinnamon
1/2 teaspoon cayenne pepper

Wash tomatoes and cut into slices an inch thick. Into a large saucepan, layer tomatoes slices; sprinkle each layer with salt. Combine water and 1 quart vinegar. Pour over salted tomatoes. Bring to a boil over medium heat. Cook 5 minutes. Drain tomatoes in a colander. In large saucepan, combine 4 quarts vinegar, brown sugar, mustard, ginger, cinnamon and cayenne pepper with drained tomato slices. Bring to a boil over medium heat. Boil gently 5 minutes. Stir gently throughout cooking time, making sure tomato slices do not overcook but remain intact and do not become mushy. Pack cooked tomatoes in syrup into hot sterilized jars which can be sealed with zinc-lined lids and rubber rings. Makes 6 to 8 pints.

# PIES

"Can she bake a cherry pie, Billy Boy, Billy Boy? Can she bake a cherry pie, charming Billy? She can bake a cherry pie, quick as a cat can wink its eye, but she's a young thing and cannot leave her mother." I remember singing that old ditty as a school kid. It was just a song, but in a way, it reminded me of how a Czech mother might have felt about teaching a daughter to bake a pie, first to please her Papa, and then to please a husband.

## TILLIE'S PIE DOUGH

"No pie is ever any better than its crust." That was Mother's opening remark when I got her lesson on making "firm, yet tender and flaky pie crust." Mother always added "a little sugar for flavor" to her pie dough. She believed it made a crust "brown better and more evenly." Much of the liquid in home-rendered lard evaporated during the processing, so pie dough made with lard necessarily required more water in proportion to flour than is found in pastry recipes made with commercial shortenings.

3 cups flour
1 cup lard
3 teaspoons salt
1 tablespoon sugar
1/2 cup cold water

Measure flour, lard, salt and sugar into a small, straight-sided bowl. Use a wide-tined cooking fork to cut lard into dry ingredients until mixture appears "mealy." Sprinkle water over mixture and stir with fork; use as few strokes as possible to mix just until mixture begins to "hold together." Turn dough out onto lightly floured board or pastry cloth and *gently* form into a soft ball. Divide ball in half. Lightly coat rolling pin with flour and roll dough out into rounds 1/8-inch thick. Makes a double-crust 9-inch pie or two single-crust 9-inch pies.

Fruit pies were filled with apples, apricots, cherries, peaches, strawberries, mulberries and rhubarb from our own yard or garden or from those of our neighbors. Whoever had an over-supply of fruit sent out the call "Come and pick..." and there were always plenty of pickers.

Fresh apple pie was a year-round favorite. Apples began ripening late in July and by September, the harvest was over. Some were eaten, some were canned as apple sauce and some were sorted to cull out those with bruised and broken skins. The solid, blemish-free apples were stowed in wooden barrels down in the cave where cooler temperatures kept them fresh and firm, good to the last apple.

If the apples in our home orchards had variety names, we didn't know them. With apples, names didn't matter to us then. An apple was an apple. When an apple was peeled to make sauce or a pie, it was tasted to see how much sugar should be added. When I make an apple pie, or any kind of fruit pie, for that matter, I still taste the fruit before I add sugar.

## FRESH APPLE PIE

Once I picked whatever variety of apples came from trees in our yard or our neighbors' yards. Now that I have a choice of apples, when I go to the store, I "pick" Jonathans, Granny Smiths or Rome Beauties when I want to bake an apple pie—

6 cups fresh apple slices
1 cup sugar
1 tablespoon cornstarch
1/8 teaspoon salt
1/2 teaspoon cinnamon
1/4 teaspoon nutmeg
2 tablespoons butter or margarine
Pie crust for double-crust 9-inch pie

Preheat oven to 425 degrees F. Line pie pan with lower crust. Cut vents in upper crust and set aside. Slice apples into a large bowl. If apples lack tartness, sprinkle with 1 tablespoon of fresh lemon juice. In a small bowl, combine sugar, cornstarch, salt, cinnamon and nutmeg. Sprinkle 2 tablespoons of sugar mixture evenly over bottom crust. Toss remaining sugar mixture with apples and put into crust-lined pan. Dot with butter. Top with vented upper crust. Seal and flute edges. Bake 45 to 50 minutes or until crust is golden brown and apples are tender. Serves 6.

## FRESH APRICOT PIE

Do not peel apricots. Dip whole fruits into boiling water for *half a minute* and peels will "slip" off easily—

12 to 14 fresh, whole apricots, peeled, halved and seeded, about three cups
3/4 cup sugar
3 tablespoons flour
1/4 teaspoon nutmeg
1 tablespoon fresh lemon juice.
1 tablespoon butter or margarine
Pie crust for double-crust 9-inch pie.

Preheat oven to 425 degrees F. Line pie pan with lower crust. Cut remaining dough into 1-inch strips for a lattice top crust and set aside. In a large bowl, combine apricot halves, sugar, flour and nutmeg and toss lightly. Add lemon juice and toss again. Turn fruit mixture into crust-lined pan. Dot with butter. Top with lattice top. Seal and flute edges. Bake 45 minutes or until crust is golden brown and fruit is tender. Serves 6.

The town of Gibbon did a bang-up job of celebrating the Fourth of July and, weather and field work permitting, we were on hand for their day-long "Glorious Fourth" activities. In the morning, we stood curbside on Center Street and watched the parade of high school bands, crepe paper decorated floats, riding horses, horse-drawn buggies and rigs and the latest in fancy new automobiles. At noon, we spread our blanket in Davis Park among hundreds of other families and ate fried chicken, potato salad, baked beans and cherry pie—at home or at the park, dessert on the Fourth of July was always fresh cherry pie—and enjoyed a band concert of, among other selections, John Philip Sousa's patriotic and rousing marches—"The Washington Post," "El Capitan," "The Stars and Stripes Forever"...

Races and games for children and adults led off the afternoon schedule of events. There were relay races, 100-yard dashes, egg races, three-legged races, sack races, wheelbarrow races, even a potato race—sprinters balanced a potato in a spoon carried in an outstretched hand as they ran a designated course. Races over and prizes awarded, the exhausted winners and losers collapsed in the grandstand and on the grass to watch two local teams take to the baseball diamond in what was always a hotly contested game.

After the game, we headed home to milk cows, gather eggs and do evening chores. Later, after dark, we were back at the park "ooohing" and "aaahing" at a flashy, glittery barrage of fireworks.

### FRESH CHERRY PIE

Pit cherries with preferably a *brand new*, clean, old-fashioned, wire hair pin. Slip the hair pin into the stem end of the cherry; slip it in under the pit and the pit will lift out quickly and easily. The cherry will hold its shape and none of its juice will be lost—

4 cups pitted fresh cherries
1-1/2 to 2 cups sugar
1/4 cup flour
1/8 teaspoon salt
1 tablespoon butter or margarine
Pie crust for double-crust 9-inch pie

Preheat oven to 450 degrees F. Line pie pan with lower crust. Cut vents in upper crust and set aside. Before adding sugar, taste a cherry to determine how much sugar to add. In a large bowl, combine cherries, sugar, flour and salt. Fill crust-lined pan. Dot with butter. Top with vented upper crust. Seal and flute edges. Bake 10 minutes. Reduce oven temperature to 350 degrees and continue baking another 30 minutes or until crust is golden brown and fruit is tender. Serves 6.

## FRESH PEACH PIE

A delicate pie that at one time could be enjoyed only a few weeks each summer but one that now can be baked any season of the year, thanks to the home freezer—

3/4 cup sugar
2-1/2 tablespoons cornstarch
1/2 teaspoon cinnamon
6 cups sliced fresh peaches
1 tablespoon fresh lemon juice
1 tablespoon butter or margarine
Pie crust for double-crust 9-inch pie

Preheat oven to 425 degrees F. Line pie pan with lower crust. Cut vents in upper crust and set aside. In a small bowl combine sugar, cornstarch and cinnamon. Slice peaches into a large bowl and toss with lemon juice. Add sugar mixture and toss again. Fill crust-lined pan. Dot with butter. Top with vented upper crust. Seal and flute edges. Bake 40 minutes or until crust is golden brown and fruit is tender. Serves 6.

## FRESH RHUBARB PIE

Almost every garden had a few clumps of the pinkish-red stalked plant with the huge umbrella-like leaves. The young stalks were early risers; they often peeked through the last snow of winter. By early May, the tender but tart, rosy stems were turning up in sauces, jams and pies—

3 cups rhubarb, cut into 3/4-inch chunks
1-1/4 cups sugar
1/2 teaspoon freshly grated orange peel
3 tablespoons flour
1/8 teaspoon salt
2 tablespoons butter or margarine
Pie crust for double-crust 9-inch pie

Preheat oven to 450 degrees F. Line pie pan with lower crust. Cut vents in upper crust and set aside. In a large bowl, combine rhubarb, sugar, orange peel, flour and salt. Fill crust-lined pan. Dot with butter. Top with vented upper crust. Seal and flute edges. Bake 10 minutes. Reduce temperature to 350 degrees. Bake 30 minutes or until crust is golden brown and fruit is tender. Serves 6.

I remember kneeling between rows and rows of ground-hugging plants in the strawberry bed, wearing a broad-brimmed straw hat and swatting at insects that hovered nearby. I watched my step, taking care not to squash any "runners," shoots trying to become new little strawberry plants, as my fingertips riffled through the leaves, searching out only the ripe berries and leaving behind those that needed one more day in the sun.

Berry picking was slow and tedious but as I picked, I dreamed, dreams of the sweet, sweet berries swimming in cream, over flaky, still-warm shortcakes or half-buried in whipped cream drifts or hiding inside a pie.

## FRESH STRAWBERRY PIE

An old-fashioned, double crust pie—actually any berry pie, raspberry, gooseberry, blackberry, mulberry or loganberry—can be made with this recipe. Taste the berries first and then decide how much sugar to use—

1 to 1-1/2 cups sugar
2-1/2 tablespoons cornstarch
1/8 teaspoon salt
4 cups fresh strawberries, washed, hulled and halved
1 tablespoon butter or margarine
Pie crust for double-crust 9-inch pie

Preheat oven to 425 degrees F. Line pie pan with lower crust. Cut vents in upper crust or cut into 1-inch strips for a lattice top and set aside. In a small bowl, combine sugar, cornstarch and salt. In a large bowl *gently* toss berries with sugar mixture. Fill crust-lined pan. Dot with butter. Top with vented upper crust or lattice strips. Seal and flute edges. Bake 40 minutes or until pie is golden brown and fruit is tender. Serves 6.

## RAISIN PIE

When fresh fruits weren't available, pies were made with dried fruits. A raisin pie was Walter's first choice—

2 cups dark, seedless raisins
1 cup brown sugar
1-1/3 cups water
1/8 teaspoon salt
Juice of one orange
1 tablespoon fresh lemon juice
3 tablespoons cornstarch
Pie crust for double-crust 9-inch pie

Preheat oven to 450 degrees F. Line pie pan with lower crust. Cut vents in upper crust and set aside. In a small saucepan, combine raisins, sugar, water, salt, orange and lemon juices and cornstarch. Cook over medium heat until thick. Cool. Pour into crust-lined pan. Top with vented upper crust. Seal and flute edges. Bake 10 minutes. Reduce temperature to 350 degrees. Bake 30 minutes or until crust is golden brown and pie tests done. Serves 6.

## CARRIE'S MINCEMEAT PIE FILLING

Sometime in the fall, after apples were harvested, kettles of mincemeat simmered on the stove. Its tantalizing aroma let everyone know that pie would be on the holiday dessert table and provoked those who were especially fond of it to ask, "Why do we have to wait until Thanksgiving or Christmas to have mincemeat pie?"—

6 cups ground beef or 3 pounds of meaty beef neck bones
12 cups chopped apples, Jonathans are my choice
6 cups dark, seedless raisins
1 cup currants
1 cup apple cider
1 tablespoon fresh lemon juice
1 tablespoon nutmeg
1 tablespoon cinnamon
1 tablespoon allspice
3-1/2 cups sugar

Cook the beef thoroughly *but do not brown*. Use the finest blade of a food chopper to grind meat and apples. In a large saucepan, combine beef, apples, raisins, currants, cider, lemon juice, nutmeg, cinnamon, allspice and sugar. Bring to a simmer over low heat; simmer 45 minutes. Seal in hot sterilized pint jars. Adjust jar lids and process in a pressure cooker at 10 pounds of pressure 10 minutes or in a hot water bath 45 minutes. Even though it takes 4 cups of canned mincemeat to make a 9-inch pie, pint jars process in less time and are a little easier to handle than quart jars.

## MINCEMEAT PIE

4 cups canned mincemeat
Pie crust for double-crust 9-inch pie

Preheat oven to 400 degrees F. Line pie pan with lower crust. Cut vents in upper crust and set aside. Fill crust-lined pan with mincemeat. Top with vented upper crust. Seal and flute edges. Bake 35 minutes or until crust is golden brown and tests done. Serves 6.

## LEMON MERINGUE PIE

Whenever fresh lemons showed up in grocery store produce bins, this pie was bound to show up on the dinner table. It was a welcome taste of a spring morning in the middle of winter—

1 cup sugar
1-1/4 cups water
1 tablespoon butter or margarine
1/4 cup cornstarch
3 tablespoons cold water
6 tablespoons fresh lemon juice
1 teaspoon freshly grated lemon peel
3 eggs, separated
2 tablespoons milk
6 tablespoons sugar
1 teaspoon fresh lemon juice
1 baked 9-inch pie crust

To bake an unfilled pie crust, preheat oven to 425 degrees F. Roll out half a recipe of pie crust dough to make one round which will extend 2 inches beyond the rim of the pie pan when it is inverted over the rolled dough. The extension allows for shrinkage during the baking of an "empty" crust. Place crust in pan and gently but firmly ease dough into place. Trim off excess dough and use thumb and forefinger to press dough to the rim of the pan. To keep the crust from heaving and browning unevenly, prick bottom and sides of crust generously with a fork. Bake 12 to 15 minutes or until crust is golden brown. Cool completely before filling.

In a small saucepan, combine sugar, 1-1/4 cups water and butter. Place over medium heat and heat just until sugar dissolves and butter melts. In a cup, mix cornstarch and 3 tablespoons water together and add to hot mixture. Cook slowly until mixture is clear and thick, about 8 minutes. Add lemon juice and peel; cook 2 minutes more. In a small bowl, beat egg yolks with 2 tablespoons milk. Slowly add to hot mixture; stir constantly. Bring mixture to a full boil. Remove from heat. Cool. Pour into baked crust. Preheat oven to 350 degrees F. In a medium bowl, beat egg whites with 6 tablespoons sugar and 1 teaspoon lemon juice until stiff peaks form. Spread meringue over filling making sure meringue overlaps crust edges completely. Bake 12 to 15 minutes until meringue peaks are golden brown. Cool thoroughly before serving. Serves 6.

## CREAM PIE

Cream pies are popular as stand-by desserts because they can be made from ingredients which can be kept on hand in the cupboard or pantry allowing a pie to be prepared, baked and ready to serve on short notice. Many cream pies can be made from this one basic recipe—banana, butterscotch, chocolate, coconut, pineapple. Place a sheet of waxed paper or plastic directly on the surface of the cooked cream pudding to prevent a scum from forming during the cooling period—

1/3 cup flour
2/3 cup sugar
1/4 teaspoon salt
2 cups milk, scalded
3 eggs, separated
2 tablespoons butter or margarine
1/2 teaspoon vanilla
1/2 teaspoon cream of tartar
Dash of salt
6 tablespoons sugar
One baked 9-inch pie crust

Preheat oven to 350 degrees F. In a small saucepan, combine flour, sugar and salt. Gradually stir in milk. Cook over medium heat; stir constantly until mixture boils and thickens; then cook 2 minutes longer. Remove from heat. In a small bowl, beat egg yolks. Stir a small amount of hot mixture into yolks then stir yolk mixture into cooked pudding and return to heat. Cook over medium heat 2 minutes; stir constantly. Remove from heat. Add butter and vanilla. Stir until butter melts and is thoroughly blended. Cool pudding to room temperature. Pour into cooled baked pie crust. In a medium bowl, beat egg whites with cream of tartar and dash of salt until frothy. Gradually beat in 6 tablespoons of sugar, 1 tablespoon at a time; beat until stiff peaks form. Spread meringue over filling, making sure meringue overlaps the crust edges completely. Bake 12 to 15 minutes or until meringue peaks are golden brown. Serves 6.

## CREAM PIE VARIATIONS

## BANANA CREAM PIE

Slice 2 large or 3 medium bananas into cooled filling.

## BUTTERSCOTCH CREAM PIE

Replace 2/3 cup of sugar with 1 cup brown sugar and increase butter or margarine to 3 tablespoons.

## CHOCOLATE CREAM PIE

Increase sugar to 1 cup. Add 2 one-ounce squares of unsweetened chocolate or 2 tablespoons of cocoa to scalded milk.

## COCONUT CREAM PIE

Add 1 cup moist shredded or flaked coconut to cooled filling. Sprinkle 1/2 cup shredded or flaked coconut over meringue just before meringue is browned.

## PINEAPPLE CREAM PIE

Add 1/2 cup thoroughly drained crushed pineapple to cooled filling.

## OLD-FASHIONED CUSTARD PIE

Or as some call it, "cussed pie." The first time I made a custard pie, I pricked the unbaked pie crust before I poured in the filling. When I took the pie out of the oven, the crust had risen to the top and formed a rather soggy, crumb-like "topping." Without a word of explanation or apology, I spooned the "pie" into small individual bowls and served it as pudding—

3 eggs
1/2 cup sugar
1/4 teaspoon salt
1/4 teaspoon nutmeg
1/2 teaspoon vanilla
2 cups milk, scalded
Pie crust for single-crust 9-inch pie

Preheat oven to 450 degrees F. Line pie pan with crust. *Do not prick the unbaked crust.* In a medium bowl, beat eggs and combine with sugar, salt, nutmeg and vanilla. Slowly add to scalded milk. Cool until a hand can be held comfortably on the bottom of the saucepan. Pour into crust-lined pan. Bake 10 minutes. Reduce oven temperature to 325 degrees. Bake 25 minutes or until pie tests done. Pie is done when a silver or stainless table knife inserted halfway between outer edge and center of custard comes out clean. Cool baked pie on a cooling rack 30 minutes then refrigerate until serving time. Serves 6.

## SIDE DISHES

What few salads I made in the 1920s and 1930s were lumped into a category called "side dishes," dishes intended to "fill in and fill out" meals, meals prepared almost exclusively with either fresh, home-grown or home-canned and preserved foods. Without an icebox or a refrigerator, fresh, home-grown summer vegetables could seldom be held from one day to the next; most had to be eaten the same day they came out of the garden. A few more fortunate cooks, like my mother-in-law, had an Iceless to help avoid summer's wilting and melting ways with food. Carrie's iceless was located on the side porch near the kitchen.

An Iceless was a round, metal cylinder, about fourteen inches in diameter and six feet high. Inside the cylinder behind a full-length door, six shelves held containers of food. The cylinder was lowered in an upright position into a hole in the ground. The hole extended several feet into the dirt floor of the cellar underneath the porch. Temperatures at the bottom of the hole got as low as the upper thirties, cool enough to keep butter firm, cream and milk sweet and fruits and vegetables fresh until they were eaten.

In a noisy clatter, the cylinder was raised and lowered by cranking a link chain over pulleys. And the person handling the crank better be strong. It took plenty of muscle-power to raise a loaded Iceless or to lower it. Keeping an Iceless steady and under control as it was lowered prevented it from crash landing at the bottom of the pit.

Lettuce always got the front-row in my garden. Its tiny seeds were the first ones I planted every spring. Early in May, as soon as the plot could be spaded and raked, the fine seeds, as fine as ground black pepper, went into the ground and, if it was a "good spring," with normal rainfall and lots of sunshine, three weeks later I'd be picking the three-to-four-inch crinkled, light green oval leaves. I didn't cut lettuce with a knife or pull it up in clumps; each leaf was carefully selected and hand-picked, leaving the small, immature leaves behind and undisturbed so they could go on growing and be ready for the next picking. Once lettuce was established, the plants could be picked every day from then on until the middle of July when heat and humidity wiped them out.

## LEAF LETTUCE SALAD

The most delicate and popular early summer garden treat, ours was served only at the noon meal—

4 cups freshly picked, sorted, rinsed and drained leaf lettuce
1/2 cup light cream
1/4 cup sugar
2 to 3 tablespoons cider vinegar
Dash of salt
Few shakes of pepper

Pick lettuce early in the day, before the sun gets a chance to wilt the fragile leaves. Sort carefully. Look over every leaf and flick out any insects the leaves may harbor. Rinse leaves over and over; plunge them up and down through several changes of fresh, cold water or rinse under cold, running water. When water runs clear, free of any dirt particles, immerse lettuce in a pan of shallow cold water. Set aside to crispen at room temperature or refrigerate at least 30 minutes. Drain and dry lettuce leaves in a clean towel or on paper towels or in a salad spinner and place in a large bowl. Measurements for dressing are approximate and may be varied to suit personal taste. In a small bowl combine cream, sugar, vinegar, salt and pepper. Pour over lettuce. Gently toss lettuce and dressing together. Serves 4.

## CUCUMBERS IN SOUR CREAM

Goes great with fried chicken, roast pork and beef—

2 or 3 6 to 7-inch "slicer" cucumbers
2 to 3 tablespoons salt
1 cup sour cream
1/2 cup cider vinegar
1/4 teaspoon pepper

Peel and slice cucumbers into very thin slices into a small but deep bowl. Sprinkle with salt. Use hands to mix salt through cucumber slices. Cover with a plate. Set aside 1 hour. Drain off accumulated salt water. Add sour cream, vinegar and pepper; blend well. Taste and adjust seasonings.

## *BABICKY'S* CREAMY COLESLAW

Grandmother Miller said, "Coleslaw's best when it's whipped to a froth." Vary sugar and vinegar amounts to make a sweeter or a more tart dressing—

1 head of cabbage, sliced and chopped, the finer the better
1 cup thick cream, whipping cream
1/2 cup sugar
1/4 cup cider vinegar
Dash of salt
Sprinkling of pepper

In a large bowl, combine cabbage, cream, sugar, vinegar, salt and pepper. Use a spoon to blend vigorously; stir until cream appears slightly frothy. Serves 6.

## "TASTE-AS-YOU-MAKE" POTATO SALAD

Potatoes vary greatly in how they absorb flavors depending on variety, size and maturity so dressing measurements must be taken as approximate. Like the recipe's title says, the cook will have to taste and then decide "How much...how many..." Do not use "bakers," mealy-textured potatoes which may be great to bake or mash but which become mushy in a salad. Use boiling potatoes, those with a somewhat waxy, smooth-textured interior, ones that will hold their shape through cooking, peeling, dicing and stirring—

10 medium-sized boiling potatoes
1/4 cup sugar
1 teaspoon salt
1/8 teaspoon pepper
4 green onions, include some of the tops
1/2 cup chopped celery
1 cup Carrie's Homemade Mayonnaize

In large saucepan, cook potatoes in their skins until just tender; *do not overcook.* Drain. As soon as potatoes are cool enough to handle, peel and dice into a large bowl. Layer potatoes into bowl; sprinkle lightly with sugar, salt and pepper. It's very important to season the potatoes while they are still warm, when they "take on" favors more readily and more uniformly. When potatoes are cool, add onions, celery and mayonnaise. With light, gentle folding strokes, coat potatoes thoroughly with dressing without mashing or breaking them up. Taste. Adjust seasonings. For a very moist salad, add 1 to 2 tablespoons of light cream, Half and Half. Serves 8.

## CARRIE'S HOMEMADE MAYONNAIZE
It's spelled with a "Z" on the original recipe card—

2 whole eggs or 4 egg yolks left over from baking, well beaten
1 cup sugar
1/2 cup cream, sweet or sour
1/2 cup flour
1 teaspoon prepared mustard
1 teaspoon salt
1/2 cup vinegar

In a medium saucepan, combine eggs, sugar, cream, flour, mustard, salt and vinegar. Cook over medium heat until mixture is bubbly and thick. Remove from heat. Cool completely before using. Keeps two weeks in refrigerator. Makes 2 cups.

## C-T-C (CLOSE TO CARRIE'S) MAYONNAIZE
When there's no time to cook mayonnaise, a commercial dressing can be spiked with seasonings to make a reasonable facsimile—

1 cup Miracle Whip Salad Dressing
1 teaspoon prepared mustard
2 to 3 tablespoons cider vinegar
2 tablespoons light cream, Half and Half

In a small bowl, combine salad dressing, mustard, vinegar and cream. Mix thoroughly.

## TILLIE'S HOT POTATO SALAD

Mother never used a recipe to make this wintertime supper stand-by which she served with hot cornbread and scrambled eggs—

6 large potatoes, allow one potato per person
2 tablespoons bacon drippings
2 tablespoons butter or margarine
1/2 cup chopped onion
1/2 teaspoon salt
1/8 teaspoon pepper
1/4 cup sugar
1/4 cup cider vinegar
1/2 cup light cream, Half and Half

In a large saucepan, boil potatoes in their skins just until tender. Cool. Peel and cut into slices 1/4-inch thick. In a large heavy skillet, melt drippings and butter. Add potatoes; *do not brown* but immediately add onion, salt, pepper, sugar, vinegar and cream. Cook over medium heat. Stir occasionally; take care not to break up potato slices. Taste and adjust seasonings as necessary. For a moist, juicy salad, add more cream. Serves 6.

## COTTAGE CHEESE

Along with home-canned pickles and relishes, a small bowl of homemade cottage cheese was quite often on the table for noon and evening meals. Farm-style cottage cheese, made the way we used to make it, did not taste like today's commercially prepared cottage cheese, partly because of how it was made and also because it was made from *unpasteurized* whole milk. Milk was allowed to sour until it reached the "clabber stage," the point at which the curds and whey will separate if the milk is placed over *very low* heat. Commercial cottage cheese made with pasteurized milk requires the addition of a lactic acid starter.

Making cottage cheese, or more accurately, "watching the cottage cheese," was one of my first kitchen assignments as a child. Early in the day, the already sour milk was poured into a shallow, three-quart pan and placed over low heat "way to back of the stove." Several times during the morning, I used a small ladle to carefully remove watery whey that accumulated, taking care not to stir or break up the thick, shiny white curds being formed. After four or five hours when no more whey was extracted and the curds were fully cooked, the cheese was removed to a bowl and allowed to cool before it was lightly seasoned with salt. To improve the flavor, the finished cheese was placed in a cool spot for several hours or overnight before it was served. For variation, at serving time a few tablespoons of minced winter yellow or white onions, fresh green onions, diced celery or sliced radishes were stirred into the cottage cheese.

## MACARONI AND CHEESE

This perennial favorite was served any time of the year but it was more likely to be served during winter months and it was *always* on the menu when I fed shellers. The original recipe called for "2 cups medium white sauce," but one time when I was in a big hurry, I skipped making the white sauce and added two cups of milk instead. After the casserole was baked, I found I liked the lighter, not-so-thick sauce that resulted from using only milk. Now, even when I have time to make white sauce, I make only one cup of white sauce and combine it with one cup of milk—

2-1/2 quarts water
3 teaspoons salt
1 8-ounce package of small elbow macaroni
1 cup medium white sauce, optional
1 or 1-3/4 cups milk, use 1-3/4 if white sauce is omitted
Salt
3 or 6 tablespoons butter or margarine, use 6 if white sauce is omitted
1 heaping cup of cubed Cheddar cheese
1/3 cup fine bread crumbs
1 tablespoon butter or margarine, melted

Preheat oven to 325 degrees F. Butter a two-quart casserole. In a large saucepan, combine water and salt. Bring to boil over high heat. Add macaroni and cook just until tender; about 8 minutes. Pour into a colander and run cold water over until macaroni cools slightly. Place half of macaroni in prepared casserole and sprinkle lightly with salt to taste. Dot with half of butter. Sprinkle with half of cheese cubes. Repeat macaroni, salt, butter and cheese layers. If white sauce is being used, at this point combine it with 1 cup milk and pour over all. If only milk is being used, add just enough to cover the macaroni; the macaroni should not float in milk. In a small bowl, combine bread crumbs and melted butter and sprinkle evenly over casserole. Bake *uncovered* 45 minutes or until crumbs are *very lightly browned* and a good deal of the liquid has been absorbed. *The macaroni should not be dry; it should be very moist and in a light cheesy sauce.* Serves 6.

## SOUPS

Soups were made from scratch. It took several hours to make a good pot of soup and soup alone didn't make a complete meal; there'd better be bread and dessert to go with it. Considering the total preparation time of a soup supper, it often seemed to me that it was easier to fix a regular meal. The soups I did make were hearty ones and I made them mostly in the wintertime when there was a fire in the cookstove all day long and a kettle of soup could simmer on the back of the stove for hours with little or no attention from me.

## VEGETABLE BEEF SOUP

Fresh green pepper wasn't in the original recipe. It was added after it became more available in the stores and at a reasonable price—

1 large beef soup bone
3 quarts cold water
4 tablespoons butter or margarine
1 green pepper, chopped
1 cup chopped onion
1-1/2 cups chopped celery
1 cup diced carrots
1 cup chopped cabbage
2 cups diced potatoes
2 cups canned tomatoes
3 teaspoons salt
1/4 teaspoon pepper

In a large saucepan or soup kettle, cover bone with cold water and bring to a quick boil over high heat. Remove foamy scum with a clean damp cloth wrapped around a fork. Reduce heat so stock barely simmers. Simmer 2 to 3 hours. Remove bone from broth. For a clear stock or soup, strain broth through a strainer or colander lined with cheesecloth. In large saucepan over medium heat, melt butter and lightly cook green pepper and onion, *do not brown*. Add broth, celery, carrots, cabbage, potatoes, tomatoes, salt and pepper. Bring soup to a simmer over low heat. Simmer until vegetables are tender but not mushy, about 45 minutes. Serves 8.

## CHICKEN STOCK for CHICKEN NOODLE or CHICKEN RICE SOUP

Stew the chicken, then decide which kind of soup to make—

1 4 to 6-pound chicken
8 cups cold water
1 carrot, diced
2 stalks celery, coarsely chopped, include some leaves
1 onion, sliced
3 whole peppercorns
2 teaspoons salt

In a large saucepan or soup kettle, place chicken, breast side up, in water. Add carrot, celery, onion, peppercorns and salt. Bring quickly to a full boil over high heat. Remove foamy scum with a clean damp cloth wrapped around a fork. Reduce heat so stock barely simmers; simmer 1-1/2 hours or until chicken is tender. Remove chicken pieces from broth and set aside. Strain broth.

## CHICKEN NOODLE SOUP

3 cups chicken broth
1 to 2 cups *uncooked* noodles
1 cup diced cooked chicken
Salt and pepper to taste

In a large saucepan, bring broth to boil over medium heat. Add noodles. Cook until noodles are tender, about 20 minutes. Lower heat. Stir in chicken. Simmer 10 minutes. Adjust seasoning. Serves 4.

Noodles didn't come from the grocery store in cellophane or plastic bags. When I wanted noodles for soup or to go with stewed chicken or beef, I had to make them. At first I tried making them like my mother and my grandmother made them—without a recipe and by using egg yolks left over from other baking or cooking. To two or three egg yolks, I added one or two tablespoons of water, a dash of salt and enough flour to make a very stiff dough. The dough was so stiff, it took a lot patience and a lot of hard but careful rolling to roll the dough out paper thin, or as Mother said, "so thin you can read a newspaper through it." When it was finally rolled out into one big sheet, it was draped over newspaper hung on the back of a kitchen chair and allowed to dry for an hour or more. When the dough was dry enough so it did not to stick to itself, it was folded over and over to make one long, three-inch wide strip. With a sharp knife, the strip was cut crosswise into narrow, one-quarter-inch strips. Cooks took great pride in who could cut the finest, narrowest noodles—sometimes Mother's uncooked noodles were so fine, they looked like heavy string. After taking a couple of cracks at making noodles, I knew if I ever hoped to turn out thin and tender noodles every time I made them, I had to have a recipe to go by. A few attempts and many scribbled notes later, this is the recipe I settled on and it's one I still use.

## ALICE'S HOMEMADE NOODLES
Recipe can be doubled—

1 egg, well beaten
2 tablespoons milk
1/2 teaspoon salt
1 to 1-1/4 cups of flour

In a small bowl, combine egg, milk and salt. Add flour, enough to make a stiff dough. Turn dough out onto lightly floured board or pastry cloth. Knead a couple of minutes. Divide dough in half. Roll each portion out into a very thin rectangle, as thin as the dough can be rolled without cracking or breaking. Allow rolled dough to dry at least 30 minutes. Lightly fold and roll dough over and over itself so it looks like a flattened jelly roll. Cut rolled strip into 1/4-inch slices. Separate slices. Let dry an hour or more before dropping into boiling beef or chicken stock. Boil gently 10 minutes or until noodles are tender. Serves 4.

## CHICKEN RICE SOUP

3 cups chicken broth
1/2 cup *uncooked* rice
1 carrot chopped
1 cup chopped celery
1 cup diced cooked chicken
Salt and pepper to taste

In a large saucepan, bring broth to boil over medium heat. Add rice, carrot, celery and onion. Cook until rice is fluffy and vegetables are tender, about 45 minutes. Lower heat. Stir in chicken. Simmer 10 minutes. Adjust seasonings. Serves 4.

## HAM HOCKS AND NAVY BEAN SOUP

Walter liked this soup poured over a thick slice of home-made bread—

1/2 pound dried navy beans
1 quart water
1 ham hock
1 medium onion, thinly sliced and diced
Salt and pepper to taste

Sort and wash beans. In a large saucepan, combine beans, water and ham hock. Bring quickly to a boil over high heat. Remove foamy scum with a clean damp cloth wrapped around a fork. Reduce heat so soup barely simmers. Simmer until beans are tender, 2 to 3 hours. Add onion during last 30 minutes of cooking time. Serves 6.

Christmas started for the Hendricksons with a Christmas Eve supper of fresh oyster stew. It was a "light supper," one that was easy to prepare, sparing the cook's time and energy for the family's Christmas feast at noon the next day.

After supper, we gathered around the Christmas tree—a bottom-heavy yet very fragrant cedar tree cut from a neighbor's grove—for our gift exchange. I don't remember whose name I drew my first Christmas in the family, but I *do* remember who drew my name—it was my new father-in-law! He gave me a big, sixteen-inch, round, black cast iron pancake griddle. It was big enough to bake six five-inch pancakes at a time. It came with a broad, rounded pancake turner with an extra long handle. I couldn't have been more pleased. We didn't have a griddle, but because Walter really liked pancakes, I had tried baking them one at a time in a skillet and that was a real nuisance. "Papa," as his children called him, had heard me talking about my pancake trial and errors and, though he only smiled and nodded when I thanked him for the gift, Carrie told me later the pancake griddle and flipper had been his own idea. He'd gone to Walker's hardware store in Gibbon and picked it out himself. He made the perfect choice for this brand new bride.

Walter and I carried on the tradition of an oyster supper on Christmas Eve with our family and now our children and our grandchildren make it a part of their Christmases, too.

Years ago, fresh oysters had to be ordered at a meat market. The order would be placed early in December for a morning pick-up on the twenty-fourth. If it should happen, as sometimes it did, that a shipment never came in, the stew was made with canned oysters.

Before the fresh oysters were cooked, a few select ones were held back and put into individual sauce dishes for Walter and his father and "anyone else man enough to eat a raw oyster." The men doused the oysters generously with cider vinegar and salt and pepper before they ate them.

There were puffy little, nickel-sized oyster crackers to float on the bowls of hot soup and also plenty of soda crackers or saltines to go with trays of assorted cheeses and relishes. When the grocer's shipment of fresh celery arrived in time for the holidays, he knew even without seeing "celery" written on the order that he should put a couple of stalks in the Hendricksons' box of groceries. Refreshed in icy-cold water, the crisp and crunchy celery was a bit of a splurge, one reserved for the holidays. It was a welcome addition to the relish tray of home-canned pickles and spiced beets.

## FRESH OYSTER STEW

Ingredients were doubled and tripled as the family grew—

1 quart fresh oysters in their own liquid
2 tablespoons butter or margarine
2 quarts milk
1/4 cup butter or margarine
Salt and pepper to taste
Dash of Worcestershire Sauce

DO NOT DRAIN OYSTERS. Use only the fingertips to handle the oysters carefully to check for stray pieces of oyster shell. Put oysters, their liquid and 2 tablespoons butter in a medium saucepan. Simmer over low heat until the edges of the oysters open up slightly and the edges appear to curl and ruffle. WATCH CAREFULLY. OYSTERS ARE QUICK TO SCORCH. In a large soup kettle, combine milk and 1/4 cup butter; season with salt, pepper and Worcestershire Sauce. Heat over low heat. To avoid scorching such a large quantity of milk, set soup kettle in a shallow pan of water at least 2 inches deep. When oysters are done and milk is hot, stir cooked oysters, liquid and all, into milk. Taste and adjust seasonings. Serve in warmed soup bowls. Serves 6.

## VEGETABLES

Preparing vegetables, like preparing meats, did not require recipes. Canned vegetables were reheated in their canning liquid to which butter or bacon drippings were added. Fresh vegetables were cooked in lightly salted water to cover until they were tender, then they were drained and seasoned with pats of butter or dabs of bacon drippings. Vegetable cookery was changed somewhat by the coming of the Wear-Ever Man.

Jobs were so scarce in the 1930 Depression, that any unemployed man who had a car and a dollar to put gas in that car could always take a crack at selling door to door. It was the poor selling to the poor. They came with brooms and brushes, carpet sweepers and hand tools, dishes and housewares. The best pitchman to ever call on us was a young man in his early twenties. He was selling Wear-Ever cookware. He stopped one summer day and set up an appointment to return the next day and prepare our noon meal. I was to provide the food and he would do all of the preparation, serving and clean-up, and oh yes, I could invite guests, too, as many as I wanted. If those guests either bought cookware or agreed to let the salesman come to their homes and cook a meal, too, then I got points credited towards the purchase of cookware.

Sounded like a good deal to me.

I invited a couple of neighbors and their families to come for dinner and got ready to do something I'd never done before—sit down and watch someone else, and a man at that, cook a meal in my kitchen.

The cook arrived the next morning before nine o'clock, lugging a huge, black foot locker filled with flannel-wrapped, bright and shiny, heavy-duty aluminum demonstration pots and pans. He glanced around my teeny weeny kitchen looking for a spot to set up his traveling cabinet. The only spot where it would fit and not take up any floor space and yet would be handy for him to get things out of was *under* the white enamel-topped table.

Fortunately, he'd grown up on a farm so cooking with corncobs was not a problem for him. In no time at all, he had braised a beef pot roast and had it simmering in a roaster on top of the stove. He peeled carrots and onions which were to be steam-cooked in separate pans in the roaster's top deck, scrubbed potatoes to be boiled in their skins and then put through a ricer, shredded cabbage to be boiled, and pared and sliced apples for dessert.

He was tall and slim and he was quick on his feet and fast with his hands. His motions were smooth and fluid. He whirled and glided from the stove to the table to the cupboard and swooped low, reaching under the table to snag pans out of the open foot locker. He cracked his head on his first few swoops but he shrugged off the pain and soon was able to dip and swoop without clobbering himself.

"He reminds me of a dancer," I whispered to Walter, who had come in from irrigating to watch the cooking show.

"Looks more like a gopher darting into his hole," Walter said.

It did seem to me, that while Walter wanted to be present, wanted to see what was going on, he was at the same time a bit uneasy, maybe even a little embarrassed to see a MAN cooking in my kitchen.

Part of the Wear-Ever sales pitch touted cooking fruits and vegetables in a small amount of water over low heat for the shortest length of time. It was, according to the young man's spiel and his printed hand-outs, very important to know exactly when, without lifting the lid to look, food reached the proper cooking point. That was to be determined, as he demonstrated, by grasping the handle of the lid and with a twist of the wrist, giving the lid a swift spin. If the lid kept on spinning as though it were suspended over the pan, that meant it was time to cut the heat down, or in the case of a cob-fired stove, time to move the pan to the back of the stove. The young man incorporated the lid twist-and-spin movement into his routine without missing a beat or a word. From the second he hit the back door, he'd been talking. He had the words all down pat. They rolled out of his mouth like a song. He sang about the merits of Wear Ever cookware, its good looks, durability, low price  and about how cooking with it would contribute to our family's good health. He was so entertaining, I thought he could have been a song-and-dance man in a stage show.

He did an encore while we and our guests ate and as we pondered which pots and pans to buy—*of course, we were buying*—who could resist such an enticing performance—he cleared the table and washed his pots and pans as well as my dishes. He left my kitchen looking just like he'd found it. Walter couldn't let that go unnoticed.

"Someday," he told the young man, "you'll make some woman a good wife."

Still, in general, when it came to cooking vegetables, there were very few dishes that called for even the simplest list of ingredients and instructions and for the most part, I knew those recipes by heart.

## BAKED BEANS
From scratch—

2 cups dried Navy beans
1 cup brown sugar
Salt and pepper to taste
4 strips bacon
2 tablespoons butter or margarine

To shorten cooking time, sort beans, place in a large saucepan and soak overnight in deep cold water. The next morning, do not drain but cook beans in the soaking liquid. Bring beans to a full boil over high heat; reduce heat so mixture barely simmers. Simmer until beans are tender, about 2 hours. Drain off all but about a cup of the boiling liquid. Preheat oven to 350 degrees F. Butter a deep round two-quart casserole. Pour beans into casserole. Stir in brown sugar, salt and pepper. Lay strips of bacon on top of beans. Dot with butter in between bacon strips. Bake uncovered 1-1/2 to 2 hours until bacon is browned but beans are still moist—do not bake until beans are dry. Serves 6.

Fresh corn on the cob was and is the first choice of all summer vegetables in Nebraska and the midwestern cornbelt, maybe the entire country. It also has a mighty short fresh season. In Nebraska corn doesn't "come on," isn't ready to eat, until late July or the first of August. By Labor Day, it's past its prime.

Rather than spend money for sweet corn seed, enough to plant a couple of short rows in the garden, we usually ate field corn. If it's picked at the right time, it can be just as milky and sweet as sweet corn, particularly the varieties which were available in the 1920s and 1930s.

Field corn or sweet corn, either way, select ears for eating by stripping back the outer husks and piercing a kernel with a thumbnail. If the kernel squirts a milky juice, the corn is ready to eat but it will still be young and tender. If there's no juice in the corn, leave it for the cows and hogs; it's too old to be people food. The size and color of the kernels are also indications of corn's maturity—ears with small, pale yellow kernels are sweeter and more tender than ears with large rounded, bright yellow kernels.

## CORN ON THE COB

Nothing beats fresh corn on the cob served steaming hot and lacquered with butter and spattered with salt and pepper—

Strip away husks and gently remove silks. Fill a large deep saucepan two-thirds full of cold water. Bring to a full boil over high heat. Add 1/2 teaspoon of sugar. Ease corn into boiling water, one ear at a time, so as not to stop the boiling action of the water. Cover. Boil 5 minutes. Begin timing *after* the last ear has been added and water has returned to a full rolling boil. Serve steaming hot.

## RICE SUPPER

On rainy days when Walter couldn't work in the fields, he sharpened spades and mower teeth and repaired machinery and harnesses. After a day of what he called "light work," he wanted a light supper.

"How about rice tonight?" he'd say and I knew that meant a three-course rice supper. Late in the afternoon, I put two cups of dry raw, unprocessed rice—not quick-cook or pre-cooked— in a large saucepan and added just enough water to cover the rice. I added a little salt, covered the pan and set it on the back of the cookstove where it barely simmered. It was checked of- ten and water was added if it was needed. By evening, the rice was just tender and at that point, I stirred in a few spoons of milk, just enough milk to make the rice fluffy and light.

The first bowl was served with dabs of butter; the second, with butter, sugar and a light sprinkling of cinnamon; and, the third and last bowl, which was dessert, with sugar and rich, heavy cream, so thick it almost looked like whipping cream.

## GREASY RICE

Despite its name, this dish is not greasy, it is not even juicy. I don't know how it got the name but I do know of all of our mother's old stand-by supper dishes, this is the one we kids requested most often—

3 to 4 cups chicken broth
2 cups uncooked rice

In a medium saucepan, bring broth to a boil. Add rice. When mixture returns to a boil, reduce heat so mixture barely simmers. Simmer until rice is tender, about 45 minutes. Serves 4.

By the middle of June, potatoes planted the last of March or first of April had new potatoes the size of large walnuts or small eggs. The small potatoes were washed and boiled twelve to fifteen minutes in their skins to hold in all of their delicate, sweet flavor. Cooked and drained and still in their thin skins, the new potatoes could be served whole with plenty of butter or, if time permitted, while the potatoes were still hot, their loose skins were removed and they were quickly browned on all sides in butter or, better yet, in skillet drippings in which chicken had been fried and then served with butter or chicken gravy. Or, if the new crop of peas were ready, the potatoes were combined in a cream sauce with the fresh peas.

## CREAMED FRESH PEAS WITH NEW POTATOES

A wonderful combination of the garden's top vegetables of June and a delicious way to stretch fresh peas when the early pickings are skimpy—

12 new potatoes
2 to 3 tablespoons butter or margarine
1 cup shelled fresh peas
2 tablespoons butter or margarine
2 tablespoons flour
1 cup milk
1/8 teaspoon salt
Dash of pepper

Wash potatoes and boil until tender, 15 to 20 minutes. Drain and remove loose skin. Toss hot peeled potatoes in 2 to 3 tablespoons butter until each potato is lightly coated. Place in serving bowl and keep hot. While potatoes cook, cook peas in lightly salted water and prepare white sauce. In a small saucepan over medium heat, melt 2 tablespoons butter. Stir in flour. Gradually add milk; stir constantly until sauce thickens. Add salt and pepper. Add peas and pour over potatoes. Serves 4.

## HOMINY

Not long after my mother-in-law taught me how to make hominy from scratch, it was on grocery store shelves in cans. So while I actually only made hominy a couple of times, I remember the old procedure clearly. First we selected choice, dry mature ears of white field corn—yellow corn could be used to make hominy but white corn was preferred—and then we hand-shelled the kernels from the cobs and poured the kernels from one container to another to get rid of the chafe. Then the corn was put to soak overnight in a brine. For every quart of corn being processed, the brine called for one teaspoon salt and two teaspoons Lewis lye dissolved in enough water to cover the corn. The next morning, the mixture was poured into a large heavy saucepan, placed over high heat and brought to a full boil. Then the pan was pushed to back of the stove where it simmered three or four hours until the kernels were tender and their hulls had loosened. The mixture was stirred occasionally and water added as needed throughout the cooking time. When the corn was tender, it was washed in several changes of cold water. As it was washed, kernels were rubbed gently between the fingers to remove any remaining hulls. The white, swollen corn kernels, called "hominy" at that stage, were returned to the saucepan, covered with cold water and brought to a full boil. After boiling five minutes, the hominy was drained. This process—covering the hominy with cold water, boiling it and then draining it—was repeated several times to make sure all traces of the lye were washed and boiled out.

To serve, heat hominy in melted butter, bacon or ham drippings or top with gravy.

## SAUERKRAUT

By the middle of August, before swollen cabbage heads burst in the garden, it was time to make sauerkraut—

Strip cabbage heads of thick, coarse outer leaves. Quarter each head and remove center cores. Position kraut cutter—a wooden tray device 9 inches wide and 27 inches long, with a pair of permanently attached knives anchored on a crosswise slant near the center of the tray—over a 10-gallon stone jar. In long, smooth strokes, slide cabbage chunks back and forth over the knives. Adjust space between the cutter's knives to shred the cabbage as fine or as coarse as desired—for my taste, finer is better.

Pack and layer cabbage into jar. After every three or four-inch layer, sprinkle generously with salt. Use hands to work salt thoroughly into the sliced cabbage. Allow 10 to 12 cups of salt for every 100 pounds of cabbage. With a small wooden mallet, tamp the freshly salted cabbage until juice is drawn out of the cabbage. When salted and packed cabbage comes to within 3 inches of the top of the jar, place a clean wooden board or a crockery plate directly on top of the cabbage; weight it down with a canning jar filled with water to put pressure on the curing cabbage. Cover jar with a clean dish towel and set in a moderately warm spot—at our house, the sauerkraut jar sat behind the pantry door—to ferment and "cure" without being disturbed for two or three weeks. To can sauerkraut, fill sterilized quart canning jars; *be sure to leave 1/2-inch head space.* Adjust lids and place in water-bath canner. Fill canner with cold water to the shoulders of the jars. Bring to a boil slowly and process 30 minutes. To serve, heat sauerkraut over low heat until it barely simmers—great with pork spareribs and Tillie's Featherlight Dumplings.

# Lou's Place

## LOU'S PLACE

Lou's Place, our home on the 120-acre Louis Macek farm from March 1923 to March 1926, was a big, two-story house set back a quarter of a mile from the road at the end of a long driveway halfway down a long, easterly slope among apple, peach and plum trees.

In addition to the big square, sixteen-by-sixteen-foot kitchen, the largest kitchen I had in all my years of cooking, the first floor of the house included a large dining room, bedroom, pantry *and* a bathroom, but that's all that it was—a room for taking baths; there was no sink or stool. Its only fixture was a narrow, five-foot, porcelain tub with an outside drain. Water for bathing still had to be heated in the cookstove's reservoir and carried to the tub in pails. Upstairs, there were two large bedrooms.

The move to the "new farm with less hilly, more rolling farm ground" located two miles east and a mile south of the Shack, didn't take long. Walter, his brothers and brother-in-law made the move in half a day with a horse-drawn caravan of three grain wagons of household goods and two flatbed hayracks carrying small tools and equipment and trailing larger machines. Neighbors were on hand at both ends of the move, at the Shack and at

Lou's to help load and unload.

Well ahead of moving day, we picked out new furniture for the dining room—a table, eight chairs and a buffet, part of my parents' wedding gift to us. It was delivered the next day after we moved along with a golden oak Sellers kitchen cabinet we'd ordered from the Sears and Roebuck's catalog and a four-foot long, white enamel-topped kitchen table. The table cost twelve dollars and, considering all the things it did, it was a bargain. It was where we ate family meals, where dishes were washed, baked goods cooled, canning and preserving operations took place and, because penciled notes could be easily erased from its surface with a damp cloth, it was the score pad for the card games played on it. It also became our family's communication center.

At first my messages were for my husband—"gone to your folks, back in an hour," "picking cherries with Ruth." In later years, the messages were for our children. If I was in the field helping Walter when they got home from school, they checked the table for after-school instructions, "change clothes," "do your chores." "Chores" covered everything from carrying in baskets of cobs, to gathering eggs, to feeding and watering chickens and pigs, to putting grain in feed boxes and hay in the bunks of horse and cattle stalls in the barn. Sometimes the chores list was followed by the most welcome message of all, "get cleaned up, we're going to grandmother's for supper." Never mind to which grandmother's house we were going, going to either one's house for supper was a treat for all of us.

The new, six-foot Sellers cabinet was my food fixing center and also provided much-needed kitchen storage. Its purpose was strictly utilitarian but it was, I thought, a very beautiful piece of furniture. It had deep-grained, varnished doors, drawers and side panels, and except for a twenty-five-by-forty-two-inch white porcelain enameled sliding worktop that could extend to thirty-four-by-forty-two-inches, it looked like a cupboard. Behind the work surface there was a disappearing wooden curtain of three-quarter-inch vertical slats. The "curtain" slid open or closed without disturbing anything on the worktop or in the cupboard. Behind the "curtain" there were glass storage containers for coffee, tea, spices and a swing-out sugar jar. Two upper cupboard shelves held baking powder and soda, cornstarch, dried fruits and other staples and a large lower compartment held pots and pans; there was even a door rack for lids, a long drawer for spoons, spatulas and knives and two other smaller drawers for potholders and towels. Before ordering the cabinet, I studied the catalog pages, reading all the fine print, looking for two features—one was a metal-lined bread and cake drawer with a perforated sliding lid and the other was a fifty-pound flour bin with a built-in sifter-dispenser. That wonderfully efficient cabinet cost only one hundred dollars and it had both features plus everything else I could hope for in a kitchen cabinet. Once I'd found it, I was willing to put off buying a new stove a little longer.

A new cookstove was at the top of Walter's list. He'd been promising me one practically since the day we got married and he was anxious to make good on his promise. Much as I wanted a new stove, I was the one who held back, who wanted "to wait and see." We had a machinery shopping list, too, and I knew we could spare only so many dollars for household spending right then and, besides the new cabinet and table, we'd already spent ten dollars for a secondhand leather couch with a built-in head rest and five dollars for a used treadle sewing machine. And now that we lived in a house with a big pantry, one with room enough for a cream separator, we planned on buying one of those, too. By using a machine to separate cream from milk instead of skimming it off, we would be able to market more cream and a higher-quality cream which would bring a higher price. In time, the separator would not only pay for itself, it would help us save up the money to buy other things on our lists. For the time being, the new cookstove had to wait.

It waited two-and-a-half years and would have been put off even longer if the firebox under the oven of the black monster had not burned through. I knew from poring over catalogs and adverments what I was looking for in a cookstove. I pictured "my stove" in my head but I hadn't yet found one in the stores to match my picture.

One day late in October 1925, my mother called to say she'd seen "my stove" in the front show window of the hardware store in Wood River.

I was still on the phone talking with Mother when Walter was out the door and headed down the road to borrow a two-wheel trailer from the neighbors. Less than an hour after we'd gotten the "stove call," the trailer was hitched to the back of our Model T and we were high-tailing it cross-country over the sixteen hilly miles that ended in flatlands near the town of Wood River. I hoped we weren't on a wild goose chase.

There was never a doubt in Walter's mind. That was the day he was finally going to buy that "pretty new cookstove" he'd been promising me and that I'd been talking about for nearly three years. While he parked the car and trailer, I stood in front of the hardware store gazing at the stove in the window. Mother was right. It was "my stove."

It was a Regal and was it classy! It was more handsome than any stove or picture of a stove I'd seen. Except for the black, permanently polished, forty-two-by-twenty-six-inch, six-lid, iron cooktop, the body of the stove as well as the warming ovens and the backsplash were all a lovely, light buff baked enamel trimmed with thin, pale blue lines. It had nickel-plated knobs and handles. There was also a guard rail, a rod across the front of the stove that protected against any bodily contact with the cooktop. The stove stood on a low, nickel-plated base with gracefully curved legs. Once I was inside the store, I tried to conceal how much I wanted the stove. I let the merchant "sell" me on the stove's "high quality construction," "heavily reinforced lids," "thirteen-quart, copper-lined reservoir" "big nineteen-by-nineteen-inch oven," "in-door oven thermometer," and "easy to clean surfaces."

"What's the price?" I asked.

"One hundred twenty dollars," he said.

That was twenty dollars more than we'd planned on spending. Walter was ready to reach for his checkbook, but before a deal was struck, I spoke up about advertisements I'd read where, with every new stove purchase, the customer got a new set of cooking utensils.

"Look around," the salesman said, waving an arm in the direction of the cookware stock. "Pick out whatever you want." I went home with a new cookstove and a cupboard full of bright and shiny new pots and pans to use on it. That stove lived up to all the claims. It was easy to clean. Enameled and nickeled surfaces needed only a swipe with a damp cloth followed by a dry clean towel and the cooktop was almost self-cleaning. Small grease spatters burned off as fast as they occurred; larger spills were sprinkled with salt. After the stove cooled and the salt was brushed away, the spots were gone, too. I polished the cooktop with leftover waxed bread wrappers to keep it black and glossy as a mirror—I could see my face in it.

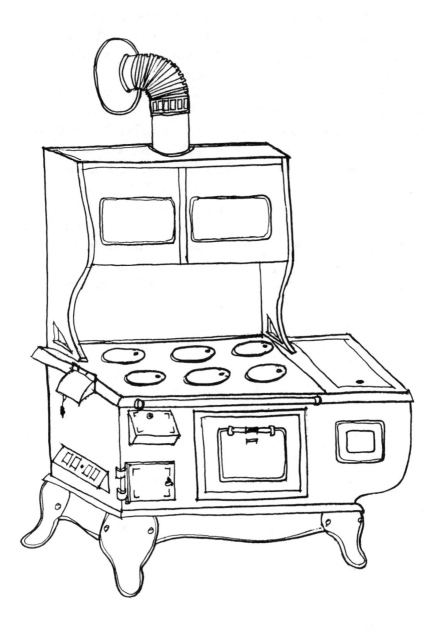

# Alice's Pretty New Cookstove

# 1935 - 1949

We didn't move once in this fourteen-year period. It began to look as though we might never move again. Still these were years marked by change, change and more change. There were changes in the nation and in the world. Some were more drastic than others, but in one way or another, they all affected our daily lives out in the fields, around the farmyard and in the house.

There were slow but noticeable changes for the better in our income. The first boost came in the middle 1930s in a year when we might least have expected it. After a late, wet spring and the forecast of an early fall frost, it appeared as though our corn crop was going to be destroyed before the ears had a chance to mature on the stalks. Walter found a way to save our crop. He bought a Letz mill and cut the green corn, ears and all, and sold it as chopped silage to cattle feeders who trucked it back to their farms and packed it into silos.

There were changes in the kinds of crops Walter raised. In 1936 he planted our first commercial crop of potatoes. It was only a five-acre plot, but with potatoes being such an unpredictable and a very perishable crop, even five acres of them could turn into a triumph or a disaster almost overnight. That year, the weather was right, the yield was above average and the July market held strong and high, making potatoes a very profitable crop, profitable enough to keep us growing them for another twenty-five years.

I didn't feed potato harvest crews. Their working day started before four o'clock in the morning and was over at noon, a "short day" compared to most days on the farm but for the crew, the truckers and the pickers, the day was long enough. It was all back-breaking work and it had to be done at a fast, steady clip. A mechanical digger passed up and down the rows, turning potatoes out of underground beds onto a flat ridge where every single potato was picked up and bagged by hand. One by one, filled bags were manually hoisted onto a slow-moving truck as it passed between the rows. If the last truckload wasn't out of the field before the heat of the day hit, you ended up with scorched and scalded spuds, cooked in their skins right there in the field. We never lost a load to the sun. Every load made it to the processing shed where potatoes were graded, hand and machine-sorted, washed, re-bagged into clean one hundred pound burlap bags and loaded into iced refrigerated railroad boxcars for next-day delivery to eastern, mainly Chicago, markets.

By the end of the harvest, all of us, family and crew alike, were relieved to see the last of the potatoes "on the rails." It called for a party. The entire crew gathered at the yard where they sat on the lawn in the shade and ate their way through the gallons of homemade ice cream hand-cranked in borrowed freezers and assorted home-baked cakes. The crew was young, most were still in their teens. They were eager, energetic and willing workers with appetites to match.

"Betcha I can eat a whole gallon..."

"Betcha can't..."

"Betcha I can eat half of that chocolate cake and..."

The party started with good-natured kidding and bantering

and ended with moaning and mumbling.

"I ate too much..."

"Now I need a nap..."

We celebrated the end of potato harvest regardless of whether that year's crop made money, lost money or broke even, but it was more fun and a whole lot easier to turn the cranks on all of those freezers of ice cream and stir up the cakes in a "good" year than it was in a "bad."

Most of our "new income" was plowed back into equipment. Each year there were new lines of tractors, tractor-pulled or mounted machinery and each year there were fewer and fewer horses working in the fields. Tractors were capable of running round after round, back and forth through the rows for hours and days on end as long there was fuel in their tanks. After they came equipped with front and back lights, farmers could run them day and night. Dan and Queen, the grays, and Daze and Blaze, the bays, couldn't keep that pace. Horses could work a twelve-hour day but they needed five-minute breaks every other round and an hour off for water and grain at noon.

Some of our new dollars went towards making changes in the house, the kitchen in particular. In 1935 I got water in the kitchen. The corner washstand was replaced by a small pitcher pump set over a built-in sink; it wasn't exactly "running water," but at least it was in the kitchen. The sink's drainpipe led directly outside.

The next spring, by squeezing the cream separator into the pantry, we were able to make room in the kitchen for a kerosene-fueled Servel Electrolux refrigerator. It was hard to believe a *flame* actually cooled the refrigerator's interior, froze ice cubes, ice cream and other desserts, but it did.

The salesman who called on us, urging us to buy the big, white, shiny enameled refrigerator showed us with paper and pencil how much money he claimed we could save by not allowing food to spoil and be thrown out and how much more money we could earn by being able to sell sweet cream instead of sour cream to the creamery.

"Take a look at these figures," he said, handing the paper to Walter, "you really can't afford *not* to buy the refrigerator."

"According to your figures," Walter told him, "we should have bought this refrigerator years ago. It's such a money-maker, we'd be rich by now."

Once we had the refrigerator, we rented a locker at the Kearney ice plant. A locker—so named because each wire box had its own padlock—measured about four feet by two feet by two feet. It was big enough to hold a side of beef and a side of pork cut into roasts, chops, steaks, ribs and still leave room for a few chickens. All of the packages were individually wrapped, labeled and dated.

When I made a trip to town for groceries, the ice plant was my last stop. It wasn't a problem going inside the sub-zero ice factory in the winter when I was wearing a heavy coat, a hat and gloves, but going in there in the summer—it felt wonderful for the *first* minute—then my teeth started chattering and I shivered and shook so hard I could scarcely turn the key in the padlock or read the labels on the packages to pick out the meats for the coming week. The packages of frozen meat were like ice chunks; they were still frozen solid when I got them home and into the Servel's freezing compartment.

Water in the kitchen!

A refrigerator!

How much more could my little kitchen hold?

While I pondered that, twenty-year old rumors were fast becoming reality. It was 1939 and another even bigger change was headed our way. Reddy Kilowatt was coming! Rural Electrification Administration poles and lines came across the corn-fields into our yard and into the house, barn, shop, chicken coop and even into the brooder house where each spring it kept hundreds of baby chicks cozy and warm under the metal "wings" of one very large, electric "mother hen," the brooder.

REA changed life on the farm for the better and it changed it forever.

For years, there'd been a lot of talk about farmers plugging into electricity, but until FDR took office, that's about all there was to it, just a lot of "talk." As Roosevelt saw it, electricity on the farm was a necessity, not a luxury. In 1935, he signed an executive order establishing the Rural Electrification Administration of 1936 which was authorized to loan money at two percent interest to public power districts or cooperatives, loans which were not only paid back, they were paid back ahead of schedule. A network of lines traced their way up and down and across the sections, lighting up rural America.

For farmers, electricity was more than an electric bulb in every room of every farm house, more than an electric refrigerator in every farm kitchen, more than an electric motor drawing water from wells so it could be heated by an electric element providing hot as well as cold running water to kitchens and indoor bathrooms. Creature comforts *did* improve; the farmer's standard of living did go up. Life *was* easier, more convenient with electricity, and it was also healthier and safer. With running water there was better sanitation; yard lights made farmyards safer at night; early and late chores were done faster and safer with light from bulbs instead of lanterns.

With a flip of a switch and a few pennies, electricity turned, lifted, pumped, ground, chopped, sharpened, chilled, froze, heated and soon made itself indispensable on the farm as a time and labor saver and as a money-maker, too.

With heftier bank accounts and fatter wallets in their hip pockets, farmers were ready to buy, try and use the latest in appliances and equipment, that is after we'd gotten over that first thrill of having "lights in the house."

Our house was "wired" for electricity for under a hundred dollars. That price included ceiling fixtures and wall switches in the kitchen, dining and living rooms; the rest of the rooms got a single bulb on a pull-chain outlet. The day we were "hooked up," and the "juice was turned on," Walter and I, right along with our children, went from room to room, turning lights on and off. That Christmas, there was a seven-bulb string of tiny electric lights on our tree and under it, an electric table lamp for the living room and a toaster for the kitchen.

That was only the beginning of all of the electric appliances we would own. Next came a small radio for the kitchen so we could catch local news and weather forecasts first thing every morning. At noon, table talk didn't start until after Walter had caught the market reports. He liked to keep up with how steers and heifers, barrows and gilts were doing on the Omaha and Kansas City markets and how corn and soybean futures were running in Chicago. The battery-operated console radio in the front room was soon replaced by a plug-in electric model and I tried coffee maker*S*—have to make that word a big plural. As a coffee lover, I was always eager to try a new way to perk, drip or brew coffee. By spring of 1940, the frost-by-fire Servel refrigerator gave way to a Philco, our first electric refrigerator.

In 1941, Cornhusker Hybrid Company offered Walter an opportunity to be one of the first farmers in south central Nebraska to grow seed corn. Walter presented the proposition to Miss Smith, our landlady, and a contract was signed assuring a market price for "commercial corn," and above market price for seed corn. "Commercial corn" included all of the corn that was harvested from "male rows," the rows of corn allowed to tassel and pollinate detasseled "female rows," and also the corn from "isolation rows," rows planted along the sides and ends of seed fields to prevent cross-pollination from corn in neighboring fields. "Seed fields" are easy to spot. In between every four rows of detasseled stalks there are two rows of tasseled stalks, creating a striped effect.

Nebraska seldom lacks for wind which is needed to spread dusty pollen from male tassels onto the fine silks of newly formed ears on female stalks to produce the hybrid kernels which will become the seed for another year's corn crop. But on those occasions when the winds didn't come at the time the pollen peaked, helicopters were brought in. They hovered above the fields while their rotating props stirred up the air and gave Mother Nature a helping hand swirling pollen from the male corn tassels to female corn silks.

Hybrid corn produces higher yields per acre and withstands diseases and pests. The ears are larger and more uniform and they mature earlier and more evenly. Because the ears grow on stronger roots and stalks which stand up better in the field, hybrid corn can be harvested with mechanical pickers with less waste.

The higher per acre returns a farmer gets for growing seed corn pays for the extra work involved at planting and harvesting. "Isolation plots" along with "male" and "female" rows all must be planted and harvested separately. The seed company furnished the seed and hired and paid detasseling crews and transported them from field to field. Farmers weren't responsible for feeding the crews, mostly teen-agers; they brought their own sack lunches.

In later years when Walter grew seed corn for DeKalb, detasselers lost their jobs, first to mechanical detasseling machines and then to the development of varieties of tassel-free female corn. With the newer varieties, two rows of male corn had the capacity to pollinate six instead of four female rows.

After trying the first seed plots, Walter was sold on the idea of growing seed corn. He persuaded Miss Smith to let him turn *all* of the farm's corn acres into seed fields. From then on, he never stopped growing seed corn. Besides the financial incentives, Walter liked being involved with the development of newer and better seed varieties that would make more money for the farmer. When we lived in the hills and were dry-land farmers, in a good year, corn yields were forty to forty-five bushels per acre; on irrigated land in the Valley, it was sixty to seventy. As more and more hybrid seed became available to farmers, the yields per acre jumped to nearly one hundred bushels in 1953; in another few years, they were over one hundred fifty bushels an acre; and, before long, it was common to hear of corn making two hundred bushels per acre.

Right when farmers' wives were in the market for more appliances, big ticket items, like stoves and refrigerators, those items fell into short supply along with farm equipment, trucks, cars, rubber tires and all of the many other commodities we had to get along without as the country geared up for the biggest and the most devastating change—World War II.

All of us, farmers and townsfolk alike, dealt with sons, brothers, fathers, cousins and friends joining the armed forces, labor shortages, price ceilings and allocations and rationing, the government's answer to wartime problems of sharing scarce or unavailable items—gasoline, shoes, rubber tires and food. Food was a powerful weapon. American farmers produced food in great quantities but there were severe cutbacks in what the civilian population could buy if our armed forces, our allies and later those in liberated countries were to be fed.

We had learned to conserve, improvise and to do without in the Depression and those lessons served us well during the war, too.

Anyone who didn't live through the frustrations and the shortages might find rationing hard to imagine today when fully-stocked, sometimes overstocked supermarkets, department stores, equipment and car dealers compete for our dollars. Rationing was hard to imagine and to understand at the time, too. The program varied from a straight-coupon system to various point systems which encouraged the purchase of products that were plentiful or not in popular demand and hopefully prevented hoarding and helped control the various factors affecting supply and demand.

At first there were separate rationing books for each member of the family. I still have a "WAR RATION BOOK NO. 3, OPA FORM NO. R-130," made out to Walter E. Hendrickson. It lists, for example, his address, serial number, age, sex, weight, height, occupation and signature along with a boxed message: "WARNING: This book is the property of the United States Government. It is unlawful to sell it to any other person, or to use it or permit anyone else to use it, except to obtain rationed goods in accordance with regulations of the Office of Price Administration. Any person who finds a lost War Ration Book must return it to the War Price and Rationing Board which issued it. Persons who violate rationing regulations are subject to $10,000 fine or imprisonment, or both."

Who knows how well the laws were enforced. No doubt there were plenty who took advantage of the system, a system that relied heavily on the honor of the individual citizen as a shopper or a retailer if it was to have any measure of success.

"WAR RATION BOOK NO. 4, OPA Form R-145," was issued with both Walter's name and my name on the cover and it came with new and separate identification serial numbers. Each time books were issued, the rules changed. Limits on meat and butter didn't affect a farm family as much as they affected town people, but rationing of coffee, cheese, sugar and dozens of other items affected everyone. Book 4 assigned specific point values to foods. Instructions accompanying "WAR RATION BOOK 4" read: "All RED and BLUE stamps in WAR RATION BOOK 4 are WORTH 10 POINTS EACH, RED and BLUE TOKENS are WORTH 1 POINT EACH. RED and BLUE TOKENS are used to make CHANGE for RED and BLUE stamps only when purchase is made. IMPORTANT! POINT VALUES OF BROWN and GREEN STAMPS are NOT changed."

I carried an extra coin purse in my handbag to hold the dime-size cardboard "tokens" I got in "change" when my purchase didn't use up the full value of the stamps used to make the purchase.

To get extra sugar for canning purposes, we were issued OPA FORM R-342 that carried this message: "READ BEFORE USING 5-POUND HOME CANNING SUGAR COU-

PONS. Before the attached coupons are used for the purchase of sugar *for home canning*, you or any member of your 'family unit' listed on the application must sign each home canning coupon. The person signing must enter the serial number of his War Ration Book Four thereon. For the purpose of identification, it will be necessary for the signer to take his War Ration Book Four with him when he purchases the sugar. These coupons are not transferable." On the reverse side: "WE MUST GET ALONG WITH LESS SUGAR THIS YEAR BECAUSE—1. Military needs are high. Each soldier actually consumes twice as much sugar as the average civilian now receives. 2. Ships which otherwise might be bringing sugar into the United States are hauling supplies to the battle fronts. 3. Manpower is scarce at sugar refineries and shipping ports. 4. Beet sugar production last year was 500,000 tons short, making the stock of sugar smaller for this year. 5. Last year many people over-applied for canning sugar. We used so much sugar that stocks at the beginning of this year were abnormally low. DO NOT APPLY FOR MORE SUGAR THAN YOU ACTUALLY NEED FOR HOME CANNING—HELP MAKE OUR WAR SHORT SUGAR SUPPLIES LAST ALL YEAR."

Throughout the war, we participated in war bond campaigns and drives to recycle fats, aluminum foil, pots and pans, scrap iron and paper—all vital materials in shipyards and munitions, airplane and arms factories that covered the country from coast to coast and border to border.

Mechanical corn pickers were available in limited numbers by 1940, the year before Pearl Harbor. Within weeks after the December 7, 1941, attack, loading docks at farm machinery factories were no longer bright with red, green, orange, yellow and gray trademark colors on tractors, plows, planters, combines, cultivators, etc. The docks had all gone "olive drab" just like the docks at car factories and many other plants as manufacturers tooled up to make weapons of war.

Walter filled out papers applying for the right to buy a two-row cornpicker, one that mounted on a tractor and plucked ears from the stalk and dropped shucked ears into a wagon pulled behind the tractor. He finally received a purchase allocation for one of the few new pickers in our area in 1943 by agreeing to help other farmers get their corn harvested.

As it happened, it was another wet fall. Fields were so muddy that Walter ran the picker at night when the wet ground was frozen so tractor and wagon wheels didn't sink in and get stuck in the mud.

Mechanical cornpickers put an end to cooking for cornpickers. Corn was still cribbed to be shelled later so I continued to cook for "shellers" for a few more years until the self-propelled grain combines that had eliminated cooking for "threshers" were outfitted with cornpicker heads. From then on, corn, too, was harvested, picked and shelled, right in the field in a one-step operation just like wheat, barley and soybeans were.

Getting electricity into the house made it possible for us, in the fall of 1943, to make another change, to take another big step toward improving life on the farm. This time it was a step down, down into a hand-dug basement.

It's no small task to dig a basement under an existing building, and putting one under a house our contractor estimated to be about eighty years old at the time and while that house was occupied was, at times, a bit precarious. It was not a job for backhoes or other excavating equipment; the hole had to be dug by men working with picks and spades. The digging started at a slanted opening under one corner of the kitchen. The opening was wide enough to permit a narrow, one-horse slip to slide down into the hole where it was loaded with dirt. One whistle from Walter and the horse eased the filled slip up out of the hole; Walter flipped it over, emptying out the dirt and then let the slip slide back down into the hole for a refill.

It was a long drawn out process. Walter and two diggers worked for several days before a mason could lay up the walls. As the excavated area got larger and larger and deeper and deeper, exposing the old beams under the house, carpenters had to crawl down in the hole with jacks and support posts and replace some beams. They took every precaution to keep the house level, steady and well-supported so everything remained stable—so floors didn't hump up or door and window frames didn't twist to the point they wouldn't open or close properly.

It wasn't a full basement; it was closer to a half basement. It was located directly below the kitchen and part of the dining room and the first floor bedroom but it was big enough for a furnace to provide central heating, a well with an electric motor to provide all the cold water needed for the house and yard and a hot water heater. Once we were assured of having hot and cold running water, we expanded the remodeling project. The back porch was enclosed to make a bathroom and built-in cupboards and a bigger sink were added to the kitchen.

I'd always done laundry on the screened back porch. Clothes were washed in a Haag washing machine powered by a small gasoline-fired engine. When the porch became a bathroom, I set up my laundry facilities in the basement with a new electric, square-tub Maytag washing machine. So as not to overburden the new water heater, I still heated extra water for wash day, at first on a small, low, black cob-fired utility stove called a "topsy" and later, on a two-burner gas outlet.

The basement was well worth all the weeks of struggle it took to dig it, wall it up and make it functional. For extra convenience, a sink and a shower stall were installed down there, too.

By then, my pretty cookstove was showing its age; its oven lining and walls were deteriorating. As long as the kitchen was torn up anyway, it seemed to be the right time to replace it. That stove had been my loyal friend in the kitchen and though it was no longer a reliable baker, it still looked great. Seeing it dismantled and carried out the door on its way to a secondhand store...I remembered how I'd felt the first time I saw that Regal beauty in the hardware store window.

A new, all-white enameled, cob-fired cookstove called a "range" took it's place. The new stove had a flat black cooktop but no warming ovens, no back splash and no reservoir—hot water from a faucet outmoded a reservoir. A new flue was installed in a much lower position in the chimney so the stove pipe was completely hidden behind the stove. At first glance, the new stove was often mistaken for an electric or a gas range.

Soon after the war ended in 1945, our son married and began his own farm and livestock operations. To Walter, who was more than willing to give up milking cows twice a day, it was time to say, "No more pigs and cattle." It didn't mean we'd be giving up beefsteaks, pork chops and roasts from farm-fed beef and hogs—we'd get those from our son. As for milk, cream and butter, we had those delivered to our door twice a week by a milkman. Imagine—a milkman *bringing* milk to the farm. The day the cows were sold, my one-gallon Daisy butter churn became an antique.

As long as we were selling off the livestock, Walter tried to convince me to get rid of my chickens and hens, too. Based on what it cost to buy the baby chicks and buy feed for them and the laying flock, I really couldn't justify keeping them. So instead of talking dollars and cents, I talked to Walter about how he'd miss fresh-from-the-nest eggs, told him he wouldn't like eating store-bought chicken that had been raised in a cage on some chicken ranch hundreds and thousands of miles away and anyway, wasn't I the one who fed, watered and killed and dressed the chickens we ate and gathered the eggs...

I won the first round of the chicken argument but I didn't take much comfort in winning. The subject would come up again.

When the war was over, appliance manufacturers along with automotive and equipment manufacturers closed out military contracts and began flooding stores and dealers with many brand new items. One I'd been waiting for was an electric food mixer, a Sunbeam Mixmaster, and once I had one, did I ever use it! I creamed, beat and whipped new recipes created especially for the mixer and I adapted and adjusted old favorites so they could be made with the mixer, too. I was crazy about the Mixmaster for all the usual reasons—it saved time, it saved the cook's strength and energy and no matter what task it was asked to do from gentle folding to whipping a meringue, it did it uniformly and thoroughly and it never had to stop and rest because a wrist or elbow or shoulder got tired. There's only one more thing to say about a Mixmaster—I wouldn't want to cook without it.

And ever since I got my first International Harvester home freezer in 1948, I don't want to be without a freezer either. I soon discovered the twelve cubic-foot chest-type freezer was too small to store meats and poultry plus all the baked products I found so convenient to keep on hand. Without benefit of a salesman—the freezer sold itself to me—I went to town and ordered a twenty-foot model delivered to our basement. I had absolutely no problem keeping both the larger freezer and the refrigerator's freezing compartment stocked with homegrown fruits and vegetables, ready-to-bake pies, baked cakes and cookies and sometimes, when there was a birthday in the family, I'd make room for a freezer canister of homemade ice cream, too.

That same fall, at Walter's urging, I got an early Christmas gift—my first electric stove, a Hotpoint with all the latest features, two of which, the oven timer and the broiler, were put to immediate and almost continual use.

In ten years, Reddy Kilowatt had become an essential and reliable worker on the farm and in the house. The slightest flicker of the lights sent uneasy shudders through all of us.

"Oh, oh, Charlie...," we'd say. "Charlie" referred to Charles Palmer, the man who headed up the Kearney office of Dawson County Public Power District that delivered electric service to Buffalo County farms.

"...don't fail us now, Charlie."

He didn't. We knew, if the lights did out go and the power did go off, we could count on Charlie's crew of linemen being out climbing poles, repairing fallen lines and restoring power as soon as it was safe to do so. Wind, rain, snow, sleet, ice and dust—those linemen weathered all the storms and kept the country lights bright and all of our electric motors humming.

# BREADS

About the time these yeast dough recipes were added to my collection, the little foil-wrapped cubes of moist, compressed yeast were disappearing from the store to be replaced by dry yeast. Dry yeast is a blend of moist yeast and a small amount of cornmeal. After the granular mixture is thoroughly blended and dried, it is sealed in foil-lined envelopes. One envelope, about two teaspoons of dry yeast, can be used in place of one two-thirds-ounce cake of yeast in recipes.

## CRISPY NUT SWIRLS
Another version of *ROHLICKY*—

1 package dry yeast
1/4 cup warm water
1/4 teaspoon sugar
Dash of ginger
2-1/2 to 3 cups flour
1/4 cup sugar
1-1/2 teaspoons salt
1/2 cup shortening
1 cup creamed style, small curd cottage cheese
1 egg, slightly beaten

Filling:
1/3 cup melted butter or margarine
1 cup brown sugar
1 cup chopped walnuts
1 teaspoon vanilla

In a small bowl, dissolve yeast in warm water to which 1/4 teaspoon sugar and ginger have been added. Set aside 5 minutes. Into a large bowl, sift together 2 cups flour, 1/4 cup sugar and salt. Add shortening; cut in until mixture resembles coarse cornmeal. Add cottage cheese, egg and yeast mixture; beat vigorously. Gradually add only as much of remaining flour as is needed to make a soft yet firm dough. Turn out onto a lightly floured pastry board or cloth. Cover with inverted bowl; let rest 5 minutes. Knead 3 minutes. Place in greased bowl; turn to grease surface. Cover dough lightly; let rise while filling is prepared. *This dough does not need to double in bulk before it is made out.* To make filling: In a small bowl, stir together melted butter, brown sugar, walnuts and vanilla. Grease two cookie sheets generously. Punch dough down and turn out onto lightly floured pastry board or cloth. Roll dough out to form a 14 x 20-inch rectangle and spread with filling. Roll up *both* long sides of the rectangle so the two sides meet at the center. With a sharp knife, cut the 20-inch long roll into 1/2-inch slices. Place slices cut side down on prepared cookie sheets. Cover lightly; let rise 1 to 1-1/2 hours. Preheat oven to 375 degrees F. Bake 12 to 15 minutes until rolls are lightly browned and test done. Makes 40 rolls.

## DANISH STRIPS

Start fruit-filled coffee cakes one evening and bake the next morning—

1/2 package of dry yeast
1/2 cup warm water
1/4 teaspoon sugar
Dash of ginger
4 cups flour
3 tablespoons sugar
1 teaspoon salt
1/2 cup butter or margarine
1 cup milk, scalded
2 eggs, well beaten
2 cups cooked, sweetened dried apricots, dates or prunes

In a small bowl, dissolve yeast in warm water to which 1/4 teaspoon sugar and ginger have been added. In a large bowl, combine flour, sugar and salt. Use a pastry blender to cut butter into flour mixture until mixture resembles cornmeal. Allow scalded milk to cool to lukewarm, then add to flour mixture along with eggs and yeast mixture; beat well. Cover bowl tightly with plastic wrap and then with a clean towel. Refrigerate overnight. The next morning, lightly grease two cookie sheets. Turn dough out onto a lightly floured board or pastry cloth and divide into four equal portions. Roll each portion into a 9 x 12-inch rectangle; dough will be quite thin. Place two strips on each prepared cookie sheet. Spread half a cup of filling lengthwise down the *center one-third* of each strip. Fold sides over the filling so edges meet at the center of the strip. Cover lightly; let rise 2 hours. Preheat oven to 350 degrees F. When dough tests light, bake 20 minutes or until coffee cakes are lightly browned and test done. Glaze with a thin powdered sugar icing. Each coffee cake serves 8.

## PARKERHOUSE ROLLS

Richer, sweeter and lighter than bread, Parkerhouse Rolls were *THE* roll to bake when you invited guests for dinner or to take to potluck suppers—

1 package dry yeast
1/4 cup warm water
1/4 teaspoon sugar
Dash of ginger
2 cups milk, scalded
4 tablespoons butter or margarine
2 tablespoons sugar
1 teaspoon salt
1 egg, well beaten
5 to 5-1/2 cups flour
1/3 cup butter or margarine, melted

In a small bowl, dissolve yeast in warm water to which 1/4 teaspoon sugar and ginger have been added. Set aside 5 minutes. In a large bowl, combine butter, 2 tablespoons sugar and salt. Add scalded milk; stir until butter melts and sugar and salt dissolve. Cool to lukewarm. Add yeast mixture; blend well. Add egg; blend well. Use a spoon to gradually stir in flour 1 cup at a time. Beat well after each addition. Add only as much flour as is needed to make a soft dough. Turn dough out onto lightly floured board or pastry cloth. Cover with inverted bowl; let rest 5 minutes. Knead gently until dough is smooth and elastic but still soft and pliable. Place in lightly greased bowl; turn to grease surface. Cover; let rise until double in bulk. Grease two 9 x 13 x 2-inch baking pans. Turn dough out onto lightly floured board or pastry cloth. Cover with inverted bowl; let rest 5 minutes. Handle gently and as little as possible. Use fingertips to lightly pat out dough until it is 1/3-inch thick. Cut with a 2-1/2-inch round cutter. Brush each round lightly with melted butter. Dip the handle of a table knife in flour and make a crease through the middle of each round. Fold the round on the crease and press edges together to shape the rolls into a half-circle. Place in prepared pans in rows close together. Cover; let rise until almost double in bulk. Preheat oven to 375 degrees F. Bake 15 to 20 minutes or until rolls are golden brown and test done. Turn rolls out of pan and serve hot. Makes 3 dozen.

# QUICK BREAD

## BANANA COFFEE CAKE
This coffee cake smells so good when it's baking, it draws a hungry crowd before it's even out of the oven—

1/3 cup shortening
2/3 cup sugar
2 eggs, well beaten
1-3/4 cups flour
2 teaspoons baking powder
1/4 teaspoon baking soda
1/2 teaspoon salt
1 cup mashed banana, 3 medium bananas

Topping:
2 tablespoons sugar
1/4 teaspoon cinnamon
1 teaspoon *freshly* grated orange peel
1/4 cup chopped walnuts

Preheat oven to 350 degrees F. Grease a 10-inch round cake pan. In a large bowl, cream shortening and sugar until light and fluffy. Add eggs; beat well. Sift flour, baking powder, baking soda and salt together 3 times. Add to creamed mixture alternately with bananas; start and end with dry ingredients. Mix well after each addition. Pour into prepared pan. In a small bowl, combine 2 tablespoons sugar, cinnamon, orange peel and nuts. Sprinkle topping evenly over batter. Bake 35 minutes or until cake tests done. Serves 12.

# CAKES

### ALADDIN LAYER CAKE
A tall, light and delicate cake with a lively lemony frosting—

3 cups sifted cake flour
1-2/3 cups sugar
4 teaspoons baking powder
1/4 teaspoon salt
3 eggs, well beaten
1-1/4 cups milk
1 teaspoon vanilla
1/2 cup butter, softened but *not* melted

Preheat oven to 375 degrees F. Grease three round 9-inch cake pans. Crisscross two 2-inch wide strips of waxed paper in each pan; the strips will aid in removing these very delicately textured cake layers from the pans. Sift and measure cake flour. Add sugar, baking powder and salt and sift together 3 times; on the last sifting, sift into a large bowl. In a small bowl, combine eggs, milk and vanilla. Add to flour mixture along with butter. Use a spoon to stir just until all of the flour is moistened, then beat vigorously 1 minute. Pour batter into prepared pans. Bake 25 minutes or until cake tests done. Cool cake in pans 10 minutes before removing to cooling racks. When cool, fill and frost with Lemon Frosting. Serves 16.

Lemon Frosting:
4 tablespoons butter
4-1/2 cups sifted powdered sugar
1/4 teaspoon freshly grated lemon peel
1 teaspoon yellow food coloring
1-1/2 teaspoons fresh lemon juice
5 tablespoons water

In a medium bowl, cream butter to soften. Add 1 cup powdered sugar and cream until fluffy. Add lemon peel, yellow coloring and lemon juice. Add remaining powdered sugar alternately with water; add water a tablespoon at a time. Beat well after each addition.

## MRS. GLANTZ'S MILK CHOCOLATE CAKE

This cake was a big hit at PTA! A neighbor brought it to a Parent-Teacher Association meeting at the country school our children attended and she gladly shared her recipe for a cake with just the right, light touch of chocolate—

1/2 cup shortening
3/4 teaspoon salt
1 teaspoon vanilla
1-1/2 cups sugar
2 eggs
1 1-ounce square of unsweetened chocolate, melted
2 cups sifted cake flour
2-1/2 teaspoons baking powder
1 cup evaporated milk

Preheat oven to 350 degrees F. Grease two round 9-inch cake pans. In a large bowl, combine shortening, salt and vanilla. Add sugar gradually and cream until light and fluffy. Add eggs one at a time; beat well after each addition. Add chocolate; blend thoroughly. Sift cake flour and baking powder together 3 times. Add to creamed mixture alternately with milk; start and end with dry ingredients. Bake 25 minutes or until cake tests done. Cool cake in pans 10 minutes before removing to cooling racks. When cool, frost with Creamy Chocolate Butter Frosting. Serves 12.

Creamy Chocolate Butter Frosting:
4 cups sifted powdered sugar
1 tablespoon cocoa
1/3 cup butter or margarine
1 egg yolk
1-1/2 teaspoons vanilla
2 tablespoons light cream, Half and Half

Sift powdered sugar and cocoa together. In a small bowl, cream butter. Gradually add half of powdered sugar-cocoa mixture; beat until light and fluffy. Beat in egg yolk and vanilla. Add remaining powdered sugar-cocoa alternately with light cream; add only as much of cream as is needed to reach spreading consistency.

## PINEAPPLE CAKE

This was the first cake I mixed up after I got my first electric mixer. It comes with its own glorious frosting—

2-1/2 cups sifted cake flour
1-1/3 cups sugar
3-1/2 teaspoons baking powder
1 teaspoon salt
2 teaspoons freshly grated orange peel
1/2 cup butter or margarine
2 teaspoons vanilla
1 cup milk
4 egg whites
1/3 cup sugar

Preheat oven to 375 degrees F. Grease two round 9-inch cake pans and line with waxed paper; lightly grease and flour waxed paper. This cake may also be baked as a loaf cake in a lightly greased and floured 9 x 13-inch pan. Sift together cake flour, 1-1/3 cups sugar, baking powder and salt. Stir in orange peel. In a large bowl and with mixer at high speed, cream butter until light and fluffy. Add flour mixture, vanilla and 3/4 cup of milk; beat at low speed just until dry ingredients are moistened, *at that point begin counting time* and continue to beat at medium 2 minutes. In small bowl beat egg whites at high until soft peaks form. Gradually beat in 1/3 cup sugar; beat at high until stiff peaks form. Add beaten egg whites, remaining 1/4 cup of milk to creamed mixture; mix at low speed 1 minute. Pour batter into prepared pans. Bake 25 to 30 minutes or until cake tests done. Cool cake in pans 10 minutes before removing to cooling racks. When cool, frost with Pineapple Frosting. Serves 16.

Pineapple Frosting:
1/4 cup orange juice, heated to very hot but *not boiling*
1/2 cup butter or margarine
4 cups sifted powdered sugar
Pinch of salt
1 8-ounce can crushed pineapple, drained and pressed very dry
1 small package flaked coconut

In a small bowl, add hot juice to butter. Cool. At low speed, gradually beat in half of powdered sugar. Add salt. Add pineapple and remaining powdered sugar. Beat well at medium speed until powdered sugar completely dissolves and mixture reaches spreading consistency. Frost cake. Sprinkle top of cake with coconut.

## WHITE MOUNTAIN ICING

With an electric mixer, it's possible to make perfect Seven-Minute Icing every time—

1 tablespoon white corn syrup
1 cup sugar
1/3 cup water
1 egg white
1 teaspoon vanilla

In a medium saucepan, combine syrup, sugar and water. Stir until sugar dissolves. Cook *covered* over high heat until syrup boils rapidly. In a small bowl, beat egg white 2 minutes at high speed. While mixer continues to beat, gradually add about 3 tablespoons of hot syrup mixture. Cover. Return remaining syrup mixture to high heat and boil 3 minutes. Uncover and continue to boil until syrup spins a thin thread that curls back on itself as syrup falls from a spoon. Pour remaining hot syrup in a thin, steady stream into egg white mixture and beat at high speed. Beat in vanilla. Continue to beat until icing reaches spreading consistency; will frost a two-layer, 8 or 9-inch cake or a 9 x 13-inch loaf cake.

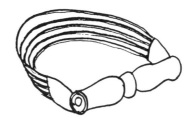

# COOKIES

## SURPRISE DOUBLE COOKIES

Two slices of cookie dough self-seal during baking and make one delicious fruit-filled cookie—

1 cup sugar
1 cup brown sugar
1 cup butter or margarine
3 eggs
4 cups flour
1 teaspoon baking soda
1/2 teaspoon cream of tartar
1/2 teaspoon salt
1 teaspoon vanilla

In a large bowl, cream sugar, brown sugar and butter together until light and fluffy. Add eggs; beat well. Sift flour, baking soda, cream of tartar and salt together. Add to creamed mixture; beat well. Add vanilla; blend thoroughly. Refrigerate dough 1 to 2 hours before dividing into four equal portions. On a *very lightly* floured board or pastry cloth, use hand to roll each portion out into a long roll that is 2 inches in diameter. Refrigerate rolls another 2 hours before baking. Preheat oven to 375 degrees F. Grease two cookie sheets. Cut two rolls of dough into 1/4-inch thick slices and place an inch apart on prepared cookie sheets. Place 1/2 teaspoon of date or raisin filling on each slice. Cut two remaining rolls of dough into 1/4-inch thick slices and place on top of filling. Use fingertips to *lightly* press edges of cookies together. During baking the slices of dough will seal together. Bake 10 minutes or until cookies are delicately browned and test done. Makes about 4 dozen.

Date Filling:
1 cup dates, cut up
1/2 cup sugar
1 cup water
1 tablespoon flour
1/4 teaspoon salt
1/3 cup finely chopped walnuts

In a medium saucepan, combine dates, sugar, water, flour and salt. Cook over medium heat until thick, about 10 minutes. Stir in walnuts. Set aside to cool.

Raisin Filling:
1 cup chopped raisins
1/2 cup sugar
1/2 cup water
1 tablespoon flour
Dash of salt

In a medium saucepan, combine raisins, sugar, water, flour and salt. Cook over medium heat until thick, about 10 minutes. Set aside to cool.

## WAXY NUT COOKIES
Crisp and thin, airy and nutty wafers—

1/2 cup butter or margarine
1 cup brown sugar, firmly packed
1/4 teaspoon salt
1 egg, well beaten
1 cup flour
1/2 cup chopped walnuts

Preheat oven to 375 degrees F. Lightly grease two cookie sheets In a large bowl, cream butter and sugar until light and fluffy. Add salt. Add egg; beat well. Add flour; mix until smooth. Fold in walnuts. Drop dough by teaspoon onto prepared cookie sheets; *allow 3 inches between drops.* Bake 10 minutes. Let cookies cool *5 minutes* on cookie sheet before carefully removing with a wide spatula to a cooling rack. Makes 2 dozen. Note: Altitude affects this recipe resulting in a thicker, less airy cookie.

# DESSERTS

## DOUBLE DATE HOLIDAY PUDDING
There are dates in the pudding and dates in the topping—

1 cup boiling water
1 cup seeded and chopped dates
3/4 cup sugar
2 tablespoons butter or margarine
1 egg
1-3/4 cups flour
1 teaspoon baking soda
Dash of salt

Preheat oven to 350 degrees F. Butter a 7 x 10-inch baking pan. In a small bowl, pour boiling water over dates. Set aside to cool. In a medium bowl, cream sugar and butter until light and fluffy. Add egg; beat well. Add dates and water mixture. Sift flour, baking soda and salt together. Add to creamed-date mixture; blend thoroughly. Pour batter into prepared pan. Bake 25 minutes. Serve warm or cold topped with Date Sauce and a dollop of whipped cream.

Date Sauce:
1 cup seeded and chopped dates
1 cup water
1/2 cup sugar
1 tablespoon butter or margarine
1/2 cup chopped walnuts

In a small saucepan, combine dates, water and sugar. Cook over medium heat until sauce thickens. Remove from heat. Stir in butter and nuts. Sauce maybe served hot or cold. Serves 8.

## BANANA ICE CREAM
Make this smooth, rich ice cream in any regular hand-cranked or electric ice cream freezer and store it in a home freezer. It will not become hard as a rock or crystalline—

6 eggs
2 cups sugar
1/2 teaspoon lemon extract
1/4 cup vanilla
3 cups milk
3 12-ounce cans of evaporated milk
3 medium bananas, mashed to yield 1 cup

In a large bowl, beat eggs until they are a light lemony color. Gradually beat in sugar. Add lemon extract, vanilla, milk and evaporated milk. Add bananas; stir until thoroughly blended. Rinse container and dasher of a one-gallon ice cream freezer and pour in mixture. Secure container in freezer tub, attach crank and gear assembly or electric motor head. Add six parts cracked ice to one part rock salt to within an inch of the lid. Add ice and salt as necessary throughout freezing time, 20 to 25 minutes. Remove dasher. Drain off water. Repack with ice and salt. Let stand a couple of hours for ice cream to ripen. Makes 1 gallon.

## CHOCOLATE ICE CREAM
Quick and easy—

6 eggs
2 cups sugar
3 cups milk
2 12-ounce cans evaporated milk
1 16-ounce can Hershey's chocolate syrup
1/4 cup vanilla

In a large bowl, beat eggs until they are a light lemony color. Gradually beat in sugar. Add milk, evaporated milk, chocolate syrup and vanilla; blend thoroughly. Rinse dasher and container of a gallon freezer and pour in mixture. Secure container in freezer tub, attach crank and gear assembly or electric motor head. Add six parts cracked ice to one part rock salt to within an inch of the lid. Add ice and salt as necessary throughout freezing time, 20 to 25 minutes. Remove dasher. Drain off water. Repack with ice and salt. Let stand a couple of hours for ice cream to ripen. Makes 1 gallon.

## CREAM PUFF SHELLS

Have eggs at room temperature and keep baked puffs away from drafts as they cool—

2 cups water
2/3 cup butter or margarine
1-1/2 cups flour
1/4 teaspoon salt
5 eggs

Preheat oven to 450 degrees F. Grease a cookie sheet. In a medium saucepan, combine water and butter and bring to a full boil over medium heat. Remove from heat and stir in flour and salt *all at one time*; beat hard to blend thoroughly. Return to heat and again bring to a full boil; stir constantly. Cook until batter pulls away from the sides of the pan, *about a minute*. Remove from heat. Cool slightly before adding eggs, *one at a time*. Beat vigorously after each addition until mixture is smooth and satiny. Drop onto prepared cookie sheet by tablespoonful; allow 2 inches between puffs. Bake 15 minutes; then reduce oven temperature to 325 degrees F. and bake 25 minutes or until beads of moisture no longer appear on surface of dough. *Do not open oven door until within 5 to 10 minutes of the end of the baking time*. Remove puffs to a cooling rack. When puffs are completely cool, use a knife with a serrated blade to cut off top. Remove any membrane inside the puff. For dessert, fill with whipped cream topped with sweetened fresh strawberries, raspberries, blackberries or blueberries or fill with a cream custard. Replace top. For a luncheon, fill puffs with ham or chicken salad. If puffs are not used the same day they are baked, cool completely then package in an airtight container. Puffs also freeze well and can be stored in the freezer for a month. Makes 12 to 15 puffs.

## MERINGUE SHELLS

An electric mixer whips up perfect meringue every time—

6 egg whites at *room temperature*
1/4 teaspoon salt
1/2 teaspoon cream of tartar
1-1/2 cups sugar
1/2 teaspoon vanilla

Preheat oven to 250 degrees F. Cut brown paper to cover cookie sheet. In a large bowl, beat egg whites at low speed until frothy. Add salt and cream of tartar. Beat at high speed until soft peaks form. Continue to beat while slowly adding 3/4 cup sugar *1 tablespoon at a time*; then beat 5 minutes at high speed. Add vanilla and remaining 3/4 cup sugar *1 tablespoon at a time*. Continue to beat at high speed. Beating time should total 35 minutes! Drop meringue onto brown paper in mounds; allow 2 inches between mounds. Use the back of a teaspoon to flatten mounds and shape into nests. Bake 1 hour. Turn off oven and let shells dry in the oven, *with the door closed*, another hour. The baked meringue *should not brown but should be a delicate creamy color* Baked meringues will retain crispness if stored in a plastic bag or an air-tight container. To serve, lightly coat and fill inside of meringue nests with sweetened fresh strawberries, raspberries, blackberries or blueberries and top with a small scoop of ice cream. Makes 12 shells.

## MEATS

In the middle 1930s, when we began growing potatoes by acres instead of by so many rows in the garden, for a few weeks late in March and early April, I was part of a small temporary crew that hand-cut the seed potatoes.

We cutters sat at a table built just for that job. It was three feet wide, six feet long and had a recessed center section that created a bin large enough to hold two one hundred-pound bags of seed potatoes. There were two cutting positions on opposite sides near the end of the table; at each position, a thin-bladed knife was anchored into a slot with the knife sticking straight up out of the table, its cutting edge facing the cutter. One by one, every single seed potato was pushed against the knife *two* times, first to cut the potato in half and second to quarter it. Cut potatoes fell through holes and were caught in burlap sacks hanging from the underside of the table top. We wore white cotton work gloves to protect our hands. The rough potatoes were hard on gloves, too; we wore out at least a pair a day.

Potato cutting may sound like a slow, tedious and maybe even a hazardous job. It was, but for me, it was never boring. I actually looked forward to those few weeks each spring. My cutting partner, the one at the other end of the cutting table, was usually my sister-in-law Elsie. While she and I shared cutting duty, her husband Clinton Betebenner and Walter exchanged planting chores. They took turns driving the tractor or riding the planter.

The hours at the cutting table gave us uninterrupted visiting time, time to talk about our children, plan that year's garden and discuss recipes as we planned the next day's dinner. Bar-B-Q-ed Ribs, popular anytime of the year, were particularly well-suited to dinners during potato cutting-planting season when the weather was cool, damp and breezy. Our husbands came in from the field chilled and hungry and, even though we'd been working in the shed all morning, we still wanted to give them a hot meal at noon. The rib dish was assembled after breakfast and went into a slow oven to cook all morning. A couple of times during the morning, the cook made a quick run from the cutting table back to the house to drop a few cobs on the fire to maintain the low heat in the oven.

## BAR-B-Q-ED RIBS

Serve with baked beans, coleslaw and thick slices of home-made bread—

4 pounds of pork spareribs or country-style ribs
2 large onions, peeled and sliced into rings
1 cup catsup
1 cup water
1 teaspoon celery seed
1 tablespoon salt
1 teaspoon pepper
1/4 teaspoon prepared mustard
1/4 teaspoon chili powder

Preheat oven to 325 degrees F. Wipe ribs with a damp paper towel. In a large roaster or a covered baking dish, layer ribs and onion rings. In a small bowl, combine catsup, water, celery seed, salt, pepper, mustard and chili powder. Blend thoroughly and pour over ribs and onions. Bake 3 to 4 hours. Serves 6.

## PORK CHOP SKILLET SUPPER

After chops are browned and simmering, peel and split twelve carrots and six potatoes and add to the skillet for a complete meal—

6 pork loin chops, 1/2 to 3/4-inch thick—
3/4 cup flour
1 teaspoon salt
1/2 teaspoon pepper
Prepared mustard
2 to 3 tablespoons shortening
1 10-1/2-ounce can of chicken with rice soup
1 can of water

Trim away excess fat from outer edges of pork chops. In a shallow bowl, combine flour, salt and pepper. Spread a thin coating of prepared mustard on both sides of chops. Dip in seasoned flour. In a large heavy skillet with a tight-fitting lid, melt shortening and brown chops on both sides. Use a wide spatula to lift chops carefully so browned coating is not disturbed as chops are turned. Add soup and water. Cover. Simmer 1-1/2 to 2 hours or until chops are tender. Add more liquid as needed during cooking time. Serves 6.

# PICKLES

### TREE STUMP PICKLES

Called "Chunk Pickles" when it came to me, this recipe for very attractive, shiny dark green pickles was renamed by a sweet-pickle lovin' grandson—

50 medium-sized Boston pickling cucumbers, a firm, small-seeded cucumber
Soak one week in a two-gallon stone jar in a salt brine, a brine strong enough to float an egg. *Keep cucumbers submerged through all of the processes by weighing them down with a plate.* On the eighth day, drain off the salt brine and soak cucumbers in clear water 3 days. Cut cucumbers crosswise into inch slices and boil 30 minutes in an alum water solution—2 tablespoons of alum to whatever amount of water it takes to cover the pickles in a large saucepan. At the end of the cooking time, drain and run cold water over the hot pickles until the pieces are cool to the touch.

Pickling syrup:
5 pounds sugar
1 quart water
1 pint cider vinegar
2 teaspoons mixed pickling spices

In a large saucepan, combine sugar, water, vinegar and spices. Bring to a full boil over medium heat. Add pickles and continue to boil 30 minutes. Pour pickles and syrup into stone jar. The next day, drain syrup into a large saucepan. Heat to boiling and pour over pickles in the jar. Repeat this step the next day. On the third morning, drain syrup into a large saucepan but before it is boiled, pack pickles into hot sterilized pint jars. Then heat syrup to boiling. Pour over pickles and seal. Makes 7 or 8 pints.

# PIES

Since I've had a home freezer, I rarely make just one pie. When I *have* the time or *take* the time so I can really enjoy making and rolling out the dough and preparing fillings, I make two, three or as many as eight pies at a time. By making extra pies, I can keep a fresh stock of *ready-to-bake* frozen fruit pies in the freezer. I keep one or two unbaked pie crusts in the freezer, too, so a cream pie or a custard pie or a quiche can be baked on short notice, too.

About the time the freezer changed how, when and how many pies I made, I found a new pie crust recipe.

## FLAKY TENDER PIE CRUST

Of all the recipes and methods I've tried for pie crust, this one tops them all—

3 cups flour
1 teaspoon salt
1-1/4 cups shortening
1 egg, well beaten
5 tablespoons ice water
1 teaspoon vinegar

In a small straight-sided bowl, combine flour and salt. Add shortening. Use a pastry blender to cut in shortening until mixture resembles coarse crumbs. Combine egg, ice water and vinegar; *add to flour mixture all at one time.* Use a fork to stir briskly—*not more than 10 strokes*—or until mixture forms a loose ball. Turn dough out onto a sheet of waxed paper or plastic wrap and use hands to gently compress dough into a ball. Refrigerate dough at least 30 minutes before rolling out on a well-floured board or pastry cloth with a cloth-covered rolling pin. Makes a double-crust pie or 2 single-crust pies.

## FLAKY TENDER PIE CRUST MIX

Speed up pie making by tripling flour, shortening and salt amounts in the original recipe to make a make a pie crust mix—

9 cups flour
1 tablespoon salt
3-3/4 cups shortening

In a large bowl, combine flour and salt. Add shortening. Use a pastry blender to cut in shortening until mixture resembles coarse crumbs. Store in an air-tight container on a dry, cool cupboard shelf for two months or in a freezer for twelve months. Date and label container so mix will be used while it is fresh. Makes 16 cups of mix, enough to make 3 double-crust 9-inch pies or 6 single-crust, 9-inch pies.

To make a double-crust 9-inch pie or two single-crust 9-inch pies:

2-1/2 cups Flaky Tender Pie Crust Mix
1 egg, well beaten
1/4 cup ice water
1 tablespoon cider vinegar

Crumble mix into medium bowl. In a small bowl, combine egg, water and vinegar. Add to flour mixture all at one time. Use a fork to stir briskly—*not more than 10 strokes*—or until mixture forms a loose ball. Turn dough out onto plastic or waxed paper. Use hands to gently press dough into a ball. If time permits, refrigerate 30 minutes before rolling out with a cloth-covered rolling pin on a lightly floured board or pastry cloth. Divide in half and roll out.

## PUMPKIN PIE

Before canned pureed pumpkin became available, I didn't like to make pumpkin pie. Making pumpkin pie, a *good* pumpkin pie, from scratch was a long process. The process really started before the garden was planted in the spring when the pumpkin seeds were selected. The variety of a pumpkin made a big difference in the color, flavor and texture of the cooked pumpkin pulp; you looked for a variety that yielded deep orange, mild-flavored, fine-textured, string-free pulp.

After fall's first frost, pumpkins were picked. To use, a pumpkin was split, seeded and baked in the shell in a moderate oven, 350 degrees Farenheit, until tender. The baked pulp was scooped into a heavy iron skillet and the skillet was pushed to the back of the stove where the pumpkin then simmered slowly for a couple of hours to reduce the moisture and thicken.

To make a pumpkin pie from either homegrown or canned pumpkin so the pie has the true pumpkin color, be sure to combine the ingredients in the precise order in which they are listed in the recipe—

2 eggs
1 16-ounce can pumpkin or 2 cups cooked pumpkin pulp
3/4 cup sugar
1/2 teaspoon salt
1/2 teaspoon cinnamon
1/4 teaspoon ground ginger
1/4 teaspoon ground cloves
1 12-ounce can evaporated milk or 1-2/3 cups light cream, Half and Half
Unbaked crust for a single-crust 9-inch pie

Preheat oven to 425 degrees F. Line pie pan with crust. In a large bowl, beat eggs. Add pumpkin; stir to blend well. Add sugar, salt, cinnamon, ginger and cloves; blend thoroughly. Add milk; blend thoroughly. Pour filling into prepared crust. Bake 15 minutes. Reduce heat to 350 degrees F. and bake 45 minutes or until pie tests done when a silver or stainless steel table knife inserted in the middle of the pie comes out clean. Serves 6.

## RHUBARB CREAM PIE
Tangy fruit in a mellow custard—

3 cups fresh rhubarb, cut into 1/2-inch slices
1-1/2 cups sugar
3 tablespoons flour
1/2 teaspoon nutmeg
1 tablespoon butter or margarine, softened but not melted
2 eggs, well beaten
Unbaked crust for a double-crust 9-inch pie

Preheat oven to 450 degrees F. Line pie pan with lower crust. Use a cookie cutter to cut remaining crust into fancy pieces. Pile sliced rhubarb into crust-lined pan. In a medium bowl, blend sugar, flour, nutmeg and butter. Add eggs; beat until smooth. Pour over rhubarb. Top with pastry cutouts. Bake 10 minutes. Reduce oven temperature to 350 degrees F. and bake 30 minutes or until pie tests done. Serves 6.

## SOUR CREAM RAISIN PIE
This pie *must* be made with large, puffy Muscat raisins—

1 cup light cream, Half and Half
1 tablespoon cider vinegar
1-1/2 cups Muscat raisins
1/4 teaspoon salt
2 tablespoons flour
1 tablespoon cornstarch
1 cup plus 2 tablespoons sugar
Scant 1/2 teaspoon cinnamon
Scant 1/2 teaspoon nutmeg
3 egg yolks, well beaten
1 teaspoon vanilla
1 baked 9-inch pie crust

In a small bowl, combine cream and vinegar. Set aside 5 minutes. In a medium saucepan, combine raisins with enough water to cover. Bring raisins to a full boil over medium heat. Reduce heat and boil gently 7 to 10 minutes. Remove from heat. Add salt and set aside. In a medium saucepan, combine flour, cornstarch, sugar, cinnamon and nutmeg. Add eggs; blend thoroughly. Add soured cream; blend thoroughly then cook over medium heat until mixture thickens. Add vanilla. Set mixture aside to cool until a hand can be held comfortably on the bottom of the saucepan. Pour into baked pie crust. Top with meringue. Preheat oven to 325 to 350 degrees F.

Meringue:
3 egg whites
1/2 teaspoon cream of tartar
Dash of salt
6 tablespoons sugar

In a small bowl, beat egg whites with cream of tartar and salt until foamy. Gradually add sugar, one tablespoon at a time; beat until egg whites stand in peaks that curl slightly at the tip when beaters are lifted. Spread meringue over filling; make sure meringue overlaps edges of crust completely. Bake 10 minutes or until peaks are a golden brown. Serves 6.

# SALADS

It took more than a refrigerator in the kitchen to get rid of the notion that leafy, green, crispy vegetables were more than "rabbit food" or "fodder." Leaf lettuce and cabbage slaw were "okay" in the summer but it took time for salads to find a regular spot on our tables. But no one, not even the men, shied away from hearty salads like Macaroni Salad.

## MACARONI SALAD
The dressing makes the taste difference in this salad. Use Carrie's Homemade Mayonnaize or use the salad dressing recipe that accompanies this recipe—

2 cups cooked and cooled small elbow or shell macaroni
1 slicing cucumber, peeled and diced
3 or 4 green onions, chopped, include some of the tops
1/4 cup finely chopped green pepper
2 whole fresh tomatoes, peeled, seeded and diced,
1/2 cup finely diced celery
3/4 cup cubed American cheese
1/2 teaspoon celery salt
Salt and pepper to taste
3/4 cup Carrie's Homemade Mayonnaize or salad dressing
    recipe given below

In a large bowl, combine macaroni, cucumber, onion, green pepper, tomatoes, celery, cheese and celery salt. Sprinkle lightly with salt and pepper. Add mayonnaise or salad dressing. Stir with a large spoon or rubber spatula in a gentle lifting and folding motion; blend thoroughly. Serves 8.

Salad Dressing:
3/4 cup Miracle Whip salad dressing
1 tablespoon vinegar
1 teaspoon prepared mustard
1 tablespoon sugar

In a small bowl, combine salad dressing, vinegar, mustard and sugar; blend thoroughly.

## SOUP

### CHILI

In December, as soon as temperatures fell below freezing and stayed there for several days, Walter flooded a pond he'd banked up near one of the irrigation wells and made an ice skating rink. From December until March or for as long as there was solid ice on the rink, neighborhood kids came to skate after school, on Friday nights and all day on Saturdays. I ran a short-order kitchen, serving hamburgers and hot dogs to the kids. On Saturdays, I doubled or tripled this recipe so there'd be plenty of fiery chili to warm the shivering, red-cheeked skaters. After a chili-time-out, they hit the rink again and skated on into the night by the light of a big bonfire built by the side of the pond—

1 pound lean ground beef
2 tablespoons shortening
2 medium onions, chopped
Half a green pepper, seeded and chopped
1 quart canned whole tomatoes
2 15-ounce cans of red kidney beans
1 teaspoon salt
1-1/2 teaspoons chili powder
Dash of cayenne pepper
Few shakes of garlic salt

In a large heavy saucepan or soup pot, brown ground beef in shortening. Add onions and green pepper and saute lightly. Add tomatoes, beans, salt, chili powder, cayenne pepper and garlic salt. Cover. Simmer over low heat 2 to 4 hours. Serves 4.

## COOKING WITH HONEY

During World War II's sugar rationing, honey didn't automatically substitute for sugar across the cookbooks or recipe cards. It couldn't. The two sweeteners are quite different. One is a liquid, a thick liquid, but a liquid just the same, and the other is a dry ingredient and that affects how they are measured and when and how they are combined with other ingredients. In addition to contributing sweetness to a recipe, honey also adds flavor. The best results were achieved by using recipes specifically devised to be made with honey.

When the war was over, I switched back to using sugar in almost all of my recipes. These "made with honey" recipes survived World War II and are still part of my collection.

## CHOCOLATE HONEY CAKE
Mix and beat with a spoon or with an electric mixer—

2 cups sifted cake flour
1-1/2 teaspoons baking soda
1 teaspoon salt
1/2 cup shortening
1-1/4 cups honey
2/3 cup water
2 eggs
2-1/2 one-ounce squares of unsweetened chocolate, melted
1 teaspoon vanilla

Preheat oven to 350 degrees F. Grease and flour two 9-inch cake pans. Sift cake flour, baking soda and salt together. Set aside. In a large bowl, stir shortening to soften. In a small bowl, combine honey and water; add half of the mixture to creamed shortening. Stir to blend thoroughly. Add eggs; beat well. Add dry ingredients. Stir slowly until well blended, then beat hard one minute. Add remaining honey and water mixture along with melted chocolate and vanilla. Blend well, then beat hard 2 minutes. It is important to count only the actual beating time, not blending time, regardless of whether the mixing is being done by hand with a spoon or with an electric mixer. For hand beating, allow 150 full around-the-bowl strokes per 1 minute of beating with a mixer. The finished batter will be thin. Pour into prepared pans. Bake 30 minutes or until cake tests done. Cool cake in pans 10 minutes before turning out onto cooling racks. When cake is cool, frost with Easy Honey Frosting. Serves 16.

Easy Honey Frosting:
1 egg white
Dash of salt
1/2 cup honey
1/2 teaspoon vanilla


In a small bowl, beat egg white with salt until stiff peaks form. Add honey in a fine stream; beat constantly 4 minutes or until frosting holds shape and is of spreading consistency. Beat in vanilla.

## HONEY-APRICOT CAKE
A fruity surprise—


1/2 cup dried apricots, diced
1 cup water
1/2 cup mayonnaise
3/4 cup honey
1 teaspoon freshly grated lemon peel
2 cups sifted flour
1/3 cup sugar
1 teaspoon baking soda
1/2 teaspoon salt
1/4 teaspoon cinnamon
1/4 teaspoon nutmeg
1/4 cup chopped walnuts


Preheat oven to 350 degrees F. Grease a 4 x 5 x 9-inch loaf pan. Line bottom of pan with a double thickness of waxed paper; grease waxed paper. In a small saucepan, combine apricots and water. Bring to simmering over low heat; simmer 10 minutes. Drain; reserve liquid. In a large bowl, blend mayonnaise and honey. Beat until fluffy. Add lemon peel. Sift flour, sugar, baking soda, salt, cinnamon and nutmeg together and add alternately with reserved liquid; start and end with dry ingredients. Beat well after each addition. Add apricots and walnuts; blend thoroughly. Pour into prepared pan. Bake 1 hour or until cake tests done. Cool cake 10 minutes in pan before turning out onto cooling rack. When cake is cool, frost with Lemon-Orange Butter Frosting. Serves 12.

Lemon-Orange Butter Frosting:
2 cups sifted powdered sugar
1 teaspoon freshly grated orange peel
1/2 teaspoon freshly grated lemon peel
Dash of salt
1 egg yolk
3 tablespoons softened, not melted, butter or margarine
1-1/2 teaspoons lemon juice
2-3 tablespoons orange juice

In a small bowl, combine sugar, orange and lemon peel and salt. Add egg yolk, butter, lemon juice and 2 tablespoons of orange juice; blend thoroughly. Gradually add remaining orange juice until frosting is of spreading consistency. Beat until smooth and fluffy.

## HONEY ORANGE ROLLS
There's honey in the dough and honey in the filling—

2 packages of dry yeast
1/4 cup warm water
1/4 teaspoon sugar
Dash of ginger
1 cup milk
1/4 cup shortening
1/4 cup sugar
1/4 cup honey
1-1/2 teaspoons salt
5 cups sifted flour
2 eggs, well beaten

Filling:
1/2 cup honey
2 tablespoons freshly grated orange peel

In a small bowl, dissolve yeast in water to which 1/4 teaspoon of sugar and ginger have been added. In a small saucepan, scald milk. Add shortening, sugar, honey and salt to milk. Cool to lukewarm. Add 2 cups flour; beat well. Add yeast mixture and eggs; mix thoroughly. Add 2 more cups of flour; mix thoroughly. Add only as much of the remaining cup of flour as is needed to make a soft dough. Turn dough out onto lightly floured board or pastry cloth. Cover with inverted bowl; let rest 5 minutes. Knead until smooth and satiny. Place dough in greased bowl; turn to grease surface. Cover; let rise until double in bulk. Punch dough down and turn out onto lightly floured board or pastry cloth. Cover with inverted bowl; let rest 10 minutes. While dough rests, grease generously three 12-muffin muffin pans. On a lightly floured board or pastry cloth, roll dough out into a 9-inch wide rectangle that is 1/4-inch thick. Spread with 1/2 cup honey. Sprinkle with grated orange peel. Start with a long side and roll dough up as for a jelly roll; pinch to seal edges. Use a sharp knife to cut into 1-inch slices. Place slices cut side down in prepared pans. Cover; let rise until double in bulk. Preheat oven to 375 degrees F. Bake rolls 20 minutes or until they are lightly browned and test done. Makes 3 dozen.

## HONEY PUMPKIN PIE

The honey flavor blends perfectly with cinnamon and ginger—

1 1-pound can pumpkin, 2 cups
2 cups evaporated milk
1 cup honey
3 eggs, well beaten
1/2 teaspoon salt
1 teaspoon cinnamon
1/2 teaspoon ginger
1 unbaked 9-inch pie crust

Preheat oven to 350 degrees F. Line pie pan with crust. In a large bowl, combine pumpkin, milk, honey, eggs, salt, cinnamon and ginger; blend thoroughly. Pour into crust. Bake 1 hour or until tip of silver knife inserted in center of the pie comes out clean. Serves 6.

## HONEY OATMEAL CRISPIES
With coconut, too—

1/2 cup sugar
1/2 cup brown sugar
1 cup shortening
1 cup honey
1 teaspoon vanilla
2 eggs, well beaten
2 cups flour
1 teaspoon baking soda
1/2 teaspoon baking powder
1/2 teaspoon salt
3 cups quick-cook oatmeal
1 cup flaked coconut

Preheat oven to 350 degrees F. Grease cookie sheets. In a large bowl, cream sugar, brown sugar and shortening until light and fluffy. Add honey, vanilla and eggs; blend thoroughly. Sift flour, baking soda, baking powder and salt together. Add to creamed mixture; beat well. Add oatmeal and coconut; blend thoroughly. Drop by teaspoonfuls on prepared cookie sheets. Bake 10 to 12 minutes or until cookies are lightly browned and test done. Makes 6 dozen.

## FROZEN FRUIT DELIGHT
Can be a salad or dessert—

2 tablespoons sugar
1 tablespoon flour
1/2 cup honey
1/3 cup fresh lemon juice
1 egg, slightly beaten
1 20-ounce can crushed pineapple, well drained
1 banana, sliced
1/3 cup orange sections
1/4 cup maraschino cherries, halved
1 cup heavy cream, whipped

In a small saucepan, combine sugar, flour and honey. Bring to a boil over medium heat; stir constantly. In a small bowl, stir lemon juice into beaten egg. *Slowly* add a little of hot honey mixture to egg mixture; stir constantly. When mixtures are thoroughly blended, return to saucepan and cook over low heat just until mixture comes to a boil. Cool completely. Add pineapple, banana slices, orange slices and cherries. Stir gently to blend. Fold in whipped cream. Turn into a one-and-one-half-quart freezer-proof container and freeze 3 or 4 hours or overnight; can be stored in freezer a month. Serves 8.

# VEGETABLES

Of all the vegetables recommended for the freezer, none appealed to our family more than corn on the cob. The idea of eating fresh corn on the cob after its short summer season on through fall and winter got kids and grown-ups alike excited.

## CORN ON THE COB

Freezing corn is easy. The first rule is to freeze it when it is tender and milky. When corn is ready to eat, it's ready for the freezer. The second rule is to get corn from the field to the freezer the same day it's picked. Husk ears and remove silks. There continue to be differences of opinion as to whether or not corn on the cob prepared for the freezer should be blanched, scalded, or not. I have done it both ways and according to our family taste tests, we prefer it unblanched. Wrap each clean ear individually in foil. Store up to six months in the freezer. To use, *do not thaw.* Unwrap and drop frozen ears, no more than six at a time, into deep boiling water to which one-half teaspoon of sugar has been added. When water returns to a full boil, *start timing and boil only three minutes.* Not blanching the corn before it goes into the freezer, not thawing it before it is cooked and cooking it a shorter length of time eliminates any hint of the "cobby" flavor sometimes associated with frozen corn on the cob.

If corn is to be blanched before freezing, immerse a few ears, no more than six at a time, into boiling water for seven to nine minutes, depending on the diameter of the ears; ears measuring one-and-one-half-inches across the base should be blanched seven minutes and those with a two-inch base, nine minutes. At the end of blanching, plunge hot ears into ice water or place under cold running water for fourteen to eighteen minutes; cooling time should be twice as long as blanching time. Drain cool ears and seal in plastic bags or aluminum foil, one ear to a package. To use, partially thaw ears in unopened package two hours at room temperature and then cook four to five minutes in deep boiling water into which one-half teaspoon of sugar has been added.

Eating corn on the cob in the dead of winter is a novelty and while the taste may not be one hundred percent true to summer's fresh-from-the-field corn on the cob, it's close, close enough to justify the extra space the whole ears take up in the freezer. Packaged whole kernel corn makes more efficient use of freezer space; it requires only about half the storage space taken up by the same number of servings of corn left on the cob.

If corn is to be cut from the cob and frozen, blanch ears only four to five minutes then place in ice water eight to ten minutes. As soon as the ears are completely cool—break an ear and make sure the cob is cool to the touch—drain. With a short, very sharp knife, slice kernels from the cob. *Do not cut into the cob.* Each slice should be no wider than two or three rows of kernels. Package in pint or quart freezer containers.

To use, simmer in a small amount of lightly salted water—one-fourth teaspoon for a pint and one-half teaspoon for a quart—for three to four minutes. Halfway through simmering, stir with a fork to break frozen kernels apart for more uniform cooking. Drain. Season with butter or margarine.

## CORN BAKE
Tastes like it was just cut from the cob—

1 quart frozen whole kernel corn
1/2 cup light cream, Half and Half
2 tablespoons butter or margarine
1/4 teaspoon salt

Preheat oven to 350 degrees F. Place frozen corn in a casserole with a tight-fitting lid. Add cream, butter and salt. Cover. Bake 20 to 30 minutes. Halfway through baking time stir with a fork to break frozen kernels apart for more uniform baking. Serves 6.

When home freezers first came on the market, instructions from the manufacturers were brief and sometimes sketchy. Along with directions and lists of foods recommended for the freezer, manufacturers listed foods "not completely satisfactory after freezing and thawing." Potatoes and tomatoes were on that list. But not for long. At the same time housewives experimented in their home kitchens, home economists in manufacturers' test kitchens did their own experimenting and soon came up with ways to successfully process potatoes and tomatoes for and from the freezer.

## MILLIONAIRE POTATOES
After college, our daughter was a home economist for a major appliance manufacturer who, at the time, did not recommend freezing potatoes. She told her boss, "My mother does it..." After he'd sampled these potatoes and the recipe had passed taste tests at the company test kitchen, these twice-baked potatoes became a regular demonstration feature—

6 8 to 10-ounce baking potatoes
4 tablespoons butter or margarine
1/2 to 3/4 cup light cream, Half and Half
1/2 to 3/4 teaspoon salt
1/8 teaspoon pepper
2 medium carrots, finely diced and cooked
1 cup cubed Cheddar cheese
2 tablespoons minced fresh green onions, include some of the tops

Preheat oven to 400 degrees F. Scrub potatoes. Dry with paper towels. For crispy skins, rub potatoes lightly with shortening. Insert baking nails or pierce each potato twice with a sharp cooking fork to shorten baking time and promote uniform baking. Bake 1 hour. As soon as potatoes come out of the oven, with a sharp knife, cut a small oval of skin from the flat top of each potato. Scoop pulp out into a medium bowl. Mash thoroughly, until no lumps remain. Add butter. Continue to mash until butter melts. Add half of cream; whip thoroughly. Add as much of remaining cream as is needed to whip potatoes until they are smooth and fluffy. Add salt and pepper to taste. Add carrots, cheese and onions; blend thoroughly. Spoon mixture back into shells. Cool. Package potatoes individually in plastic freezer bags or containers. Potatoes may be stored in freezer six months. To serve, preheat oven to 400 degrees F. *Do not thaw*; remove frozen potatoes from package, place on a cookie sheet and put directly into hot oven. Bake 20 to 30 minutes or until potatoes are completely heated through and tops are lightly browned. Serves 6.

## FROSTY TOMATOES

Work quickly with small quantities of fresh, vine-ripened tomatoes—

Immerse tomatoes in boiling water 30 seconds so they peel easily and quickly. Tomatoes may be left whole or quartered. Place in pint or quart-sized lidded plastic freezer containers. Do not fill containers to the top; allow 1/2-inch for expansion during freezing. Sprinkle with salt; 1/2 teaspoon for a pint and 1 teaspoon for a quart. Place lids on containers and freeze immediately. Tomatoes can be stored in freezer for a year. To use, thaw only enough to loosen outer edges so tomatoes slip easily of the container. Use as stewed tomatoes or add to soups, stews, chili or casseroles.

## FROZEN TOMATO JUICE
Make that "FRESH" Frozen Tomato Juice—

Work quickly. Process no more than 4 quarts of juice at a time. Rinse, quarter and core fresh, vine-ripened tomatoes. Place in a large saucepan. Use a potato masher to crush tomatoes slightly to squeeze out just enough juice to cover bottom of saucepan. Bring tomatoes quickly to a simmer over high heat—DO NOT BOIL—simmer just until tomatoes are soft enough to be strained. Remove from heat. Strain hot juice immediately; press tomato pulp, but not seeds and skins, through a sieve or colander. Pour juice into pint or quart freezer containers; allow 1/2-inch at the top for expansion during freezing. Add salt, 1/2 teaspoon to a pint and 1 teaspoon to a quart. Place lids on filled containers and set in a shallow pan of ice water to cool quickly. When completely cool, freeze immediately. Juice can be stored in freezer for a year. To use, allow frozen juice to thaw several hours or over-night in the refrigerator. For faster thawing, container may be placed in cold water; the depth of the water should be 1 inch below the top of the container.

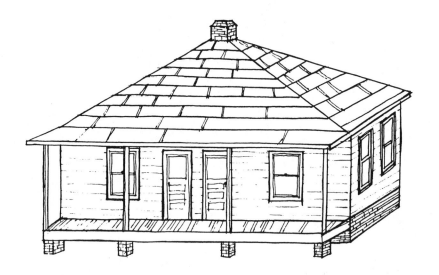

# Clayt's

# CLAYT'S

Clayt's, our third and smallest home, was a square four-room house on a 240-acre farm owned by Clayton Glazier, who owned and operated an adjoining farm. The farm was located seven miles straight north of Gibbon. We lived there four years, from March 1, 1926, to March 1, 1930. Farm rental contracts ran from March to March and, unless weather interfered, March the first was traditionally moving day for farmers. Clayt's was only three miles south and three-quarters of a mile east of Lou's Place and while it was another short move as far as distance was concerned, because we'd accumulated more household furnishings and more farm machinery in the three years since we'd last moved, it took a whole day to make the move.

The farmyard was set inside an L-shaped border of catalpa, box elder and fruit trees, mostly apple and cherry, on a slight slope near the northeast corner of the farm. The low, box-like house faced east and had a long, open porch across the front. Two doors opened off the porch, one into the kitchen and one into the dining room. Behind those two rooms were two bedrooms, one closet and a pantry. The dining room, at fourteen-by-fourteen feet, was the biggest room in the house. The kitchen was twelve-by-fourteen feet but it seemed much smaller because of its limited wall space. Four doorways opened out of that room—one to the porch, the pantry, the dining room and the bedroom. The cookstove had to go on the north wall of the kitchen because that's where the chimney was; the cabinet fit in the northwest corner of the room; the tall dish cupboard took up the space between the pantry door and the window on the south wall; the sewing machine was under the south window; the wash stand was under the east window; the enamel-topped table and four chairs were in the center of the room; and, the rocking chair floated from one spot to another. The room was so ram-jam full of furniture, if I had to open a cupboard door when people were seated at the kitchen table, they had to duck. It was hard to walk through the room without bumping into furniture and harder still to cook without bruising an elbow, knee or hipbone.

As we reminded ourselves when we bumped into each other crossing the room or sat around the table, elbow-to-elbow with our guests, the house wasn't what had attracted us to that farm. We'd moved there for the land. The farm was twice the size of Lou's and other than forty acres of hay, the rest of the land was all tillable and relatively flat, making it a very desirable farm rental property. Walter saw it as another opportunity to expand.

It did have one "stick"-ler—the land was heavily infested with the dreaded cocklebur. The pesky weed had been allowed to thrive and spread in dense patches along fence rows, ditches and low spots in the fields. Everywhere Walter went, he took his spade with him. If it wasn't on his shoulder, it was nearby. It rode beside him on the corn planter, the harrow, the go-devil or the cultivator. He whacked at every young green cocklebur plant he saw, hoping to chop it out before it had a chance to bloom and develop prickly, seed-bearing burs. He made some headway against the cocklebur crop the first year but it was two years before he could declare the farm "bur-free."

It was while we lived at Clayt's that I tied on my big, floppy straw hat, pulled on a pair of Walter's bibbed overalls and one of his shirts and began helping out in the fields, cultivating corn and making hay in the summer and picking corn in the fall. Walter drove a four-horse team on a two-row cultivator and I drove a team on a one-row. When we picked corn, we used one team and one wagon; Walter picked ears from two rows of corn and I picked from one. Now it may not seem like I was cutting a very big swath doing just one row at a time, but, as Walter reminded me, for every row I cultivated or picked, I cut his work by one-third.

We made hay two or three times each summer. My job was to drive a team of horses on the hay buck. After the hay was mowed, it was raked into long windrows and allowed to dry a couple of days before it was "bucked" to where it was to be stacked. Of all the machinery ever invented for use on the farm, the hay buck has to be one the strangest rigs to look at; it's even stranger when it's seen in action. It's a contraption of long, wooden, wide-set, ground-hugging "teeth." A team of horses pushes rather than pulls the buck through the field picking up dry, windrowed hay, carrying it to the haystack and depositing it onto the long, wooden "teeth" of the haystacker, another odd looking piece of equipment. By a combination of ropes and pullies powered by a team of horses hitched to a stacker buggy, stacker "teeth" were raised up in the air, high enough to flip the load of hay onto the top of a haystack.

Walter stood on top of the haystack, ready to receive the hay, pitch it around, shaping and leveling layers of hay to form a reasonably compact, straight-sided stack that might grow to be twenty, thirty or forty feet tall.

Walter was a whistler. He had an extensive program of distinctive whistles; some were tunes and some were merely sounds, but very specific sounds with which he could summon me, the kids, the dog and even the cows and horses. With one whistle, he signaled the horses hitched to the stacker buggy to go forward and lift up the stacker; with another, he signaled them to stop; and, with another, he signaled them to back up and lower the stacker.

When I helped in the field, Walter's parents kept the children in the daytime and occasionally overnight but they never had them at haying time; the kids wanted to be home for that. We took them out on that job with us and they loved it. They rode back and forth in the stacker buggy all day long—playing, eating and napping.

# 1950-1974

Walter and I were a twosome again. Our son had married Wilma Huffstutter and our daughter married Wayne Fritz and we became grandparents to two grandsons, Kirk and Kevin Hendrickson, and three granddaughters, Kathleen Hendrickson and Linda and Krista Fritz. The two boys grew up farming with their father and grandfather and the three girls took a liking to cooking and now they, along with my daughter, daughter-in-law and a granddaughter-in-law, Connie Swift Hendrickson, all share recipes with me.

We thought our lives couldn't get any busier than they'd been the preceding twenty-eight years but they did. Our work-loads, Walter's in the fields and mine in the house, went through various changes as to *how* the work was done but, if anything, the *size* of the loads increased at the same time we were trying to make time for grandchildren, more time for friends and clubs and more time for travel. For me, there was an extension club, church activities and a bridge club; for the two of us, there was a pinochle card club and two supper clubs.

One supper club, "The Birthday Bunch," was a six-couple,

twelve-member group that met once a month. Each month we celebrated one member's birthday with a sit-down potluck dinner followed by an evening of card games.

The other supper club, "The Wild Life Bunch"...Wait...Let me explain that name. Before it became a monthly supper club for five other couples and us, it was a monthly men-only meeting for hunters and fishermen. On the night our husbands went to their Wild Life Club meeting, we wives gathered to share a potluck supper and play cards. Dessert topped off the evening. Sometimes the fellows came to pick up their wives before we'd had our dessert and, naturally, when that happened, we politely asked the men to join us. When they tasted the good food we were eating and heard about all the fun we were having on *their* night out, it wasn't long before, at their suggestion, they began skipping their meetings to spend the whole evening with us. Out of habit, one night each month continued to be designated "Wild Life" on our calendars though the word "club" was dropped. We weren't in any way, shape or form a club. What we were was a "bunch" of friends getting together to enjoy themselves. And that's how that group got its name. The whole "bunch," men and women, ate supper together at one big dining table but afterwards, we went to separate tables where the women played canasta and the men played pitch.

In both supper clubs, the hostess prepared the entree and beverages and others took turns bringing a vegetable, salad, rolls, relishes and dessert. We cooked and baked our favorite tried-and-true recipes but we also experimented with new recipes and new methods, especially when it came to salads and vegetables. We were always looking for recipes that could be transported easily, that didn't have to be served in any split-second order, that could be held and kept hot or cold and still be delicious and look attractive even if there was a delay in the serving time. With all the great cooks in those two clubs, it was one continual round of recipe exchanges.

If I wasn't trying a new recipe, I was trying a new electric appliance—ice cream freezer, skillet, waffle iron, blender, crock pot, automatic drip coffee maker. The number of people at my table was erratic. For one meal I might be cooking for two and the next, I was cooking for a crowd. Either way, knowing I had a side of beef, half a hog, dozens of whole-bodied chickens and cut up fryers, baked breads, rolls, cakes and cookies and ready-to-bake fruit pies a few steps away down in the basement in the freezer made spur-of-the-moment cooking or long-range menu planning both "easy as pie" and "a piece of cake."

By the early 1950s, television sets with sound *and* pictures were bumping radio-record player consoles out of living rooms everywhere and that, in turn, affected when and where we ate our meals and sometimes it even determined what we ate and who we ate with. Family and company meals might be planned around favorite television shows—Saturday night's "Show of Shows" with Sid Caesar and Imogene Coca, Ed Sullivan's Sunday night "The Toast of the Town," Milton Berle's "Texaco Star Theater," Lucille Ball's "I Love Lucy..." When I heard the theme song "Bubbles in the Wine," I dropped everything in the kitchen to watch "The Lawrence Welk Show" with Walter.

For special events and programs like the New Year's Day Rose Parade and Rose Bowl football game, baseball's World Series and others, the living room became a mini-stadium. Furniture was rearranged to give every seat a front row view of the screen. Beverages and snacks were "hawked" during parades and games and when the last float rolled by or with the last out in the bottom of the ninth or a game-ending gun, "fans" moved to the dining room table for brunch, lunch, supper or dinner.

There were times when we were entertaining at home or we were away from home being entertained, that I almost forgot I had chickens to tend. Early in 1960, I decided all on my own, without one urging word from Walter, the chickens had to go.

My decision was made easier because by that time, I'd located a nearby source for home-grown fryers and farm-fresh eggs— my sister-in-law Elsie.

At the same time our social commitments were on the increase, so were Walter's farming interests. We bought and rented more land, doubling and tripling the acres he farmed. On the Smith land, his farming became more diversified. In the mid-1950s, he grew tomatoes on a twenty-acre experimental plot for the Campbell Soup Company. After several years with tomatoes, he was invited to participate in a cooperative experiment on vegetable production funded by the Kearney Chamber of Commerce and under the direction of the University of Nebraska College of Agriculture. Recording instruments were installed in plots of snap beans, green peppers, carrots, summer squash, tomatoes and onions to test the effects of wind, herbicides and fungicides and also to collect other weather data. Walter was the farmer for the project; he prepared the soil beds, oversaw planting, tilling and watering. And while he didn't keep the records, he was always right there, at the plot manager's elbow every time readings were jotted down, anxious to see and hear the latest information. He never left the vegetable plots empty handed, the manager saw to that. Other than a few rows of lettuce, radishes, green onions and peas, I no longer planted a big garden, so I appreciated getting the baskets of fresh produce from the test plots.

In 1960, Walter was cited as a "Founding Father" in the Agricultural Hall of Fame "in recognition of his contribution to agriculture." He appreciated the honor, what farmer wouldn't, but he didn't dwell on it, didn't talk about it much. I think, to him, the honor represented the past, what had been, what he'd done and Walter preferred looking ahead. The things that got his attention were new methods of irrigation, such as using gated pipes in place of open ditches or, in the case of hilly, irregular, ungraded fields, using overhead, pivot systems; new equipment to improve field work with new, bigger, faster, better, more efficient, and, yes, more expensive tractors, planters, cultivators—equipment that allowed one man on one machine to farm more and more acres. No one, not even our grandsons, got a bigger thrill than Walter did seeing a new piece of machinery delivered to the farm.

At times, I thought he got a little carried away with buying the latest model, like the time he spent a September morning in town talking with a farm equipment dealer and came home to tell me he'd traded in a tractor I thought was brand new.

"Isn't that the tractor you just bought in March? Why are you getting rid of it?" I asked.

"I never did like the seat on that damned thing," he said. "Wait 'til you see the seat on this new model—it's real comfortable and it's adjustable, too."

I'd been reading and studying ads for refrigerators, larger, two-door, frost-free models with separate lower doors for larger, freezing compartments. I didn't intend to part with the big, chest-type freezer in the basement, but I did think it would be handier to have a refrigerator with greater freezer capacity close at hand in the kitchen; it would save me running up and down the basement stairs several times every day.

I went to town that afternoon to see an appliance dealer.

The next day, when Walter came in to eat at noon, the old white Philco had been replaced by a copper-colored Frigidaire. It was a "looker." It stopped Walter right in his tracks, two feet inside the back door.

"Where'd that come from?" he asked after about a thirty-second pause.

"Swan's brought it out this morning."

"When'd you buy it?"

"Yesterday afternoon."

"Did the Philco quit working?"

"No."

"Why'd you get rid of it?"

I was ready for *that* question.

"Well," I said slowly, holding back a laugh, "I never did like the seat on that old thing."

It was a sheepish-looking Walter who hung up his hat and washed up for dinner without another word.

A few weeks later, at his suggestion, the companion piece to the new refrigerator, a copper-colored, double-deck Frigidaire electric range with two self-cleaning ovens and a glass cooktop was ordered.

I've never lost interest in new kitchen appliances and utensils—I was a sucker for slicer-dicer-chopper-juicer gizmos and gadgets demonstrated in booths at county and state fairs.

Walter never got over his fascination for new machinery. He made the rounds, checking on the latest machines at local dealerships and collecting brochures and pamphlets from machinery displays at fairs and equipment shows. With the advent of self-propelled grain combines, he predicted someday there'd be a similar machine that would harvest corn, pick it and shell it right in the field, so it could be trucked straight to town to the grain elevator. In the fall of 1963, when the first cornpicker-sheller rolled out of the machine shed and roared off toward the field guided by its own headlights on a dark autumn morning, Walter was right on the spot to see it cut through the rows—four at a time!

He reveled in the years spent plowing, harrowing and cultivating side by side in the same field with his son and grandsons until 1964. He was sixty-five and he no longer wanted to be the first one up and out in the field on a tractor in the morning or the last one to switch off an irrigation well and go to bed at night. He never quit farming; he just cut back.

In the spring of 1974, after he had already prepared the soil and done all of the ground work for that year's crops on Miss Smith's farm, a massive heart attack struck him down as he walked across the yard late one afternoon in May.

# APPETIZERS

## CRAB or CLAM DIP
Take your choice, crab or clam—

1 8-ounce package cream cheese, softened
1 tablespoon mayonnaise
1 teaspoon lemon juice
1 teaspoon onion salt
1/2 teaspoon garlic salt
1/8 teaspoon Worcestershire sauce
Dash of Tabasco sauce
1 6-1/2-ounce can of cooked crab or clams, drained well

In a medium bowl, combine cheese, mayonnaise, lemon juice, onion and garlic salts, Worcestershire sauce and Tabasco sauce; blend thoroughly. Stir in crab or clams. Serve with assorted crackers. Makes 2 cups.

## DAZZLE DIP
For dipping chips, crackers or fresh vegetables—

1 6-ounce jar of pimento cream cheese
1/2 cup sour cream
1/2 teaspoon paprika
1/4 teaspoon Tabasco sauce
1/2 teaspoon Worcestershire sauce
1/2 teaspoon salt
1/4 cup catsup
1/3 cup seeded and minced cucumber
1/3 cup finely chopped celery
1/4 cup finely chopped green pepper

In a medium bowl, combine cream cheese, sour cream, paprika, Tabasco sauce and Worcestershire sauce, salt and catsup. Refrigerate 2 to 3 hours to allow flavors to blend. At serving time, stir in cucumber, celery and green pepper. Makes 2 cups.

# BEVERAGES

## AUTUMN GOLD PUNCH
Served at our fiftieth wedding anniversary reception—

2 12-ounce cans apricot nectar
1-1/2 cups orange juice
3/4 cup lemon juice
1-1/2 quarts sweet apple cider

In a three-quart pitcher or container, combine nectar, orange and lemon juice and cider. Stir to blend thoroughly. Pour over ice ring in a chilled punch bowl. Makes 15 6-ounce servings.

## CRANBERRY PUNCH
For Christmas—

1 46-ounce can grapefruit juice
1 46-ounce can pineapple juice
6 16-ounce bottles cranberry juice
2 28-ounce bottles gingerale

Chill juices and gingerale several hours in refrigerator. Pour over ice block or ring in a chilled punch bowl. Makes 40 6-ounce servings.

## PINK PUNCH
It's frosty and it's pretty—

4 8-ounce bottles strawberry soda pop
1 cup sugar
1/2 cup water
1 cup orange juice
1 cup pineapple juice
1/2 cup concentrated lemon juice
3 quarts gingerale

Pour soda pop into ice cube trays and freeze until slushy. In a small saucepan, combine sugar and water and boil until sugar is completely dissolved. Set aside to cool. Add orange, pineapple and lemon juices. To serve, place slushy cubes of soda pop in a chilled punch bowl. In a large container, combine juice mixture with gingerale and pour over soda pop cubes. Makes 24 6-ounce servings.

## SPICED TEA
Hot tea for a large group—

12 cups boiling water
6 whole cloves
6 teaspoons allspice
12 teaspoons black tea leaves
4 6-ounce cans frozen orange juice
3 6-ounce cans frozen *lemon juice*, do not use lemonade
4-1/2 cups sugar
12 quarts boiling water

In a large coffee pot or saucepan, pour 12 cups boiling water over cloves, allspice and tea. Steep 15 minutes. Add undiluted orange and lemon juice, sugar and 12 quarts of boiling water. Stir to blend thoroughly. Serve immediately. Serves 50.

## RHUBARB PUNCH
Sparkling punch with a refreshing nip—

8 cups diced rhubarb
5 cups water
2 cups sugar
Pinch of salt
About 1 cup sugar
1 6-ounce can frozen orange juice
3 ounces, half of a 6-ounce can, frozen lemonade
1 quart 7-UP
1 quart gingerale

In a medium saucepan, combine rhubarb, water, 2 cups of sugar and salt. Simmer until rhubarb is very soft and mushy. Strain. Measure liquid and add 1/3 cup of sugar for each cup of liquid. In a large saucepan, cook over medium heat until sugar dissolves. Cool. Add undiluted orange juice and lemonade; blend thoroughly. Pour into ice cube trays or ring molds and freeze. To serve, place frosty slush in chilled punch bowl and pour over equal parts of 7-UP and gingerale. Serves 16 to 20.

# BREADS

### ANGEL BISCUITS
Easy to make, good to eat—dough can be refrigerated for up to three days—

2-1/2 cups flour
1 teaspoon baking powder
1 teaspoon salt
1/2 cup sugar
1/2 cup shortening
1 package dry yeast
1/4 cup warm water
1/4 teaspoon sugar
Dash of ginger
1 cup buttermilk

In a large bowl, combine flour, baking powder, salt and 1/2 cup sugar. Add shortening; cut into flour mixture with a pastry blender until mixture resembles coarse cornmeal. In a small bowl, dissolve yeast in warm water to which 1/4 teaspoon sugar and ginger have been added. Set aside 5 minutes. Add buttermilk to flour mixture along with yeast mixture; blend thoroughly. At this point, dough may be covered and refrigerated or the process may continue on through baking. If that is the case, preheat oven to 400 degrees F. Grease a cookie sheet. Turn dough out onto a lightly floured board or pastry cloth. Cover with inverted bowl; let rest 5 minutes. Knead gently 5 or 6 times, then roll out until 1/2-inch thick. Use a 1-1/2 to 2-inch round cookie cutter to cut biscuits. Place on prepared cookie sheet. Cover; let rise 20 to 30 minutes until biscuits are light but not quite double in bulk. If dough has been refrigerated, it will take biscuits a little longer to rise. Bake 15 minutes or until biscuits are lightly browned and test done. Makes 18 biscuits.

## BASIC SWEET DOUGH

One dough made with the help of an electric mixer can be turned into many different sweet breads—

1-1/2 packages of dry yeast
1/4 cup warm water
1/4 teaspoon sugar
Dash of ginger
1/4 cup margarine
1 tablespoon shortening
1/4 cup sugar
1 teaspoon salt
1 cup milk, scalded
1 egg, well beaten
3-1/2 to 4 cups flour

In a small bowl, dissolve yeast in warm water to which 1/4 teaspoon sugar and ginger have been added. Set aside 5 minutes. In a large bowl, combine margarine, shortening, sugar and salt. Add scalded milk; stir to dissolve sugar and salt and blend melted margarine and shortening. Set aside to cool to lukewarm. Add yeast mixture, egg and 2 cups flour. Combine ingredients at low speed then beat at high speed *1 minute.* Use a spoon to stir in 1 cup flour to make a *very soft dough.* Gently ease dough out onto a floured board or pastry cloth. Cover with inverted bowl; let rest 10 minutes. Gently knead in only as much of the remaining flour as is needed to make a smooth yet a very soft dough. Place dough in a well-greased bowl; turn to grease surface. Cover; let rise until double in bulk. Punch down and turn out onto lightly floured board or pastry cloth. Cover with inverted bowl; let rest 5 minutes before making out into Cinnamon Twists, Crispies, *Kulich, Kolaches* or a Tea Ring.

## CINNAMON TWISTS

Half of Basic Sweet Dough
1/2 cup margarine, softened
1/2 cup sugar
1 teaspoon cinnamon

Preheat oven to 375 degrees F. Grease two cookie sheets generously. Roll dough out to make a 10 x 14-inch rectangle 1/2-inch thick. Spread dough with softened margarine. In a small bowl, combine sugar and cinnamon. Sprinkle over margarine. Fold the long sides of the rectangle together so they overlap down the center to form a 3 x 14-inch rectangle. Press and pinch edges together to seal. Use a knife to cut rectangle into 3/4-inch crosswise slices. Twist each slice 2 times and place on prepared cookie sheet. Do not crowd rolls; allow 2 inches between slices. Cover lightly; let rise until double in bulk. Bake 15 minutes or until rolls are lightly browned and test done. Makes 18 rolls.

## CRISPIES

Half of Basic Sweet Dough
1/2 cup margarine, softened
1/2 cup sugar
1 teaspoon cinnamon
1/2 cup chopped walnuts

Preheat oven to 375 degrees F. Grease a cookie sheet generously. Roll dough out to a 12 x 20-inch rectangle. Spread dough with softened margarine. In a small bowl, combine sugar and cinnamon; reserve one-third of the mixture. Sprinkle two-thirds of the sugar-cinnamon mixture and walnuts over margarine. Start with a long side of the rectangle and roll up as for a jelly roll. Use a knife to cut dough crosswise into inch slices. Dip slices in reserved sugar-cinnamon mixture. Cover each slice with waxed paper and roll until it is about 1/8-inch thick. Place flattened slices on prepared cookie sheet. Cover lightly; let rise until double in bulk. Bake 10 to 12 minutes until rolls are crisp, lightly browned and test done. Makes 20 rolls.

## *KULICH*
Bake in a 1-pound coffee can—

Cut off a piece of dough half the size of the coffee can and to
    that amount of dough, add the following:
1/4 cup golden raisins
1/4 cup chopped walnuts
1/2 teaspoon vanilla
1 tablespoon tiny, multi-colored sugar candies

Preheat oven to 350 degrees F. Grease one-pound coffee can generously. In a small bowl, "plump" raisins by covering with boiling water for 5 minutes. Drain thoroughly on paper towels. Knead dough on a lightly floured board or pastry cloth. Knead in raisins, walnuts and vanilla until evenly distributed. Place dough in prepared can. Cover; let rise until the dough reaches top of can. Bake 30 minutes or until bread is golden brown and tests done. Remove bread from can and while it is still warm, frost with a thin powdered sugar icing and immediately sprinkle with colored sugar candies. Makes 1 loaf.

## TEA RING

Half of Basic Sweet Dough
1/2 cup sugar
1 teaspoon cinnamon
1/2 cup margarine, melted
1/2 cup raisins *or*
1 cup cooked, pitted, sweetened, dried prunes *or*
1 cup cooked, sweetened, dried apricots
1/4 cup red or green candied cherry halves

Preheat oven to 375 degrees F. Grease a cookie sheet. Roll dough out into an oblong 1/2-inch thick. In a cup combine sugar and cinnamon. Brush dough with melted margarine; sprinkle with sugar-cinnamon mixture and top with raisins *or* prune *or* apricot filling. See Page 55 for recipes. Start with a long side of the oblong and roll up as for a jelly roll. Place rolled dough on prepared cookie sheet and shape into a circle. Join ends and pinch edges together to seal. Use sharp kitchen shears or a knife to cut *almost* through rolled dough at 2-inch intervals. Separate and twist sliced sections slightly so cut sides are up. Cover lightly; let rise until double in bulk. Bake 25 minutes or until bread is golden brown and tests done. Remove to a cooling rack and glaze with a thin powdered sugar icing. Decorate with red or green candied cherry halves. Makes 1 ring.

## KOLACHES

One *full* recipe of Basic Sweet Dough

Fillings:
2 cups dried prunes, cooked, pitted, sweetened and pureed
2 cups dried apricots, cooked, sweetened and pureed
1 cup poppy seeds, ground, cooked, sweetened and flavored

Topping: (optional)
1 cup cottage cheese, fine curd, *not creamed style*
1/4 cup sugar
1/2 teaspoon cinnamon

Preheat oven to 425 degrees F. Grease three cookie sheets. Use hands to gently press dough out until it is 1/2-inch thick. Use a knife to cut off small pieces of dough about the size of a golf ball. Lightly roll dough pieces between the palms of the hands to smooth. Place balls 2 inches apart on prepared cookie sheets. Cover lightly; let rise until double in bulk. While dough rises make topping. In a small bowl, combine cottage cheese, sugar and cinnamon; blend thoroughly. Set aside. With the first two fingers of each hand, make an indentation in the center of each ball and gently flatten and spread dough slightly to form a shallow hole. Fill with prune, apricot or poppy seed fillings—fillings should be at room temperature. Use canned commercial fillings or see Page 55 for filling recipes. Top with 1/2 teaspoon of cottage cheese topping. Cover lightly; let rise until double in bulk. Bake 12 to 15 minutes until rolls are lightly browned and test done. Makes 3 dozen.

## BUTTERMILK RAISIN BREAD
Smells so - o - o - o good while it's baking—

1-1/2 cups buttermilk or
9 tablespoons dried buttermilk reconstituted with 1-1/2 cups
   water and mixed thoroughly
1 package dry yeast
1/4 cup warm water
1/4 teaspoon sugar
Dash of ginger
1/2 cup margarine
1-1/2 teaspoons salt
1/3 cup sugar
1 teaspoon baking soda
2 eggs, well beaten
1 cup dark, seedless raisins
5 to 5-1/2 cups flour
2 tablespoons margarine, melted

Measure buttermilk into top of a double boiler and scald over boiling water. In a small bowl, dissolve yeast in warm water to which 1/4 teaspoon sugar and ginger have been added. Set aside 5 minutes. In a large bowl, pour hot buttermilk over margarine, salt, 1/3 cup sugar and baking soda; stir until margarine melts. Cool to lukewarm. Stir in eggs, yeast mixture, raisins and 2 cups flour; beat vigorously. Gradually add only as much of remaining flour as is needed to form a soft dough that cleans the bowl. Turn dough out onto a well-floured board or pastry cloth. Cover with inverted bowl; let rest 10 minutes. Knead gently for a few minutes. Place dough in a well-greased bowl; turn to grease surface. Cover; let rise until double in bulk, about 1-1/2 hours. Grease two 9 x 5 x 3-inch loaf pans generously. Punch dough down, turn out onto floured board or pastry cloth. Cover with inverted bowl; let rest 5 minutes. Divide in half, shape into loaves and place in prepared pans. Cover; let rise until light and almost double in bulk, about an hour. Preheat oven to 350 degrees F. Bake 45 to 60 minutes or until loaves are golden brown and test done. Turned baked loaves out of pans onto cooling racks and brush tops with melted margarine. Makes 2 loaves.

## GERMAN SOUR CREAM TWISTS
A crispy, sweet treat—

1 package dry yeast
1/4 cup warm water
1/4 teaspoon sugar
Dash of ginger
3-1/2 cups flour
1 teaspoon salt
1/2 cup shortening
1/2 cup margarine
3/4 cup sour cream
1 whole egg
2 egg yolks
1 teaspoon vanilla
1 cup sugar

In a small bowl, dissolve yeast in warm water to which 1/4 teaspoon sugar and ginger have been added. Set aside 5 minutes. In a large bowl, combine flour and salt. Use a pastry blender to cut in shortening and margarine until mixture resembles coarse cornmeal. In a small bowl, beat whole egg and yolks together. Add to flour-salt mixture along with sour cream and vanilla. Use a spoon to blend thoroughly, then beat hard until large bubbles rise and burst on the surface. Cover bowl with a damp cloth and refrigerate 2 hours. Preheat oven to 375 degrees F. Have *ungreased cookie sheets* at hand. Punch dough down and while dough is still in the bowl, divide in half. Sprinkle board or pastry cloth lightly with sugar and roll out each portion of dough to form an 8 x 16-inch rectangle. Fold long sides of rectangle toward center, overlapping the sides. Sprinkle lightly with half of sugar and again, roll dough out, fold in long sides and sprinkle with remaining sugar. Roll folded dough out one more time until it is about 1/4-inch thick then cut crosswise into 1 x 4-inch strips. Twist ends of each strip in opposite directions, stretching slightly; place on cookie sheets in the shape of a horseshoe; press ends down onto cookie slightly to help dough holds its shape. *Bake as soon as rolls are shaped.* Bake 15 minutes or until rolls are delicately browned and test done. Remove twists from cookie sheets to cooling racks immediately. Makes 4 dozen.

## NO-KNEAD ICEBOX ROLLS
Dough may be refrigerated up to two weeks—

2 cups boiling water
3/4 cup sugar
1 heaping teaspoon salt
1/4 cup margarine
1 package dry yeast
1/4 cup warm water
1/4 teaspoon sugar
Dash of ginger
2 eggs, well beaten
7 cups flour

In a large bowl, pour boiling water over sugar, salt and margarine. Cool to lukewarm. In a small bowl, dissolve yeast in 1/4 cup water to which 1/4 teaspoon sugar and ginger have been added. Set aside 5 minutes. Add yeast mixture, eggs and *2 cups* flour to sugar-margarine mixture; beat hard until large bubbles rise and burst on the surface. Add only as much of remaining flour as is needed to form a *very soft* dough. Cover and refrigerate. Dough should be refrigerated several hours or overnight before it is used the first time and it may be refrigerated up to two weeks. To use, preheat oven to 375 degrees F. Grease cookie sheets or baking pans, whichever is appropriate according to the kind of rolls to be made. Punch dough down and remove the amount of dough needed to make dinner rolls or sweet rolls. Turn dough out onto lightly floured board or pastry cloth. Cover with inverted bowl; let rest 10 minutes. Shape rolls and place in prepared pans. Cover; let rise until double in bulk. Since dough is chilled, allow 1-1/2 to 2 hours for rising. Follow baking time and temperature suitable for rolls baked in muffin pans, on cookie sheets or in a baking pan. This dough is too soft to be shaped into bread loaves. Makes 3 dozen.

## KELLOGG'S BRAN ROLLS

Extra special, light and nutritious dinner rolls that freeze beautifully—

2 packages dry yeast
1 cup warm water
1/4 teaspoon sugar
Dash of ginger
1 cup Kellogg's All-Bran cereal
6 tablespoons margarine
6 tablespoons shortening
3/4 cup sugar
1-1/2 teaspoons salt
1 cup boiling water
2 eggs, well beaten
6 cups flour
1/2 cup margarine, melted

In a small bowl, dissolve yeast in warm water to which 1/4 teaspoon of sugar and ginger have been added. Set aside 5 minutes. In a large bowl, combine bran, margarine, shortening, 3/4 cup sugar and salt. Pour boiling water over. Stir to dissolve sugar and melt margarine and shortening. Cool to lukewarm. Add yeast mixture, eggs and 2 cups of flour; beat well. Gradually add only as much of remaining flour as is needed to form a soft dough. Turn dough out onto lightly floured board or pastry cloth. Cover with inverted bowl; let rest 10 minutes. Knead 5 or 6 minutes or until dough is smooth. Place in a well-greased bowl; turn to grease surface. Cover; let rise until double in bulk. Preheat oven to 425 degrees F. Grease two 9 x 13-inch baking pans. Turn dough out onto lightly floured board or pastry cloth. Cover with inverted bowl; let rest 5 minutes. Divide dough in half. Roll each portion out until it is 1/4-inch thick. Use a 3-1/4-inch round cutter to cut rolls. Brush half of each dough circle with melted margarine and fold over the other half, pinching edges to seal. Place half circles of dough in prepared pan in three lengthwise rows, eight rolls in each row, and with all the folded edges facing the same direction. Cover; let rise until double in bulk. Bake 12 minutes or until rolls are light golden brown and test done. Turn rolls out of pan onto cooling rack immediately and brush tops with melted margarine. Makes 4 dozen.

## NINETY-MINUTE ROLLS
Short order rolls—

1/2 cup milk
2 tablespoons sugar
2 tablespoons margarine
1 package dry yeast
1/4 cup warm water
1/4 teaspoon sugar
Dash of ginger
1 egg, well beaten
3 to 3 1/2 cups flour
2 tablespoons margarine, melted
1/2 cup raisins
1/4 cup sugar
1/2 teaspoon cinnamon

Grease a 10-inch round baking pan. In a small saucepan, heat milk *just until steam begins to rise; do not scald.* Add sugar and margarine. Stir to dissolve sugar and melt margarine. Cool to lukewarm. In a small bowl, dissolve yeast in warm water to which 1/4 teaspoon sugar and ginger have been added. Set aside 5 minutes. In a large bowl, combine milk-sugar-margarine mixture and yeast mixture. Add egg and 1 cup flour; beat vigorously. Stir in only as much of remaining flour as is needed to make a *very soft* dough. Turn dough out onto lightly-floured board or pastry cloth. Cover with inverted bowl; let rest 10 minutes. Knead 2 minutes. Roll dough out into a rectangle that is 1/2-inch thick. In a cup, combine 1/4 cup sugar and cinnamon. Brush dough with melted margarine and sprinkle with raisins and sugar-cinnamon mixture. Start with a long side and roll dough up as for a jelly roll; pinch cut edges to seal. Use a knife to cut roll into 12 equal slices and place slices, cut side up, in prepared pan. Cover; let rise until rolls are light and almost double in bulk, about 45 to 60 minutes. Preheat oven to 375 degrees F. Bake 25 to 30 minutes until rolls are lightly browned and test done. Turned rolls onto cooling rack and while they are still warm, frost with a powdered sugar icing. Makes 1 dozen.

## RYE BREAD
Can be shaped into loaves or dinner rolls—

2 packages dry yeast
1 quart warm water
1 teaspoon sugar
Dash of ginger
4 cups flour
4 tablespoons melted shortening
1 cup brown sugar
4 tablespoons molasses
Pinch of baking soda
1 tablespoon salt
3 cups rye flour
1 tablespoon anise seed
5 to 6 cups flour

In a large bowl, dissolve yeast in warm water to which a teaspoon of sugar and ginger have been added. Set aside 5 minutes. Add 4 cups flour; mix vigorously. Set aside *45 minutes* after which time mixture will be bubbly. In a small saucepan, combine shortening, brown sugar, molasses and baking soda. Heat just until warm, *do not allow to boil*. Add to yeast-flour mixture along with salt, rye flour, anise seed and only as much of remaining white flour as is needed to make a soft dough. Turn dough out onto lightly-floured board or pastry cloth. Cover with inverted bowl; let rest 10 minutes. Knead until smooth and firm, about 10 minutes. Place in well-greased bowl; turn to grease surface. Cover; let rise until double in bulk, about an hour. Punch dough down. Cover; let rise until *almost* double in bulk, about 40 to 45 minutes. Preheat oven to 350 degrees F. for loaves or 375 degrees for rolls. Grease generously four 9 x 5 x 3-inch loaf pans if making bread or three 9 x 12-inch baking pans if making rolls. Turn dough out onto lightly-floured board or pastry cloth and shape. Cover; let rise until double in bulk, about 30 minutes. Bake loaves 45 to 50 minutes or until bread is a rich brown color and tests done. Bake rolls 15 to 18 minutes or until they are a rich brown color and test done. Makes 4 loaves or 5 to 6 dozen rolls.

## WHOLE WHEAT BREAD
The best whole wheat bread ever—

2 packages dry yeast
1/2 cup warm water
1/4 cup packed brown sugar
Dash of ginger
2-1/2 cups warm water
1/2 cup packed brown sugar
4 cups flour
4 teaspoons salt
1 cup hot water
1/2 cup margarine, melted
8 cups whole wheat flour

In a large bowl, dissolve yeast in 1/2 cup warm water to which 1/4 cup brown sugar and ginger have been added. Set aside 5 minutes. Add 2-1/2 cups warm water, 1/2 cup brown sugar, 4 cups flour and salt. Beat until smooth. Cover; let rise until light and double in bulk. Stir down. Add 1 cup hot water, margarine and only as much of whole wheat flour as is needed to make a very soft yet a kneadable dough. Turn dough out onto lightly-floured board or pastry cloth. Cover with inverted bowl; let rest 10 minutes. Knead until smooth, 5 or 6 minutes. Place dough in well-greased bowl; turn to grease surface. Cover; let rise until double in bulk. Punch dough down and turn onto well-floured board or pastry cloth. Grease generously three 9 x 5 x 3-inch loaf pans. Divide dough into thirds; shape each portion into a loaf and place in prepared pans. Cover lightly; let rise until *almost* double in bulk. Preheat oven to 350 degrees F. Bake 30 to 35 minutes or until loaves are golden brown and test done. Makes 3 loaves.

# QUICK BREADS

## BANANA BREAD
Just *banana* banana bread, without nuts—

1-3/4 cup flour
2 teaspoons baking powder
1/4 teaspoon baking soda
1/2 teaspoon salt
1/3 cup shortening
2/3 cup sugar
2 eggs
1 cup mashed ripe banana, 3 medium bananas

Preheat oven to 350 degrees F. Grease a 9 x 5 x 3-inch loaf pan. Sift flour, baking powder, baking soda and salt together. In a large bowl, cream shortening and sugar until light and fluffy. Add eggs; beat well. Add flour mixture alternately with bananas; start and end with dry ingredients. Beat well after each addition. Pour into prepared pan. Bake 1 hour and 10 minutes or until loaf is golden brown and tests done. Makes 1 loaf.

## BUTTERMILK CARAWAY RAISIN BREAD
Delicious! With a subtle yet distinctive caraway flavor—

2-1/2 cups raisins, plumped 5 minutes in boiling water to cover
5 cups sifted flour
1 cup sugar
1 teaspoon baking soda
1 tablespoon baking powder
1-1/2 teaspoons salt
1/2 cup butter or margarine
3 tablespoons caraway seeds
2-1/2 cups buttermilk
1 egg, slightly beaten

Preheat oven to 350 degrees F. Grease generously an 11-inch round oven-proof skillet or dutch oven; heavy cast iron is best. In a small bowl, "plump" raisins by covering with boiling water for 5 minutes. Drain thoroughly on paper towels. In a large bowl, sift flour, sugar, baking soda, baking powder and salt together. Use a pastry blender to cut in butter until mixture resembles coarse cornmeal. Stir in raisins and caraway seeds. Combine buttermilk and egg. Add to dry ingredients. Blend only until mixture is well-moistened; mixture will appear lumpy. Put into prepared pan. Bake 1 hour or until bread is golden brown and tests done. Makes 1 loaf.

## CRANBERRY SOUR CREAM COFFEE CAKE
For Christmas breakfast or a holiday brunch—

1 cup margarine
3 eggs, separated
1 cup sugar
1 cup sour cream
1-3/4 cups sifted flour
1 teaspoon baking soda
1 teaspoon baking powder
1/2 teaspoon salt
1 cup chopped cranberries
1 tablespoon margarine

Topping:
1/4 cup sugar
1/2 teaspoon cinnamon
1/2 cup chopped walnuts

Preheat oven to 325 degrees F. Grease a Bundt pan generously and lightly dust with flour. In a large bowl, cream margarine and sugar until light and fluffy. Add egg yolks and sour cream; beat until light and fluffy. Sift flour, baking soda, baking powder and salt together. Fold into creamed mixture; beat hard 1 minute. Fold in cranberries. Pour into prepared pan and sprinkle with topping. To make topping: In a small bowl, combine 1/4 cup sugar, cinnamon and walnuts. Dot with 1 tablespoon margarine.Bake 1 hour or until cake tests done. Cool cake in pan 15 minutes before turning out onto cooling rack. Serves 12.

## VIENNA WALTZ COFFEE CAKE

Get ready for the compliments and requests for the recipe—

5 tablespoons margarine
2/3 cup sugar
2 eggs
1 teaspoon vanilla
1-1/2 cups flour
3/4 teaspoon baking soda
1/2 teaspoon baking powder
1/2 teaspoon salt
1 cup sour cream

Preheat oven to 325 degrees F. Grease and lightly flour a 9-inch square cake pan. In a large bowl, cream margarine and sugar until light and fluffy. Add eggs, one at a time. Beat well after each addition. Add vanilla. Sift flour, baking soda, baking powder and salt together. Add alternately with sour cream; start and end with dry ingredients. Beat well after each addition. Spread batter gently into prepared pan. Bake 40 minutes or until cake tests done. Cool cake in pan 5 minutes before turning out onto cooling rack.

While cake cools, prepare filling and topping.

Filling:
1 3-1/4-ounce package *instant* coconut pudding
1 cup milk
1 teaspoon freshly grated lemon peel
1/4 cup margarine, softened but *not melted*

Prepare pudding according to directions on package, using *1 cup of milk*. Stir in lemon peel. Chill. Cream margarine until it is very soft and light and gradually blend into chilled pudding. Reserve 1/4 cup of filling.

Topping:
1/4 cup flour
1/4 cup brown sugar
1/2 teaspoon cinnamon
2 tablespoons margarine

In a small bowl, combine flour, brown sugar, cinnamon and margarine with a fork until mixture resembles tiny peas. Cool cake completely then split in half horizontally and place bottom half on plate. Spread with the *larger portion* of the filling and replace top half of cake. Spread with reserved 1/4 cup of pudding. Sprinkle with topping and refrigerate. Serves 10 to 12.


## GOLDEN RAISIN TEA BREAD

Spread with cream cheese to make dainty, delicately flavored sandwiches—

1 cup golden seedless raisins
Boiling water to cover
Juice of one medium orange plus enough boiling water to make 1 cup
2 cups flour
1/4 teaspoon salt
1 teaspoon baking powder
1/2 teaspoon baking soda
1 cup sugar
2 tablespoons melted margarine
1 teaspoon vanilla
1 egg, well beaten
1/2 cup finely chopped pecans

Preheat oven to 350 degrees F. Grease a 9 x 5 x 3-inch loaf pan. In a small bowl, "plump" raisins by covering with boiling water for 5 minutes. Drain thoroughly on paper towels. Add boiling water to orange juice to make 1 cup. Set aside to cool. Combine flour, salt, baking powder, baking soda and sugar. Sift together into a large bowl. Combine orange juice-water mixture, margarine, vanilla and beaten egg and add to dry ingredients all at one time. Mix just until dry ingredients are well-moistened. Fold in raisins and nuts; blend thoroughly. Pour into prepared pan. Bake 1 hour or until bread is browned and tests done. Makes 1 loaf.

## FRESH CRANBERRY MUFFINS

Tart and tasty triumphs for a holiday breakfast, brunch or coffee party—

1 cup halved fresh cranberries
3 tablespoons sugar
2 cups sifted flour
3/4 cup sugar
2 teaspoons baking powder
1/2 teaspoon baking soda
3/4 teaspoon salt
1/2 cup chopped walnuts
1 teaspoon freshly grated orange peel
1 egg, well beaten
1/2 cup freshly squeezed orange juice
1/4 cup melted margarine
1/4 cup milk

Preheat oven to 425 degrees F. Grease generously a 12-muffin muffin pan. In a small bowl, sprinkle cranberry halves with 3 tablespoons sugar. Set aside. Combine flour, 3/4 cup sugar, baking powder, baking soda and salt. Sift together into a large bowl. Add cranberries, walnuts and orange peel; blend thoroughly. Combine egg, orange juice, margarine and milk. Add to flour mixture all at one time. Mix just until dry ingredients are well-moistened. Spoon into prepared muffin pan; fill cups two-thirds full. Bake 18 to 20 minutes or until muffins are lightly browned and test done. Cool muffins in pan 5 minutes before removing. Serve hot. Makes 12.

## FRESH BLUEBERRY MUFFINS

Summer "blues," a hot bread to go with salads—

3/4 cup blueberries
2 cups flour
1/2 teaspoon salt
3 teaspoons baking powder
2 tablespoons sugar
3/4 cup milk
1 egg, well beaten
3 tablespoons margarine, melted

Preheat oven to 400 degrees F. Grease generously a 12-muffin muffin pan. Rinse blueberries; dry on paper towels. Combine flour, salt, baking powder and sugar. Sift together into a large bowl. Combine milk, egg and margarine. Add to flour mixture all at one time. Stir just until dry ingredients are well-moistened. Fold in blueberries. Spoon into prepared muffin pan; fill cups two-thirds full. Bake 25 minutes or until muffins are lightly browned and test done. Cool muffins in pan 5 minutes before removing. Serve hot. Makes 12.

## MASTER MIX

On the very same day this Nebraska State Extension Service recipe was presented as the lesson for Buffalo County Extension Club members, I went home, made a batch of the mix and it's been a stand-by in my freezer ever since. With measuring and cutting-in already done—both time-consuming steps in many quick bread recipes—this mix not only saves a lot of preparation time but it also lets the cook choose *when* those steps are done. It can be used like any commercial biscuit mix to make biscuits, shortcakes, muffins, pancakes, waffles, or nut bread or coffee cake by adding a liquid, egg, flavoring, nuts or fruits. The cook is limited only by her imagination.

Grocery store shelves are lined with a variety of commercial baking mixes, I know, but there are at least five very good reasons for making your own mix. One, you know exactly what ingredients are in the mix; two, you know they are fresh; three, you know there are no preservatives in it; four, it's there, you don't have to run to the store to get it; and, five, it costs less. If the mix is made with a commercial vegetable shortening that does not require refrigeration, the mix can be stored in an airtight container on a cupboard or pantry shelf for a week or two or it can also be stored in the refrigerator three months. I prefer to keep it in the freezer where it can be stored for as long as a year. I say "can" because, quite frankly, I use Master Mix so often, I've never had a batch last that long; my Master Mix container gets a refill once, sometimes twice a month.

## MASTER MIX

9 cups sifted flour
1/4 cup baking powder
1 tablespoon salt
1 cup dry whole milk powder
2 teaspoons cream of tartar
2 cups shortening

In a *large* bowl, combine flour, baking powder, salt, milk powder and cream of tartar. Stir to blend thoroughly then sift mixture together *3 times.* Use a pastry blender to cut in shortening until mixture look like coarse cornmeal. Store in an air-tight container; keeps three months in refrigerator and a year in freezer. NOTE: Since Master Mix is made with dry milk powder, when it is used, it can be prepared by adding only water, however, I prefer to add whole, fresh milk which yields a richer, lighter dough.

## BISCUITS
### Made with Master Mix—

3 cups Master Mix
3/4 cup milk

Preheat oven to 450 degrees F. Have ungreased cookie sheet at hand. Measure Master Mix into a bowl. Add milk. *Stir with a fork just until mix is well-moistened—no more than 10 strokes.* Turn dough out onto a lightly floured board or pastry cloth. Knead gently 10 times. Use fingers to gently pat dough out until it is 1/2-inch thick. Cut with a 2-inch biscuit or round cookie cutter. Place biscuits 1/2-inch apart on cookie sheet. Bake 10 to 12 minutes or until biscuit tops are golden brown and test done. Makes 24.

## SHORTCAKE NUMBER ONE
### Made with Master Mix—

2 cups Master Mix
1/4 cup sugar
2/3 cup light cream, Half and Half

Preheat oven to 425 degrees F. Have ungreased cookie sheet at hand. Measure Master Mix into a bowl. Stir in sugar. Add cream. *Stir with a fork just until mix is well-moistened—no more than 10 strokes.* Turn dough out onto a lightly floured board or pastry cloth. Knead gently 10 times. Use fingers to gently pat dough out until it is *3/4-inch thick* and cut with a 2-1/2-inch round cutter. Place shortcakes 3/4-inch apart on cookie sheet. Bake 10 to 12 minutes or until shortcake tops are golden brown and test done. Makes 8.

## SHORTCAKE NUMBER TWO
A softer, richer shortcake—

2 cups Master Mix
1/4 cup sugar
3 tablespoons melted margarine
1/2 cup milk

Preheat oven to 425 degrees F. Have ungreased cookie sheet at hand. Measure Master Mix into a bowl. Stir in sugar. Combine melted margarine and milk. Add to dry ingredients. *Stir with a fork just until mix is well-moistened—no more than 10 strokes.* Turn dough out onto a lightly floured board or pastry cloth. Knead gently 10 times. Use fingers to gently pat dough out until it is *3/4-inch thick* and cut with a 2-1/2-inch round cutter. Place shortcakes 3/4-inch apart on cookie sheet. Bake 10 to 12 minutes or until shortcake tops are golden brown and test done. Makes 8.

## SHORT-CUT SHORTCAKE
Made with Master Mix, these shortcakes are every bit as good as made-from-scratch biscuit shortcakes—

2-1/4 cups Master Mix
1/2 cup sugar
3/4 cup milk
1/4 cup melted margarine
Option: Substitute 1 cup light cream, Half and Half, for milk and margarine

Preheat oven to 400 degrees F. Have an ungreased cookie sheet at hand. Measure mix into a large bowl. Add sugar; blend thoroughly. Combine milk and margarine. Make a hole in center of dry ingredients. Add milk-margarine mixture all at one time. Use a fork to stir just until dry ingredients are moistened. Turn dough out onto a board or pastry cloth which has been *lightly* dusted with a few tablespoons of Master Mix. Knead gently 4 or 5 times. With a 2-1/2-inch round cutter, cut eight shortcakes. Place shortcakes 1/2-inch apart on cookie sheet. Bake 12 to 15 minutes or until shortcakes are lightly browned and test done. Makes 8.

## MUFFINS
Made with Master Mix—

3 cups Master Mix
3 tablespoons sugar
1 cup milk
1 egg, well beaten

Preheat oven to 425 degrees F. Grease generously a 12-muffin muffin pan. In a large bowl, combine Master Mix and sugar. Combine milk and egg and add to dry ingredients. *Stir with a fork just until mix is well-moistened; do not stir until lumps disappear.* Spoon batter into prepared muffin pan; fill cups two-thirds full. Bake 18 to 20 minutes or until muffins are lightly browned and test done. Makes 12.

## NEVER FAIL NOODLES
Easy to make noodles that do not need to be dried and can be stored in freezer three months—

2 egg yolks
1 teaspoon softened margarine
2 tablespoons light cream, Half and Half
1/4 teaspoon salt
1/4 teaspoon baking powder
3/4 to 1-1/4 cups flour

In a medium bowl, beat egg yolks. Add margarine and cream; mix thoroughly. Add salt and baking powder and enough flour to make a soft dough which is not sticky; one that can be rolled out. Turn dough out onto lightly floured board or pastry cloth and roll out until it is very thin. Lightly fold rolled dough into flat, 3-inch wide turns. Use a sharp knife to cut folded dough crosswise into 1/8-inch wide strips. Noodles may be cooked immediately or packaged in plastic bags and stored in the freezer for up to three months. At cooking time, sift a very light dusting of flour over noodles before adding to boiling broth. Cook 10 minutes or until noodles are tender. Serves 4.

# CAKES

Angel food cakes call first for a heavy hand to beat egg whites to stiff peaks and then for a light hand to fold dry ingredients into the beaten eggs whites. Folding is a particularly crucial step. The action must be gentle but thorough, easy but firm and solid and it must be smooth and quick.

Never use accumulated egg whites leftover from other cooking and baking; use only freshly cracked and separated eggs. And a special reminder for country cooks who gather eggs fresh from the hen house—*eggs used to make an angel food cake should be at least three days old.*

## BROWN SUGAR ANGEL FOOD CAKE
An extra-ordinary cake with a delicate difference—

1-1/4 cups sifted cake flour
1 cup brown sugar, firmly packed
1-1/2 cups egg whites, whites from 12 to 14 eggs
1-1/2 teaspoons cream of tartar
1 teaspoon salt
1 cup brown sugar, firmly packed
2 teaspoons vanilla

Preheat oven to 350 degrees F. Have an ungreased 10-inch tube pan at hand. Combine cake flour and 1 cup brown sugar. In a large bowl, beat egg whites with cream of tartar and salt until foamy. Gradually add second cup of brown sugar. Continue to beat until stiff peaks form. Add vanilla; blend well. Divide flour-brown sugar mixture into four portions. Use a large rubber spatula to fold each portion in separately; gently lift meringue up and roll it over onto itself. Fold just until no traces of dry ingredients can be seen. Gently push batter into pan. With a long, sharp knife, make five or six vertical cuts through batter to get rid of large air pockets. Bake 45 minutes or until top of cake springs back after it is lightly touched with a finger. As soon as cake is removed from the oven, *immediately* invert pan. If pan does not have legs, place the center tube over the neck of a large, heavy bottle. *Do not remove from pan until cake is completely cool—takes at least an hour.* Dust with sifted powdered sugar or frost with a favorite icing. Serves 16.

## CHOCOLATE ANGEL FOOD CAKE
An unforgettable Angel Food Cake for chocolate lovers—

3/4 cup sifted cake flour
3/4 cup plus 2 tablespoons sugar
1/4 cup cocoa
1-1/2 cups egg whites, whites from 12 to 14 eggs
1-1/2 teaspoons cream of tartar
1/4 teaspoon salt
1-1/2 teaspoons vanilla
3/4 cup sugar

Preheat oven to 375 degrees F. Have an ungreased 10-inch tube pan at hand. Sift cake flour, 3/4 cup plus 2 tablespoons sugar and cocoa together 3 times. In a large bowl, beat egg whites, cream of tartar, salt and vanilla together until foamy—5 to 7 minutes with an electric mixer at high speed or 10 minutes with a rotary hand beater. Add 3/4 cup plus 2 tablespoons sugar, 2 tablespoons at a time. Beat hard *10 seconds* after each addition. After the last addition, beat hard until stiff, straight peaks form when beaters are lifted; beating in sugar may take a total of 10 minutes. Use a large rubber spatula to gradually fold in flour-sugar-cocoa mixture; gently lift meringue up and roll it over onto itself; fold until no traces of dry ingredients can be seen. Gently push batter into pan. With a long, sharp knife, make 5 or 6 vertical cuts through the batter to get rid of any large air pockets. Bake 30 to 35 minutes or until the top of the cake springs back after it is lightly touched with a finger. Remove cake from oven and *immediately* invert the pan. If the pan does not have legs, place the center tube over the neck of large, heavy bottle. *Do not remove cake from pan until the cake is completely cool—takes at least an hour.* Split cooled cake crosswise into 3 layers. Spread tops of layers and the sides of the cake with Chocolate Fluff.

Chocolate Fluff:
2/3 cup sifted powdered sugar
1/2 cup cocoa
1/8 teaspoon salt
2 cups whipping cream

Sift powdered sugar, cocoa and salt together. In a small *well-chilled bowl* and with *chilled* beaters, beat cream just until it is frothy. Gradually add dry ingredients. Beat at high speed until cream is whipped and frosting is of spreading consistency. Store frosted cake in the refrigerator. Serves 16.

## CHOCOLATE BUTTERMILK CAKE
The most delightfully delicate chocolate cake ever—

1 cup margarine
2-1/4 cups sugar
2 eggs
1 teaspoon vanilla
3 cups sifted cake flour
2 teaspoons baking soda
1/3 cup cocoa
1 teaspoon salt
2 cups buttermilk

Preheat oven to 350 degrees F. Generously grease three 8-inch or two 10-inch round cake pans. Lightly dust greased pans with a small amount of sifted cocoa. In a large bowl, cream margarine and sugar together until light and fluffy. Add eggs; beat thoroughly. Add vanilla; blend well. Sift cake flour, baking soda, cocoa and salt together. Add to creamed mixture alternately with buttermilk; start and end with dry ingredients. Beat well after each addition. Pour batter into prepared pans. Bake 25 to 30 minutes or until cake tests done. Cool cake in pans 10 minutes before turning out onto cooling racks. When cake is cool, spread Fluffy Filling between the layers and frost top and sides of the cake with a chocolate frosting.

Fluffy Filling:
1/4 cup margarine
3/4 cup sifted powdered sugar
1 scant tablespoon cocoa
1 egg

In a small bowl, combine margarine, powdered sugar, cocoa and egg. Beat at high speed until filling is fluffy and thick. Serves 16.

## COCONUT BUTTERMILK CAKE
A light, moist cake—

2-1/4 cups sifted cake flour
1-1/2 cups sugar
1/2 teaspoon salt
1 teaspoon baking soda
1 teaspoon baking powder
1/4 cup margarine
1/4 cup shortening
1 teaspoon coconut extract
1/4 teaspoon almond extract
1 cup buttermilk
4 egg whites, *unbeaten*

Preheat oven to 350 degrees F. Generously grease and lightly flour two round 8-inch cake pans. In a large bowl, sift together cake flour, sugar, salt, baking soda and baking powder. Add margarine, shortening, coconut extract, almond extract and 3/4 cup buttermilk. Beat at medium speed 2 minutes. Add remaining buttermilk and egg whites. Beat 2 minutes at medium speed. Pour batter into prepared pans. Bake 30 to 35 minutes or until cake tests done. Cool cake in pans 10 minutes before turning out onto cooling racks. When cake is completely cool, fill and frost with Coconut Icing.

Coconut Icing:
2 cups sifted powdered sugar
Dash of salt
1 teaspoon coconut extract
1/3 cup shortening
1 egg white, *unbeaten*
1 tablespoon hot water
1 7-ounce package of flaked coconut

In a small bowl, combine powdered sugar, salt, coconut extract, shortening, egg white and hot water. Beat at high speed until icing reaches spreading consistency. Fill and frost top and sides of cake. Before frosting sets, sprinkle top and sides of cake with flaked coconut. Serves 16.

## DEVIL'S FOOD CAKE
Another "Devil's" cake, this one's made with *hot* water—

2 1-ounce squares unsweetened chocolate
1 cup boiling water
1/2 cup milk
1/2 teaspoon cider vinegar
2 cups brown sugar
1/2 cup margarine
2 eggs, well beaten
2 teaspoons baking soda
2 cups sifted cake flour
1/4 teaspoon salt
1 teaspoon vanilla

Preheat oven to 350 degrees F. Grease two round 9-inch cake pans. Line pans with waxed paper; grease and lightly flour waxed paper also. In a small saucepan, dissolve chocolate in boiling water. Set aside to cool. In a small bowl, combine milk and vinegar. Set aside 5 minutes. In a large bowl, cream brown sugar and margarine until light and fluffy. Add eggs; beat well. Dissolve baking soda in sour milk. Sift flour and salt together. Add to creamed mixture alternately with milk mixture; start and end with dry ingredients. Beat well after each addition. Stir in chocolate-water mixture and vanilla; blend thoroughly. This is a *thin* batter. Pour into prepared pans. Bake 20-25 minutes or until cake tests done. Cool cake in pans 10 minutes before turning out onto cooling racks. When cake is cool, frost with a chocolate or fudge frosting. Serves 16.

## HEAVENLY WHITE CAKE
As light as a cloud—

1/2 cup butter, do not substitute margarine
1/2 teaspoon salt
2 cups sugar
2 tablespoons boiling water
3 cups sifted cake flour
1 cup cold water
1 tablespoon milk
1 teaspoon vanilla
4 egg whites, unbeaten
2 teaspoons baking powder

Preheat oven to 350 degrees F. Grease and flour two round 9-inch cake pans. In a large bowl, cream butter, salt and sugar. Add hot water. Beat until fluffy. *Sift flour 7 times after it has been measured.* Combine cold water, milk and vanilla. Add flour to creamed mixture alternately with water-milk mixture; start and end with flour. Blend well after each addition; beat hard 2 minutes after the last addition. In a small bowl, beat egg whites until foamy. Gradually beat in baking powder and continue to beat until stiff peaks form. Use a large rubber  spatula to gently fold into prepared batter until well blended. Pour into prepared pans. Bake 30 to 35 minutes or until cake tests done. Cool cake in pans 10 minutes before turning out onto cooling racks. When cake is cool, frost with Peerless Icing.

Peerless Icing:
2 egg whites, unbeaten
1-1/2 cups sugar
5 tablespoons cold water
1 tablespoon white corn syrup
1/2 teaspoon salt
1-1/2 teaspoons vanilla
1 teaspoon almond extract
1/2 teaspoon orange extract

In the top of a double boiler, combine egg whites, sugar, cold water, syrup and salt. Use a rotary beater to beat thoroughly. Place over rapidly boiling water and continue to beat 7 minutes. Remove from heat. Add vanilla, almond extract and orange extract; beat until icing is cool, thick and of spreading consistency. Serves 16.

## SOUR CREAM CAKE

A quick cake delicious enough to serve unfrosted—

2 eggs
1 cup sugar
1 cup sour cream
1-1/2 cups sifted cake flour
1/2 teaspoon salt
1/2 teaspoon baking powder
1/2 teaspoon baking soda

Preheat oven to 350 degrees F. Grease an 8-inch square cake pan. In a large bowl, beat eggs until light. Add sugar; beat until mixture is light and fluffy. Add sour cream; blend thoroughly. Sift cake flour, salt, baking powder and baking soda together. Add to egg mixture all at one time; blend thoroughly then beat hard 2 minutes. Pour into prepared pan. Bake 30 minutes or until cake tests done. Cool cake in pan. When cool, frost with favorite icing. Serves 8.

## $25 CHOCOLATE CAKE

A prize winner for some lucky contestant and it'll be a winner for you, too—

1-1/2 cups milk
1 teaspoon cider vinegar
1/4 cup margarine
3 tablespoons cocoa
1-1/2 cups brown sugar, firmly packed
1 egg, well beaten
1 teaspoon baking soda
2 cups cake flour
1/2 teaspoon salt
1 teaspoon vanilla

Preheat oven to 350 degrees F. Grease two round 9-inch cake pans and lightly dust with sifted cocoa. In a small bowl, combine milk and vinegar. Set aside 5 minutes. In a large bowl, cream margarine, cocoa and brown sugar *with your hands*. The warmth of your hands gets rid of all the brown sugar lumps, even the tiny ones. Add egg; beat thoroughly. Dissolve baking soda in sour milk. Sift flour and salt together. Add to creamed mixture alternately with sour milk; start and end with dry ingredients. Beat well after each addition. Stir in vanilla. Pour into prepared pans. Bake 25 minutes or until cake tests done. Cool cake in pans 10 minutes before turning out onto cooling racks. When cake is cool, frost with Soft Chocolate Frosting.

Soft Chocolate Frosting:
4 1-ounce squares semi-sweet chocolate
1-1/4 cups cold milk
4 tablespoons cake flour
1 cup sugar
2 tablespoons margarine
1 teaspoon vanilla

In top of double boiler, combine chocolate and milk. Place over boiling water to melt chocolate. Beat well with a rotary egg beater. Sift flour and sugar together into a small bowl. Add a small amount of hot chocolate mixture to flour-sugar mixture and return all to top of double boiler. Add margarine. Cook over boiling water until frosting thickens to spreading consistency. Stir in vanilla. Serves 16.

# FROSTINGS

## COFFEE FROSTING
Just a hint of coffee flavor—

1/2 cup margarine
4 cups sifted powdered sugar
2 to 4 teaspoons instant coffee
2 to 3 teaspoons hot milk

In a small bowl, cream margarine until soft and fluffy. Add powdered sugar gradually. Beat until smooth after each addition. Stir in coffee. Gradually beat in milk until frosting reaches spreading consistency; will frost a two-layer, 8 or 9-inch cake or a 9 x 13-inch loaf cake.

## CHOCOLATE FUDGE FROSTING
The "real" thing, rich and velvety—

2 1-ounce squares unsweetened chocolate
3 cups sugar
3 tablespoons white corn syrup
Dash of salt
1 cup milk
1/4 cup butter
1 teaspoon vanilla

In a large heavy saucepan, combine chocolate, sugar, syrup, salt and milk. Cook over low heat; stir just until chocolate melts. Cook *without stirring* until mixture reaches "soft ball stage." Remove from heat. Add butter *but do not stir*. Set aside until mixture cools to lukewarm—until a hand can be comfortably held on the bottom of the saucepan. Add vanilla. Beat until frosting reaches spreading consistency; will frost a two-layer, 8 or 9-inch cake or a 9 x 13-inch loaf cake.

## FUDGE FROSTING

1-1/2 1-ounce squares of unsweetened chocolate
1/4 cup water
Pinch of salt
2 tablespoons butter
12 marshmallows, quartered
1 teaspoon vanilla
2 cups sifted powdered sugar

In a small heavy saucepan, combine chocolate, water, salt, butter and marshmallow pieces. Place over low heat and stir constantly until ingredients melt and are thoroughly blended. Remove from heat. Add vanilla. Gradually beat in powdered sugar until frosting reaches spreading consistency; will frost a two-layer, 8 or 9-inch cake or a 9 x 13-inch loaf cake.

## GLOSSY CHOCOLATE FROSTING
Watch the clock! This frosting *boils only a minute—*

3/4 cup sugar
2 tablespoons cornstarch
1/8 teaspoon salt
3/4 cup boiling water
1 6-ounce package semi-sweet chocolate pieces
2 tablespoons margarine
1 teaspoon vanilla

In a small heavy saucepan, combine sugar, cornstarch and salt. Add boiling water. Cook over moderate heat; stir constantly until mixture comes to a full boil. Stop stirring and *boil just 1 minute*! Remove from heat. Add chocolate pieces and margarine. Stir until chocolate and margarine are completely melted. Blend in vanilla. Will frost a two-layer, 8 or 9-inch cake or a 9 x 13-inch loaf cake.

## LIGHTNING ICING

2 1-ounce squares of semi-sweet chocolate
1 teaspoon butter or margarine
3 tablespoons hot milk
2 cups sifted powdered sugar
1/2 teaspoon vanilla

In the top of double boiler over simmering water, melt chocolate. Add butter and hot milk. When butter melts and mixture is steaming hot, remove from heat. Gradually beat in powdered sugar until frosting reaches spreading consistency. Blend in vanilla. Makes 1 cup, enough to frost a single layer 8 or 9-inch cake.

## NEVER-FAIL CHOCOLATE FROSTING
This recipe *cannot* be doubled—

1 cup sugar
1/4 cup butter, *do not substitute margarine*
1/4 cup cocoa
1/4 cup milk
1 teaspoon vanilla

In a small, heavy saucepan, combine sugar, butter, cocoa and milk. Bring mixture to a full, rolling boil over medium heat. *Stir until mixture boils, then stop stirring and boil exactly 1 minute.* Remove from heat. Add vanilla. Beat hard until frosting thickens to spreading consistency; will frost a two-layer, 8 or 9-inch cake or a 9 x 13-inch loaf cake.

## 7-MINUTE ICING
White corn syrup greatly improves the chances of success with this version of an old favorite—

2 cups sugar
1 tablespoon white corn syrup
3/4 cup water
Dash of salt
2 egg whites
1 teaspoon vanilla

In a small, heavy saucepan, combine sugar, syrup, water and salt. Cook over low heat until sugar dissolves. Cover; simmer 2 or 3 minutes to dissolve any sugar crystals. Remove cover and bring to a full boil over medium heat. *Do not stir*! Cook until mixture reaches "soft ball stage." While syrup cooks, use a rotary beater to beat egg whites in a small bowl until stiff peaks form. While continuing to beat at high speed, pour hot syrup into egg whites in a narrow but steady stream. Blend in vanilla. Continue to beat until frosting reaches spreading consistency; will frost a two-layer, 8 or 9-inch cake or a 9 x 13-inch loaf cake.

## SOUR CREAM VELVET FROSTING

1 6-ounce package semi-sweet chocolate pieces
1/4 cup margarine
1/2 cup sour cream
1 teaspoon vanilla
1/4 teaspoon salt
2-1/2 to 2-3/4 cups sifted powdered sugar

In the top of a double boiler over simmering water, combine chocolate pieces and margarine. Place over boiling water to melt. Remove from heat. Add sour cream, vanilla and salt. Gradually beat in powdered sugar until frosting reaches spreading consistency; will frost a two-layer, 8 or 9-inch cake or a 9 x 13-inch loaf cake.

# COOKIES

More than a cookie but not quite a cake, bars are quick to make, fast to bake and easy to eat—no plate or fork is needed—they can be eaten out-of-hand right from the cookie plate.

## BANANA BARS
Moist and full-of-banana bars—

1/2 cup margarine
1-1/2 cups sugar
2 eggs, well beaten
1 cup mashed banana, 3 medium bananas
1 teaspoon vanilla
2 cups flour
1/2 teaspoon salt
1 teaspoon baking soda
3/4 cup buttermilk

Preheat oven to 350 degrees F. Grease a 9 x 15-inch jelly roll pan. In a large bowl, cream margarine and sugar until light and fluffy. Add eggs one at a time; beat well after each addition. Stir in banana and vanilla. Sift flour, salt and baking soda together. Add to creamed mixture alternately with buttermilk; start and end with dry ingredients. Beat well after each addition. Spread batter evenly into prepared pan. Bake 30 minutes or until bars test done. Cool bars in pan. Frost with a butter cream frosting. Makes 4 dozen.

## BUTTERSCOTCH SQUARES
The bars with the shiny tops—

1 cup margarine, melted
2-1/4 cups brown sugar, firmly packed
3 eggs
2-3/4 cups flour
2-1/2 teaspoons baking powder
1/2 teaspoon salt
1 cup chopped walnuts
1 6-ounce package chocolate chips

Preheat oven to 350 degrees F. Grease a 9 x 15-inch jelly roll pan. In a large bowl, combine melted margarine and brown sugar. Cool. Beat in eggs one at a time; beat well after each addition. Sift flour, baking powder and salt together. Add to creamed mixture; beat well. Stir in nuts and chocolate chips; blend thoroughly. Pour into prepared pan. Bake 25 to 30 minutes or until bars test done. Cool bars in pan 20 minutes before cutting into squares. Makes 4 dozen.

## HERSHEY'S CHOCOLATE SYRUP BROWNIES
Rich and moist with a fail-proof frosting—

1 cup sugar
1/4 cup margarine
4 eggs
1 cup flour
1/2 teaspoon salt
1 16-ounce can Hershey's Chocolate Syrup
1 teaspoon vanilla
1/2 cup chopped walnuts

Preheat oven to 350 degrees F. Grease a 9 x 15-inch jelly roll pan generously with margarine. In a large bowl, combine sugar and 1/4 cup margarine. Cream until thoroughly blended. Add eggs one at a time; beat well after each addition. Add flour and salt; beat thoroughly. Stir in chocolate syrup and vanilla; blend thoroughly. Stir in nuts. Pour into prepared pan. Bake 20 to 25 minutes or until brownies test done. Cool brownies in pan. When cool, frost with Fail-Proof Frosting. Makes 3 dozen.

Fail-Proof Frosting:
1-1/2 cups sugar
6 tablespoons margarine
6 tablespoons milk
1/2 cup milk chocolate chips.

In a small saucepan, combine sugar, margarine and milk. Bring to a boil over medium heat; *boil 1 minute*. Add milk chocolate chips; stir until chips melt and are thoroughly blended. Beat hard 2 or 3 minutes before spreading over brownies.

## LEMON COOKIE BARS
Squeeze a lemon to give these bars the freshest flavor—

2 cups flour
1/2 cup sifted powdered sugar
1 cup margarine
4 eggs, well beaten
2 cups sugar
1/3 cup fresh lemon juice
1/4 cup flour
1/2 teaspoon baking powder

Preheat oven to 350 degrees F. Have a 9 x 13-inch baking pan at hand. In a large bowl, combine 2 cups flour, powdered sugar and margarine. Stir with a fork until mixture is crumbly. Press into pan. Bake 20 minutes; crust will be only slightly browned. While crust bakes prepare cookie layer. In a large bowl combine eggs, sugar and lemon juice. Stir 1/4 cup flour and baking powder together. Add to egg-sugar-juice mixture; blend thoroughly. Pour over baked crust and return to oven. Bake 25 minutes or until cookie layer tests done. Sprinkle warm bars with sifted powdered sugar. Makes 2 dozen.

## MARILYN'S DREAM BARS
A layered bar for coconut lovers—

1/2 cup margarine
1/2 cup brown sugar, firmly packed
1 cup flour
Dash of salt
3 eggs
1 cup brown sugar, firmly packed
2 tablespoons flour
Dash of salt
1/2 cup chopped walnuts or pecans
1 cup coconut
1 teaspoon vanilla

Preheat oven to 375 degrees F. Have an ungreased 9-inch square pan at hand. In a large bowl, cream margarine until light and smooth. Gradually add 1/2 cup brown sugar and cream until light and fluffy. Sift flour and dash of salt together. Add to creamed mixture; beat well. Pour into pan. Bake 10 minutes. While bottom layer bakes, prepare top layer. In a medium bowl, beat eggs until frothy. Add 1 cup brown sugar, 2 tablespoons flour and dash of salt; beat until smooth. Stir in nuts, coconut and vanilla. Remove bottom layer from oven; reset oven temperature to 425 degrees F. Spread baked layer with top layer. Return to oven and bake 15 to 18 minutes. Cool bars in pan 1 to 2 hours before cutting. Makes 16.

## ROCKY ROAD BROWNIES
A mellow, mallow bar—

6 tablespoons margarine
1 1-ounce square unsweetened chocolate
1 cup sugar
1 teaspoon vanilla
2 eggs
3/4 cup flour
1/2 teaspoon salt
1/2 teaspoon baking powder
1/2 cup chopped walnuts
2 cups miniature marshmallows

Preheat oven to 350 degrees F. Grease a 7 x 11-inch baking pan. In a small saucepan, combine margarine and chocolate. Melt over low heat. In a large bowl, combine sugar and vanilla. Add eggs, one at a time. Beat well after each addition. Add margarine-chocolate mixture; blend thoroughly. Sift flour, salt and baking powder together. Add to creamed mixture; beat well. Stir in walnuts. Pour into prepared pan. Bake 20 to 25 minutes or until brownies test done. Remove brownies from oven and *IMMEDIATELY* cover with marshmallows. While marshmallows melt, prepare frosting. Makes 20.

Frosting:
1 1-ounce square unsweetened chocolate
1/2 cup brown sugar, firmly packed
1/4 cup water
3 tablespoons margarine
1-1/2 cups sifted powdered sugar

In a small saucepan, combine chocolate, brown sugar and water. Bring to a boil over medium heat; reduce heat and simmer 3 or 4 minutes. Remove from heat. Add margarine. Allow margarine to melt and mixture to cool to lukewarm. Beat in powdered sugar until frosting reaches spreading consistency. Spread over brownies. When frosting sets, cut into bars.

## SUGAR CRUST RAISIN BARS
With a baked-on topping—

3/4 cup seedless raisins
1 egg
2/3 cup brown sugar, firmly packed
1/3 cup margarine
1 cup flour
1/2 teaspoon baking powder
1/4 teaspoon salt
1 teaspoon vanilla
2 tablespoons sugar
1/2 teaspoon cinnamon

Preheat oven to 325 degrees F. Grease a 9-inch square baking pan. In a small saucepan, combine raisins and water to cover. Bring quickly to a full boil over high heat; remove from heat. Set aside 5 minutes. In a large bowl, beat egg slightly. Stir in brown sugar and margarine; beat well. Sift flour, baking powder and salt together. Add to egg-sugar-margarine mixture; beat well. Drain raisins; dry on paper towels. Stir in vanilla and raisins. In a cup, combine 2 tablespoons sugar and cinnamon. Sprinkle over batter. Bake 25 minutes or until bars test done. Makes 15.

## WALNUT BANANA BROWNIES
Chocolate, nuts, bananas—these brownies have it all—

1/3 cup margarine
1 6-ounce package semi-sweet chocolate pieces
1 cup sifted flour
1/2 teaspoon baking powder
1/2 teaspoon salt
2 eggs
3/4 cup sugar
1 teaspoon vanilla
1/2 cup mashed banana, 1 large banana
1 cup chopped walnuts

Preheat oven to 350 degrees F. Grease generously a 9 x 13-inch baking pan. In the top of a double boiler, combine margarine and chocolate pieces. Melt over hot water. Remove from heat and cool slightly. Sift flour, baking powder and salt together. In a large bowl beat eggs with sugar and vanilla until mixture is light and fluffy. Stir in mashed banana. Stir in flour mixture. Beat well. Stir in 3/4 cup nuts; reserve 1/4 cup nuts. Spread batter into pan. Sprinkle with reserved nuts. Bake 35 to 40 minutes or until bars test done. Cool completely before cutting. Makes 2 dozen.

## CARROT COOKIES
A frosted, quick-mix teatime cookie—

3/4 cup sugar
3/4 cup shortening
1 egg
1 cup cooked, mashed carrots
2 cups sifted flour
1/2 teaspoon salt
2 teaspoons baking powder

Preheat oven to 375 degrees F. Grease cookie sheets. In a large bowl, combine sugar, shortening, egg and carrots; beat well. Sift flour, salt and baking powder together. Add to sugar-shortening-egg-carrot mixture; beat well. Drop by teaspoonfuls onto prepared cookie sheets. Bake 8 to 10 minutes. *Cookies should not be browned on top.* Remove cookies to cooling racks and while still warm, frost with Orange Butter Frosting. Makes 4 dozen.

Orange Butter Frosting:
2 tablespoons margarine
1/2 cup fresh orange juice
1/2 teaspoon freshly grated orange peel
2 cups sifted powdered sugar

In a small bowl, combine margarine, juice, peel and powdered sugar and beat well until smooth and of spreading consistency.

## CHERRY WINKS
Measure corn flakes before crushing—

1 cup sugar
3/4 cup shortening
2 eggs
2 tablespoons milk
2 teaspoons vanilla
2-1/4 cups flour
1/2 teaspoon baking soda
1 teaspoon baking powder
1/2 teaspoon salt
1 cup chopped pecans
1 cup chopped dates
2-1/2 cups corn flakes, crushed
1/3 cup quartered maraschino cherries

Preheat oven to 350 degrees F. Grease cookie sheets. In a large bowl, cream sugar and shortening until light and fluffy. Add eggs; beat well. Add milk and vanilla; blend thoroughly. Sift flour, baking soda, baking powder and salt together. Add to creamed mixture; mix thoroughly. Stir in nuts and dates. Use hands to shape dough into balls the size of a walnut. Roll balls in crushed corn flakes and place on prepared sheets. Top each ball with a piece of maraschino cherry. Bake 12 minutes or until cookies test done. Remove to cooling racks. Makes 4 dozen.

## DATE-FILLED DROP COOKIES

An easy, self-sealing filled cookies—there's no rolling or cutting—

Date Filling:
2 cups dates, finely chopped
3/4 cup sugar
3/4 cup water
1/2 cup chopped pecans or walnuts

In a small saucepan, combine dates, sugar and water. Cook over medium heat until mixture is thick; stir constantly. Stir in nuts. Set aside to cool completely.

1 cup shortening
2 cups brown sugar, firmly packed
2 eggs
1/2 cup buttermilk
1 teaspoon vanilla
3-1/2 cups sifted flour
1 teaspoon salt
1 teaspoon baking soda
1/4 teaspoon cinnamon

Preheat oven to 350 degrees F. Have cookie sheets at hand. In a large bowl, cream shortening and brown sugar until light and fluffy. Add eggs; beat well. Stir in buttermilk and vanilla; blend thoroughly. Sift flour, salt, baking soda and cinnamon together. Add to creamed mixture; beat well. Drop by teaspoonfuls onto cookie sheets; allow 2 inches between drops. Place half a teaspoon of filling on dough. Cover filling with another half a teaspoon of dough. Bake 10 to 12 minutes or until cookies are lightly browned and test done. Remove to cooling racks. Makes 5 to 6 dozen.

## LEMON DAINTIES
They're light, they're lemony and they're frosted—

3/4 cup margarine
1/2 cup sugar
1 egg yolk
1 teaspoon vanilla
1/2 teaspoon lemon extract
2 cups flour
1-1/2 cups flaked coconut

Preheat oven to 350 degrees F. Grease two cookie sheets. In a large bowl, cream margarine and sugar until light and fluffy. Add egg, vanilla and lemon extract; beat well. Blend in flour. Stir in coconut. Use hands to shape dough into walnut-sized balls. Place balls 2 inches apart on prepared cookie sheets; flatten balls with a fork. Bake 8 minutes or until edges of cookies are *faintly browned* and test done. Remove cookies to cooling racks. Allow cookies to cool then frost with Lemon Butter Frosting. Makes 4 dozen.

Lemon Butter Frosting:
1/4 cup margarine
1/2 teaspoon freshly grated lemon peel
1/8 teaspoon salt
2 cups sifted powdered sugar
1-1/2 to 2 tablespoons fresh lemon juice

In a small bowl, cream margarine with lemon peel and salt until soft and light. Add powdered sugar alternately with lemon juice. Beat well after each addition. After last addition continue to beat until frosting is smooth and of spreading consistency.

## MANDELFLAM, "LACY" DANISH COOKIES
Dainty to look at and delightful to eat—

2/3 cup finely chopped almonds
7 tablespoons margarine, half a cup less 1 tablespoon
1 cup sugar
1 tablespoon flour
2 tablespoons milk
1 tablespoon freshly grated orange peel

Preheat oven to 325 degrees F. Grease and flour two cookie sheets. In a medium saucepan, combine almonds, margarine, sugar, flour and milk. Cook over low heat; stir constantly until margarine melts. Remove from heat. Add orange peel. Drop by scant teaspoonfuls onto prepared cookie sheets; allow *5 inches between drops.* Have oven rack in the top position; bake 8 to 10 minutes. Cool cookies slightly on cookie sheets but while they are still warm, use a broad spatula to carefully slip them off the cookie sheet. Wrap aluminum foil around 8 inches of a round wooden broomstick handle an inch in diameter—large *metal, not plastic,* knitting needles an inch in diameter will work, too. Use fingers to gently roll warm cookies, one at a time, on the prepared round. *WORK FAST!* Cookies must be rolled while they are warm and pliable so they will not break. If cookies aren't warm enough to roll without breaking, return to cookie sheet and reheat at 325 degrees F. 1 to 2 seconds. *Carefully slip rolled cookies from the round and allow to cool completely on cooling racks.* Store in an airtight container. Makes 3 dozen.

## SCOTCH OATMEAL COOKIES
Chuck-full of raisins—

1 cup raisins
3/4 cup water
1 teaspoon baking soda
1 cup shortening
1 cup sugar
2 eggs
2 cups sifted flour
1 teaspoon salt
2 cups quick-cook oatmeal

Preheat oven to 350 degrees F. Grease cookie sheets. In a small saucepan, combine raisins and water. Bring to a boil over medium heat; simmer 5 minutes. Drain; *reserve raisin juice.* In a cup, combine 5 tablespoons of raisin juice with baking soda. Set aside. In a large bowl, cream shortening and sugar until light and fluffy. Add eggs, one at a time; beat well after each addition. Sift flour and salt together. Add to creamed mixture; mix thoroughly. Add juice-baking soda mixture; blend thoroughly. Stir in oatmeal and raisins; blend thoroughly. Drop by teaspoonfuls onto prepared cookie sheets; allow 2 inches between drops. Bake 10 minutes or until cookies are lightly browned and test done. Remove to cooling racks. Makes 4 dozen.

# DESSERTS

## APPLE PUDDING
Topped with a warm Brown Sugar Sauce—

1/2 cup raisins
1 cup sugar
1/4 cup margarine
1 egg, well beaten
1 cup flour
1/2 teaspoon nutmeg
1 teaspoon baking soda
Pinch of salt
3 medium apples, pared and chopped
1/2 cup chopped walnuts

Preheat oven to 350 degrees F. Grease a 7 x 11-inch or an 8-inch square baking pan. In a small bowl, "plump" raisins by covering with boiling water 5 minutes. Drain; dry on paper towels. In a large bowl, cream sugar and margarine until light and fluffy. Add egg; beat well. Sift flour, nutmeg, baking soda and salt together. Add to sugar-margarine-egg mixture; mix thoroughly. Add raisins, apples and nuts; blend thoroughly. Batter will be quite thick. Pour into prepared pan. Bake 30 minutes. Serve warm topped with warm Brown Sugar Sauce. Serves 8.

Brown Sugar Sauce:
1/2 cup margarine
1/2 light cream, Half and Half
1/2 cup brown sugar, firmly packed
1/2 cup sugar
1-1/2 teaspoons vanilla

In a small saucepan, combine margarine, cream, brown sugar and sugar. Cook over medium heat until mixture is thick and bubbly. Remove from heat. Stir in vanilla. Serve warm.

## BAKED FRUIT COMPOTE
Just right for a winter brunch—

1 1-pound can freestone peaches, drained, reserve syrup
1 1-pound can whole apricots, seeded and drained
1 1-pound can blue plums, seeded and drained
2 bananas, peeled and sliced
3 oranges, peeled and sectioned
Juice of one lemon

Preheat oven to 350 degrees F. In a shallow three-quart baking dish, combine peaches, apricots, plums, bananas and oranges. Combine reserved peach syrup and lemon juice. Pour over fruits. Bake 25 minutes. Serves 12.

## CHILLED FRUIT COMPOTE
Just right for a summer brunch—

16 ounces of dried fruits—any combination of apricots, peaches,
    pears or apples
3/4 cup sugar
1 teaspoon freshly grated lemon peel
1/4 teaspoon mace
3 cups water

Custard:
2 eggs, well beaten
3 tablespoons sugar
2 tablespoons cornstarch
2 cups milk
2 teaspoons vanilla
1/4 teaspoon lemon extract
1/4 cup toasted, slivered almonds

In a medium saucepan, combine fruit, 3/4 cup sugar, lemon peel, mace and water. Cover; simmer over low heat until fruit is just tender but still holds its shape, about 45 minutes. Chill cooked fruit in cooking liquid. While fruit cooks, prepare custard. In the top of a double boiler, combine eggs, 3 tablespoons sugar, cornstarch and milk. Cook over simmering water until sauce thickens and coats a metal spoon. Remove from heat. Add vanilla and lemon extract. Chill. To prevent a "skin" from forming on the sauce as it chills, place a sheet of plastic wrap or waxed paper directly on top of the sauce. Preheat oven to 400 degrees F. Place almonds in a single layer on an *ungreased* cookie sheet and bake a few minutes. *Watch carefully; shake cookie sheet a couple of times to stir and turn the nuts so they do not burn!* Drain fruits thoroughly; layer fruit and custard in a glass serving bowl. Sprinkle with almonds. Serves 8.

## LEMONY CRUMB SQUARES
In a nutty, graham crust—

1 cup finely crushed graham cracker crumbs
1/3 cup finely chopped pecans
2 tablespoons sugar
1/4 cup margarine, melted
1/2 cup sugar
1 package lemon flavored pudding and pie filling,
    *do not use instant pudding mix*
2-1/4 cups water
1 egg, slightly beaten
1 tablespoon margarine

Preheat oven to 375 degrees F. Have an 8-inch square baking pan at hand. In a small bowl, combine crumbs, pecans and 2 tablespoons sugar. Add margarine; mix well. Press two-thirds of crumb mixture into baking pan; reserve remaining one-third of crumb mixture. Bake 5 minutes. Cool crust completely before filling. In a medium saucepan, combine 1/2 cup sugar, pudding mix and water. Add egg. Cook over medium heat; stir constantly until mixture comes to a full boil and thickens, about 5 minutes. Remove from heat. Add 1 tablespoon margarine. Cool 5 minutes; stir twice during cooling time. Pour into crumb-lined pan. Sprinkle with reserved crumbs. Chill at least 3 hours before serving. Garnish with dollops of whipped cream. Serves 9.

## NO PEEKING ANGEL CAKE
The "No Peek" rule must be obeyed—

5 egg whites
1/4 teaspoon salt
1/2 teaspoon cream of tartar
1 cup sugar
1 teaspoon vanilla
1-1/4 cups cake flour
1 cup whipping cream
2 tablespoons sifted powdered sugar
1/4 teaspoon vanilla
1-1/2 cups fresh raspberries or fresh sliced strawberries

Preheat oven to 450 degrees F. Butter an 8-inch square baking pan. In a large bowl, beat egg whites with salt and cream of tartar until foamy. Gradually beat in 1 cup sugar; continue to beat 15 minutes. Add 1 teaspoon vanilla; blend thoroughly. Use a rubber spatula to fold in flour in *four* parts. After last addition, continue to fold gently until flour is completely moistened. Gently ease batter into prepared pan and into the oven. *Close oven door and IMMEDIATELY turn off the heat. No peeking for at least 8 hours or until the next morning.* At serving time, use small chilled bowl and beater to whip cream until frothy. Gradually beat in powdered sugar until cream is thick and of spreading consistency. Stir in 1/4 teaspoon vanilla. Top cake with whipped cream and fresh fruit. Serves 8.

## HOT MILK SHORTCAKE
A quick-mix sponge cake—

1 cup flour
1 teaspoon baking powder
1/4 teaspoon salt
2 eggs
1 cup sugar
2 tablespoons margarine
1/2 cup hot milk
1 teaspoon vanilla

Preheat oven to 350 degrees F. Grease and line an 8-inch square baking pan with greased waxed paper. Sift flour, baking powder and salt together.

In a large bowl, beat eggs until thick. Gradually add sugar; beat well until sugar dissolves and mixture thickens. Fold in dry ingredients. Add margarine to hot milk; stir until margarine melts. Add vanilla to milk-margarine mixture. Stir into batter; blend thoroughly. Pour batter into prepared pan. Bake 25 minutes or until cake tests done. Cool cake in pan 15 minutes before cutting into squares. Top with sweetened, sliced fresh strawberries and pass a pitcher of light cream. Serves 8.

## STRAWBERRY FLUFF ROLL
Taking fresh strawberries beyond shortcakes—

4 eggs, separated
3/4 cup sugar
1/2 teaspoon vanilla
1 cup flour
1 teaspoon baking powder
1/4 teaspoon salt
1 cup sifted powdered sugar

Preheat oven to 375 degrees F. Grease generously a 15 x 10-1/2-inch jelly roll pan. Line pan with greased waxed paper. In a small bowl, beat egg yolks until thick. Gradually add sugar; beat well until sugar dissolves and mixture thickens. Stir in vanilla. In a large bowl, beat egg whites until *almost* stiff peaks form. Sift flour, baking powder and salt together. Use a rubber spatula to fold egg-sugar mixture into egg whites. Blend gently but thoroughly. Fold in dry ingredients; blend gently but thoroughly. Pour batter into prepared pan. Bake 12 minutes or until cake tests done. Sprinkle a towel generously with sifted powdered sugar. Loosen sides of cake from pan and turn cake onto sugared towel. Peel off waxed paper. Trim crusts from sides and ends of cake. Start at a narrow end of cake and carefully roll up cake up with the towel inside. Place on a cooling rack. When cake is completely cool, unroll and fill.

Filling:
3/4 cup whipping cream, whipped
2 tablespoons sugar
1 cup sliced, fresh strawberries

In a small *chilled* bowl, use *chilled* beater to whip cream until it begins to thicken. Gradually beat in sugar; continue to beat until cream is thick and quite stiff. Fold in strawberries. Spread on cake. Carefully roll up cake. To hold rolled cake securely, wrap with waxed paper or plastic wrap. Refrigerate filled cake 2 hours before frosting; the filled cake can be packaged in freezer paper or aluminum foil and stored a month in the freezer. At serving time, place *unwrapped* frozen roll in refrigerator for *1 hour.* Unwrap cake and frost with topping.

Frosting:
1 egg white
1/2 cup sugar
1/8 teaspoon salt
3/4 cup sliced, fresh strawberries

In a small bowl, combine egg white, sugar, salt and berries. Beat 7 to 10 minutes until topping is thick and of spreading consistency. Serves 12 to 14.

## STRAWBERRY NAPOLEONS
Layered, high, light and lovely—

Pastry:
2 cups sifted flour
1/2 teaspoon salt
1/3 cup margarine
1/3 cup shortening
5 tablespoons ice water

Preheat oven to 425 degrees F. Have a large cookie sheet at hand. In a small bowl with straight sides, sift flour and salt together. Use a pastry blender to cut in margarine and shortening until mixture resembles cornmeal. Sprinkle water over mixture. Use a fork to stir quickly and gently just until dough begins to hold together in a ball. Turn dough out onto a lightly floured board or pastry cloth. Divide into four equal portions. Roll each portion out to form a 4 x 8-inch rectangle. Trim edges of rectangles where necessary to make rectangle measurements uniform and even. *Bake pastry strips one at a time.* Place one rectangle on cookie sheet and prick evenly with a fork. Cover with brown paper so pastry will bake evenly without browning. Bake 15 minutes. Remove baked pastry to cooling rack. Bake three remaining pastry strips. Cool strips completely before assembling with filling.

Filling:
1 pint fresh strawberries, stemmed, rinsed and quartered
1/2 cup sugar
5 tablespoons flour
Pinch of salt
2 cups milk
2 tablespoons margarine
2 egg yolks, beaten
1/2 cup whipping cream
1/2 teaspoon almond extract

In a medium saucepan, combine sugar, flour and salt. Stir in milk. Add margarine. Cook over medium heat; stir constantly until mixture becomes a thick custard. Stir a few tablespoons of custard into beaten egg yolks. Blend well before returning to custard in pan; cook 2 more minutes. Remove from heat and chill. In a small *chilled* bowl, use *chilled* beater to whip cream until very stiff. Add almond extract and strawberries and fold into cooled custard. To assemble, place one sheet of baked pastry on serving platter or tray and spread with one-third of filling. Repeat with two more strips; end with a plain strip. Spread icing over top strip.

Icing:
1 cup sifted powdered sugar
2 tablespoons water
1/8 teaspoon almond extract
1/2 cup chopped walnuts

In a small bowl, combine powdered sugar, water and almond extract. Beat until icing reaches spreading consistency. Spread over top pastry strip. Before icing sets sprinkle with chopped nuts. To serve, slice crosswise into eight 1-inch slices. Garnish each slice with a whole fresh strawberry. Serves 8.

## STRAWBERRY PIE IN MERINGUE CRUST
This pie looks like it's going to a party—

3 egg whites
1 cup sugar
1/2 teaspoon baking powder
10 saltine crackers, finely crushed
1/2 teaspoon chopped pecans

Preheat oven to 300 degrees F. Butter a 9-inch pie pan. In medium bowl, beat egg whites until stiff peaks form. Combine sugar and baking powder. Use a rubber spatula to fold sugar-baking powder mixture into egg whites; then fold in cracker crumbs and nuts. Push meringue gently into prepared pan; spread evenly over the bottom and up the sides of pan. Bake 30 minutes. Crust will be delicately browned. Cool completely before filling.

Filling:
4 cups strawberries, washed and stemmed
1/2 cup sifted powdered sugar
1 cup water
1/2 cup sugar
1 tablespoon cornstarch
3 drops red food coloring

In a large bowl, combine *3 cups* of strawberries with powdered sugar. Set aside. In a small saucepan, cook remaining cup of strawberries in water over low heat just until strawberries are tender. Strain. Combine sugar and cornstarch. Add to strawberry juice and return to saucepan. Cook over medium heat until juice is thick and clear. Add coloring. Arrange reserved whole strawberries in crust and pour over glaze. Serve with lightly sweetened whipped cream or ice cream. Serves 6.

## BANANA SPLIT SQUARES
Rich, rich, rich but good, good, good—

2 cups crushed cream filled chocolate cookies (Oreos)
3 tablespoons softened margarine
3 large bananas, peeled and sliced crosswise
2 tablespoons fresh lemon juice
6 cups vanilla ice cream
1 cup Thick Fudge Sauce
6 cups strawberry ice cream

Butter a 9 x 13-inch pan. In a medium bowl, combine cookies crumbs and margarine. Toss to coat crumbs with margarine. Press evenly over bottom of prepared pan. In a small bowl, sprinkle banana slices with lemon juice and toss lightly to coat slices thoroughly to prevent darkening. Set aside. Stir vanilla ice cream to soften slightly. Spread ice cream over prepared crust. Drizzle with fudge sauce. Freeze until almost firm. Top with banana slices. Stir strawberry ice cream to soften slightly and spread over bananas. Freeze until firm. To serve, top with lightly sweetened whipped cream and a drizzle of Thick Fudge Sauce. Serves 15 to 18.

Thick Fudge Sauce:
1 6-ounce package semi-sweet chocolate chips
1 cup whipping cream

In the top of a double boiler, combine chips and cream. Heat over simmering water until chips melt and blend thoroughly with cream. Keep sauce refrigerated. Makes 2 cups.

# CHOCOLATE CAKE ICE CREAM ROLL

This is a *frozen* dessert—serve right from the freezer—

1/2 cup sifted cake flour
1/2 teaspoon baking powder
1/4 teaspoon salt
4 eggs
3/4 cup sugar
1 teaspoon vanilla
2 tablespoons sugar
2 1-ounce squares unsweetened chocolate, melted
1/4 teaspoon baking soda
3 tablespoons cold water
1 quart slightly softened ice cream, vanilla, strawberry, mint or any
    other flavor that goes well with chocolate cake roll

Preheat oven to 375 degrees F. Grease generously a 10 x 15-inch jelly roll pan. Line pan with greased waxed paper. Sift cake flour, baking powder and salt together 3 times. In a large bowl, beat eggs. Gradually add 3/4 cup sugar; beat until mixture is thick and fluffy. Add vanilla; blend thoroughly. Add flour mixture all at one time and mix thoroughly. In a small bowl, combine 2 tablespoons sugar and melted chocolate. Add baking soda to cold water and stir into sugar-chocolate mixture. Stir until mixture is thick and light, then quickly fold into cake batter; blend gently but thoroughly. Pour into prepared pan. Bake 15 minutes or until cake tests done. Remove cake from the oven and *immediately, while cake is still warm, loosen edges and turn out onto a clean towel; start at a narrow end, roll up warm cake immediately with the towel inside.* Cool cake completely then unroll carefully and spread with softened ice cream. Quickly re-roll, wrap in plastic wrap and freeze. After roll is firmly frozen, over-wrap with aluminum foil or freezer paper. Roll can be stored two months in the freezer. At serving time, cut frozen roll into 1-inch crosswise slices and top with a drizzle of chocolate fudge sauce. Serves 10.

## VANILLA ICE CREAM
One more recipe for homemade ice cream—

2 tablespoons unflavored gelatin
3 cups milk
2 cups sugar
1/4 teaspoon salt
6 eggs
1-1/2 quarts light cream, Half and Half
1 3-3/4-ounce package *instant* vanilla pudding mix, use dry
5 teaspoons vanilla

In a medium bowl, soften gelatin in 1/2 cup cold milk. In a small saucepan over low heat, scald remaining 2-1/2 cups milk. Stir into gelatin-milk mixture until gelatin dissolves and is thoroughly blended. Add sugar and salt; stir to dissolve. In a very large bowl, beat eggs 5 minutes. Add cream, pudding mix, vanilla and milk mixture. Rinse container and dasher of a gallon ice cream freezer. Pour in ice cream mixture. Set container lid in place and place container in freezer tub. Pack with six parts of crushed ice to one part rock salt and freeze. When ice cream is frozen, drain water from freezer tub and repack with ice and salt using three parts ice to one part salt. Allow ice cream to age at least 2 hours before serving. Makes one gallon.

# MEATS

Butchering activities had vanished from our farm by 1950. Any time of the year that our meat stock ran low, we delivered a home-fed steer or hog to a professional butcher where, in a well-equipped plant, the animal was slaughtered and the meat was cut into family-sized portions which were then packaged and frozen, ready for storage in our home freezer. The processing plant also cured hams and bacon, ground and seasoned sausage and rendered lard. With someone else handling those big jobs, I had more time to cook and to collect and try new recipes, like the one for Big Onion Roast Beef.

The old recipe was, at one time, a trade secret of the once-famous Big Onion Saloon and Cafe located on the ground floor of the Ravenna Opera House at the corner of Utica Street and Grand Avenue on Ravenna's main street. Sometimes called "Havlicek's Hall" for its builder, Frank Havlicek, the opera house was constructed in 1886. Its second-floor auditorium had a seating capacity of three hundred and was the scene of plays and musical productions staged by touring companies whose actors and actresses recited lines and sang songs in the Czech and Bohemian languages as well as in English. In addition to professional shows, the opera house had an almost continual run of concerts by local bands, wedding anniversaries, masquerade balls and other benefit performances. After the curtain came down on a stage show, the auditorium floor was cleared of chairs for dancing that same evening.

Over the years, the opera house had many owners and went through various additions, renovations and remodeling until it was condemned in the 1960s and was finally torn down in the early 1970s.

## BIG ONION ROAST BEEF

It's claimed that this secret recipe was passed down from owner to owner. It wasn't handed out to the public until the Big Onion Saloon and Cafe closed just prior to the Ravenna Opera House being torn down—

1 6 to 8-pound boneless beef rump roast
Water
2 to 3 tablespoons Worcestershire sauce
1 teaspoon ground sage
1 teaspoon chili powder
1 teaspoon salt
1/2 teaspoon pepper
3 bay leaves
1 large onion, sliced and separated into rings

Set oven temperature for 250 degrees F.; oven does not need to be preheated. Wipe roast with a damp cloth and place in a shallow pan. Add water to a depth of 1/4-inch in the pan. Add Worcestershire sauce to water.

In a small bowl, combine sage, chili powder, salt and pepper. Sprinkle evenly over roast. Lay bay leaves on roast. Lay onion slices on and around roast. Roast 4 to 5 hours or until roast is done to personal taste. Strain pan juices and serve hot with sliced roast. Delicious as a main course and equally delicious when served as cold or hot beef sandwiches. Serves 12.

## SHERRY MARINADE FOR BEEF

After we received the gift of an outdoor gas grill, steaks and chops got more than a quick and easy turn on the grid when I discovered the tantalizing and tenderizing effects of marinades—

1/4 cup salad oil
1/4 cup sherry wine
1/2 teaspoon crushed rosemary
1/2 teaspoon crushed sweet basil
1/2 teaspoon garlic powder
1/2 teaspoon seasoned salt
One whole beef tenderloin

In a shallow *glass* baking dish, combine oil, wine, rosemary, basil, garlic powder and salt. Stir until garlic powder and salt dissolve. Place tenderloin in marinade; turn to coat surface. Cover dish with plastic wrap and refrigerate 5 or 6 hours. Turn tenderloin 2 or 3 times during marinating time. Remove from refrigerator 30 minutes before grilling. Grill grid should be about 4 inches above hot coals. Length of grilling time varies from 20 to 50 minutes depending on the degree of doneness desired. To serve, cut into 1-inch slices. Serves 4 to 6.

## BAKED CHICKEN BREASTS
Marinate chicken overnight in the refrigerator—

8 chicken breast halves, skinned and boned
1 cup sour cream
1 tablespoons Worcestershire sauce
1/2 teaspoon Tabasco sauce
1 clove garlic, crushed
2 teaspoons salt
1 teaspoon paprika
1 cup fine, dry bread crumbs

Rinse chicken pieces and pat dry with paper towels. In a shallow, glass baking dish, combine sour cream, Worcestershire sauce, Tabasco sauce, garlic, salt and paprika; blend thoroughly. Place chicken pieces in marinade; turn each piece to coat completely. Cover dish with plastic wrap and refrigerate overnight. Turn chicken 2 or 3 times during marinating time. Remove chicken pieces from marinade 1-1/2 hours before it is time for it to go into the oven. Allow marinade to cling to chicken and roll pieces in bread crumbs to coat generously on all sides. Place in a single layer in an *ungreased* 9 x 12-inch baking dish. Cover with plastic wrap and refrigerate 1-1/2 hours. Preheat oven to 325 degrees F. Bake *uncovered* 1-1/4 hours or until chicken tests done. Serve with Baked Rice Pilaf. Serves 8.

## OVEN FRIED CHICKEN IN POTATO FLAKES
As crispy as skillet-fried chicken—

1 2-1/2 pound whole chicken cut into pieces or
    2-1/2 pounds of chicken pieces of your choice
2 eggs
2 tablespoons water
3 cups dried potato *flakes*, do not substitute dried potato granules
1 teaspoon paprika
1 teaspoon garlic salt
1 tablespoon grated Parmesan cheese
1 teaspoon salt
1 teaspoon pepper
1/2 cup margarine

Preheat oven to 375 degrees F. Rinse chicken pieces; pat dry with paper towels and place on waxed paper. In a shallow bowl, beat eggs and water together. Measure potato flakes into a shallow bowl. In a small bowl, combine paprika, garlic salt, cheese, salt and pepper; blend thoroughly. Sprinkle seasonings over all sides of chicken pieces. Melt margarine in 9 x 12-inch baking pan. Dip chicken pieces in egg-water mixture; dredge in potato flakes; and place skin side up on melted margarine in baking pan. Bake 30 minutes then turn chicken carefully with a spatula so as not to disturb the coating. Bake another 30 minutes or until chicken is golden brown and tender. Serves 4.

## CHICKEN BREASTS IN CRANBERRY SAUCE

When fresh cranberries are in season, stock the freezer and serve this tasty, colorful dish the year 'round—

3 whole chicken breasts, halved, boned and skinned
1 cup flour
1/2 teaspoon salt
1/4 teaspoon pepper
1/4 cup margarine
1 cup *fresh* cranberries
1 cup water
1 tablespoon red wine vinegar
1/2 cup brown sugar
Dash of nutmeg

Rinse chicken. In a shallow bowl, combine flour, salt and pepper; blend thoroughly. In a heavy skillet, melt margarine. Dredge chicken pieces in flour mixture and brown lightly on both sides. Remove chicken from skillet and keep warm. To skillet drippings, add cranberries, water, wine vinegar, brown sugar and nutmeg; stir to blend and dissolve brown sugar. Cover. Cook until cranberries burst, about 5 minutes. Return chicken to skillet; baste each piece with cranberries and sauce. Cover. Simmer 30 to 40 minutes or until chicken is tender and sauce is thick. Serves 6.

## CHICKEN BAKED IN A PAPER BAG
Chicken bakes to a crisp, rich golden brown—

1 3 to 5-pound roasting chicken
1 cup dried potato flakes
1 cup chopped celery
3 tablespoons melted margarine
1/4 cup minced onion
1 tablespoon fresh minced parsley
1/2 teaspoon salt
1/4 teaspoon poultry seasoning

Preheat oven to 325 degrees F. Rinse chicken inside and out. Pat skin dry with paper towels. In a small bowl, combine potato flakes, celery, margarine, onion, parsley, salt and poultry seasoning. Spoon into chicken's body cavity. Close opening with skewers or tie legs down with heavy string. Place chicken inside a large brown paper bag being careful that breast does not touch the bag. Fold open end of bag over to close; fasten shut with large paper clips and place on a cookie sheet. Bake 2-1/2 to 3 hours or until chicken is tender. Serves 4.

## CHICKEN BARBECUED IN A PAPER BAG
The sauce bakes into the chicken instead of onto the sides of the oven—

1 2-1/2 to 3-pound chicken cut into serving pieces
1 large, heavy brown paper bag
1/2 cup salad oil
3 tablespoons sugar
3 tablespoons catsup
2 tablespoons Worcestershire sauce
2 tablespoons cider vinegar
1 tablespoon lemon juice
1/4 cup water
1 tablespoon paprika
1 teaspoon dry mustard
1 teaspoon salt
1 cup flour

Preheat oven to 350 degrees F. Place paper bag on a jelly roll pan or a cookie sheet with sides and coat the inside of bag with salad oil. In a shallow bowl, combine sugar, catsup, Worcestershire sauce, vinegar, lemon juice, water, paprika, mustard and salt; mix thoroughly. Place flour in a shallow bowl. Dip each piece of chicken in barbecue sauce, then roll in flour and place inside the bag. Pour remaining sauce over chicken pieces in the bag. Fold open end of bag over to close; fasten shut with large paper clips. Bake 2 hours or until chicken is tender. Serves 4.

## NEW YEAR'S DAY ROAST DUCK
After goose or turkey for Christmas, switch birds and start the New Year off with duck—

2 4-1/2 to 5-pound ducks cut into serving pieces
2 cups flour
2 teaspoons salt
1 teaspoon pepper
1/4 cup margarine
1 cup orange juice
3 ripe fresh tomatoes, peeled, seeded and chopped or
    2 cups canned whole tomatoes, seeded and chopped
2 garlic cloves
1 bay leaf
1 teaspoon thyme
1/2 cup fresh chopped parsley

Preheat oven to 350 degrees F. Rinse duck pieces. Remove excessive fat. In a shallow bowl, combine flour, salt and pepper. In a heavy skillet, melt margarine. Dredge duck pieces in seasoned flour and brown in margarine until golden brown on all sides. Place duck in heavy baking dish or a roaster with a tight-fitting lid. In a small bowl, combine orange juice, tomatoes, garlic, bay leaf and thyme. Pour over duck. Sprinkle with parsley. Cover. Bake 1-1/2 to 2 hours or until duck is tender. Serves 8.

## SUMMER SAUSAGE
Sausage that is shaped, not stuffed—

2 pounds ground beef
1 cup water
3 tablespoons Morton's Quick Salt
1/8 teaspoon garlic salt
1/8 teaspoon onion salt
1 tablespoon liquid smoke

In a large bowl, combine beef, water, Morton's Quick Salt, garlic salt, onion salt and liquid smoke; mix thoroughly. Divide mixture into three equal portions. Form each portion into a roll 3 inches in diameter. Wrap each roll separately in aluminum foil and refrigerate 24 hours. Place rolls—still in foil—in a pan of boiling water; if the pan is large enough, all three rolls can be cooked at the same time. Simmer rolls over low heat 1-1/4 hours. Remove from water and drain. Unwrap and rewrap rolls with fresh aluminum foil and refrigerate. Refrigerated sausage will keep several months. Use in sandwiches, salads or as snacks. Makes 3 rolls.

## DELUXE SCALLOPED OYSTERS
With extra seasonings—

3 8-ounce cans of oysters
1/2 cup margarine
2 tablespoons minced green pepper
2 teaspoons minced onion
2 tablespoons flour
Half a clove of garlic, pressed
1 tablespoon lemon juice
1 tablespoon Worcestershire sauce
1 teaspoon salt
1/8 teaspoon pepper
1-1/4 cups coarsely crushed cracker crumbs
Milk, enough to measure 3/4 cup when combined with oyster liquid
2 tablespoons margarine

Preheat oven to 375 degrees F. Butter a deep two-quart casserole. Drain oysters; reserve liquid. In a small saucepan, melt 1/2 cup margarine and saute green pepper and onion until slightly limp but not browned. Add flour, garlic, lemon juice, Worcestershire sauce, salt and pepper; blend thoroughly. Place one-third of oysters in prepared casserole. Sprinkle with one-third of seasonings and one-third of crumbs. Continue to layer ingredients; end with a layer of crumbs. Combine oyster liquid and milk; pour over layered ingredients in casserole. Dot with 2 tablespoons margarine. Bake 20 to 25 minutes. Serves 6.

# PIES

### FRESH PEACH CHIFFON PIE
Use fresh peaches only—

3/4 cup sugar
1-1/2 cups peeled, chopped fresh peaches
1 envelope unflavored gelatin
1/4 cup cold water
1/2 cup hot water
1 tablespoon lemon juice
Dash of salt
1/2 cup whipping cream, whipped
1 9-inch Corn Flake Crust

In a large bowl, combine sugar and peaches. Set aside 30 minutes. In a small bowl, soften gelatin in cold water. Dissolve in hot water. Cool gelatin completely and add to sugar-peach mixture along with lemon juice and salt. Chill until partially set. Fold in whipped cream. Pour into Corn Flake Crust. Chill 2 to 3 hours before serving. Keep uneaten portions refrigerated. Serves 6.

Corn Flake Crust:
1 cup crushed corn flakes
1/4 cup sugar
1/3 cup margarine, melted

Butter a 9-inch pie pan generously. In a small bowl, combine corn flakes, sugar and margarine; mix thoroughly. Press firmly into prepared pie pan.

## HONEY RHUBARB PIE
Looks like a picture—

4 cups fresh, diced rhubarb
2-1/2 teaspoons quick-cooking tapioca
1/2 cup honey
1/2 cup sugar
1/4 teaspoon salt
1 tablespoon fresh lemon juice
Pie crust for a double-crust, 9 or 10-inch pie

Preheat oven to 425 degrees F. Line pie pan with lower crust. Cut remaining crust into 1/2 to 3/4-inch lattice strips. Preheat oven to 425 degrees F. In a large bowl, combine rhubarb, tapioca, honey, sugar, salt and lemon juice; mix thoroughly. Pile into crust-lined pan. Work quickly to weave lattice strips over filling; see "Pie Tips" in Special Reminder Section for further information. Bake 15 minutes. Reduce oven heat to 350 degrees F. and bake 40 to 45 minutes or until pie is lightly browned and tests done. Serves 6.

## MINCEY PEACH PIE
A fruity touch to one of winter's favorite pies in an orange-flavored crust–

Pie crust:
2 cups flour
3/4 cup shortening
1 teaspoon salt
1/3 cup plus 1 tablespoon cold water

Preheat oven to 425 degrees F. Have a 9-inch pie pan at hand. In the large bowl for an electric mixer, combine flour, shortening and salt. Mix at low speed until mixture resembles small peas. Add water. Mix at low speed just until dough begins to form a ball. Use hands to form dough into a ball. Divide dough in half. On a lightly floured board or pastry cloth, roll out crusts. Line pie pan with lower crust. Cut vents in top crust and slip onto waxed paper. Refrigerate both crusts while filling is prepared.

Filling:
1 9-ounce package dry mincemeat
1/2 cup water
1 1-pound 6-ounce can peach pie filling
2 tablespoons light cream, Half and Half
1 teaspoon freshly grated orange peel
1 tablespoon sugar

In a medium saucepan, combine mincemeat and water. Bring to a boil over medium heat; cook 1 minute. Remove from heat and stir in pie filling. Cool until a hand can be comfortably held on the bottom of the pan. Pour filling into prepared bottom crust. Fit top crust into place and crimp edges of crusts together. Brush top with light cream. Sprinkle with orange peel and sugar. Bake 30 to 35 minutes or until crust is lightly browned and pie tests done. Serves 6.

# SALADS

### CORNED BEEF SALAD
Salads aren't just "for ladies only" any more. Even Dinty Moore would go for this one–

1 3-ounce package lime gelatin
1-1/2 cups hot water
1 12-ounce can corned beef
3 hard-cooked eggs, chopped
1/2 cup grated cucumber
1/4 cup grated onion
1/2 cup finely chopped celery
1/4 cup finely chopped green pepper
1/4 teaspoon salt
1/2 cup mayonnaise

Butter an 8-inch square baking dish or an 8-cup salad mold. In a large bowl, dissolve gelatin in hot water. Cool. In another bowl, use a fork to break corned beef into small chunks. Add eggs, cucumber, onion, celery, green pepper and salt. Stir with a fork until well mixed. When gelatin begins to congeal, stir in mayonnaise; blend well. Stir in corned beef mixture; blend thoroughly. Pour into prepared baking dish or mold. Serves 8.

## CUCUMBER RINGS
A garnish for beef and pork roasts or poultry–

1 gallon of large cucumbers
2 cups of lime
8-1/2 quarts water
1 cup cider vinegar
1 tablespoon alum
Half of a bottle of red food coloring

Syrup:
1 pint cider vinegar
9-1/2 cups sugar
6 whole cinnamon sticks
1 package red hot candies
3 cups water

Wash and peel cucumbers. Cut into crosswise slices 1/2-inch thick. Use a donut hole cutter to remove seeds. In a 2-gallon crockery jar, combine lime and 8-1/2 quarts of water. Soak cucumber rings in lime solution for 24 hours. Drain. Wash rings in cold water; rinse thoroughly 2 or 3 times then soak in cold water 3 hours. In a large saucepan, combine 1 cup vinegar, alum, food coloring and rings with enough water to cover. Simmer over medium heat 2 hours. Drain and discard vinegar solution. To make syrup: In a large saucepan, combine 1 pint vinegar, sugar, cinnamon sticks, candies and 3 cups water. Bring to a boil over medium heat; reduce heat and simmer until mixture makes a light syrup. Turn cucumber rings back into crockery jar and pour hot syrup over. Let stand 24 hours. On three successive days, reheat rings in syrup. At the end of heating time on the third day, pack rings into hot sterilized pint jars and seal immediately. Green food coloring may be used as a variation. Makes 4 to 5 pints.

## GOLDEN FRUIT SALAD
A do-ahead salad combining fresh and canned fruits–

1 1-pound 5-ounce can peach pie filling
1 cup mandarin oranges, drained
1 8-ounce can pineapple tidbits, drained
1-1/2 cups miniature marshmallows
1 cantaloupe, cut into balls
3 bananas, peeled and sliced
1 pint fresh strawberries, washed and hulled or 2 cups seedless green grapes
Lettuce leaves, rinsed and chilled

Three hours before serving time or the night before, in a large bowl, combine pie filling, oranges, pineapple, marshmallows and cantaloupe. Chill. At serving time, slice bananas and stir into chilled fruit mixture along with fresh strawberries or grapes. Line individual salad plates or a large glass serving bowl with lettuce leaves and spoon on fruits. Serves 12.

## HORSERADISH SALAD
Goes with chicken or ham salad sandwiches for a luncheon or with pork chops, ham or roast beef for dinner—

1 3-ounce package lemon gelatin
1 3-ounce package lime gelatin
2 cups boiling water
1 cup mayonnaise
1 8-ounce can crushed pineapple, drained
1 cup cottage cheese
2 tablespoons horseradish
1 12-ounce can evaporated milk
1 cup chopped pecans

In a large bowl, combine lemon and lime gelatin. Add boiling water; stir to dissolve gelatins completely. Cool. When gelatin mixture is cool but *not yet congealed*, stir in mayonnaise, pineapple, cottage cheese, horseradish, milk and nuts; blend thoroughly. Pour into a 9 x 12-inch baking dish that has been rinsed with cold water. Chill until salad is firm, about 3 hours. Serves 12.

# DOUBLE "O" SALAD
Oranges and onions brought together by a touch of rosemary—

3 tablespoons mayonnaise
1-1/2 tablespoons fresh orange juice
1-1/2 teaspoons fresh lemon juice
1 teaspoon crushed rosemary
Dash of salt
Fresh ground pepper
3 oranges, peeled and sliced into thin rounds
1 red onion, thinly sliced and separated into rings
Lettuce leaves, rinsed and chilled

An hour or two ahead of serving time in a small bowl or jar, combine mayonnaise, orange juice, lemon juice, rosemary, salt and pepper; mix thoroughly. Refrigerate to allow seasonings to blend. At serving time, arrange lettuce leaves on individual salad plates. Top with orange rounds and onion rings. Drizzle with dressing. Serves 6.

# PARTY CHEESE RING
For a buffet party—

1 1-ounce pack of unflavored gelatin
1 cup cold water
1 cup sour cream
1/2 cup Miracle Whip salad dressing
8 ounces sharp Cheddar cheese, shredded
2 tablespoons finely chopped green pepper
2 tablespoons finely chopped pimentos
1 tablespoon finely chopped onion
1 teaspoon Worcestershire sauce
1/4 teaspoon salt
2 tablespoons butter

In a small saucepan, sprinkle gelatin over cold water. Place pan over low heat; stir constantly until gelatin dissolves, 3 or 4 minutes. In a small bowl, combine sour cream and salad dressing. Gradually add to gelatin mixture; blend thoroughly. Stir in cheese, green pepper, pimentos, onion, Worcestershire sauce and salt; blend thoroughly. Chill until mixture thickens slightly. Butter a four-cup ring mold generously. Gently spoon mixture into prepared mold. Chill until firm, about 4 hours. Unmold and serve with assorted crackers. Serves 14.

## PIMENTO CHEESE SALAD
Goes with ham, chicken or turkey—

1 3-ounce package of lemon gelatin
1 cup hot water
1 teaspoon cider vinegar
1 cup mayonnaise
1 5-ounce jar pimento cream cheese
3/4 cup cold water
1/2 cup chopped celery
1/4 cup chopped onion
1 cup diced green pepper

Butter generously a glass 9 x 5 x 3-inch loaf baking dish or an 8-inch square baking dish. In a large bowl, dissolve gelatin in hot water. Add vinegar, mayonnaise and cheese. Use an electric mixer at low speed or a rotary beater to blend thoroughly. Add cold water, celery, onion and green pepper; use a spoon to blend thoroughly. Pour into prepared mold. Chill until firm, about 3 hours. Serves 8.

## SALAD DELIGHT
Frosted with a creamy, zesty topping—

1 3-1/2-ounce package lemon gelatin
1 cup hot water
1 cup cold water
1 8-ounce can crushed pineapple, drain and reserve juice
1 cup pineapple juice, add water to make 1 cup of liquid
1 tablespoon sugar
2 tablespoons flour
2 tablespoons butter
1 tablespoon fresh lemon juice
1 egg, well beaten
8 large marshmallows, quartered
2 or 3 medium bananas, peeled and sliced
1 cup whipping cream, whipped
1 cup shredded Cheddar cheese

In a large bowl, dissolve gelatin in hot water. Add cold water. Chill until partially set. Add enough water to pineapple juice to make 1 cup of liquid. In a medium saucepan, combine pineapple juice-water mixture, sugar, flour, butter, lemon juice and egg. Cook over medium heat until mixture is thick and bubbly; stir constantly. Cool. Fold pineapple, marshmallows and banana slices into partially set gelatin. Pour into a 7 x 11-inch baking dish which has been rinsed with cold water. Chill until firm. Fold whipped cream into cooled topping; blend thoroughly. Spread on set gelatin mixture. Sprinkle with cheese. Serves 12.

## TACO SALAD
A north-of-the-border version of Mexican tacos—

1 pound ground beef
1 tablespoon shortening
Salt
Pepper
1 head iceberg lettuce, rinsed, chilled and torn into bite-sized pieces
2 fresh tomatoes, chopped
1/2 medium onion, chopped
1/2 pound Cheddar cheese, grated
1 15-ounce can kidney beans, drained
Half to three-fourths 8-ounce bottle of Catalina or Taco Salad Dressing
1 12-ounce package of regular corn chips

In a heavy skillet, brown ground beef in shortening until crumbled and well done. Season to taste with salt and pepper. In a large salad bowl, combine lettuce, beef, tomatoes, onion, cheese and beans. Add dressing and toss to mix thoroughly. Refrigerate at least 30 minutes before serving. Add corn chips and toss lightly. Serves 6.

# SANDWICHES AND PIZZA

Late night refreshments for our couple's pinochle club calls for heartier foods than for my ladies' bridge club and these hot sandwiches fill the bill.

## BUMSTEADS
Foil-wrapped sandwiches can be held a few hours in the refrigerator or four weeks in the freezer—

1/4 pound American cheese, cubed
3 hard cooked eggs, chopped
1 7-ounce can tuna fish, flaked
2 tablespoons finely chopped green peppers
2 tablespoons chopped onions
2 tablespoons chopped stuffed olives
1/2 cup mayonnaise
6 hot dog buns
Butter or margarine

In a medium bowl, combine cheese, eggs, tuna fish, green peppers, onions and olives. Add mayonnaise; blend thoroughly. Split buns and spread lightly with butter. Fill generously with prepared filling. Wrap each bun individually in aluminum foil. At this point, sandwiches can be frozen and stored a month in the freezer. To serve, preheat oven to 300 degrees F. Heat sandwiches 20 to 25 minutes. Frozen sandwiches can go directly from the freezer to the oven; allow 30 to 35 minutes to heat and thaw at 300 degrees F. Serves 6.

## HAM-SOMES

Ham-filling baked in a spiraled, caraway dough and topped with a hot cheese sauce—

Filling:
2-1/2 cups ground baked ham, *do not use boiled ham*
1 medium onion, ground, about 1/4 cup
2 tablespoons chopped fresh parsley
1 tablespoon ground horseradish
2 teaspoons prepared mustard
1/8 teaspoon cayenne pepper
1 egg, well beaten

Dough:
2 cups flour
3-1/2 teaspoons baking powder
1 teaspoon salt
2 teaspoons sugar
1/2 cup shortening
2 teaspoons caraway seeds
1 egg, well beaten
Milk, combine enough milk with egg to measure 2/3 cup

Hot Cheese Sauce:
3 tablespoons butter or margarine
3 tablespoons flour
2 cups milk
1 cup grated Cheddar cheese
2 teaspoons Worcestershire sauce
Salt to taste

To make filling:  In a medium bowl, combine ham, onion, parsley, horseradish, mustard and pepper. Use a fork to blend thoroughly. Add beaten egg; use a fork to blend thoroughly. Preheat oven to 425 degrees F. Grease a cookie sheet.

To make dough:  In a medium bowl, combine flour, baking powder, salt and sugar. Add shortening; use a pastry blender to cut in until mixture resembles coarse cornmeal. Stir in caraway seeds. Combine egg and milk; add all at one time to flour mixture. Use a fork to stir 10 to 12 times, just until dry ingredients are moistened. Turn dough out onto lightly floured board or pastry cloth. Knead gently 3 or 4 times. Roll dough out to a 10 x 12-inch rectangle. Spread with ham filling. Start with a long side of the dough and roll up as for a jelly roll. Cut roll crosswise into 8 slices. Place on prepared cookie sheet. Bake 20 minutes or until dough is a light brown and tests done. Serve hot with Hot Cheese Sauce. Serves 8.

While Ham-somes bake, make sauce. In a small saucepan, melt margarine over medium heat. Add flour and cook 1 to 2 minutes, then gradually stir in milk. Cook over medium heat; stir constantly until sauce is thick and smooth. Remove from heat. Add cheese, Worcestershire sauce and salt. Stir until cheese melts. Keep warm over hot water.

Note:  2 cups of Master Mix, see Page 280, can be substituted for flour, baking powder, salt and shortening; add caraway seeds, combine egg and milk and proceed according to remaining directions for making the dough.

## STUFFED PICNIC ROLLS
Serve these juicy 'wiches in their foil wraps—

1 tablespoon shortening
1 pound ground beef
1/2 cup chopped onion
1 tablespoon chopped green pepper
1/2 cup catsup
1/4 cup water
1/2 teaspoon salt
1 tablespoon Worcestershire sauce
6 hot dog buns
Prepared mustard
1/2 cup shredded Cheddar cheese

In a skillet, melt shortening and brown ground beef. Add onion and green pepper; cook just until soft. Add catsup, water, salt and Worcestershire sauce. Simmer uncovered for 15 minutes. Preheat oven to 400 degrees

F. Split buns and spread with mustard. Stir cheese into meat mixture. Fill buns with meat-cheese mixture. Wrap each bun individually in aluminum foil; seal ends securely. Heat 15 minutes. Serves 6.

## *RUNZAS*

Ground beef, cabbage and onions wrapped in dough and baked—

Filling:
1/2 pound ground beef
1 small onion, chopped
2 tablespoons butter or margarine
2 cups chopped cabbage
1/2 teaspoon salt
1/8 teaspoon pepper

In a skillet, brown ground beef and onions. In a saucepan, melt butter; add cabbage and place over low heat just long enough to wilt cabbage. Add to beef-onion mixture along with salt and pepper; blend well.

Dough:
2 to 2-1/2 cups flour
1/4 cup sugar
1/2 teaspoon salt
1 package dry yeast
6 tablespoons milk
1/4 cup water
1/4 cup shortening
1 egg

In a large bowl and with an electric mixer, combine 1 cup flour, sugar, salt and yeast. In a small saucepan, heat milk, water and shortening until shortening melts and mixture is very warm but not hot. Add to flour mixture along with egg. Beat at low speed 1 minute; then beat 3 minutes at high speed. Use a spoon to stir in remaining flour; dough will be soft. Turn out onto a lightly floured board or pastry cloth. Knead 3 minutes. Cover dough with inverted bowl; let rest 20 minutes before rolling out. Preheat oven to 350 degrees F. Grease a cookie sheet generously. Roll out dough until it is about 1/4-inch thick. Cut into 6-inch rounds. Place 3 tablespoons of filling in the center of each round and fold dough over to form a half circle; pinch edges of dough together to seal. Place *runzas* on prepared cookie sheet *smooth sides up.* Cover lightly; let rise 20 to 30 minutes. Bake 20 minutes or until *runzas* are lightly browned and dough tests done. Serve immediately. Makes 6. To freeze, bake, cool completely and package individually in foil. Store in freezer 2 weeks. To use, *do not unwrap;* frozen *runzas* should go directly from the freezer into an oven preheated to 350 degrees F. for 20 to 30 minutes to thaw and reheat.

# PIZZA
For those who like thick and yeasty pizza dough—

Dough:
4-1/2 to 5 cups flour
1/2 cup sugar
1 teaspoon salt
2 packages dry yeast
3/4 cup milk
1/2 cup water
1/2 cup margarine
2 eggs

In a large bowl and with an electric mixer, combine 1-3/4 cups flour, sugar, salt and yeast. In a small saucepan, heat milk, water and margarine until margarine melts and mixture is very warm but not hot. Add to flour mixture along with eggs. Beat at low speed 1 minute; then beat 3 minutes at high speed. Use a spoon to stir in remaining flour; dough will be very soft. Turn dough out onto lightly floured board or pastry cloth. Knead 3 minutes. Place dough in a well-greased bowl; turn to grease surface. Cover with waxed paper and a damp towel; let rise 20 minutes. Divide dough in half. Press dough into two 14 or 15-inch round deep pizzas pans. For shallow pans, push edges of dough up slightly to hold sauce and toppings of your choice. Let dough rise 15 minutes in pan before filling.

Sauce:
Makes enough for *one* pizza; *double the recipe to make two pizzas.*

1/2 cup minced onion
1 tablespoon shortening
1 8-ounce can tomato sauce
1 6-ounce can tomato paste
1 teaspoon salt
1/2 teaspoon oregano
1/4 teaspoon garlic salt
1/4 teaspoon pepper

In a medium saucepan, saute onion in shortening. Add tomato sauce, tomato paste, salt, oregano, garlic salt and pepper. Simmer 5 minutes over low heat.

Toppings:
Enough for *one* pizza; *double to make two pizzas.*

2 cups shredded Mozzarella cheese
1 pound pork sausage or 1 pound ground beef or 1 pound sliced pepperoni
    sausage

For pork sausage or ground beef, brown in a skillet until meat is no longer pink but is only slightly browned. Season lightly with salt and pepper to taste.
Preheat oven to 400 degrees F.

To assemble pizza:
Sprinkle *1 cup* of cheese over dough. Spread on pizza sauce. Arrange browned meat over sauce. Sprinkle with remaining cheese. Bake 12 to 15 minutes. Garnish with sliced stuffed olives or chopped ripe olives. Sprinkle with grated parmesan cheese. One pizza serves 2 very hungry pizza eaters; with a salad, it can serve 3 or 4 not-so-hungry pizza eaters.

## TUNA PIZZA

A non-traditional pizza—there's no tomato sauce, just tuna and cheese—a big hit with the grandchildren—

Half of prepared Pizza Dough
Topping: Enough for *one* pizza.
2 6-1/2-ounce cans of water-packed tuna, flaked
3 hard-cooked eggs, chopped
1/4 cup chopped stuffed olives
1/4 cup chopped green onions, include some of tops
1 cup shredded Cheddar cheese

Press dough into *one* 14-inch pizza pan. Let dough rise 15 minutes before filling. Preheat oven to 400 degrees F. To make topping: In a medium bowl, combine tuna, eggs, olives, onion and *1/2 cup* cheese; blend thoroughly. Spread over prepared dough. Sprinkle with remaining cheese. Bake 15 to 20 minutes. Serves 2 to 4.

# SOUPS

## TOMATO SOUP

Homemade, canned cream of tomato soup—

2 pecks ripe tomatoes, washed and quartered, *do not peel*
10 to 12 medium onions, coarsely chopped
2-1/2 tablespoons celery seed tied in a cloth bag

Thickening Sauce:
1-1/4 cups flour
1-1/4 cups sugar
1/3 cup salt
1 cup butter

In a large stewing pot, combine tomatoes, onions and celery seed. *Do not add water; juice from tomatoes will provide adequate cooking liquid.* Cook over low heat until tomatoes and onions are completely tender. Remove and discard bag of celery seed. Press tomatoes and onions through a fine sieve. Set aside 4 cups of puree to cool. Measure remaining puree and return to stewing pot. For every 5 quarts of puree, make 1 recipe of thickening sauce. In a medium bowl, combine flour, sugar and salt. Add to the 4 cups of *cooled puree*; stir briskly to make a smooth paste. Add paste and butter to puree in stewing pot. Cook over medium heat 15 to 20 minutes; stir occasionally. Pour into hot sterilized pint jars and seal. Makes about 12 pints.

At serving time, add a pint of milk to a pint of canned soup. Heat over low heat *just to simmering—DO NOT BOIL.* Serve in warmed soup bowls. Serves 2 to 3.

## CREAMY POTATO SOUP
More than potatoes—

6 cups peeled and sliced potatoes, about 5 large potatoes
1/2 cup peeled and sliced carrots
6 slices bacon, fried crisp
1 cup chopped onion
1 cup sliced celery
1-1/2 teaspoons salt
1/4 teaspoon pepper
2 cups milk
2 cups light cream, Half and Half
1 cup shredded Cheddar cheese
Parsley sprigs

In a large saucepan and in water to cover, cook potatoes and carrots together until tender. Do not drain cooked vegetables; most of the water will be absorbed during cooking and what little remains will be full of flavor. In a skillet, fry bacon until crisp. Drain on paper towels. Cool, then crumble. Pour off all but 2 tablespoons of bacon drippings. Saute onion and celery in drippings. Add onion, celery, bacon, salt, pepper, milk and cream to cooked potatoes and carrots. Bring to serving temperature over low heat. *Watch carefully so soup does not scorch.* Serve in warmed soup bowls. Garnish with sprinkles of cheese and a sprig of parsley. Makes 2 quarts. Serves 4 generously.

# VEGETABLES

More and more on through the 1950s, fewer and fewer vegetables came to our table from the home garden. Farm women picked fresh vegetables year 'round from the grocer's produce section or they selected packages from the grocer's frozen food section. As the source of vegetables changed, so did vegetable cookery. The new general rules called for one inch of water in the saucepan with one-half teaspoon of salt for every cup of water used. Vegetables were cooked only until *barely tender* and crisp. For my family's tastes, the new guidelines are fine for all vegetables except green beans. We still prefer fresh green beans simmered two to three hours until they have the appearance and flavor of home canned green beans. It was during this period that vegetable farmers from coast to coast developed and shipped more new, improved varieties of vegetables, and with better, faster transportation facilities, midwestern markets began to offer fresh and frozen vegetables we'd never seen or tasted before, like broccoli and cauliflower, to mention just two.

## BROCCOLI WITH HORSERADISH SAUCE
This relative to the cabbage never grew in my garden, still it has become a family favorite when topped with a zippy sauce—

3 pounds fresh broccoli or
2 16-ounce packages frozen whole broccoli spears,
    *do not use chopped broccoli*
3 tablespoons margarine
3 tablespoons flour
1/4 teaspoon dry mustard
1-1/2 cups milk
2 tablespoons horseradish, well drained
Salt and pepper to taste

In a large saucepan, cook fresh broccoli in lightly salted water just until tender. Drain. Prepare frozen broccoli according to package directions. In a small saucepan over low heat, melt margarine. Stir in flour and mustard; mix until smooth. Gradually add milk; stir constantly. When sauce is thick and smooth, stir in horseradish, salt and pepper. Arrange cooked broccoli in a serving dish. Pour sauce over. Serves 8.

## LAZY WAY BAKED BEANS
Skip presoaking and cooking—

4 1-pound cans of canned, cooked navy or northern beans
1-1/2 cups brown sugar
Salt and pepper to taste
4 strips of bacon
2 tablespoons margarine

Preheat oven to 350 degrees F. Butter a deep two-quart casserole. Pour beans into casserole. Add brown sugar, salt and pepper. Lay strips of bacon over beans. Dot beans with margarine in between bacon strips. Bake uncovered 1-1/2 hours. Beans should not be baked dry; they should be moist but not soupy. Use more or less brown sugar according to taste. Serves 6 to 8.

## CABBAGE SUPREME
Fresh cabbage casserole with a very short baking time—

4 cups chopped cabbage
1 cup water
1 cup crisp fried and crumbled bacon
4 cups soft, fresh bread crumbs
1/4 teaspoon celery seed
1 can cream of celery soup, undiluted
1/2 cup milk

Preheat oven to 400 degrees F. Butter an 8-inch square casserole. In a medium saucepan, combine cabbage and water. Bring to a boil over high heat; reduce heat and simmer 5 minutes. Drain. In a small bowl, combine bacon, bread crumbs and celery seed. In another bowl, combine soup and milk. Spread half of cabbage in prepared casserole. Top with half of crumb mixture. Pour over half of soup mixture. Repeat layers with remaining crumb and soup mixtures. Bake 15 minutes. Serves 6.

## CABBAGE ROYALE
Even cabbage haters love this royal dish—

6 cups finely sliced cabbage
1/2 cup water
1/2 teaspoon salt
1/2 cup chopped green onion, include some of the tops
3 tablespoons margarine
3 tablespoons flour
2 cups canned tomatoes
2 teaspoons Worcestershire sauce
3/4 teaspoon salt
1/2 teaspoon sugar
1/4 teaspoon pepper
3 slices bread, cubed
1 tablespoon margarine
1/4 pound American cheese, cubed

Preheat oven to 375 degrees F. Butter a three-quart casserole. In a medium saucepan, cook cabbage in water with 1/2 teaspoon salt. Drain. In a medium saucepan, saute onion in 3 tablespoons margarine until just tender but not browned. Add flour and blend until smooth. Add tomatoes, Worcestershire sauce, 3/4 teaspoon salt, sugar and pepper. Cook over medium heat until thick and smooth; stir constantly and carefully so tomatoes remain in recognizable pieces and do not become mushy. In a small skillet, lightly brown bread cubes in 1 tablespoon margarine. Cool completely before combining with cheese cubes. Arrange in layers in prepared casserole; begin with cabbage, top with a layer of tomato mixture and end with a layer of bread and cheese cubes. Bake 30 minutes. Serves 8.

## HOT CREAMED CABBAGE
Cooked, sauced and ready-to-eat in minutes—

1 large head of cabbage, cored and coarsely chopped
1/2 cup water
1/2 teaspoon salt
1/2 cup margarine
Salt and pepper
1-1/2 cups light cream, Half and Half

In a large saucepan, cook cabbage in water with 1/2 teaspoon salt until cabbage is just tender, about three minutes. Drain well. Leave drained cabbage in saucepan and add margarine, salt and pepper to taste. Add light cream to barely cover cabbage; do not use all of cream if it is not needed. Reheat over low heat—*do not boil*—and serve at once. Serves 8.

## CARROT CASSEROLE
Versatile, colorful carrots go with everything—

12 carrots, peeled and split lengthwise and crosswise
2 tablespoons chopped onion
2 tablespoons chopped fresh parsley
2 tablespoons margarine
1 teaspoon chicken stock base
1 cup boiling water
1 tablespoon cornstarch
3 tablespoons cold water
1/2 teaspoon salt

Preheat oven to 350 degrees F. Grease a deep two-quart casserole. In a medium saucepan in water to cover, cook carrots until barely tender. Drain and place in prepared casserole. In a small saucepan, saute onion and parsley in margarine until onion is tender but not browned. Dissolve chicken stock base in boiling water. Add to onion-parsley mixture. Dissolve cornstarch in cold water and stir into onion-parsley-chicken stock mixture. Add salt. Bake uncovered 20 to 30 minutes. Serves 6.

## GREEN BEANS AU GRATIN
Ordinary canned green beans become extraordinary—

2 cups canned green beans, drained
2 tablespoons butter or margarine
1 tablespoon flour
1/2 cup milk
2 teaspoons minced onion
1 teaspoon chopped pimentos
1 tablespoon Cheez Whiz
Half 10-1/2-ounce can cream of mushroom soup, undiluted
1/2 cup crushed potato chips

Preheat oven to 350 degrees F. Butter a one-quart casserole. Place beans in casserole. In a small saucepan, melt 2 tablespoons butter. Blend in flour. Gradually add milk. Cook over low heat until mixture is bubbly and thick; stir constantly. Add onion, pimentos, Cheez Whiz and soup; blend thoroughly. Pour sauce over beans. Top with crushed potato chips. Bake 45 minutes. Serves 4.

## HOMINY CASSEROLE
An unusual buffet dish—great accompaniment to roast pork—

3 cups canned hominy, drained
2 tablespoons margarine
2 tablespoons flour
1 cup milk
1 8-ounce jar of Cheez Whiz
1/4 teaspoon Worcestershire sauce
Salt and pepper to taste
1-1/2 cups corn flakes, crushed

Preheat oven to 325 degrees F. Butter a deep two-quart casserole. Place hominy in a large bowl. In a small saucepan, melt margarine. Stir in flour; blend until smooth. Gradually add milk. Cook over medium heat until sauce is thick and smooth; stir constantly. Stir in Cheez Whiz, Worcestershire sauce, salt and pepper. Pour over hominy. Blend thoroughly and turn into prepared casserole. Top with crushed corn flakes. Bake 1 hour. Serves 6.

## HONEYED ONIONS
They'll be back for seconds—

4 large white onions, peeled and quartered
1 cup hot water
1 teaspoon chicken stock base
1 tablespoon margarine
2 teaspoons honey
1 teaspoon salt
1/4 teaspoon freshly grated lemon peel
1/4 teaspoon paprika
1/8 teaspoon pepper
1 tablespoon snipped fresh parsley
1 cup shredded Cheddar cheese

In a skillet with a tight-fitting cover, arrange onions stem ends up. In a medium bowl, combine hot water, chicken stock base, margarine, honey, salt, lemon peel, paprika, pepper and parsley. Pour over onions. Cover. Bring to simmering over medium heat; simmer an hour or until onions are tender. At serving time, place onions and sauce in serving dish and sprinkle with cheese. This dish may also be prepared in the oven. Preheat oven to 325 degrees F. Butter a shallow two-quart, covered casserole. Arrange onions in casserole. Pour over sauce. Cover. Bake 1 hour. Uncover and sprinkle with cheese. Return to oven for 10 minutes. Serves 8.

## ESCALLOPED ONIONS
Especially good with roast leg of lamb—

4 cups small white onions, about 2 pounds
3 tablespoons margarine
3 tablespoons flour
1-1/2 cups chicken broth
1/4 teaspoon salt
Dash of white pepper
1/2 cup shredded Cheddar cheese
1/4 cup finely chopped walnuts

Preheat oven to 375 degrees F. Butter a one-and-a-half-quart baking dish. Arrange onions in dish. In a small saucepan, over medium heat melt margarine. Stir in flour; blend until smooth. Add chicken broth, salt and pepper. Cook until sauce is thick and bubbly; stir constantly. Pour sauce over onions. Sprinkle with cheese and walnuts. Bake 30 minutes. Serves 6.

## PINWHEEL CASSEROLE
The perfect potluck vegetable casserole—

3 cups frozen mixed vegetables
1 10-1/2-ounce can cream of celery soup, undiluted
2/3 cup milk
1-1/4 cups biscuit mix or Master Mix
1/3 cup milk
2 tablespoons chopped pimentos
1/2 cup grated Cheddar cheese

Preheat oven to 425 degrees F. Butter a 9 x 13-inch baking dish. Cook vegetables according to package directions. Drain well. In a medium saucepan, combine soup and 2/3 cup milk. Bring soup mixture just to a boil over medium heat; stir constantly. Add vegetables and pour into prepared baking dish. Bake until sauce becomes bubbly, about 25 minutes. While casserole bakes, make biscuits. Measure mix into a small bowl. Make a hole in the center of the mix. Add 1/3 cup milk. Use a fork to quickly stir in milk just until mix is moistened; *about 10 strokes*. Turn dough out onto a floured board or pastry cloth lightly dusted with extra mix. Knead gently 4 or 5 times. Roll dough out to form an 8 x 12-inch rectangle. Sprinkle with pimentos and cheese. Start with a long side and roll up as for a jelly roll. Cut crosswise into sixteen 3/4-inch slices. When sauce is hot and bubbly, remove casserole from oven and place biscuit slices around the edges of baking dish; leave the center open. Return to oven. Bake 20 to 25 minutes or until biscuits are lightly browned and test done. Serves 12.

## BAKED RICE
Instead of potatoes—

1 cup regular, *uncooked*, long grain rice
3 green onions, chopped fine, include some of the tops
1 teaspoon chopped fresh parsley
1/2 teaspoon salt
1/8 teaspoon pepper
1/4 teaspoon garlic salt
1/4 teaspoon celery salt
1 teaspoon Worcestershire sauce
1 10-1/2-ounce can beef consomme
1 soup can of water
3 tablespoons margarine

Preheat oven to 350 degrees F. Butter a two-quart casserole. In casserole, combine rice, onion, parsley, salt, pepper, garlic salt, celery salt and Worcestershire sauce. In a small saucepan combine consomme, water and margarine. Heat until margarine melts and mixture is well-blended. Pour over rice mixture; blend thoroughly. Cover. Bake 1 hour or until rice is tender and liquid has been absorbed. Serves 6.

## BAKED RICE PILAF
Ready for the oven in no time—

1 cup regular, *uncooked*, long grain rice
1 10-1/2-ounce can onion soup
1 soup can of water
1 4-ounce can sliced water chestnuts, drained
2 tablespoons margarine, melted

Preheat oven to 325 degrees F. Butter a two-quart casserole. In casserole, combine rice, soup, water, water chestnuts and margarine; mix thoroughly. Cover. Bake 1-1/4 hours or until rice is tender and liquid has been absorbed. Serves 8.

## SPANISH RICE
Main dish for a light supper—

3/4 pound ground beef
1 tablespoon shortening
1 teaspoon salt
Dash of cayenne pepper
3 tablespoons bacon drippings or margarine
1 cup regular, *uncooked*, long grain rice
1/2 cup chopped green pepper
1/2 cup chopped onion
1 garlic clove, pressed
2-1/2 cups canned tomatoes
1/2 cup chopped pimentos
1/8 teaspoon saffron

In a large heavy skillet, brown ground beef lightly in shortening. Season with salt and cayenne pepper. Remove from skillet and set aside. Melt bacon drippings or margarine in skillet. Add rice. Cook 10 minutes; stir constantly. Add green pepper, onion and garlic. Continue to cook until onion is tender and lightly browned. Add tomatoes, pimentos, saffron and beef. Cover; simmer 25 minutes or until rice is tender. Preheat oven to 375 degrees F. Butter a shallow three-quart casserole. Turn rice-beef mixture into prepared casserole. Bake 30 minutes. Serves 8.

## ZUCCHINI ITALIAN STYLE
An electric skillet dish—

2 pounds zucchini, washed, stemmed and cut into crosswise slices 1/4-inch
   thick
2 medium onions, sliced and separated into rings
1 cup thinly sliced celery
3 tablespoons margarine
1/4 teaspoon salt
1/2 teaspoon garlic salt
Dash of pepper
1 8-ounce can tomato sauce
Grated Parmesan cheese

In a large skillet, saute zucchini, onion and celery in melted margarine; stir constantly and cook only until squash is *barely golden* and just tender. Add salt, garlic salt, pepper and tomato sauce; blend well. Cover; simmer 30 minutes. To serve, spoon into serving dish and sprinkle with Parmesan cheese. Serves 8.

## ZUCCHINI SPECIAL
You can't have too many zucchini recipes—

3/4 pound zucchini, washed, stemmed and cut into crosswise slices
    1/2-inch thick
2 to 3 tablespoons margarine
1/4 cup minced onion
1 garlic clove, pressed
2 medium fresh tomatoes, peeled, cored and diced
Pinch of basil
Pinch of oregano
1/4 teaspoon salt
Dash of pepper
1/2 cup grated Cheddar cheese

In a large skillet, saute zucchini in melted margarine. Add onion and garlic. Cook 10 minutes; stir constantly, until zucchini is barely golden and just tender. Add tomatoes, basil, oregano, salt and pepper; blend thoroughly. Cover; simmer 15 minutes or until sauce is condensed. Turn into serving dish and sprinkle with cheese. Serves 4.

Gladys's

## GLADYS'S

Gladys's was the fourth and the last farm Walter and I would rent or live on. It was a half section of flat, irrigated land south of the Lincoln Highway, U. S. 30, six miles west of Gibbon and seven miles east of Kearney in the Platte River Valley. Of all the farms we rented, it was the only one owned by a woman. Gladys Smith, as it turned out, was our landlady for more than fifty years, from March 1930 until September 1980. We eventually became land-owners ourselves though we never lived on any of the farms we owned.

Gladys's was more than thirteen miles, about a twenty-seven-mile round trip, from Clayt's. A hired truck hauled the livestock—cows, hogs and chickens—but for everything else, it was another horse-and-wagon move made over several days near the end of February. Fortunately, the weather was very mild that year. March the first, the final day of the move, was an unseasonably warm and balmy, sunny and bright day. We couldn't have picked a better day to start a new life on a new farm. It was a day filled with all the "right signs" and lots of "good feelings."

There was, however, one thing we weren't prepared for. No one warned us about living two city blocks from the main line of the Union Pacific railroad. Trains remained a vital part of the country's transportation system in the 1930s. They ran so often and so regularly, we could almost set our clocks by them. Day and night, coal-fired, fleet passenger trains and long freights rumbled, thundered and tooted east and west, up and down the tracks. We saw them, heard them and sometimes, when the wind came from the north, we smelled their smoke and even when we couldn't see, hear or smell them, we *felt* them passing by—the ground shook, the house trembled, curtains quivered, beds vibrated and dishes rattled in the cupboard. As unsettling as trains were our first couple of days *and nights* at Gladys's, in a short time, we scarcely noticed them. Now and then, when we had overnight guests, they complained about being tired in the morning because the trains kept them awake all night.

"There's just one cure for that," Walter told them, "stay another night, milk a few cows, cut a few weeds and after you follow me around for a day, you'll be so tired, you'll sleep right through, the trains won't bother you at all."

In the fifty years we lived in it, the two-story wooden frame house went through many renovations, renovations that went far beyond springtime paint-and-wallpaper spruce ups. The house got a new roof, new siding, new windows, new floors and new beams; it was wired for electricity; walls were removed; the front porch was removed and the front door was relocated; the side porch was enclosed to make a bathroom; and, a hand-dug basement was excavated under a portion of the first floor where a shallow, man-drilled well supplied running water and a furnace furnished central heat and later air conditioning. Each renovation improved the overall structural condition of the house to the point where it seldom creaked, squeaked or quaked when a train passed by, not even in the two upstairs bedrooms where train tremors had been the most noticeable.

Downstairs, on the first floor, there was a dining room, living room, one bedroom and closet, pantry and kitchen, the smallest of all the kitchens I've had. On moving day, the cookstove was set up first; it took up most of the east wall; the stove's reservoir and the washstand were separated by only inches. The kitchen cabinet and cream separator filled the north wall and the dish cupboard the west. That left a narrow path around the white enamel-topped table and its four chairs in the center of the eleven-by-twelve-foot room. As it turned out, the smallest of all my kitchens became the kitchen where I did the biggest share of my lifetime cooking. From that tiny kitchen and for over fifty years, I fed our own little family of four, assorted large and small, planned and unplanned gatherings of Hendricksons and Mickishes—parents, brothers, sisters, aunts, uncles, cousins—friends and neighbors, hired men, corn shelling and threshing crews.

Walter guessed that I cooked "more food to feed more people out of that kitchen in one year than some women cook in five, maybe even ten years." Maybe I did, I don't know, and maybe I did do it in a cramped and inconvenient kitchen. That never diminished my pleasure in cooking.

Once I had married, had my own kitchen and was in charge of everything that went on in that kitchen, I discovered something that hadn't occurred to me in any of my girlish, childhood dreams—I *really* liked to cook. Liking to cook didn't mean I liked doing it with limited facilities and sometimes under trying conditions. Wherever we lived, I tried to make each kitchen work more efficiently, always hoping for the day we could afford an icebox...a refrigerator...hot and cold running water...an electric stove...a freezer...anything to help me cook better and easier.

I was glad to see a "house pump" six steps from the back porch at Gladys's. Having water nearby eased housekeeping chores even though the water still had to be pumped by hand. Somehow, pumping seemed easier and took less time than lugging five-gallon pails of water from the windmill near the barn. There were days when the little pump got a work-out and so did I—on the end of its pump handle. Besides water for cooking, cleaning, clothes washing and bathing, the pump furnished water to fill chicken watering cans, watered rows of leaf lettuce, green onions and red and white radishes in an early spring garden planted beside the pump—a big summer garden was planted in a field near one of the irrigation wells—and also provided water for a few fast-growing Chinese elm trees we set out later to shield the south windows of the house from the hot summer sun.

Only a couple of low, sprawling, scraggly box elders, one old elm and a lightning-riddled cottonwood north of the house kept the farmyard from being treeless. It took several years of transplanting "volunteer" Chinese elm seedlings and regular weekly waterings to establish a three-row, L-shaped, wind and snow break north and west of the house. In the Platte Valley's sandy and light soil, everything—crops, gardens, even trees—needed irrigation.

Irrigation! It was the Great Debate! The word was the center of every conversation Walter and I had with each other and with families and friends during the months between the time we first heard the Smith farm was going to be available and the day Walter signed the contract to move there. Could we come up with the extra money irrigation entailed? Could Walter learn to irrigate? Could we afford to buy additional equipment and attachments needed to "ridge" and "ditch" the crops? Would the financial gains offset the extra expense and extra work?

Irrigation spared crops from drought but it couldn't protect them from everything. Irrigated crops might still drown in downpours, get hammered by hail, flattened by winds or eaten by grasshoppers. Still, the odds favored the farmer who irrigated and thereby improved his chances of harvesting a top quality, high-yield crop, which, in a good year when market prices were steady or climbing, meant more money in the bank. For dry-land farmers like us, moving to an irrigated farm wasn't an easy decision. Our annual operating expenses would naturally go up to allow for the cost of fuel and oil burned by tractor engines that supplied the belt-power that turned the turbines that lifted thousand gallons of water from wells twenty, thirty and forty feet deep. Before we worried about how we would pay for tractor fuel, we had to worry about finding the money to buy the tractors and that was a major investment. Gladys's farm had two wells. We needed *two* tractors! That was a *major, major* investment.

After dickering and dealing, Walter struck a bargain with Gladys's previous renter to buy two huge Titan tractors he had used to "pull" the wells. Those tractors looked like small locomotives and from the way their throbbing engines shook the ground when their flywheels were cranked up and spinning, you would have sworn there were trains passing by.

Besides the extra expenses connected to it, irrigation also changed how Walter farmed. He studied "the lay of the land," so he'd know where to locate and how deep to cut the "laterals," open ditches three to four feet across which carried water from well spill boxes to the crops where, by gravity flow, water trickled down ridged rows from one end of a field to the other. The process sounds simple, but in practice, at least for a beginning irrigator, watering days were one crisis after another—ditches broke out, tractors overheated, belts broke, wells lost their "prime." And there were times when *all* of those things happened in *one* day.

Irrigation extended each working day of summer and it extended the whole farming season. With dryland farming, corn, cane and other row crops were usually "laid by," no longer cultivated, well ahead of the middle of July. Except for a few days of threshing and haying, the only field work a dryland farmer did between cultivating and cornpicking was plowing under stubblefields where wheat, barley or oats had grown. With irrigation, the long, hard days of watering usually started in June; in a dry year, they might start in May and run on into September. At times, the wells ran day and night. At the same time, there was livestock to tend, cows to milk, grain crops to harvest and thresh. There were a few weeks every summer when Walter put in more than his share of eighteen and twenty-four-hour days.

When Walter's work patterns changed, so did mine. I still cooked three big meals a day but I also prepared extra food so there was always a stock of quick, walk-away food handy, food that could be eaten out of hand, on the run at mid-morning, mid-afternoon or midnight.

When summer's blistering heat blew in, the cave at Gladys's lost its "cool." Underground water levels were so high in the Valley at that time, caves could not be dug much more than eight or ten feet deep without hitting water. The shallow cave was deep enough and cool enough to store eggs and keep them fresh for the weekly trip to town during summer months, but it wasn't cool enough to keep cream and milk sweet more than a day or two or to keep butter from melting and running off the plate.

After one summer with a warm cellar, I was ready to spend a few dollars to buy a small, secondhand, rather decrepit, oak icebox. There wasn't room in the kitchen for the icebox, so we tried putting it on the screened porch just off the kitchen. When the first hot spell of the summer hit, in less than a day the fifty-pound chunk of ice inside the box had completely melted. Then we moved the icebox down into the cellar, a less convenient location for me but it was much better for the icebox and the ice to be in cooler temperatures and away from the hot, withering south winds. If I were stingy and didn't chip at the block of ice more than once a day to make iced tea or lemonade, one block of ice would last for five, sometimes six days.

# 1974—

There I was, seventy years old and for the first time in my life, living alone.

Walter and I had spent very few days and nights apart in our nearly fifty-two years of marriage. Like most widows, I found meals-for-one and evenings by myself lonely. Still I felt very fortunate that I did not have to move, at least not right away. Though Walter worked the fields and tended summer irrigation on Gladys's after he officially retired in 1964, our son had assumed the rental contract with Miss Smith. There was an unwritten, three-way agreement, an understanding between Gladys Smith, our son and us allowing Walter and me to continue to occupy the buildings on the farm. Upon Walter's death, Miss Smith came to me immediately to say I was free to stay on at the farm for as long as I wanted. I was very grateful for her offer. Her farm had been our home for so long and it was still "home" to me. Within a year, I was finding my way along a different road with new signposts. I sewed more.

After years of watching granddaughters model in sewing contests, I took to the contest runways myself, collecting ribbons in local, district and state Federated Women's Clubs and Make It With Wool contests. When three granddaughters and one grandson married—when Kathleen Hendrickson married Don Colburn, Connie Swift married Kirk Hendrickson, Krista Fritz married Barry Rogers and Linda Fritz married Noel Corkery—at each wedding the bride walked down the aisle in a wedding gown and veil I made especially for her.

And I gave more hours to offices and committees of clubs and organizations, became a hospital volunteer and a certified parliamentarian and traveled more. I began to take short and long trips to see my family which so far includes eight great-grandchildren—Angela Hendrickson, Darr, Carrie and Kirk Colburn, Benjamin and Katherine Rogers, and Allison and Elizabeth Corkery.

At the end of a day or a week or a month away, it always felt good to get back home to the farm. Just being there, in familiar surroundings and watching the seasonal changes in the field work and the crops comforted me.

There was and is one thing I've never adjusted to—cooking for one. Frankly, most of the time I don't even try. When I cook or bake, *really* cook and bake, I'm not talking about making a quick sandwich or fixing myself a plate of leftovers, I'm talking about preparing full recipes, a complete meal. Usually relatives or friends come to share it with me. If not, I eat what I want and freeze the rest. I haven't stopped cooking, I haven't stopped baking and as long as there are family and friends to cook and bake for, I won't.

I never seriously considered where I would go if I should ever leave the farm. From time to time, well-meaning friends suggested this house or that apartment in town, but I didn't give any of the suggestions a second thought. I seldom bothered to look at any of them until one July day in 1980 when I got a call about a "spacious, two-bedroom apartment."

"It's all on ground level...has an attached two-car garage with automatic doors...separate utility room...large rooms...lots of closets and cupboards...convenient kitchen...dishwasher...garbage disposal..."

I'd never needed one of those on the farm where the cats and dogs got the table scraps and the chickens and pigs got the kitchen leavings.

"...microwave oven..."

I wondered if I could learn to use one of those.

The apartment had a lot to offer someone. Was that someone me? I wouldn't know unless I took a look.

One look and I was ready to move, ready to leave the farm.

The rooms of my new home are large, large enough to hold all of my furniture, except for one bedroom set, and there is room to stretch the dining room table to seat twelve; there is even room for my freezer.

As the lease was being signed, the apartment complex manager asked how long I'd lived at my previous address.

"More than fifty years as a renter," I told him, "but I don't think I can promise you I'll stay here fifty years."

# APPETIZERS

Dips and spreads—hot ones and cold ones—can't have a party without 'em!

## CHEESE BALL
Surround it with an assortment of crackers—

1 8-ounce package cream cheese
4 ounces shredded Cheddar cheese
1/8 teaspoon pepper
1/2 teaspoon salt
5 shakes Tabasco sauce
2 teaspoons Worcestershire sauce
2 tablespoons minced onion
3 ounces dried beef, finely minced

Allow cream cheese and Cheddar cheese to come to room temperature. In a small bowl, stir cheeses together. Add pepper, salt, Tabasco sauce, Worcestershire sauce and onion; blend thoroughly. Form mixture into a ball and roll in minced dried beef. Makes 1 ball.

## HOT CHIPPED BEEF SPREAD
With a nutty topping—

2 8-ounce packages of cream cheese, softened
4 tablespoons milk
6 ounces dried beef, finely chopped
1 cup sour cream
1/2 cup chopped green pepper
4 tablespoons minced green onions, include some of tops
1/2 teaspoon pepper
1/2 teaspoon garlic salt
1 cup chopped pecans
4 tablespoons margarine

Preheat oven to 350 degrees F. Butter a shallow one-quart baking dish. In a medium bowl, combine cheese, milk, dried beef, sour cream, green pepper, onion, pepper and garlic salt; blend thoroughly. Turn into prepared baking dish. In a skillet, saute pecans in margarine and sprinkle over cheese-beef mixture. Bake 20 minutes. Serve hot with an assortment of crackers. Makes about 4 cups.

## BACON BUTTER
A snack to go with soup or salad—

1/2 cup margarine
3/4 teaspoon prepared mustard
5 slices bacon, fried crisp and crumbled

In a small bowl, cream margarine to soften. Add mustard; blend well. Stir in bacon and spread on hot toasted English muffin halves. Makes 2/3 cup.

## PARSLEYED CHEESE AND HAM PATE
Many delicately-colored layers under a chilled glaze—

2 8-ounce packages cream cheese, softened
1 cup grated Swiss cheese
1 4-1/2-ounce jar stuffed olives, drained, *reserve juice*
1/4 teaspoon pepper
1 teaspoon basil leaves, crushed
1 envelope unflavored gelatin
1/4 cup water
1 8-ounce package boiled ham slices

Parsley Glaze:
1 envelope unflavored gelatin
1/4 cup water
1 10-1/2-ounce can condensed chicken broth, undiluted
1/2 cup dry white wine
1/4 teaspoon tarragon leaves, crushed
1 tablespoon wine vinegar
2 tablespoons finely minced fresh parsley

Lightly butter a 9 x 5 x 3-inch loaf baking dish. In a large bowl and with an electric mixer, beat cream cheese at low speed until smooth. Add Swiss cheese; blend at low speed. Chop olives. Add to cheese mixture along with reserved juice, pepper and basil. Blend at low speed. In a small bowl, sprinkle an envelope of gelatin over 1/4 cup water. Set aside 5 minutes. Place over boiling water to dissolve gelatin. Cool slightly then stir into cheese mixture; blend thoroughly. Arrange one-third of ham slices on bottom of prepared baking dish. Spoon one-third of cheese mixture over. Add another layer of ham slices; top with cheese mixture; add last layer of ham slices; and, finish with last portion of cheese mixture. Cover with plastic wrap and refrigerate overnight. Next day, prepare glaze. To make glaze: In a small bowl, sprinkle an envelope of unflavored gelatin over 1/4 cup water. Set aside 5 minutes; then place over hot water to dissolve. In a small bowl, combine chicken broth, wine, tarragon, wine vinegar, parsley and gelatin. Place bowl over ice cubes to thicken glaze slightly. Use a thin spatula to gently loosen pate loaf around the edges and carefully unmold onto a serving platter. Reserve 2 or 3 tablespoons of Parsley Glaze. Spoon remaining glaze over loaf; tip platter from side to side so glaze covers loaf completely. Refrigerate 30 minutes. Spoon reserved glaze around bottom of loaf to seal it to serving platter. Serve at room temperature with small rye bread rounds. Makes 16 1/2-inch slices.

## VEGGIE DIP
Quick and easy and very tasty—

1 4-ounce jar pimento cheese spread
1/2 teaspoon garlic salt
Dash of Worcestershire sauce
Dash of Tabasco sauce
1/2 cup mayonnaise
2 tablespoons catsup

In a small bowl, combine cheese, garlic salt, Worcestershire sauce, Tabasco sauce, mayonnaise and catsup; blend thoroughly. Serve with crisp and icy celery and carrot sticks, green pepper strips or cauliflower and broccoli florets or assorted crackers. Makes 1 cup.

## SAUSAGE CHEESE BALLS
Store baked or unbaked balls one month in the freezer—

3 cups Master Mix
1 pound seasoned "hot" pork sausage
10 ounces sharp Cheddar cheese, grated

In a large bowl, combine mix, crumbled but *uncooked* sausage and cheese. Allow mixture to stand until it comes to room temperature; stir to blend thoroughly. Preheat oven to 350 degrees F. Have *ungreased* jelly roll pan at hand. Use hands to shape mixture into walnut-sized balls; place on pan. Bake 15 minutes. Gently shake pan midway through baking time to turn balls as they brown. Serve hot. Makes 48 balls.

# BREADS

### BEST EVER CINNAMON ROLLS
A fast, one-pan-full for when a cinnamon roll craving strikes—

1/4 cup sugar
1 teaspoon salt
1/4 cup margarine
1/2 cup milk, scalded
1 package dry yeast
1/2 cup warm water
1/4 teaspoon sugar
Dash of ginger
1 egg, well beaten, *be sure it is at room temperature*
3 to 3-3/4 cups flour
2 tablespoons margarine, softened
2 cups whipping cream

Filling:
3/4 cup raisins
1 cup brown sugar, firmly packed
1/2 teaspoon cinnamon

In a large bowl, combine sugar, salt and 1/4 cup margarine. Add scalded milk to sugar-margarine mixture. Stir until sugar and salt dissolve and margarine melts. Cool to lukewarm. In a small bowl, dissolve yeast in warm water to which 1/4 teaspoon sugar and dash of ginger have been added. Set aside 5 minutes. Cool sugar-margarine-milk mixture to luke-warm then add yeast mixture, egg and 1-1/2 cups flour; beat until smooth. Gradually add as much of remaining flour as is needed to make a soft dough that cleans the sides of the bowl. Turn dough out onto lightly floured board or pastry cloth. Cover with inverted bowl; let rest 5 minutes. Knead gently 5 minutes. Place in a greased bowl; turn to grease surface. Cover; let rise until double in bulk, about 30 minutes. Prepare filling: In a small bowl, "plump" raisins by covering with boiling water for 5 minutes. Drain; dry on paper towels. In a small bowl, combine brown sugar and cinnamon. Pour whipping cream into an *ungreased* 9 x 13-inch baking pan. Turn dough out onto lightly floured board or pastry cloth and roll out to a 12 x 15-inch rectangle. Spread with softened margarine and sprinkle evenly with brown sugar-cinnamon filling and raisins. Start with a long side of rectangle and roll up dough as for a jelly roll. Cut crosswise into 1-inch slices. Place slices cut side down on cream in prepared baking pan. Cover; let rise until light and double in bulk, about 30 minutes. Preheat oven to 350 degrees F. Bake 25 minutes or until rolls are golden brown and test done. Let rolls stand in pan 10 minutes before turning out onto a serving tray. Serve warm. Makes 15 rolls.

## CHEESY MINI WHEAT LOAVES
No-kneading—

1 package dry yeast
1/4 cup warm water
1/4 teaspoon sugar
Dash of ginger
3/4 cup milk
1 tablespoon margarine
1 tablespoon instant minced onion
2 tablespoons sugar
1 teaspoon salt
1 egg, slightly beaten
1-1/8 to 1-1/4 cups unsifted flour
1-1/8 to 1-1/4 cups whole wheat flour
1/3 cup grated Parmesan cheese
1-1/2 cups grated Cheddar cheese

In a large bowl, dissolve yeast in warm water to which 1/4 teaspoon sugar and dash of ginger have been added. Set aside 5 minutes. In a small saucepan, combine milk, margarine, onion and 2 tablespoons sugar. Heat over low heat just until steamy. Cool to lukewarm then stir into yeast mixture. Add salt and egg. Gradually beat in white and whole wheat flours until a stiff yet somewhat sticky dough forms. Stir in Parmesan cheese and *1 cup* Cheddar cheese; blend thoroughly. Cover; let rise until almost double in bulk, about an hour. Grease generously six 1-cup custard cups or baking dishes. Stir dough down. Divide into six equal portions and place in prepared baking dishes. Cover; let rise until almost double in bulk, 20 to 30 minutes. Preheat oven to 350 degrees F. Just before loaves go into the oven, sprinkle with remaining Cheddar cheese. Bake 25 to 30 minutes or until loaves are golden brown and test done. Remove from baking dishes. Cool a few minutes before serving. Makes 6 mini loaves.

## CHICKEN LITTLE BREAD
Unusual loaves with delicious flavor and distinctive texture—

2 teaspoons chicken stock granules
1 cup boiling water
2 packages dry yeast
1/4 teaspoon sugar
Dash of ginger
1 2-ounce package of dried potato with leeks soup
1/4 cup sugar
1-1/2 teaspoons salt
1/4 cup minced fresh parsley
1 2-ounce jar pimentos, chopped
6 to 6-1/2 cups flour
2 eggs
2 tablespoons melted margarine

In a small saucepan, and over high heat, dissolve chicken stock granules in boiling water. Cool broth until it is lukewarm. In a small bowl, dissolve yeast in 1/2 cup of warm broth to which 1/4 teaspoon sugar and dash of ginger have been added. Set aside 5 minutes. Return remaining broth to heat; heat over low heat until steamy. Set aside 1 tablespoon of dry soup mix. In a large bowl, combine remaining dry soup mix, sugar, salt, parsley and pimentos. Add hot broth; stir to dissolve soup mix, sugar and salt. Cool to lukewarm. Stir in 2 cups of flour and yeast mixture. Add eggs; beat vigorously. Gradually add only as much of remaining flour as is needed to form a soft dough. Turn dough out onto lightly floured board or pastry cloth. Cover with inverted bowl; let rest 10 minutes. Knead dough until smooth, about 8 minutes. Place in greased bowl; turn to grease surface. Cover; let rise until double in bulk. Grease generously two 9 x 5 x 3-inch loaf pans. Punch dough down; turn out onto floured board or pastry cloth. Cover with inverted bowl; let rest 10 minutes. Divide in half and shape into loaves. Place in prepared pans. Cover; let rise until almost double in bulk.

Preheat oven to 375 degrees F. Bake 45 minutes or until loaves are golden brown and test done. Remove from pans onto cooling racks. Brush tops with 2 tablespoons melted margarine and sprinkle with reserved soup mix. Makes 2 loaves.

## GOLDEN SESAME ROLLS
One dozen clover leaf rolls with a difference—

2 packages dry yeast
3-1/2 cups sifted flour
1/2 cup milk
1/2 cup water
1/2 cup margarine
1/4 cup sugar
2 teaspoons salt
1 egg, slightly beaten
1 cup grated Parmesan cheese
1 egg yolk, slightly beaten
1 teaspoon water
Sesame seeds

In a large bowl, combine yeast and 1 cup flour. In a small saucepan, combine milk, 1/2 cup water, margarine, sugar and salt. Heat over low heat until mixture is very warm and bubbles form where liquid touches sides of pan. Add hot mixture to flour-yeast mixture; beat with electric mixer at medium speed until mixture is smooth, about 3 minutes. Blend in egg, cheese and 1 cup of flour at low speed, then beat 2 minutes at medium speed. Use a spoon to stir in as much of remaining flour as is needed to make a stiff yet soft dough. Cover; let rise until double in bulk, about an hour. Grease a 12-muffin muffin pan generously. Turn dough out onto lightly floured board or pastry cloth. Cover with inverted bowl; let rest 5 minutes. Divide into four equal portions. Divide each portion of dough into nine equal pieces. Grease palms of hands well and shape pieces of dough into smooth balls by rolling gently between the palms of the hands. Place three dough balls in each prepared muffin pan. In a small bowl beat egg yolk with teaspoon of water. Use a pastry brush to lightly brush tops of rolls with yolk mixture then sprinkle with sesame seeds. Cover lightly; let rise until *almost* double in bulk. Preheat oven to 325 degrees F. Bake 30 minutes or until rolls are golden brown and test done. Makes 1 dozen.

## HEARTY HURRY-UP WHEAT ROLLS
Dinner rolls, mini rolls or hamburger buns in a hurry—

2 cups flour
2 packages dry yeast
1 cup milk
3/4 cup water
1/2 cup vegetable oil
1/4 cup sugar
1 tablespoon salt
2-1/2 to 3 cups whole wheat flour

Grease generously two 9 x 13-inch baking pans for dinner rolls; two 12-muffin muffin pans for mini rolls; or, two cookie sheets for buns. In a large bowl, combine 2 cups flour and yeast. In a small saucepan, combine milk, water, oil, sugar and salt. Warm over medium heat until mixture is very warm and bubbles form at sides of pan. Add milk mixture to flour-yeast mixture. Beat with an electric mixer at medium speed until dough is smooth. Use a spoon to gradually stir in only as much of whole wheat flour as is needed to form a soft dough. If dough seems too sticky to handle, cover bowl with a towel and let stand *15* minutes. Turn dough out onto lightly floured board or pastry cloth and roll out to 1/2-inch thickness. Cut or shape into individual rolls of your choice and place in prepared baking pans; for mini buns, cut with 1-1/2-inch round cutter and place in prepared muffin pans; and, for hamburger buns, cut with a 2-1/2-inch round cutter and place on cookie sheets allowing 2 inches between rounds so buns do not touch during rising and baking. Cover; let rise 30 minutes. Preheat oven to 400 degrees F. Bake dinner rolls and mini buns 12 to 15 minutes and hamburger buns for 15 to 18 minutes. Makes 30 dinner rolls or mini buns or 24 hamburger buns.

## HERB BREAD

When baked in clay, heart-shaped baking dishes, this bread was a blue ribbon winner at a fund raiser Bread Fair called "Raising the Dough," sponsored by Kearney Area Arts Council—

1 package dry yeast
1-2/3 cups warm water
1/4 teaspoon sugar
Dash of ginger
2 teaspoons chicken stock base or 2 crumbled chicken bouillon cubes
1 tablespoon vegetable oil
1/4 cup sugar
1/4 cup chopped pimentos
1/4 cup dried onion flakes
1/4 cup dried mixed vegetable flakes
1 egg
2-1/2 teaspoons salt
4 to 5 cups flour
2 tablespoons margarine, softened
Cornmeal

In a small bowl, dissolve yeast in 1/4 cup warm water to which 1/4 teaspoon sugar and ginger have been added. Set aside 5 minutes. In a large bowl, combine remaining water, chicken stock and oil; blend thoroughly. Add yeast mixture, 1/4 cup sugar, pimentos, onion flakes, vegetable flakes, egg and salt; blend thoroughly. Add flour, 1 cup at a time, until 4 cups have been added. Beat well after each addition. Coat board or pastry cloth with remaining flour. Turn dough out onto floured surface. Cover with inverted bowl; let rest 5 minutes. Knead in only as much flour as is needed to make a soft dough. Place dough in greased bowl; turn to grease surface. Cover; let rise until double in bulk. Punch dough down. Cover; let rise again. Use softened margarine to grease two clay baking dishes heavily. Dust dishes with cornmeal. Turn dough out onto floured board or pastry cloth and divide in half. To form heart-shaped loaves, roll each portion of dough out into a round and turn the outer, lower edges of the round to the center to form a point at the bottom. Place dough into prepared dishes with folded seams on the underside. Cover; let rise until double in bulk. Preheat oven to 350 degrees F. Bake 50 minutes or until bread is golden brown and tests done. Turn loaves out onto cooling racks. Makes 2 heart-shaped loaves.

Dough can be shaped into single loaves and baked in two 9 x 5 x 3-inch loaf pans. Makes 2 loaves.

## HONEY WHOLE WHEAT BREAD
Quick-mix casserole bread—serve hot from the oven—

1 cup milk
3/4 cup margarine
1/2 cup honey
2 teaspoons salt
2 packages dry yeast
3/4 cup warm water
1/4 teaspoon sugar
Dash of ginger
3 eggs, lightly beaten
4-1/2 cups flour
1-1/2 cups whole wheat flour
1 teaspoon softened margarine

In a small saucepan, heat milk over medium heat just until bubbles form around sides of pan. Remove from heat. Add 3/4 cup margarine, honey and salt. Stir until margarine melts; blend well. Cool to lukewarm. In a large bowl, sprinkle yeast over warm water to which 1/4 teaspoon sugar and dash of ginger have been added. Set aside 5 minutes. Add milk mixture and eggs. Combine the flours and add 4 cups of the mixture to yeast-egg-milk mixture; with an electric mixer, blend at low speed 2 minutes. Use a spoon to stir in remaining flour; blend thoroughly. Cover with waxed paper and a towel; let rise until double in bulk, about an hour. Lightly grease a three-quart round casserole. Punch dough down and beat with a spoon until smooth. Turn into prepared casserole. Cover; let rise until double in bulk. Preheat oven to 375 degrees F. Just before bread goes into oven, use a sharp knife to cut a 1/2-inch deep slash in the shape of a 4-inch cross in the center of the loaf. Bake 45 to 50 minutes or until loaf is a rich golden brown and tests done. Spread softened margarine on hot loaf and remove to a cooling rack. Serve hot. Makes 1 loaf.

## UNUSUAL *KOLACHES*
Traditional, Old World rolls with a surprise ingredient—

1 3-1/2-ounce package vanilla pudding mix, *do not use instant pudding*
1-1/2 cups milk
1/2 cup margarine
2 packages dry yeast
1/2 cup warm water
1/4 teaspoon sugar
Dash of ginger
2 eggs, well beaten
2 teaspoons salt
5 to 5-1/2 cups flour
1/2 cup margarine, melted

Cook pudding according to package directions *using only 1-1/2 cups of milk*. Remove from heat. Add margarine; stir until margarine melts. Cool to lukewarm. In a large bowl, dissolve yeast in warm water to which 1/4 teaspoon sugar and ginger have been added. Set aside 5 minutes. Add pudding mix and with electric mixer at low speed; blend well. Add eggs and salt. Beat 1 minute at medium speed. Add 2 cups of flour. Beat 2 minutes at medium speed. Stir in only as much of remaining flour as is needed to make a soft dough. Turn dough out onto floured board or pastry cloth. Cover with inverted bowl; let rest 5 minutes. Knead gently 5 minutes. Place dough in greased bowl; turn to grease surface. Cover; let rise until double in bulk. Grease four cookie sheets. Turn dough out onto floured surface and punch down. Cover with inverted bowl; let rest 5 minutes. Use a sharp knife to cut off pieces of dough the size of a large walnut. Flour hands and roll dough pieces between the palms of the hands to make smooth balls. Place dough balls 2 inches apart on prepared cookie sheets. Brush dough with melted margarine. Cover with waxed paper. Let rise until double in bulk. With tips of first two fingers on each hand, punch down centers of balls to make a well to hold cooked prune, apricot or poppy seed fillings. See Page 55 for filling recipes or use commercial fillings. Top with Cottage Cheese Topping if desired. See Page 55 for topping recipe. Let rise until dough is light to the touch, about 30 minutes. Preheat oven to 400 degrees F. Bake 10 to 12 minutes or until rolls are *lightly browned* and test done. Before removing baked rolls from cookie sheets, brush lightly with melted margarine. Cool *kolaches* on several thicknesses of newspaper covered with waxed paper. Makes 5 dozen.

## OATMEAL REFRIGERATOR ROLLS

Start dough the night before and serve hot Butterscotch or
Orange Spiral Rolls for breakfast or brunch—

2 packages dry yeast
1/2 cup warm water
1/4 teaspoon sugar
Dash of ginger
1-1/2 cups milk, scalded
1/2 cup brown sugar, firmly packed
2 teaspoons salt
5 to 5-1/2 cups flour
2 eggs, well beaten
1/2 cup margarine, melted
1-1/2 cups quick-cook oatmeal
1 tablespoon margarine, melted

In a small bowl, dissolve yeast in warm water to which 1/4 teaspoon
sugar and ginger have been added. Set aside 5 minutes. In a large bowl,
combine milk, brown sugar and salt. Stir to dissolve sugar and salt. Cool to
lukewarm. Add 1 cup flour, eggs and yeast mixture; use a spoon to beat
hard. Fold in 1/2 cup melted margarine and oatmeal; blend thoroughly. Add
only as much of remaining flour as is needed to make a soft dough. Turn
dough out onto lightly floured board or pastry cloth. Cover with inverted
bowl; let rest 5 minutes. Knead 5 to 6 minutes. Place dough in greased
bowl; turn to grease surface. Cover; let rise until double in bulk. Punch
down; brush with 1 tablespoon melted margarine. Cover with waxed paper
and a damp cloth. Refrigerate overnight. *Dough can be refrigerated up to 4
days before it is baked.* Shape dough into dinner rolls, cinnamon rolls or
Butterscotch or Orange Spirals.

Butterscotch Spirals:
Half of Oatmeal Refrigerator Rolls dough
1/2 cup brown sugar, firmly packed
2 teaspoons cinnamon
1/2 cups chopped walnuts
4 tablespoons margarine, melted

Grease a 9 x 13-inch baking pan. On a lightly floured board or pastry
cloth roll dough out to make a 14 x 18-inch rectangle. In a small bowl,
combine brown sugar, cinnamon and walnuts. Brush dough with half of

melted margarine and sprinkle evenly with sugar mixture. Start with a long side and roll up as for a jelly roll. Use a sharp knife to cut into 1-inch slices. Place slices in prepared pan cut side down. Brush with remaining melted margarine. Cover; let rise until light, about an hour. Preheat oven to 400 degrees F. Bake 15 to 20 minutes or until rolls are lightly browned and test done. Makes 18 rolls.

Orange Spirals:
Half of Oatmeal Refrigerator Rolls dough
1/2 cup softened margarine
2 tablespoons freshly grated orange peel
3 tablespoons fresh orange juice
2 cups sifted powdered sugar

In a small bowl, combine margarine, orange peel, juice and powdered sugar. Reserve one-fourth of the mixture. Grease a 9 x 13-inch baking pan. On a lightly floured board or pastry cloth, roll dough out to make a 14 x 18-inch rectangle. Spread remaining three-fourths of filling over rectangle. Start with a long side and roll up as for a jelly roll. Use a sharp knife to cut into 1-inch slices. Place slices in prepared pan cut side down. Sprinkle with reserved sugar mixture. Cover; let rise until light, about an hour. Preheat oven to 400 degrees F. Bake 15 to 20 minutes or until rolls are lightly browned and test done. Makes 18 rolls.

## ORANGE ROLLS
Goes with chicken salad for a luncheon as well as for breakfast, brunch or morning coffee—

1 package dry yeast
1/4 cup warm water
1/4 teaspoon sugar
Dash of ginger
1 cup milk
4 cups flour
1 cup margarine
1/2 cup sugar
Freshly grated peel of one orange

In a small bowl, dissolve yeast in warm water to which 1/4 teaspoon sugar and ginger have been added. Set aside 5 minutes. In a small saucepan over medium heat, scald milk. Cool to lukewarm. In a large bowl, combine flour, margarine, orange peel and 1/2 cup sugar. Use a pastry blender to cut in margarine until mixture resembles coarse cornmeal. Stir lukewarm milk and yeast mixture together and add to flour mixture; beat well until mixture is smooth. Cover bowl; refrigerate overnight. The next morning, grease two 9 x 13-inch baking pans and prepare filling.

Filling:
1 cup sifted powdered sugar
1 tablespoon cinnamon
1 tablespoon margarine

In a small bowl, combine powdered sugar, cinnamon and margarine. Use a fork to blend into a crumbly mixture. Turn dough out onto lightly floured board or pastry cloth and divide in half. Roll each portion out into an 8 x 12-inch rectangle; sprinkle with filling. Start with a long side and roll up as for a jelly roll. Use a sharp knife to cut into 1-inch slices. Place slices in prepared pan cut side up. Repeat with remaining dough and filling. Cover; let rise until double in bulk. Preheat oven to 375 degrees F. Bake 15 minutes or until rolls are lightly browned and test done. While rolls bake, prepare frosting. Makes 24 rolls.

Frosting:
2 tablespoons margarine
1 cup sifted powdered sugar
1 teaspoon freshly grated orange peel
3 tablespoons thawed orange juice concentrate

In a small bowl, cream margarine. Gradually add powdered sugar alternately with orange juice concentrate until frosting reaches spreading consistency. Stir in orange peel.

Turn baked rolls out of pans and frost *immediately*; frosting will appear as a glaze on the hot rolls.

## GLAZED HERB RYE BREAD
Freckled with caraway seeds and herbs—

5 cups unsifted rye flour
3 to 3-1/2 cups unsifted white flour
1 teaspoon sugar
2 teaspoons salt
1 to 2 tablespoons caraway seeds
1 tablespoon dried onion flakes
1 tablespoon dill seed
1 tablespoon celery seed
1 tablespoon dried parsley flakes
2 packages dry yeast
2-1/2 cups water
1/4 cup cider vinegar
1/4 cup dark molasses
1/4 cup margarine

Glaze:
1 teaspoon cornstarch
1/2 cup water

In a large bowl, combine rye and white flour. In another large bowl, combine 2-1/2 cups of flour mixture, sugar, salt, caraway seeds, onion flakes, dill seed, celery seed, parsley flakes and dry yeast. In a medium saucepan, combine 2-1/2 cups water, vinegar, molasses and margarine. Heat over medium heat until mixture is steamy. Gradually add to dry ingredients with an electric mixer at medium speed. Beat 2 minutes. Add 1/2 cup flour mixture. Beat 2 minutes at high speed. Use a spoon to stir in only as much of remaining flour as is needed to make a soft dough. Turn out onto lightly floured board or pastry cloth. Cover with inverted bowl; let rest *15* minutes. Knead until smooth and elastic, about 8 to 10 minutes. Place in greased bowl; turn to grease surface. Cover; let rise until double in bulk, about an hour. Grease generously two round 8-inch pans. Punch dough down and turn out onto lightly floured board or pastry cloth. Divide in half. Shape each portion into a flat ball. Place in prepared pans. Cover; let rise until double in bulk, about an hour. Preheat oven to 350 degrees F. Bake 45 to 50 minutes or until bread tests done. While bread bakes, make glaze. In a small saucepan, combine cornstarch and 1/2 cup water. Cook over medium heat until mixture boils; stir constantly. Cook 1 minute. When bread is done and *while bread is still in pans* brush glaze over top of loaves and return bread to oven. Bake 2 to 3 minutes to set glaze. Turn loaves out onto cooling racks. Makes 2 loaves.

## SPIRAL HERB BREAD
The seasonings are in the filling—

1-1/2 cups milk
1/4 cup sugar
2 teaspoons salt
1/2 cup margarine
2 packages dry yeast
1/2 cup warm water
1/4 teaspoon sugar
Dash of ginger
3 eggs, lightly beaten
7-1/2 cups unsifted flour

Filling:
2 cups finely chopped fresh parsley
1 cup finely chopped chives or scallions
2 tablespoons margarine
3/4 teaspoon salt
1/8 teaspoon pepper
Dash of Tabasco sauce
1 egg, slightly beaten
1/4 cup margarine, melted

In a small saucepan, heat milk until bubbles form at sides of pan. Remove from heat. Add 1/4 cup sugar, salt and margarine; stir until margarine melts. Cool to lukewarm. In a large bowl, dissolve yeast in warm water to which 1/4 teaspoon sugar and ginger have been added. Set aside 5 minutes. Add milk-sugar-salt-margarine mixture along with 3 eggs and 4 cups of flour. Use a spoon to beat vigorously until mixture is smooth. Add only as much of remaining flour as is needed to make a soft dough. Turn dough out onto lightly floured board or pastry cloth. Cover with inverted bowl; let rest 5 minutes. Knead until smooth. Place in greased bowl. Cover; let rise until double in bulk, about 1-1/2 hours. While dough rises, make filling. In a small saucepan, combine parsley, chives or scallions and margarine. Saute over medium heat; stir constantly so mixture does not brown. Remove from heat; cool 5 minutes. Stir in salt, pepper and Tabasco sauce. Reserve 2 tablespoons of 1 slightly beaten egg and add remaining egg to parsley-chive-margarine mixture. Grease generously two 9 x 5 x 3-inch loaf pans. Turn dough out onto floured surface and divide in half. Roll each portion out to make an 8 x 16-inch rectangle. Brush rectangles with reserved beaten egg and spread with filling. Start at a narrow end and roll up as for a jelly roll; pinch edges to seal. Tuck ends of spiral under to make smooth loaves and place in prepared pans. Brush top of loaves lightly with half of 1/4 cup melted margarine. Cover; let rise until sides of loaves reach top of pan sides. Preheat oven to 375 degrees F. *Lightly* brush loaves with remaining melted margarine. Bake 35 to 40 minutes or until loaves are golden brown and test done. Remove from pans *immediately* and place on cooling racks away from cool air drafts. Makes 2 loaves.

## WHOLE WHEAT POTATO BREAD
Without peeling or boiling a single potato—

1-1/2 cups water
1-1/4 cups milk
1/4 cup margarine
1/4 cup honey
3-1/2 cups flour
1-1/2 cups mashed potato *flakes*
2-1/2 teaspoons salt
2 packages dry yeast
2 eggs, well beaten
2-1/2 to 3 cups whole wheat flour

In a medium saucepan, heat water, milk, margarine and honey over medium heat until very warm. In a large bowl, combine 2 cups flour, potato flakes, salt, yeast and eggs. Add warm liquids; beat vigorously with a spoon or with an electric mixer at medium speed. Use a spoon to stir in whole wheat flour and only as much of the remaining all-purpose flour as is needed to make a soft dough. Turn dough out onto lightly floured board or pastry cloth. Cover with inverted bowl; let rest 5 minutes. Knead until smooth and elastic, about 5 minutes. Place in a greased bowl; turn to grease surface. Cover; let rise until double in bulk, about an hour. Grease generously two 9 x 5 x 3-inch loaf pans. Turn dough out onto floured surface and divide in half. Shape each portion into a loaf and place in prepared pans. Cover; let rise until double in bulk, about 45 minutes. Preheat oven to 375 degrees F. Bake 35 to 40 minutes or until loaves are golden brown and test done. Makes 2 loaves.

# QUICK BREADS

## HORSERADISH LOAF

Dyed-in-the-wool horseradish lovers of yesterday like *Opa* Mickish, *Dececek* Miller and my father, spiked thick slices of roast beef and smoked ham with freshly ground horseradish to "clear the head," "tickle the throat," and "stimulate the appetite." They liked their horseradish "straight" from a small glass or china relish cup and spoon—ground horseradish blackens silver—and would never have considered diluting its bite by putting it in a sauce. The pungent, creamy white herb looks innocent enough but one small dab of the fiery condiment can cause an unsuspecting diner to grab his throat and grope for a water glass through tear-filled eyes. Just one teaspoon puts a zesty nip in this bread and made it a blue ribbon winner at a local festival—

3 cups flour
1/4 cup sugar
2 tablespoons baking powder
1 tablespoon mustard seed
1-1/2 teaspoons salt
3 eggs, well beaten
3/4 cup milk
1/4 cup margarine, melted oil
1 tablespoon prepared mustard
1 teaspoon prepared horseradish

Preheat oven to 375 degrees F. Grease a 9 x 5 x 3-inch loaf pan. In a large bowl, combine flour, sugar, baking powder, mustard seed and salt; blend thoroughly. In a small bowl, combine eggs, milk, oil, mustard and horseradish; blend thoroughly. Add liquid mixture to dry ingredients all at one time. Stir only until dry ingredients are moistened. Pour into prepared pan. Bake 65 minutes or until bread tests done. Cool in pan 15 minutes before removing to cooling rack. Makes 1 loaf.

## OVERNIGHT COFFEE CAKE

Measure and mix, put it in a pan and then in the "frig."
Come morning, this quick bread is ready for the oven—

2 cups flour
1 teaspoon baking powder
1 teaspoon baking soda
1/2 teaspoon salt
1 teaspoon cinnamon
2/3 cup margarine
1 cup sugar
1/2 cup brown sugar, firmly packed
2 eggs
1 cup buttermilk

Crumb Topping:
1/2 cup brown sugar, firmly packed
1/2 cup chopped walnuts
1/2 teaspoon cinnamon
1/4 teaspoon nutmeg

Grease a 9 x 13-inch baking pan or two round 8-inch cake pans. Sift flour, baking powder, baking soda, salt and cinnamon together. In a large bowl, combine margarine, sugar and 1/2 cup brown sugar. Cream until fluffy. Add eggs one at a time; beat well after each addition. Add dry ingredients alternately with buttermilk; start and end with dry ingredients. Beat well after each addition. Spread batter in prepared pan or pans. To make topping: In a small bowl, combine 1/2 cup brown sugar, walnuts, 1/2 teaspoon cinnamon and nutmeg. Sprinkle evenly over batter. Cover with plastic wrap and refrigerate overnight. The next morning, preheat oven to 350 degrees F. Remove plastic and bake 35 to 40 minutes or until coffee cake is lightly browned and tests done. Serves 12.

## APPLE-CRANBERRY BREAD

For the holidays when fresh cranberries are on the market—

1/2 cup shortening
1 cup sugar
1 egg
2 cups flour
2 teaspoons baking powder
1/2 teaspoon baking soda
1/2 teaspoon salt
1/2 teaspoon cinnamon
1/2 teaspoon mace
1/2 cup orange juice
1 cup peeled and shredded Golden Delicious apples
1 cup fresh cranberries, chopped fine, makes about 1/2 cup
1 tablespoon freshly grated orange peel

Preheat oven to 340 degrees F. Grease a 9 x 5 x 3-inch loaf pan. In a large bowl, cream shortening. Add sugar and continue to cream until mixture is light and fluffy. Add egg; beat well. Sift flour, baking powder, baking soda, salt, cinnamon and mace together. Add dry ingredients to creamed mixture alternately with orange juice; start and end with dry ingredients. Beat well after each addition. Blend in apple, cranberries and orange peel. Turn batter into prepared pan. Bake 1-1/4 hours or until bread is golden brown and tests done. Cool bread in pan 5 minutes before turning out onto cooling rack. Makes 1 loaf.

## PEACHY MUFFINS

When it's the fresh peach season, make these muffins with the sugary tops—

2 cups flour
1/3 cup brown sugar, firmly packed
1 teaspoon baking powder
1/2 teaspoon salt
1/4 teaspoon baking soda
1/8 teaspoon allspice
1 fresh peach, peeled and chopped, enough to make 1/2 cup
1 egg
1/4 cup melted butter
1 cup sour cream
2 tablespoons brown sugar, firmly packed

Preheat oven to 375 degrees F. Grease a 12-muffin muffin pan. In a large bowl, sift flour, brown sugar, baking powder, salt, baking soda and allspice. Make a well in the center of the dry ingredients. Add peaches. In a small bowl, beat egg. Add butter and sour cream; blend well. Pour into center of dry ingredients. Stir just to moisten dry ingredients, about 12 strokes—batter will appear lumpy. Put batter into prepared pan; fill muffin cups two-thirds full. Sprinkle evenly with 2 tablespoons of brown sugar. Bake 20 to 25 minutes or until muffins are browned and test done. Makes 12 muffins.

## THREE-HERB MUFFINS

A not-too-sweet muffin for dinner or to go with ham, chicken or other luncheon salads—

1-1/2 cups unsifted flour
1 cup wheat germ
1/4 grated Parmesan cheese
2 tablespoons sugar
3 teaspoons baking powder
1 teaspoon salt
1/2 teaspoon marjoram leaves, crushed
1/2 teaspoon thyme leaves, crushed
1/4 teaspoon rosemary leaves, crushed
1 egg, slightly beaten
1 cup milk
1/4 cup margarine, melted

Topping:
1 teaspoon margarine, melted
2 tablespoons wheat germ
1 teaspoon grated Parmesan cheese
1/2 teaspoon sugar

Preheat oven to 400 degrees F. Grease a 12-muffin muffin pan. In a large bowl, combine flour, 1 cup wheat germ, 1/4 cup Parmesan cheese, 2 tablespoons sugar, baking powder, salt, marjoram, thyme and rosemary; blend thoroughly. In a small bowl, combine egg, milk and margarine. Add to dry ingredients all at one time. Stir just until dry ingredients are moistened, 10 to 12 strokes. Turn batter into prepared pan; fill muffin cups only two-thirds full. To make topping: In a small bowl, combine 1 teaspoon margarine, 2 tablespoons wheat germ, 1 teaspoon Parmesan cheese and 1/2 teaspoon sugar; blend thoroughly. Sprinkle evenly over batter. Bake 15 to 18 minutes. Makes 12 muffins.

# CAKE

### MASTERPIECE CAKE

A good old cake recipe made even better by switching "lard" to "shortening," "vanilla" to "almond and coconut extracts," adding a packet of dry "Dream Whip" and letting an electric mixer do the beating and mixing. "Dream Whip" is the secret ingredient that makes this a very fine-textured cake yet one that is easy to handle, making it particularly well-suited for wedding cakes, anniversary cakes or other multi-layered and decorated cakes. *Do not double the original recipe*; but repeat it as many times as is necessary to make the desired number of layers in the sizes and shapes needed. See Cake Tips for further information—

1/2 cup plus 2 tablespoons shortening
1 cup sugar
2 cups flour, *do not use cake flour*
2 tablespoons cornstarch
2 teaspoons baking powder
1/2 teaspoon salt
4 egg whites
1 cup milk
1/2 teaspoon almond extract
1 teaspoon coconut extract
1 envelope Dream Whip, in dry, powdered form

Preheat oven to 350 degrees F. Grease two round 9-inch cake pans, two square 8-inch cake pans or a 9 x 13-inch pan. Line pan or pans with waxed paper which has been greased and floured. In a large bowl, cream shortening and sugar at high speed until light and fluffy. *Sift flour before measuring*. Sift flour, cornstarch, baking powder and salt together. Add to creamed mixture along with egg whites, milk, almond and coconut extracts and Dream Whip—*ADD ALL AT ONE TIME*. Beat 4 minutes at medium speed. Pour batter into prepared pan or pans. Bake 25 to 30 minutes or until cake tests done. Cool cake in pan or pans 10 minutes before turning out onto cooling racks. Cool cake completely then frost with favorite icing or with White Frosting. Serves 16.

White Frosting:
3/4 cup flour
2 tablespoons cornstarch
1 cup shortening
1/2 teaspoon salt
3/4 cup cold water
2 pounds sifted powdered sugar
1/2 teaspoon almond extract
Few drops of lemon extract to taste

In a medium bowl, sift flour and cornstarch together. Add shortening and salt. Blend at low speed until well mixed; then cream at high speed until mixture is light and creamy. Add water *very slowly, 1 to 2 teaspoons at a time*. Gradually beat in powdered sugar; continue beating until frosting is very light and smooth. Blend in almond and lemon extracts. Unused frosting will keep indefinitely in refrigerator in a sealed container. Allow refrigerated frosting to soften at room temperature briefly so it will spread more easily.

# CANDY

## CRUNCH BALLS

Snap, crackle and pop! And peanut butter, too, all dipped in chocolate—

2 cups creamy style peanut butter
1/2 cup margarine, melted
1 1-pound box powdered sugar
3-1/2 cups Rice Krispies cereal, crushed
1 8-ounce plain Hershey candy bar
Half of 4-ounce bar of paraffin
1 6-ounce package of semi-sweet chocolate chips

In a very large bowl combine peanut butter and margarine; blend thoroughly. Add powdered sugar; cream thoroughly. Add cereal; blend thoroughly. Use hands to shape mixture into balls 1-inch in diameter. In top of double boiler combine candy bar, paraffin and chips. Melt over simmering water; stir to blend thoroughly. Use a toothpick and a spoon to dip each ball separately into hot chocolate sauce. Leave chocolate sauce over hot water while dipping balls. Place dipped balls on waxed paper to set; chocolate sauce sets up very quickly. Makes 50 to 60 balls.

# COOKIES

## GOOD-BETTER-BEST 100 COOKIES
Grease all the cookies sheets you have—this recipes makes LOTS of cookies and they freeze very well, too—

1 cup sugar
1 cup brown sugar, firmly packed
1 cup margarine
1 egg
1 cup vegetable oil
3-1/2 cups flour
1 teaspoon salt
1 teaspoon baking soda
1 teaspoon cream of tartar
3 teaspoons vanilla
1 cup quick-cook oatmeal
1 cup Rice Krispies cereal
1 cup flaked coconut
1 cup chopped walnuts

Preheat oven to 350 degrees F. Grease cookies sheets. In a large bowl, cream sugar, brown sugar and margarine until light and fluffy. Add egg; beat well. Add oil; blend thoroughly. Sift flour, salt, baking soda and cream of tartar together. Add to sugar-margarine-egg-oil mixture; beat well. Add vanilla; blend thoroughly. Use a spoon to stir in oatmeal, Rice Krispies, coconut and walnuts; mix thoroughly. Drop by teaspoonfuls onto prepared cookie sheets; press down with a fork dipped in flour. Bake 8 to 10 minutes or until cookies are slightly browned and test done. Makes 100 cookies.

## CHOCOLATE LACE COOKIES
A cookie to dress up any tea table—

1/2 cup flour
2/3 cup sugar
1/4 cup cocoa
1/2 cup white corn syrup
1/2 cup margarine, softened to room temperature
1/2 teaspoon rum extract or vanilla

Preheat oven to 375 degrees F. Lightly grease two or three cookie sheets. In a small bowl, combine flour, sugar and cocoa. In a small saucepan over high heat, bring syrup quickly to a boil. Remove from heat. Add margarine; stir until it melts. Stir in rum extract or vanilla. Add flour mixture; mix thoroughly. Allow 2 teaspoons of batter for each cookie; drop batter *7 inches* apart on prepared cookie sheets. Batter spreads during baking to make 4-1/2-inch cookies; bake no more than 4 cookies on each cookie sheet. Bake 5 to 7 minutes. Remove from oven. Cool cookies on cookie sheet 2 minutes, then, *work quickly* to gently loosen cookies from cookie sheet with a wide spatula and roll around a round, foil-covered object that is about an inch in diameter—a *metal, not plastic,* knitting needle or the handle of a wooden spoon will do. If cookies harden on cookie sheet, return sheet to oven for *1 minute* to soften cookies slightly so they can be rolled without breaking. Makes 3 dozen.

## COFFEE BARS
Coffee in the bars, coffee in the frosting—

1 cup golden raisins
2/3 cup fresh, hot coffee
1/2 teaspoon cinnamon
1 cup sugar
2/3 cup margarine
2 eggs
1-1/2 cups flour
1/2 teaspoon baking powder
1/2 teaspoon baking soda
1/2 teaspoon salt

Frosting:
1 cup sifted powdered sugar
1 to 2 tablespoons fresh, hot coffee

Preheat oven to 350 degrees F. Grease a 10 x 15-inch baking pan. In a small bowl, combine raisins, coffee and cinnamon. Set aside. In a large bowl, cream sugar and margarine until light and fluffy. Add eggs one at a time; beat well after each addition. Sift flour, baking powder, baking soda and salt together. Add to sugar-margarine-egg mixture; beat well. Use a spoon to stir in raisin-coffee mixture; blend thoroughly. Spread batter into prepared pan. Bake 20 to 25 minutes or until bars test done. To make frosting: In a small bowl, combine powdered sugar and coffee to make a thin frosting. *Frost bars as soon as they are removed from the oven. Cool completely before cutting into bars.* Makes 3 dozen.

# DESSERTS

## BAKED APPLE CUSTARD
Whole apples baked in a custard—

6 small, tart baking apples
1 cup water
1 tablespoon fresh lemon juice
5 eggs
4 cups milk
3/4 cup sugar
1 teaspoon vanilla
1/4 teaspoon nutmeg

Preheat oven to 350 degrees F. Have a shallow two-quart baking dish at hand. Pare and core apples. In a skillet over medium heat, bring water to boil. Add lemon juice and apples. Simmer gently until apples are just tender; baste occasionally. Use a slotted spoon to remove apples and place in baking dish. In a large bowl, beat eggs. Add milk, sugar, vanilla and nutmeg; blend thoroughly until sugar dissolves. Pour over apples. Place baking dish in a pan containing 1/2-inch of water. Bake 50 minutes or until a silver table knife inserted in custard half an inch from edge of baking dish comes out clean. Cool at least 20 minutes before serving. Serves 6.

## RASPBERRY LEMON ICE CREAM BOMBE
Festive and fancy-looking but so easy to make—

1 package of lady fingers
1 quart raspberry ice cream, softened
1 pint lemon sherbet, softened

Sauce:
1 10-ounce package frozen raspberries, thawed
1 cup raspberry juice
2 tablespoons cornstarch
Dash of salt
2 teaspoons fresh lemon juice
Red food coloring

Split lady fingers. Cut rounded tips off one end of enough lady fingers so they stand on end to line the sides of a 9 x 5 x 3-inch loaf pan. Trim rounded tips off both ends of remaining lady fingers so they fit snugly on the bottom of the pan. Freeze. Spoon raspberry ice cream over frozen lady fingers; push ice cream into grooves between lady fingers. Freeze. Spread lemon sherbet over frozen raspberry ice cream—be sure raspberry ice cream is *frozen solid.* Freeze. To make sauce: Drain raspberries; reserve the juice. Add enough water to juice to make 1 cup. In a medium saucepan, combine juice-water mixture, cornstarch and salt. Cook over medium heat; stir constantly until mixture thickens. Stir in lemon juice. Add raspberries and stir gently so as not to break up berries. Cool and refrigerate. At serving time, unmold bombe by dipping pan into deep warm water. Place platter over pan and turn out bombe. Slice bombe into 1-inch slices and spoon over raspberry sauce. Serves 8.

## VANILLA ICE CREAM FOR SALTON FREEZER

This little ice cream maker can turn out homemade ice cream—enough to serve two or enough for pie or cake ala mode to serve four—without ice or salt in about an hour. Exact freezing time depends on the inside temperature of the home freezer or the refrigerator's freezer compartment—

1-1/4 cups milk
1/2 cup sugar
1-1/2 teaspoons unflavored gelatin
1/4 cup water
2 cups heavy cream, whipping cream
1 teaspoon vanilla

In a small saucepan over low heat, scald milk. Add sugar; stir until sugar dissolves. Soften gelatin in water; stir until gelatin completely dissolves. Add to hot milk. Cool completely. Add cream and vanilla; blend thoroughly. Pour into ice cream maker. Plug cord for freezer motor into a wall outlet and set ice cream maker inside home freezer or freezer compartment of refrigerator. Let freezer churn until motor stops; check frequently during freezing time, about an hour. When motor stops, remove ice cream maker from freezer and transfer the soft ice cream to a plastic container and place in home freezer. Makes 2 whole servings or 4 small servings.

# BEEF, LAMB, PORK— AND POULTRY

## CRISP BACON
For crisp, flat, uncurled bacon, cook it in the oven—

Preheat oven to 400 degrees F. Have a 9 x 13-inch baking pan and two wire cooling racks at hand. Place one cooling rack inside the 9 x 13-inch baking pan. Place strips of bacon on the rack and cover with second cooling rack—the wire of the top rack must be perpendicular to the wires of bottom rack. Length of baking time depends on how thick and lean the bacon is. Watch carefully and remove from oven when bacon reaches desired degree of crispness.

## BEEF OR LAMB COFFEE ROAST
Coffee adds intriguing flavor to roasts and wait until you taste the gravy—

1 5-pound beef rump roast or leg of lamb
1 small onion
2 garlic cloves
1 cup cider vinegar
3 tablespoons shortening
2 cups strong, hot coffee
2 cups water
Salt and pepper to taste

Use the tip of a sharp knife to cut slits in meat and insert slivers of onion and garlic. Place meat in a glass or ceramic bowl—*do not use a stainless steel bowl*—and pour vinegar over. Cover with plastic wrap and refrigerate 24 hours. For a beef roast: In a Dutch oven or heavy roaster, melt shortening and brown roast all sides. Add coffee and water. Cover. Reduce heat and simmer slowly on top of stove 6 hours; add water as needed; or, place in a preheated 325 degree F. oven 4 hours. Serves 8. For a leg of lamb: Preheat oven to 450 degrees F. In the bottom of a Dutch oven or heavy roaster, cook lamb *uncovered* at high temperature *30 minutes*, then add coffee and water. Cover. Reduce oven heat to 350 degrees F. Allow 30 minutes per pound total cooking time for lamb; it should not be overcooked and *it must be served hot*! *Do not season beef or lamb with salt and pepper until the last 20 minutes of roasting time.* Serves 8.

## HAM WELLINGTON

Ham baked in a dough crust was one of the entrees I prepared and served at a buffet dinner at my home for my 1922 high school graduating classmates and their spouses for our sixtieth-year class reunion—

2 cups Master Mix or biscuit mix
1/2 cup cold water
1 8-pound fully cooked boneless ham
1 egg yolk

Preheat oven to 325 degrees F. Place ham on a cookie sheet. In a small bowl, combine Master Mix or biscuit mix and water to form a soft dough. Beat vigorously *30 seconds*. Add another 1 to 2 tablespoons of mix if dough seems too sticky to handle. Turn dough out onto board or pastry cloth lightly floured with a few tablespoons of mix. Knead 10 times. Roll or pat out into a 12 x 16-inch rectangle. Dough will be easier to handle if the long sides are folded toward the center; then lift it gently and place it over the ham. Unfold dough and press it firmly onto and around the ham—*do not press dough underneath the ham*. Trim off the bottom edge of the dough and press firmly onto cookie sheet to seal. Roll dough trimmings out on floured surface until they are 1/8-inch thick. Use a knife or cookie cutter to cut dough into shapes resembling leaves and petals of flowers. Arrange shapes in designs on top of dough. In a small bowl, beat egg yolk. Brush over entire surface of dough; take care not to dislodge or misshape the overlaid pieces of dough. Bake 1 hour and 50 minutes. Dough will be a deep golden brown. Use a sharp knife to carefully slice ham into 1/2-inch serving slices; each slice should be served in its own crust. Serves 20.

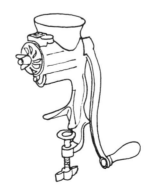

## ISLAND CHICKEN
With a perky pineapple flavor—

2 whole chicken legs, legs and thighs attached
2 whole chicken breasts, split into four halves
1 cup flour
1-1/2 teaspoons salt
1/2 teaspoon pepper
1/3 cup shortening
1 1-pound 4-ounce can sliced pineapple, drained, reserve juice
Water
1 cup sugar
2 tablespoons cornstarch
3/4 cup cider vinegar
1 tablespoon soy sauce
1/4 teaspoon ginger
1 teaspoon chicken stock base or 1 chicken bouillon cube
1 large green pepper, sliced crosswise into 1/4-inch wide rings

Preheat oven to 350 degrees F. Have 9 x 13-inch baking dish at hand. Bone chicken pieces. In a shallow bowl, combine flour, salt and pepper. Dredge chicken pieces in flour mixture. In a large heavy skillet, melt shortening and brown chicken on all sides. Remove chicken to baking dish; arrange with skin side up. Drain pineapple; reserve juice. Add enough water to juice to make 1-1/4 cups of liquid. In a medium saucepan, combine pineapple-water mixture with sugar, cornstarch, vinegar, soy sauce, ginger and chicken stock base. Bring to a boil over medium heat. Cook 2 minutes; stir constantly. Pour sauce over chicken. Bake *uncovered* 30 minutes. Arrange pineapple slices and green pepper rings over chicken. Return to oven. Bake another 30 minutes. Serves 4.

## CHICKEN AND DRESSING CASSEROLE
While the casserole bakes, prepare Mushroom Sauce—

1 8-ounce package of herb-seasoned stuffing
1 cup hot water
1/2 cup butter or margarine
3 cups cubed cooked chicken or turkey
1/2 cup butter or margarine
1/2 cup flour
1/4 teaspoon salt
Dash of pepper
4 cups chicken broth
6 eggs, slightly beaten

Mushroom Sauce:
1 10-1/2-ounce can cream of mushroom soup
1/4 cup milk
1/4 cup chopped pimentos
1 cup sour cream

Preheat oven to 325 degrees F. Butter a 9 x 13-inch baking dish. In a large bowl, combine stuffing, water and 1/2 cup butter. Spread into prepared pan. Top with chicken pieces. In a medium saucepan, melt 1/2 cup butter over moderate heat. Blend in flour, salt and pepper; stir constantly. Gradually add broth. Cook until sauce is thick; stir constantly. Stir a small amount of sauce into beaten eggs. Mix thoroughly before returning all of egg mixture to saucepan. Heat until sauce thickens; *do not over-cook sauce*. Pour sauce over stuffing and chicken. Bake 40 to 45 minutes or until casserole is set. At serving time, cut into squares and top with Mushroom Sauce. To make Mushroom Sauce: In a medium saucepan, combine soup and milk; stir until smooth. Stir in pimentos. Cook over low heat until bubbly. At serving time, stir in sour cream and heat through; *do not allow sauce to bubble after sour cream has been added*. Serves 12.

## CASHEW CHICKEN CASSEROLE
With plenty of crunch—

1 10-1/2-ounce can cream of mushroom soup
1/4 cup water
2 cups cooked, diced chicken
1 cup thinly sliced celery
1/2 cup chopped salted cashew nuts
1/4 cup finely chopped onion
1/4 cup chopped green pepper
Pepper to taste
3 ounces chow mein noodles

Preheat oven to 375 degrees F. Have a 7 x 11-inch shallow two-quart casserole at hand. In a small bowl, combine soup and water; blend thoroughly. In a large bowl, combine chicken, celery, nuts, onion, green pepper, pepper and *half of the noodles*; blend thoroughly. Put into casserole; sprinkle with remaining noodles. Bake 25 to 30 minutes. Serves 4 to 6.

## NOODLE TUNA CASSEROLE
Cream cheese and celery soup improve the flavor of an old stand-by—

3 quarts boiling water
1 tablespoon salt
8 ounces egg noodles
1/2 cup milk
1 3-ounce package chive-flavored cream cheese, softened
1 10-1/2-ounce can cream of celery soup
1 tablespoon prepared mustard
2 tablespoons finely chopped onion
2 6-1/2-ounce cans tuna, drained
1 tablespoon minced chives or green onions

Preheat oven to 350 degrees F. Butter a one-and-a-half-quart casserole. In a large saucepan, cook noodles in boiling water with salt until tender according to package directions. Drain; place in a large bowl. In a medium bowl, combine milk and cream cheese; mix thoroughly. Add soup, mustard, onion and tuna; blend thoroughly. Add to noodles; blend thoroughly. Turn into prepared casserole. Bake 25 minutes. At serving time, garnish with minced chives. Serves 8.

# PICKLES

## HAMBURGER DILL PICKLES
Use a slicer so cucumbers are sliced uniformly thin—

Fresh cucumbers, 1-1/2-inches in diameter
1 large onion
Garlic cloves
1 pint water
1 quart cider vinegar
1/4 teaspoon alum
1-1/2 cups sugar
1/2 cup coarse pickling salt

Wash and slice *unpeeled* cucumbers into very thin slices. Peel and slice onion. In the bottom of sterilized pint jars, place a slice of onion and 1 small garlic clove. Fill jars with cucumber slices to within 1/2-inch of the top. In a large saucepan, combine water, vinegar, alum, sugar and salt. Heat to bubbling. Pour over cucumbers. Seal jars immediately. Recipe makes liquid for 7 pints of pickles.

## REFRIGERATOR SWEET PICKLES
Fast and easy—there's no cooking—

Fresh cucumbers, 1-inch in diameter and three inches long
1 large onion
4 cups sugar
1/2 cup salt, scant
1-1/3 teaspoons celery seed
1-1/3 teaspoons mustard seed
1-1/3 teaspoons tumeric
4 cups white vinegar

Wash and slice *unpeeled* cucumbers with a slicer so they are uniformly thin. Peel and slice onion. In the bottom of six sterilized pint jars, place one or two onion slices. Fill jars with cucumber slices to within 1/2-inch of the top. In a large bowl, combine sugar, salt, celery seed, mustard seed, tumeric and vinegar. *Do not heat this solution.* Stir until sugar and salt dissolve. Pour over cucumber slices. Let pickles stand at least 5 days in refrigerator before using. Pickles keep several months. Makes 6 pints.

# SALADS

## FRUIT SALAD DRESSING
A tangy topping for fresh fruits—

1 3-ounce package cream cheese, softened
1/4 teaspoon cinnamon
1 cup sour cream
1/2 teaspoon freshly grated tangerine peel
1 tablespoon fresh tangerine juice
1/3 cup chopped walnuts
2 tablespoons honey

In a small bowl, stir softened cheese briskly. Add cinnamon, sour cream, tangerine peel and juice, nuts and honey; blend thoroughly. Arrange fruit on a bed of lettuce leaves and spoon on dressing. Goes well with fresh oranges, grapefruit and tangerine sections, apples, pears, watermelon, cantaloupe, honeydew melon, strawberries, peaches, plums, apricots, bananas, grapes, any fresh fruit will do. Makes 1-1/2 cups.

## GOOSEBERRY SURPRISE SALAD
You have to try it to believe it—

1 16-ounce can gooseberries in syrup
1/2 cup sugar
1 3-ounce package lemon-flavored gelatin
1 3-ounce package lime-flavored gelatin
2 cups boiling water
1/2 teaspoon lemon extract
1 cup diced celery
1/2 cup chopped pecans
1 cup shredded Cheddar cheese

Dressing:
1/2 cup mayonnaise
1 tablespoon honey
2 to 3 tablespoons French dressing

In a medium saucepan, combine gooseberries in syrup with sugar. Stir until sugar dissolves. Bring gooseberry-sugar mixture just to boiling over medium heat. Remove from heat. Cool. In a large bowl, dissolve lemon and lime-flavored gelatins in boiling water. Cool. Add lemon extract. Add cooled gooseberry-sugar mixture to cooled gelatin mixture; blend thoroughly. Fold in celery, nuts and cheese. Turn into a rinsed 7 x 11-inch or 6 x 10-inch glass baking dish. Refrigerate until set. Allow salad to chill at least 3 hours before serving. To make dressing: In a small bowl, combine mayonnaise and honey; blend thoroughly. Add just enough French dressing to make a dressing thin enough to stream from a spoon. Serves 8.

## POPPY SEED DRESSING
Super with fresh spinach salad—

1-1/2 cups sugar
2 teaspoons dry mustard
2 teaspoons salt
2/3 cup cider vinegar
1 small onion, chopped fine
2 cups vegetable oil
3 tablespoons poppy seeds

In an electric blender, combine sugar, mustard, salt, vinegar, onion and oil; blend 1 minute. Add poppy seeds; blend a few seconds. Refrigerate. Makes 4 cups.

## TUNA MOLD
Serve as an appetizer or a main course salad—

1 10-1/2-ounces can tomato soup
1 8-ounce package cream cheese
1-1/2 envelopes unflavored gelatin
1/2 cup cold water
1 cup mayonnaise
1-1/2 cups diced celery
1/2 cup diced onion
2 6-1/2-ounces cans tuna fish, drained
1 tablespoon mayonnaise
1 small cucumber, peeled, seeded and diced
1 cup sour cream

In a small saucepan and over medium heat, bring undiluted soup to simmering. Add cream cheese; heat until cheese melts. In a cup, dissolve gelatin in cold water. Add to hot soup-cheese mixture; blend thoroughly. Add mayonnaise, celery, onion and tuna; blend thoroughly. Coat a six-cup ring salad mold with 1 tablespoon mayonnaise. Pour in salad mixture. Refrigerate at least 3 hours before serving. At serving time, dip ring mold in hot water and unmold onto serving tray. In a small bowl, combine diced cucumber and sour cream; heap in the center of the molded tuna ring. Serves 8.

## SPINACH SALAD

If you don't grow your own spinach, find the freshest, crispest bunch of spinach to make this salad—

Fresh spinach, rinsed and chilled
8 to 12 fresh red radishes, rinsed, stemmed and sliced thin
4 chopped green onions, include some of tops
8 strips of bacon, fried crisp and crumbled
2 hard-cooked eggs, split, reserve yolks
1 cup vegetable oil
1/4 cup sugar
1/4 cup cider vinegar
1 tablespoon freshly grated onion
3 tablespoons catsup
1 teaspoon Worcestershire sauce
1/4 teaspoon salt
Dash of pepper

Prepare as much spinach as is needed to make a full bed on four large salad plates. Add a layer of sliced radishes. Sprinkle onions over radishes. Sprinkle bacon over onions. Sieve egg yolks over all. Sliver egg whites into half-moon shaped pieces and arrange as garnishes on salads. In a two-cup *lidded* jar combine vegetable oil, sugar, vinegar, onion, catsup, Worcestershire sauce, salt and pepper. Shake to blend thoroughly. At serving time, pass dressing in a pitcher. Makes 1-1/2 cups.

When fresh, ripe Bartlett pears are plentiful, they can be the center of attraction on a summer salad plate. Here's a trio of glazed pear recipes.

## PEARS WITH CRAN-APPLE GLAZE
And a touch of cinnamon, too—

6 fresh ripe, blemish-free pears with stems still attached
2 cups cranberry-apple juice
1/2 cup water
1 2-inch long cinnamon stick
Fresh mint leaves

Wash and pare pears; leave stems on. In a large saucepan, combine pears, juice, water and cinnamon stick. Bring to a boil over medium heat; *cook uncovered.* Reduce heat so syrup barely simmers. Cook until pears are tender, 20 to 30 minutes. Test carefully with a toothpick. Turn pears occasionally so they cook evenly. Use a slotted spoon to lift pears from syrup and place in a deep bowl. Discard cinnamon stick. Return juice to heat and continue boiling to reduce syrup to 1-1/2 cups. Pour over pears. Refrigerate pears in syrup. Chill until completely cool. Turn pears occasionally during chilling time so color is absorbed evenly. To serve place each pear upright in a small glass dish and garnish with a mint leaf placed on the stem end. Serves 6.

## APRICOT-GLAZED PEARS
A sweet way with pears—

6 or 8 fresh, ripe, blemish-free pears with stems still attached
4 cups sugar
1 teaspoon vanilla
2 cups water
1 12-ounce jar apricot preserves
Fresh mint leaves

Wash and pare pears; leave stems on. In a large saucepan, combine sugar, vanilla and water. Heat over medium heat; stir until sugar dissolves. Add pears. Simmer *uncovered* until pears are tender, about 20 to 30 minutes. Test carefully with a toothpick. Turn pears occasionally so they cook evenly. Use a slotted spoon to remove pears from syrup; drain thoroughly. Discard syrup. In a small saucepan, heat apricot preserves just to a boil over low heat. Boil gently one minute. Press through a sieve. Brush pears with hot preserves; coat well. Refrigerate several hours before serving. To serve, place each pear upright in a small glass dish and garnish with a mint leaf placed on the stem end. Serves 6 to 8.

## ELEGANT GLAZED PEARS
And one more version—

6 fresh, ripe, blemish-free pears with stems still attached
2 tablespoons fresh lemon juice
3 cups water
1 cup sugar
4 tablespoons fresh lemon juice
4 whole cloves
1 12-ounce jar orange marmalade
1 16-ounce can apricot halves, drained
Fresh green grapes

Wash, pare and core pears. Rub gently with 2 tablespoons lemon juice to prevent discoloration. In a large saucepan over medium heat, boil water, sugar, lemon juice and cloves 5 minutes. Add pears; simmer until tender. Test carefully with a toothpick. Turn pears occasionally during cooking time so they cook evenly. Use a slotted spoon to remove pears; place in a shallow bowl. Discard cloves. Simmer syrup to reduce it to 1-1/4 cups. Stir in marmalade. Cool. To serve, arrange apricot halves and grapes around pears and pour syrup over all. Serves 6.

# SOUP

## HURRY-UP VEGETABLE SOUP
Homemade soup ready in an hour—

1 pound ground beef
1 to 2 tablespoons shortening
1 quart stewed tomatoes, sieved
2 cups diced potatoes
2 large carrots, sliced
1/2 cup celery, sliced
1 medium onion, chopped
1/4 cup regular, uncooked rice
1 tablespoon salt
1/8 teaspoon pepper
1-3/4 cups water

In a large saucepan, brown ground beef in shortening. Add tomatoes, potatoes, carrots, celery, onion, rice, salt, pepper and water. Reduce heat when mixture steams; simmer an hour. Serves 6.

# VEGETABLES

## MONTEREY BROCCOLI CASSEROLE
With a touch of Mexican green chilies—

1-1/2 pounds fresh broccoli, enough to make 3 cups of small florets and
    chopped stems, use only tender stems
6 green onions, chopped, include some of the tops
2 tablespoons margarine
4 eggs, well beaten
2 cups milk
1-1/2 cups grated sharp Cheddar cheese
1 cup cooked rice
1/4 cup chopped canned green chilies
1 2-ounce jar pimentos, chopped
1-1/4 teaspoons salt
1/2 teaspoon Worcestershire sauce

Preheat oven to 350 degrees F. Butter a shallow, two-quart baking dish. In a medium saucepan, cook broccoli in lightly salted water 3 to 5 minutes; drain well. In a medium saucepan, saute onion in margarine. Remove from heat. Add eggs and milk; blend well. Stir in cheese, rice, chilies, pimentos, salt and Worcestershire sauce; blend thoroughly. Add broccoli; stir gently to blend. Pour into prepared baking dish and set in a pan of hot water. Bake 40 minutes or until custard is set so when a table knife is inserted in the center, it comes out clean. Serves 8.

## CABBAGE CASSEROLE
With lots of extras—

1 small head of green cabbage, coarsely shredded
1 teaspoon salt
2 cups boiling water
2 hard-cooked eggs, coarsely chopped
2 tablespoons margarine
1 tablespoon flour
1-1/2 cups milk
1 teaspoon mustard
1 tablespoon chopped onion
1 tablespoon chopped green pepper
1 tablespoon chopped pimentos
3/4 cup shredded American cheese

Preheat oven to 375 degrees F. Butter a deep, two-quart casserole. In a medium saucepan, bring salted water to boil over high heat; drop in shredded cabbage. *Cook uncovered* 5 minutes. Drain. Layer cabbage and eggs in prepared casserole. In a small saucepan over medium heat, melt margarine. Add flour and stir until smooth. Gradually add milk. Cook until sauce thickens; stir constantly. Stir in mustard, onion, green pepper, pimentos and cheese. Pour over cabbage and eggs. Bake 15 minutes. Serves 6.

## CHEESY CAULIFLOWER CASSEROLE
For those who claim they don't like cauliflower—

1 large head cauliflower, broken into small, bite-size florets
1/4 cup flour
1/2 cup water
2 cups chicken broth, canned or prepared with chicken stock or bouillon cubes
2 tablespoons finely chopped green onions
Salt and pepper
1 cup shredded Cheddar cheese

Preheat oven to 350 degrees F. Butter a deep, two-quart casserole. In a medium saucepan, cook cauliflower in lightly salted water until almost tender, about 7 or 8 minutes. Drain. Place in prepared casserole. In a small bowl, stir flour into water to make a thickening paste. In a small saucepan over low heat, bring chicken broth to a gentle boil. Gradually stir in thickening. Cook over medium heat until broth thickens; stir constantly. Add onion, salt and pepper. Pour over cauliflower. Top with cheese. Bake uncovered 25 minutes. Serves 6.

## CUKE CASSEROLE
A unexpected taste treat—goes great with barbecued ribs—

6 slicing cucumbers
1/4 cup chopped green onions, include some of the tops
1/4 cup chopped red onion
Dash of pepper
1/4 teaspoon garlic salt
1 8-ounce can water chestnuts, drained and sliced thin
2 tablespoons margarine
2 tablespoons flour
1/2 teaspoon salt
1 cup milk
1 cup mayonnaise
1 cup grated Cheddar cheese

Preheat oven to 350 degrees F. Butter a shallow, two-quart baking dish. Peel and quarter cucumbers lengthwise. In a medium saucepan, cook cucumbers 5 minutes in lightly salted water. Drain well. Arrange in prepared baking dish. Sprinkle with green onions, red onion, pepper, garlic salt and chestnuts. In a small saucepan over medium heat, melt margarine. Add flour and salt. Stir until smooth. Gradually add milk. Cook until sauce is thick and bubbly; stir constantly. Add mayonnaise; blend well. Pour over cucumber-onion-chestnut mixture. Sprinkle with cheese. Bake 25 to 30 minutes. Serves 6.

## YELLOW SUMMER SQUASH
Double baked—

2 medium yellow, crook-necked squashes, cut in half and seeded
1/4 cup water
1 tablespoon butter flavoring
1/2 teaspoon salt

Preheat oven to 350 degrees F. Place squash halves cut sides down in a shallow pan. Pour water around halves. Bake 30 minutes. Butter a two-quart casserole. Scoop baked pulp out of shells and mash. Add butter flavoring and salt. Turn into prepared casserole. Bake 20 minutes. Serves 4.

## EVERGREEN ZUCCHINI
Easy and full of flavor—

8 medium zucchini squashes
1 tablespoon salt
1-1/2 cups water
1/4 cup margarine
Dash of garlic powder
1/4 cup chopped green onions, include some of tops
1/2 teaspoon freshly grated lemon peel
2 tablespoons fresh lemon juice

Wash squash, trim ends and cut into 1/2-inch slices. In a medium saucepan, cook zucchini in salted water until just tender, about 8 minutes. Drain. Add margarine, garlic powder, onion, lemon peel and lemon juice; stir gently to blend. Return to low heat. When mixture is heated through, it's ready to serve. Serves 8.

# BRUNCH DISHES

Sunday dinner has become Sunday brunch for many families. A brunch is that meal where the best of breakfast—bacon, eggs, ham—is often served in new and varied combinations. These same breakfast-brunch dishes are also welcome refreshments at women's clubs and organizations that meet in the morning.

## BRUNCH IN A CUSTARD CUP
Ham and eggs and potatoes all in one dish—

4 medium baking potatoes
3 tablespoons margarine
1/2 teaspoon salt
1/3 to 1/2 cup milk
2 eggs, separated
2 tablespoons minced chives or green onions
1-1/2 cups finely chopped baked ham, do not use boiled ham
1 cup shredded Cheddar cheese

In a medium saucepan, boil potatoes in lightly salted water until tender. Drain, mash and whip with margarine, salt and milk. Preheat oven to 375 degrees F. Butter four 10-ounce custard cups or four individual souffle dishes. In a small bowl, beat egg yolks. Add chives and prepared potatoes. In another small bowl, beat egg whites until stiff. Gently fold in ham and cheese. Gently fold in potatoes. Spoon into prepared cups or dishes. Bake 30 minutes. Serves 4.

## BAKED POTATOES TOPPED WITH CHIPPED BEEF
Creamed chipped beef over potatoes instead of toast—

6 baking potatoes
1 to 2 tablespoons shortening
4 tablespoons margarine
4 tablespoons flour
3 cups milk
1 2-1/2-ounce package of dried beef, chopped
3 green onions, chopped, include some of the tops
3 hard-cooked eggs, chopped

Preheat oven to 425 degrees F. Scrub potatoes. Dry with paper towels. Rub lightly with 1 to 2 tablespoons shortening. Bake potatoes 1 hour and 15 minutes. To shorten baking time, insert 2 baking nails into each potato or pierce twice with a sharp fork. Continue to bake 30 minutes or more until potatoes test done. In a small saucepan over medium heat, melt margarine. Add flour and stir until mixture is smooth. Gradually add milk; cook until sauce is thick and bubbly; stir constantly. Stir in dried beef. Keep warm over hot water. At serving time, cut 2-inch slashes in a cross on the top of each baked potato and pop open. Top with sauce. Garnish with green onions and eggs. Serves 6.

## DEVILED EGGS AND ASPARAGUS CASSEROLE
Fresh asparagus is best—

2 pounds fresh asparagus spears, cleaned and cooked until barely tender or
    substitute 2 1-pound packages of frozen asparagus spears
10 hard-cooked eggs
2 2-1/2-ounce cans deviled ham
1/2 teaspoon Worcestershire sauce
1 teaspoon grated onion
3/4 teaspoon dry mustard
1 tablespoon light cream, Half and Half
1/2 teaspoon salt
6 tablespoons margarine
6 tablespoons flour
3 cups milk
2 cups grated Cheddar cheese
1/2 teaspoon dry mustard
1-1/2 teaspoons salt
Dash of pepper
1 cup crushed corn flakes

Preheat oven to 400 degrees F. Butter a 9 x 12-inch baking dish. Arrange cooked asparagus stalks in dish. Peel hard-cooked eggs and slice lengthwise. Remove yolks and reserve. Mash yolks. Add ham, Worcestershire sauce, onion, 3/4 teaspoon dry mustard, cream and salt; blend well. Refill egg whites. Arrange egg halves over asparagus. In a small saucepan over medium heat, melt margarine. Stir in flour; cook until smooth. Gradually add milk; cook until sauce is thick; stir constantly. Remove from heat. Add cheese, 1/2 teaspoon dry mustard, salt and pepper. Pour sauce over eggs and asparagus. Sprinkle with corn flakes. Bake 30 minutes or until sauce is bubbly and lightly browned on top. Serves 8 to 10.

## EGGS AND PEAS CASSEROLE
An attractive buffet dish—

1 medium onion, chopped
1/4 cup margarine
6 tablespoons flour
3 cups milk
2 10-ounce packages frozen peas
4 hard-cooked eggs, sliced
2 tablespoons chopped pimentos
1-1/2 teaspoons salt
1/4 teaspoon pepper
1/8 teaspoon thyme
1/2 cup shredded Swiss cheese
1/2 cup dry bread crumbs

Preheat oven to 350 degrees F. Butter a deep, two-quart baking dish. In a small saucepan over medium heat, saute onion in margarine 1 minute. Add flour; stir until smooth. Gradually add milk; cook over low heat; stir constantly until sauce thickens. Add peas, eggs, pimentos, salt, pepper and thyme. Stir gently to blend thoroughly. Pour into prepared dish. Top with cheese and bread crumbs. Bake 30 minutes. Serves 8.

## BACON AND EGG CASSEROLE
Can be prepared and refrigerated two hours ahead of serving time. Remove from refrigerator ten minutes before baking—

15 hard-cooked eggs, sliced
Salt and pepper
12 slices of bacon, fried crisp and cut into 1-inch pieces
2 cups chopped baked ham, do not use boiled ham
1-1/2 cups crushed potato chips
1 tablespoon margarine
1/2 cup chopped onion
6 tablespoons margarine
6 rounded tablespoons flour
3 cups milk
1/2 teaspoon salt
Dash of pepper
1 teaspoon dry mustard
2 cups grated Cheddar cheese

Preheat oven to 350 degrees F. Butter generously a 9 x 13-inch baking dish. Place half of eggs in prepared dish. Sprinkle lightly with salt and pepper. Add in layers half of bacon, ham and potato chips. Repeat layers. In a small saucepan, saute onion in 1 tablespoon margarine. In a medium saucepan over medium heat, melt 6 tablespoons margarine. Add flour; stir until smooth. Gradually add milk; cook until sauce thickens; stir constantly. Add 1/2 teaspoon salt, dash of pepper, mustard and 1-1/2 cups cheese; reserve 1/2 cup of cheese. Stir until cheese melts and is well-blended. Pour sauce over all. Sprinkle with reserved cheese. Bake 20 minutes. Serves 10.

## FLUFFY BAKED EGGS
A souffle-like dish prepared the night before—

8 slices white bread
8 eggs
4 cups milk
2 teaspoons salt
2 teaspoons dry mustard
2 cups baked ham, cubed
1 cup grated Cheddar cheese

Butter generously a 9 x 13-inch baking dish. Remove crusts from bread slices and cut bread into 1-inch cubes. Arrange on bottom of prepared pan. In a large bowl, combine eggs, milk, salt and mustard. Beat with a rotary beater until foamy and light. Fold in ham. Pour over bread. Reserve cheese. Cover baking dish with foil; seal well around edges of the dish. Refrigerate overnight. At baking time, preheat oven to 350 degrees F. Remove foil. Sprinkle with cheese. Bake 30 minutes. Serves 8.

## PARTY EGG SCRAMBLE

Serve with a platter of fresh fruit, hot cinnamon rolls and coffee—

2 tablespoons margarine
2 tablespoons flour
2 cups milk
1 cup shredded Cheddar cheese
1/2 teaspoon salt
1/8 teaspoon pepper
2-1/2 cups soft bread crumbs
4 tablespoons margarine, melted
1/4 teaspoon paprika
4 tablespoons margarine
1-1/2 cups diced Canadian bacon
1/4 cup chopped onion
12 eggs
1 3-ounce can mushroom stems and pieces, drained
1/3 cup dry, finely grated and seasoned bread crumbs

Preheat oven to 350 degrees F. Butter a 7 x 11-inch baking dish. In a medium saucepan, melt 2 tablespoons of margarine. Add flour; blend until smooth. Gradually add milk; cook until sauce is thick and bubbly; stir constantly. Add cheese; stir until cheese melts. Add salt and pepper. Set sauce aside. In a medium bowl, combine bread crumbs, 4 tablespoons of melted margarine and paprika. Set aside. In a skillet, melt 4 tablespoons of margarine and saute bacon and onion—*do not brown*. Beat eggs slightly and add to bacon-onion mixture. Cook and scramble just until eggs are set. Fold in mushrooms and cheese sauce. Pour into baking dish. Top with seasoned bread crumbs. Bake 30 minutes. Serves 8.

## HAM AND BROCCOLI STRATA
Ham and eggs plus a vegetable—

8 slices white bread, crusts removed
2 cups fresh broccoli florets, cooked until barely tender and drained or
    1 10-ounce package frozen broccoli cooked according to
    package directions
1/2 cup finely chopped baked ham
2 tablespoons finely chopped onion
4 eggs, well beaten
1/2 cup milk
1 8-ounce jar of Cheez Whiz

Place bread slices on bottom of an *ungreased*, 8-inch square baking dish; top with broccoli, ham and onion. In a medium bowl, combine eggs, milk and Cheez Whiz. Pour over bread, broccoli and ham. Cover and refrigerate overnight. At baking time, preheat oven to 350 degrees F. Uncover and bake 40 minutes. Let stand 10 minutes before serving. Serves 4 to 6.

## SAUSAGE PIE CASSEROLE
In a cracker crust—

1-1/2 cups coarsely crushed Saltine crackers
6 tablespoons melted margarine
1/2 pound bulk seasoned pork sausage, do not use link sausage
1/2 cup chopped green chilies, do not use seeds
4 eggs, well beaten
1-1/2 cups grated Cheddar cheese
1/4 teaspoon pepper
1/4 teaspoon onion powder
1 cup sour cream
4 bacon slices, fried crisp and crumbled

Preheat oven to 325 degrees F. Have a 7 x 11 inch baking dish at hand. In a medium bowl, combine cracker crumbs and margarine. Press into baking dish. Bake 8 to 10 minutes. Remove from oven. Set aside to cool. Increase oven heat to 350 degrees F. In a skillet, crumble sausage and brown over medium heat. Set aside to cool. In a medium bowl, combine chilies, eggs, cheese, pepper and onion powder; blend thoroughly. Fold in sour cream. Spread sausage over crust. Pour egg-sour cream mixture over sausage; top with crumbled bacon. Bake 30 minutes. Serves 8.

## SAUSAGE SCRAPPLE
Prepared scrapple can be refrigerated several days—

2 pounds bulk seasoned pork sausage
1-2/3 cups evaporated milk
3 cups water
1-1/2 cups yellow cornmeal
1/2 teaspoon salt
1/4 teaspoon pepper
2 eggs, well beaten
2 cups crushed corn flakes
3 to 4 tablespoons margarine or bacon drippings

Butter generously a 9 x 5 x 3-inch loaf pan. In a skillet over medium heat, brown crumbled sausage until sausage is no longer pink but is not hard and dry. In a medium bowl, combine milk and water; reserve 2/3 cup. In a medium saucepan, combine 4 cups of liquid and sausage. Bring to a boil over medium heat; slowly stir in corn meal, salt and pepper. Continue to cook until mixture is very thick, about 5 minutes; stir constantly. Pour into prepared pan. Chill several hours or overnight. At serving time, in a small bowl, combine reserved liquid and eggs. Unmold scrapple and cut into 3/4-inch slices. Dip slices first in crushed corn flakes, then in egg-milk mixture and then dip again in corn flakes. In a large, heavy skillet over medium heat, melt margarine or bacon drippings and fry scrapple. The skillet should not be so hot that scrapple begins to brown as soon as it is placed in the skillet. Scrapple should brown *slowly* on both sides. Serve with hot maple syrup. Serves 4 to 6.

## BROILED TUNAWICHES
Makes four big sandwiches—

1 6-1/2-ounce can chunk tuna
1/3 cup mayonnaise
1/4 cup chopped green onions, include some of tops
2 teaspoons Dijon-style mustard
1/2 teaspoon garlic salt
1 3-ounce package cream cheese, softened
4 slices dark rye bread
1 cup sliced fresh mushrooms
1 large fresh tomato cut into four slices
1 cup shredded Swiss cheese

Preheat broiler. Have an ungreased cookie sheet at hand. Drain tuna and flake with a fork. In a medium bowl, combine mayonnaise, onion, mustard and garlic salt; blend thoroughly. Fold in tuna. Spread cream cheese on bread. Top with mushroom slices. Spread tuna mixture over mushrooms. Top with tomato slice and cheese. Place sandwiches on cookie sheet. Broil 3 inches from heat until cheese melts and is bubbly. Serves 4.

## MICROWAVE COOKING

I had no problems getting accustomed to using two of the new-to-me kitchen appliances—a dishwasher and a garbage disposal—when I moved into the apartment. But getting acquainted with the third new appliance—a microwave oven—took a little practice.

The microwave is a speedy way to reheat leftovers, thaw frozen foods, melt butter and chocolate or boil small amounts of water. However, when it comes to actually cooking and baking in it, out of habit, I have been slow to break away from conventional cooking and baking methods.

Because microwave ovens vary a great deal in power settings and in the size of oven interiors, both of which affect the length of cooking time and the power level that should be used, I keep a separate notebook on microwaving. In it I jot down the name of the food being prepared, the power level being used, the length of cooking time that seems most appropriate for that food in my microwave oven and I also indicate at what point the food was turned or stirred. Having that information readily available for future reference, I avoid repeating mistakes and am less likely to turn foods into mush or into brick bats by over-cooking.

## CARAMEL CORN

Popcorn and Caramel Corn are two things I now regularly prepare in the microwave—

4-1/2 to 5 quarts popped corn, the equivalent of 2 3-1/2-ounce packages of Hungry Jack popcorn for the microwave prepared according to package directions
1/2 cup margarine
1/2 cup brown sugar
1/4 cup dark corn syrup
1/4 teaspoon salt
1 teaspoon vanilla
1/4 teaspoon baking soda

Sort popped corn; remove unpopped kernels. Pour corn into a large brown paper bag and slip that bag into another brown paper bag—*corn must be double-bagged.* In a small saucepan, combine margarine, brown sugar, corn syrup and salt; mix well. On a regular cooktop burner bring to a boil over medium heat. When syrup boils, begin timing and boil *exactly 4 minutes.* Remove from heat. Add vanilla and baking soda; mix well. Pour over corn in bag. Fold ends of bag over and fasten shut with a paper clip at each end of the fold. Shake well. Place bag in microwave oven on full power for 1 minute. Remove bag from oven. Shake well. Return bag to oven at full power for 1 minute. Remove from oven. Shake well. Pour into a large container—a large bowl, roaster pan or dishpan. As corn cools, stir frequently with a fork to separate kernels. Makes about 5 quarts.

## RICE AND RAISIN PUDDING

This pudding needs to cook eight minutes on "High Power" in my microwave oven—

2 cups milk
1 3-1/2-ounce package vanilla pudding, do not use instant pudding
1/2 cup quick cooking rice
1/2 cup raisins

In a quart-and-a-half microwave-proof covered casserole, combine milk, pudding, rice and raisins. Cook on "High Power" 5 to 8 minutes. Let stand 5 minutes. Serves 4.

## BUTTERNUT SQUASH

1 butternut squash
Brown sugar
Margarine
Salt
Pepper

Wash squash and cut into bite-sized pieces according to the number of servings needed. Place in a microwave-proof baking dish. Season to taste with brown sugar, margarine, salt and pepper. If baking dish has a cover, use it or cover with plastic wrap. Cook 3 to 4 minutes on "High Power" for 1 serving. Stir once during cooking time.

# SPECIAL REMINDERS AND TIPS

Read recipe from start to finish.

Assemble equipment and ingredients called for in recipe. Line them up in the order in which they will be used. It's a good way to double check, make sure you have all the necessary ingredients, bowls, pans and utensils on hand. If something should be missing, don't be too quick to put everything back in the cupboard. By making a substitution or variation, by switching herbs or seasonings and with a little improvising, you may be creating a brand new recipe.

And there's one other very good reason for an ingredient line-up. It all but eliminates any chance of forgetting to add an ingredient or adding it twice.

# CAKES

Reading the recipe and getting equipment and ingredients ready are especially important in baking a cake. Once mixing is underway, it should proceed quickly and smoothly until the cake is in the pan and in the oven.

Have all ingredients at room temperature. Cut hard butter or margarine right out of the refrigerator into smaller chunks and it will be ready for creaming in a few minutes. Take the chill off eggs by removing them from the refrigerator an hour ahead of time or by placing them in a bowl of warm, *not hot*, water for a few minutes. Eggs separate more easily when they are cold, so when a recipe calls for eggs to be separated, separate them as soon as they come out of refrigerator and let yolks and whites come to room temperature in separate bowls.

Before mixing begins, preheat oven so it is up to temperature when the cake is ready for the oven.

Learn to recognize how creamed shortening and sugar, beaten eggs or various kinds of cake batters "look" in various stages of mixing, beating or folding. The eyes can be a big help when a cake recipe is being converted from hand-mixing to mixing with an electric mixer. One minute at medium speed in most electric mixers equals one hundred fifty full, around-the-bowl strokes of hand beating. An electric mixer is a wonderful time and labor saver; it does a beautiful and speedy job of creaming, blending, mixing, beating and folding cake batter; it can out-beat most cooks. If you don't trust your eyes to know the "right look" for cake batter when they see it, set the mixer dial at the suggested speed and also set a timer or watch the clock to avoid under-or over-beating. Generally, creaming starts at low speed and gradually increases to medium; add dry ingredients at low speed and, after all traces of dry particles disappear, increase to medium; beat egg whites at high speed; and so on. Follow instructions given in your mixer's manual. Use a *rubber or plastic* spatula to scrape down the sides of the bowl throughout mixing time. With some heavy batters, it is necessary to turn off the mixer in order to thoroughly scrape the bowl; *the mixer must always be turned off to scrape the beaters.*

When filling pans, spread batter gently and evenly to sides and corners so batter is level and not rounded up in the center. Except for angel food, chiffon, sponge and other cakes baked in tube pans, most recipes allow for pans to be half to three-quarters full. Bake cakes as near the center of the oven as possible. Place pans on the racks so each pan is at least half an inch from an oven wall. If using more than one rack, stagger pans so one is not directly above another to allow for more even heat circulation and uniform baking.

*Never, never open the oven door during the first twenty minutes a cake is in the oven.* Most ovens now have windows so you can peek at the cake without opening the oven door.

And, even though today's ovens and ranges are less apt to be jarred and shaken by the slamming and banging of doors in the house, it's still a good idea to take some precautions not to create any sudden jolts or hard vibrations that might shake a baking cake.

Rich cakes, cakes made with butter and thick cream, angel food cakes or cakes which depend on air for their structure, are all very tender and delicate cakes. It doesn't take much to cause them to "fall," causing the top to crack open after the cake has risen to its full height.

There are various ways to test a cake for doneness. For cakes made with shortening, butter or margarine, gently insert a wooden toothpick or wire tester straight down into the middle of the cake, going all the way down to the bottom of the pan. Withdraw tester gently. If it comes out clean, the cake is done. If any moist batter or crumbs stick to the tester, the cake needs to be baked longer. Test in two or three places to be sure. Some cakes may also shrink slightly and pull away from the sides of the pan when they are done. For "foam" or "air" cakes—angel food, sponge and chiffon cakes—use the "finger test." If no imprint remains when lightly touched with a finger, the cake is done.

Cool cakes made with shortening, butter or margarine in the pan or pans on wire cooling racks ten minutes. Then, with a thin knife or spatula, loosen edges, place inverted rack over cake and turn over and carefully lift off the pan. If waxed paper has been used to line the pan, remove it at this time. Put a second rack over the cake and invert it again so the top side of the cake is up. Cover lightly and let cake cool completely, at least an hour and a half, before frosting.

"Foam" or "air" cakes—angel food and chiffon cakes—must be inverted as soon as they come out of the oven to prevent excessive shrinkage and also to prevent the cake from falling out of the pan. Most tube pans have built-in "feet" for this purpose but when a pan doesn't have its own "feet," invert pan over an inverted kitchen funnel or over the neck of a heavy bottle and let cake cool *away from drafts*. And that means keep it away from the refrigerator, too; every time the refrigerator door opens, cool air escapes and that creates a sudden draft in the immediate area.

When frosting a layer cake, fill between layers first, then spread frosting over sides of the cake. Frost top of the cake last. To keep crumbs from getting into the frosting, refrigerate cooled layers thirty minutes before frosting.

To bake a "crust-less, crumb-free" cake, one that is to be frosted and then decorated, soak a terry cloth towel or towels in cold water, wring out, fold into a three-inch strip and wrap around each pan. The cloth should overlap so it can be pinned or clipped and held securely in place during baking.

All cakes can be frozen. Bake, cool completely, frost or freeze unfrosted, wrap in airtight, moisture-proof freezer wrap or packages, date and label and store in freezer six to eight months. Seven-Minute Icing and other similar frostings do not freeze well; if you plan to frost a cake with that type of frosting, do it after the cake has been thawed.

As with all baked products, *thaw frozen cakes in their wrapping or container.* As they thaw, they sweat. If they are left in the wrapping, the moisture collects on the wrapping and not on the cake, which would make it soggy.

## PIES

Tender, flaky pie crust requires no fancy ingredients, only good techniques.

Measure carefully; correct amounts and proportions make the difference between a flaky crust and a crumbly crust. Use well-chilled shortening and water or any other liquids that might be called for in a special crust.

Do not add any more liquid than is needed to hold the mealy mixture of fat and flour together.

Do not use shortening and lard interchangeably; use one and one-fourth cups shortening in place of one cup of lard. Commercially packed lard produces pie crusts with a different texture, tenderness and flavor than crusts made with home-rendered lard. Commercial lard will more closely resemble home-rendered lard in appearance and taste if it is first melted in hot water and then allowed to cool and become firm enough to drain off excess water.

Once liquids are added, mix dough quickly with a fork; over-stirring or over-working makes tough pie crust. After eight or ten strokes of the fork, the dough will begin to form a very loose ball. Gather it together with the hands and lightly press into a ball. Wrap ball loosely in waxed paper and refrigerate while preparing filling.

Divide dough into single crust portions.

When rolling pie crust, work on a lightly floured board or pastry cloth. If crust is to be rolled on marble, synthetic marble or other *smooth* counter top, dampen surface liberally and cover with a large sheet of waxed paper; lightly flour the waxed paper. Afterwards, when the pie is made up and in the oven, discard the paper along with remaining flour and pastry cuttings and the mess is quickly cleaned up.

Use a well-floured wooden or Teflon-coated rolling pin or use one that is covered with a heavily-floured knitted stockinette.

Roll out one portion of dough until it is about one-eighth-inch thick and has a diameter that is two inches larger than the pie pan. The key word is *"rolling."* Let the rolling pin actually roll; avoid pressing down on the dough with the rolling pin; lift it ever so slightly as it rolls so it does not push the dough in front of it. Stretching the dough by shoving it with the rolling pin causes big blisters to form during baking. Roll the dough from the center out; lift the pin as it nears the edge of the circle so the outer edges are not rolled too thin.

*Roll pie crust only once!* If dough should crack or break, patch it by cutting a piece of dough to fit over the break. Dampen the area slightly and press patch of dough into place. Fold rolled dough in half and lift carefully to place in pie pan. Unfold and fit lightly into pan, being careful not to stretch or puncture the dough.

Trim bottom crust with scissors or a sharp knife so extra dough hangs evenly over pan edges.

Heap filling into crust; pile it slightly higher in the center.

Roll out top crust and cut air vents inside a five-inch circle in the center of the crust. Fold crust in half. Dampen rim edge of bottom crust lightly with water and lay on top crust. Crimp edges of two crusts together with fingers or a fork.

To make a latticed upper crust, after dough is rolled out, cut into strips that are twelve inches long and one-half to three-quarters of an inch wide. Lay strips over pie filling an inch apart, first in one direction and then in a crisscross pattern. For a woven look, fold alternate strips back and weave crosswise strips over and under. Cut strips with a crimping tool for "pinked" edges; or twist strips and lay over filling at angles to form a diamond pattern. *Be careful not to pull or stretch strips of a lattice crust; lay over filling loosely to allow for shrinkage during baking.* When strips are all in place, trim edges even with outer rim of pie pan. Dampen rim edge of lower crust and fold over strips. Crimp or flute edges together to seal.

For a one-crust pie, roll dough out until circle is three inches larger than the top of the pie pan to allow an inch and a half overhang which can be doubled back onto itself to stand upright so it can be shaped with the fingers into a fluted edge. If a crust is to be baked first and filled later, after the dough has been fitted into the pan, prick it generously with a fork to keep dough from heaving and baking unevenly.

Be sure oven is fully preheated to the exact temperature called for in the recipe before putting pie into the oven. If the top crust becomes golden brown before the pie is done, cut a two-inch wide ring of plain brown paper that is at least an inch wider than the pie's diameter and lay it over the crust to prevent over-browning. The pie will continue to bake under the paper but the crust will not burn.

To prevent fruit pies from spewing over in the oven, tear muslin or sheeting into three-inch wide strips long enough to go completely around pie pan with a three-inch lap. Dip cloth in water, wring it out and wrap around the pie pan just before pie goes into the oven. As the strip is pulled snugly around the pan, be sure it cups in under the rim and also goes up and over the rim to extend over the crust about an inch—the crust will still bake and brown under the muslin. As soon as the pie comes out of the oven, *remove muslin strip immediately while the pie is still hot and before the juice cools and thickens; the strip will release and pull away without disturbing the browned crust. Discard the strip.*

An oven mess can also be avoided by baking a fruit pie in a brown paper bag. Put prepared pie in the bag, fold open end of bag over two or three times and fasten shut with paper clips. Place the bag on a cookie sheet and put it in the oven. Pies baked in a bag should be baked an hour at 425 degrees Farenheit.

To test for doneness, gently shake the pan. If the crust is fully baked, it will have shrunk just enough to allow the pie to move ever so slightly when the pan is shaken. Test pumpkin and custard pies by sticking a silver or stainless steel table knife blade in the center; if the knife comes out clean, the filling is done. Test fruit pies by sticking a wooden toothpick or wire tester carefully into center of the pie to determine if the fruit is tender. *With both methods of testing, be very careful that the tester does not pierce the bottom crust causing the filling or fruit juices to leak out and get between the crust and the pan.*

When beating meringues, "feel" a drop of the meringue between the tips of the thumb and index finger; if no sugar granules can be felt, the sugar is completely dissolved and beating can continue until meringue reaches the proper stage.

Unbaked fruit pies freeze beautifully. A pie for the freezer is made exactly the same way a pie is made for the oven *with one exception: Do not cut air vents in the top crust before laying it over the filling; cut air vents in a frozen pie just before it goes into the oven.* In the very center of the top crust, cut a hole the size of a nickel to allow steam to escape quickly and freely and to assure that the bottom crust bakes and browns evenly.

Freeze the pie right in the pan—it may be either a glass or a metal pan. I use only oven and freezer-proof glass pie pans; baking times and temperatures given in all pie recipes in this book are for glass pie pans. To protect crimped edging or fluting from being crushed in the freezer, place unwrapped pie in freezer for about an hour; when the pie is frozen solid, remove from freezer, wrap in air-tight, moisture-proof freezer wrap or container, date and label and return to the freezer. Pies may be stored in the freezer up to six months. At baking time, preheat oven to 450 degrees Farenheit. Remove the pie from freezer, *do not thaw*; unwrap and put it directly into *preheated* oven. Allow a frozen pie to bake ten to fifteen minutes longer than an unfrozen pie of the same kind.

## YEAST BREADS

It can happen with any recipe, but I find it happens most often with yeast dough recipes—someone will ask for my recipe, I pass it on and later I hear back, "Mine didn't turn out like yours."

There are many reasons why this might happen—differences in brands of flour or shortening used, size of eggs or a difference in temperatures where dough was set to rise. Or, possibly, a less than perfect product might be attributed to inexperience in working with yeast dough, something that is easily corrected with practice. When I hear a complaint, I try to help the baker figure out what might have happened so she will be encouraged to try again. Aside from all the other reasons for baking your own breads— better tasting, better for your health, saves money—baking bread is satisfying and gratifying and it's fun.

An experienced baker recognizes by sight, touch and even smell when yeast is working, when enough flour has been added, when dough is ready to knead, when it's been kneaded enough, has doubled in bulk and so on. Baking yeast breads is less "tricky and unpredictable" if a few tips are followed.

The first tip, and it just might be the best tip, is this: Do not try to race the clock. Let the dough tell you when it is ready for the next step.

Begin with all ingredients at room temperature. Adding ice cold eggs or shortening throws a chill into dough and limits the yeast's ability to "work." Yeast thrives on moisture, warmth and sugar. On all yeast dough where the procedure permits, add one-fourth teaspoon sugar and a dash of ginger to the yeast and water mixture to "test" or "proof" the yeast to make sure it is "alive" and to help activate it and speed up its action. The temperature of the water used to dissolve the yeast must be "lukewarm"; test it on your wrist; it should be warm, not hot. After standing a few minutes, "tested" or "proofed" yeast has a "yeasty" smell and a bubbly surface. Even though the amount of yeast called for in a recipe may increase, there is no need to increase the amount of sugar or ginger used to "proof" the yeast; the small amounts called for are capable of "proofing" any quantity of yeast. Both compressed or cake yeast and dry yeast make excellent bread. *Do check the expiration date on the package and never add extra yeast to a recipe hoping to speed up the action of the yeast.*

Humidity, length of storage, the kind of storage and many other considerations affect flour's ability to absorb moisture and that is why many yeast dough recipes list variations in the amount of flour to be used. Measure the smaller amount of flour out; measure and hold the extra amount of flour in reserve and if it is not needed during mixing, use it to flour the kneading surface. When you find a brand of flour you like, one you get good results with, stick with it.

Unless otherwise noted, all recipes calling for flour mean "all-purpose flour." And, unless otherwise noted, *flour is always sifted before it is measured. Do not, however, sift whole grain, cracked wheat or graham flour.*

Beat vigorously after the first addition of flour. Small bubbles will rise to the surface and burst and dough will begin to look light and satiny. Unless a recipe says otherwise, I use an electric mixer for this initial mixing; it does an excellent job of building the gluten which gives the bread its structure. I switch to a wooden spoon for remaining flour additions. When the dough begins to "follow the spoon" and "clean the bowl," it's ready to knead. Flour a pastry board or cloth lightly—allow slightly less than one tablespoon of flour for each cup of flour in the recipe. Turn dough out onto lightly floured surface and gather dough gently into a ball but before kneading begins, *cover dough and let it "rest" five minutes under the inverted bowl in which the dough was mixed or under a clean, dry towel.* The "resting" time allows the surface of dough that might seem too soft to knead or be too sticky to handle a chance to firm up without having to add a lot of extra flour which results in baked breads and rolls that are dry, dense and heavy.

Flour hands lightly and you're ready to get to the fun part of bread baking—kneading. Dough loves to be handled; don't be timid about touching it but do not abuse it; treat it kindly, with quick, light and gentle but firm motions. Flatten the ball of dough slightly. Catch hold of the back sides of the dough and fold it toward you, then, with the heel of the hands, push the dough away from you in an easy rolling motion—do not press down hard on dough. Again, fold the dough over, give it a one-quarter turn and again, push it away. Repeat folding, turning and pushing steps in a rhythmic pattern. As air is squeezed out of the dough, air blisters will appear just under the surface of the dough. Add more flour during kneading only if dough becomes too sticky to handle. When dough looks smooth, has a satiny sheen and is soft, elastic and light, tight and firm without being stiff and hard, it's been kneaded enough. A recipe may indicate how long dough should be kneaded, even so, the kneading force and action varies greatly from one baker to another. There's a test, the two-finger test, that helps avoid over-or under-kneading. With the index and middle fingers, indent kneaded dough; if dough springs back, it's been kneaded long enough; if the dent remains, continue kneading.

Place kneaded dough in a well-greased bowl. Roll and turn the ball of dough in the bowl, coating the dough lightly so the surface does not dry out during rising. Cover bowl securely with a sheet of plastic wrap and over-wrap with a clean towel or use, as I do, a lidded plastic bowl made especially for yeast dough; it keeps all the warmth of the "working dough" inside the bowl so the dough rises steadily and evenly. When the dough is double or almost double in bulk, the lid pops open.

Dough should rise in a dry, warm, 75 to 80 degrees Farenheit, draft-free spot. Finding just the right spot in a kitchen can be a problem, especially in the summer in an air conditioned home. Try placing the bowl containing the rising dough on a cookie sheet over a shallow pan of hot water; cover the entire set-up with a clean towel. Or, place the bowl on the center rack of an *UNHEATED* oven and set a shallow pan of hot water on the bottom of the oven; keep the oven door closed throughout the rising time. *Remove bowl and pan before preheating the oven.*

If you can't tell by looking if the dough has risen long enough, give it the two-finger test again—but with one difference: Press two fingertips lightly and quickly a half an inch into the dough; if the indentation remains, the dough has risen long enough. At this stage, it will be soft, satiny and very pliable, ready to be punched down for a second rising or ready to be shaped into loaves, rolls, braids, rings or coffee cakes. Punch dough down and turn out onto a lightly floured surface. *Most dough will benefit from a second "rest" under the inverted bowl before it is shaped.*

To form loaves for standard nine-by-five-by-three-inch bread pans, divide dough into loaf portions. With the hands, pat each portion into a seven-by-ten inch rectangle. Fold long sides to the center. Tuck ends of the dough under and place the roll in the pan seam side down. *Do not press dough down or try in any way to alter or reshape the top of the loaf once it is in the pan.*

If a recipe calls for the dough to be brushed or glazed *before baking*, use a soft pastry brush or a feather brush with very easy, gentle strokes to avoid puncturing the surface of the dough.

Do not put bread in the oven until the oven is fully preheated. Bake breads as near the center of the oven as possible unless recipe says otherwise. When baking several pans of bread, stagger pans so heat circulates evenly. Pans should not touch each other or the oven walls.

Rolls are done when they are a golden brown and when no moist crumbs cling to a wooden toothpick or a wire tester inserted into their centers.

Loaves of bread are done when they are a rich golden brown and sound hollow when upper crust is lightly tapped. Breads and rolls baked in a pan also tend to pull away from the sides of the pan just slightly when they are done.

Unless recipe says otherwise, remove breads and rolls from pans as soon as they come out of the oven and place on wire cooling racks, or in the case of *kolaches*, on several thicknesses of waxed paper covered newspapers. Cover lightly with clean towels and keep out of drafts. It is also important to allow room between cooling loaves of bread so air circulates and moisture does not condense on the loaves, causing soggy crusts.

Generally loaves of bread should cool two or three hours before slicing.

"Sweet dough," dough for fruited and filled rolls and coffee cakes, usually calls for more sugar, eggs and butter. Of course, sugar makes the dough sweeter, eggs make it very light so it rises higher and butter makes it tender and moist. Sweet dough is softer than bread dough and must be handled and kneaded more gently and extra care should be taken not to add any more flour than is absolutely necessary during mixing, kneading and shaping. Watch sweet dough carefully during rising so that it does not over-rise. If that should happen, punch the dough down to release the air and then let it rise again until it is *almost* double in bulk. Rich sweet doughs are delicate and should be baked at a lower temperature than bread dough.

Store home-baked bread for immediate use wrapped lightly in a clean towel or loose plastic at room temperature in a bread drawer or box.

All *baked* yeast breads and rolls can be frozen and stored in a freezer up to a year. Wrap in air-tight, moisture-proof freezer paper or foil or seal in plastic bags or containers then date and label. If loaves or rolls are to be frosted, glazed or decorated, skip that step if product is to be frozen; do it after thawing and reheating; otherwise, the frosting melts and disappears into the bread or rolls when they are reheated. Baked products frozen in foil wrap can go directly from the freezer into a 300 degree Farenheit oven for reheating. If a microwave oven is used for thawing and reheating baked products, follow oven manufacturer's directions.

## JAMS AND JELLIES

Always use enameled or stainless steel pans and glass, crockery or stainless bowls when cooking fruit or straining juice to be made into jam or jelly.

Jam is easier to make than jelly—there's only one cooking step—and it uses all of the fruit pulp, so there's no waste. To make jam that has the brightest color and the richest flavor, wash fruit, drain well and crush only enough of the fruit to cover the bottom of the pan. Add a small amount of water, just enough to cover the bottom of the pan—it may be as little as half a cup—just enough to get cooking started and prevent sticking. Add remaining fruit. Cook *uncovered*. Simmer fruit until it is soft. Add sugar and stir until sugar dissolves. Bring to a boil and reduce heat so mixture barely simmers and *does not boil*. Cook until mixture is thick, twenty to thirty minutes. Pour jam into hot sterilized jars, filling jars to within one-quarter-inch from the top and seal with melted paraffin.

To make sparkling clear, full-colored jellies, wash and drain fruit and put in a pan. Add water just until the water can be seen through the top layer of fruit; never use so much water that fruit floats. Cook *uncovered* until fruit is soft and has begun to give up color to the juice. Strain through a dampened jelly bag or several thicknesses of cheesecloth. Let juice drip from the fruit without forcing, crushing or pressing it. If cheesecloth has been used, discard it. If a jelly bag is used, *do not use soap or detergent to wash it*; clean it by rinsing in hot water until the water runs clear or by boiling it in clear water. Measure strained juice carefully to know *exactly* how much sugar is needed. Return juice to pan, bring to a rolling boil. If a scum forms, remove pan from heat and with a long-handled spoon, skim off the scum. Cook two or three minutes then gradually add sugar. When sugar dissolves, lower heat and cook until jelling consistency is reached. *Cook and strain any amount of fruit but never work with more than four cups of juice at a time when making jelly.* It takes a large amount of juice so long to reduce to jelling consistency that there is a risk the juice will overcook, causing the color of the finished jelly to be cloudy and muddy and giving the jelly a tough, chewy texture.

The most accurate way to know when the "jelling point," 220 degrees Farenheit, is reached is to use a candy thermometer. However, I still rely on a couple of other tests. One is the "sheeting" test: With a clean spoon, lift out some of the hot syrupy liquid, hold spoon twelve inches above pan and let syrup fall from the spoon back into the pan. When two large drops of syrup converge along the edge of the spoon bowl and fall as one drop, the "sheeting" stage has been reached and so has the "jelling point."

Or, I sometimes chill a clean plate in the freezer, then I spoon a little hot syrup onto the plate and return the plate to the freezer for a minute or two. If the chilled syrup wrinkles when it is pushed with a finger, the "jelling point" has been reached.

Both jams and jellies can be put into half or one-pint canning jars and sealed with two-piece lids instead of sealing with paraffin. Pour hot mixture into hot sterilized jars, wipe the rims of the jars, set a clean, hot metal lid in place and screw on the metal sealing band. Leave the band in place until the jar is opened.

## WHIPPING CREAM

Before beating begins, chill bowl and beaters in refrigerator or freezer for several minutes.

Whip cream slowly to incorporate smaller air bubbles which will make the whipped cream more stable and less likely to "weep" or become watery around the edges.

## COOKIES

To test for doneness, touch top of a cookie lightly with a fingertip; if finger imprint quickly disappears, the cookie is done. Or, with thicker, cake-like cookies, use a wooden toothpick or wire tester; if no crumbs stick to the tester, the cookie is done.

## WHEN DINNER IS LATE

This last tip could be the most important one for today's busy wives and mothers.

When I stayed too long in the garden, was delayed at the blacksmith shop waiting for the smithy to finish sharpening a set of plow shares or was detained at a meeting that ran long and I was late getting home, I didn't charge into the kitchen and begin banging pots and pans around in a rush to get a meal on the table. The first thing I did was put on my apron. The second thing I did was set the table *and then* I started fixing food.

When Walter saw me in my apron, saw the table set, he believed something was happening in the kitchen. He thought we'd soon be eating. Without a word, he picked up a newspaper—*Gibbon Reporter, Ravenna News, Kearney Daily Hub, Omaha World-Herald, Kansas City Packer*—or a magazine—*Successful Farmer, Nebraska Farmer, Wallace's Farmer, Farm Journal*—Walter was an avid reader—and was able to sit down, read and relax until I called him to the table.

## IN CLOSING

You can keep a memory alive by telling others about it, but when you write it down, you pass the memory on that others might enjoy it and benefit from glimpsing life as it was once lived in another time in history.

Here's to those who carried the cobs, built the fires and cooked the wonderful foods on the old cookstoves that also gave us warmth and comfort. Let the memories live on, knee-deep in corncobs.

# RECIPE INDEX

*1988*

Alice Mickish Hendrickson

# About the Author

E. Mae Hendrickson
Fritz is a Nebraska
native and former
Iowan who lives in
Phoenix, Arizona. She
is the author of *Prairie
Kitchen Sampler, The
Story of an Amana
Winemaker,* and *The
Family of Hy-Vee*, a
corporate history of the
Iowa-based Hy-Vee
food Stores, Inc.

A journalism
graduate of Iowa State
University, she was a
home economist for an
appliance manufacturer
and contributing editor
for *Wallace's Farmer*

*1988 Gittings*

magazine before becoming a freelance writer. Her work has appeared in many national and regional publications. She is a past
president of the Phoenix Professional Chapter of Women in Com-
munications, Inc., a member of Arizona Authors' Association, and a
member of the American Home Economics Association.

E. Mae recalls the sights, sounds and smells of Lilac Day on the
Hendrickson homestead and the sensual pleasures of her mother's
and grandmothers' farm kitchens. She never quite feels she's at
home in Nebraska until she's had her first bite of an apricot *kolache.*

For additional copies of **Prairie Kitchen Sampler** by E. Mae
Fritz send $16.95 plus $2.00 shipping and handling
charges for each book ordered (Arizona residents add
$1.19 tax) to:

Prairie Winds Press
5515 North 7th Street
Suite 5-163
Phoenix, AZ 85014

# Notes ✐

# Notes ✑

# Notes ✎

# Notes ✐

_____

_____

_____

_____

_____

_____

_____

_____

_____

_____

_____

_____

_____

_____

_____

_____

_____

_____

_____

_____

_____

_____

_____

# Notes ✑

# Notes

# Notes

# Notes ❧